WOMEN IN CRISIS
New Approach to Happiness

WOMEN IN CRISIS
NEW APPROACHES TO HAPPINESS

HARI SWARUP

GYAN PUBLISHING HOUSE
NEW DELHI—110002

WOMEN IN CRISIS

NEW APPORACH TO HAPPINESS

ISBN : 81-212-0720-7

Published in 2001 in India by
Gyan Publishing House
5, Ansari Road
New Delhi—110002

Phones : 3261060, 3282060, Fax : 3285914
E-Mail : gyanbook@del2.Vsnl.net.in
Visit Our Web Site At http:\\www.gyanbooks.com

Leser type setting at : APEX COMPUTERS
Printed at : **Mehra Offset Printers**

To
Those
Who suffer in silence

CONTENTS

PROLOGUE

Is your book finished? Asked the going lady with waning tears in her eyes and blooming smile on her lips.

No. It will finish only when every tear from every eye is wiped out, when every face lits-up with smiles, when every heart begins to beat with love.

Will that ever happen?

Yes, and then this book will finish.

It is a timeless book.

It is the continuation of that great experiment which human consciousness has been incessantly carrying on in its search for happiness.

It continues the experiment to transform agony into ecstasy, pain into pleasure, misery into joy.

This book has no beginning and no end.

INTRODUCTION

Hippocrates said that all ailments had their periods, when the humours of the body ebbed and flowed like the tide fo the sea. These tidal days he called *critical days*, and the tide itself a *crisis*... Emotions and feelings also rise and fall in the human mind like the tide of the sea. Moments in which love subsides and agony, depression and stress are on the rise make the life's *critical moments*, and the emotional tide itself constitutes the *crisis*.

In this world of unequal gender values, women face more emotional tides, live through more critical moments and suffer more crises than men. In initimate relationships, they are the ones who are scroned, slighted and dismissed, often even withouit a parting pang.

The object of the book is to help people—both men and women—enjoy happiness, prevent emotional tides and critical moemnts, and to overcome the crises if they come. The approaches to meet crisis situations are aimed at making intimate relationships more harmonious, melodious and euphoric.

The book, instead, shows the way to dive deep into the ocean of human psychology and pick up precious pearls of happiness, to fly high into sky and drink the nectar of joy falling from the heaven of intimacy, and to walk through the green meadows of peace and enjoy the sweet fragrance of flowers of love. It tells the reader how to avoid the pitfalls and remove the thorns that injure and destroy a relationship, and how to make life more fruitful and worth-living.

Women in Crisis : New Approaches to Happiness awakens the great human potential lying unused in the consciousness of every individual. It demonstrates how this hidden power can be utilized to meet every challenge and overcome every hurdle. It tries to provide necessary psychological empowerment to all particularly young women who need it most.

The real-life stories narrated in the book are the case-studies mostly of women in their youth and middle age, who have suffered agony and pain due to difficult relationships with their husbands, lovers or partners, or even otherwise.

The book is based on results obtained from communicative counselling given to a large number of persons suffering from distress and agony caused by tensions arising from disharmonious inter-personal relationsips and other psychic situations. Authentic versions of fortysix cases have been narrated in conversational style. Each case-study gives diagnositc scan, details of counselling given, coping strategies used, and the final outcome which has generally been positive.

The Book is Divided into Five Sections :

(*i*) Intimate Relationships—Sweet and Sour
(*ii*) Guilt, Shame and Fear
(*iii*) Psychio Coma
(*iv*) Death and Grief
(*v*) Anatomy of Happiness

As it is not possible to strictly conpartmentalise the cases, they have been placed along with each chapter according to the predominating emotional distress dealt with in a particular case.

The book is primarily meant for common men and women who live a normal life and suffer tension and distress in day-to-day intimate relationships and other emotional situations. The book intends to help people live a happier life. It does not deal with dogmas but real life situations, and provides easy interesting reading.

The book can be of considerable help also to sudents of behavioural psychology, research scholars, and practitioners of psychotherapy.

Names of persons whose cases have been discussed in the book have been changed. In case studies letter "C" represents the counsellor and other letters the concerned persons.

CASE STUDIES

1. Intimate Relationships—Sweet and Sour

2. Guilt, Shame and Fear

INTIMATE RELATIONSHIPS—SWEET AND SOUR

— Personal Space
— Emotional Linding Cord
— Crack and Rupture
— Violence
— Suicide

1
Intimate Relationships Sweet and Sour

"All we ask is to be let alone".
(Jefferson Davis)

All individuals need privacy–psychological privacy, a personal space, an area which must be held sacred and not encroached on.

Every person has his/her personal space, an area the individual maintains around oneself into which others are not permitted and where intrusion causes discomfort to the person whose individual space is trespassed. Persons who maintain intimate relationships however permit each other to violate their personal spaces because instead of they experience discomfort pleasure. Overlapping personal spaces become their common personal space. A relationship is deemed intimate only where the intrusion into the individual space-boundaries is permitted and welcomed, such a relationship contemplates and envisages moments of affection and endearment and a close physical presence. Couples involved in intimate relationships get a feeling of discomfort when their personal space is trespassed, intruded, or violated by any outsider.

This interpersonal distance which couples maintain varies according to the degree of intimacy they wish to maintain and the limits of intrusion they agree to permit into their common area or personal spaces. The status of a couple's relationship can be classified on the basis of the extent of their interpersonal common space and the distance between the individual spaces of the two. The status of their relationship might be that of strangers, acquaintances, friends, confidantes, or lovers.

In a normal husband-wife relationship the intrusion is quite deep, and where the two are also lovers, the two spaces merge and the distance gets reduced to minimum, leading to the maximum overlapping of their personal spaces.The situation is, however, never constant and goes on varying; it is heavily influenced by the ever-changing emotional factors and also, to some extent, by changes occurring in the family and social environment in every case, where there occurs a breach in an intimate relationship, the interpersonal common space undergoes a radical change, the character of relations' ip alters and it acquires a new dimension.

The overlapping of personal spaces of two individuals, and their merging into one instead of remaining two separate spaces, creates a new common personal space with new dimensions and special qualities. The nature and character of this common personal space depends on the kind of emotional attachment the two individuals have.

The emergence and evolution of personal spaces begins from the womb and continues till end. A child remains totally attached to the mother, both biologically and emotionally till it is delivered and the umbilical cord is cut. Then there is a biological detachment, but the more important attachment—the emotional attachment continues even after. Emotional attachment between mother and child continues across the life cycle, and does not depend on the age of the mother and the child, it may change in form and shape, may grow or wane according to the age of the mother and the child, or may even have different profiles under different circumstances.

This concept of attachment and detachment of the psychological umbilical cord cannot, however, be treated as limited to mother-child relationship, it is relevant even in interpersonal relationship among adults. It might extend to cover all relationships which are intimate and involve emotional tie-ups. Thoughts, emotions, and feelings have very wide implications and influence the behaviour of individual of all ages, and of the same or different sexes. At every age, people have emotional attachment with large number of persons. These attachments create a variety of emotional impacts, impulses, and responses. Attachments which promote love and harmony help in keeping tension at bay. They generate or tend to generate emotions, impulses, feelings, thoughts, responses and behaviours that help in making people happy.

All attachments do not promote love and harmony, some create negative emotions and bring unhappiness. They give rise to such feelings and thoughts which cause animosity, hatred, jealousy, etc., and lead to discordant responses and offensive behaviours.

Attachments *per se* also go on changing. The nature and character of an attachment or its intensity goes on varying with time and circumstances. An attachment may lose significance and even result in discord or total break. This discord may be caused by innumerable factors. It may come slowly and smoothly or by a sudden jerk. It might be just a simple end of an attachment or may cause a wound which may heal, or last the whole life. A break of relationship may come as a consequence of some event or happening, or may be voluntarily undertaken by both the parties, or may occur even when not wanted by one of the parties.

Many inter-personal relationship problems are caused by a breach in attachment, and by changes occuring in their common and individual personal spaces. Marital tensions are often the result of disharmony or unwanted partial detachments. In such cases, marital happiness disappears and the family suffers misery. When the relationship suffers a rupture, the home breaks.

Before any two persons enter into a relationship, they have separate personal spaces. When they enter into a relationship the process of merger of their spaces starts, and goes on till complete intimacy is achieved. At this stage, individual spaces disappear and joint personal space comes into being. If a third person makes an intrusion, then it has to be in this common personal space. When this occurs, their individual and common spaces begin to change their character and dimension, and their joint space begins to shrink. A part of the joint space again becomes the separate space of one of the parties and becomes open for being shared by an outsider. When that individualised space is trespassed, the entire common space undergoes a transformation. Two separate personal spaces may emerge or may become completely separate without leaving any common or joint space. It is also possible that the trespasser may be pushed out and the two personal spaces might unite again leading to revival of the old relationship.

The intimate relationship of a married couple or of two lovers gets the greatest jolt when their common personal space is violated and trespassed by a person whose intrusion is resented by one of the two. It invariably induces the feeling of sexual jealousy. If a male enters the space, the husband develops sexual jealousy and protests. He may even resort to violence against his partner and the intruder. He generally becomes aggressive and does everything to force the intruder out of their interpersonal space.

In the emotional triangle in which two men and one woman are involved, aggression is normally resorted to for ending the triangle.The woman in such a case plays an important role. In her personal space the lover gets the prime place and the husband finds himself ousted. The woman may, in a rare case, even collude with her lover to get rid of the husband. She may opt for a change in her personal space by making her lover occupy the space which had so far been occupied by her husband. In this process, she might succeed or fail. She might succeed in getting a new intimate relationship with the lover and a new common interpersonal space, or might lose even that which she had with her husband. The man is generally not ready to accept his ouster, he retaliates by using violent means.

When a female enters a couple's personal space, the woman whose joint space is violated, suffers sexual jealousy and revolts. As a first measure, she withdraws her love and tries all means to make the husband push the intruding woman out of their personal space. But being generally in a less dominating position, she continues to suffer in silence till it becomes umbearable; she might even go to the extent of committing suicide.

The aggrieved woman begins to fear loss of her husband's love, or even losing him altogether. In order to get over this fear she begins to demand more love and emotional support. But she fails to get what she demands because her husband's love at any rate to some extent, has already shifted to her rival; and as a result her jealousy is intensified. Sometimes in order to win back her private space and to force the intruder out, she makes efforts to give to her husband more love and sex, but the effort generally fails. The reason is that this interpersonal private space is the outcome of not only physical contact but also the result of emotional attachment and in such situations emotional attachment plays the decisive role.

The entry of an intruder into the personal space of a woman's husband, which she regards as her own and over which she believes and claims to have a monopoly, creates tension and discomfort in her mind. She begins to suffer various kinds of emotional problems, including some sort of depression. Her agony is enhanced by a feeling of helplessness, Many a time, her love for her children and concern for their welfare prevents her from taking any drastic step. She is generally left with only four options.

(i) to accept and tolerate the violation of their joint personal space;

(ii) to treat her husband's personal space as a space which does not belong totally or exclusively to her;

(iii) to fight for her monopoly over the couple's common personal space, and to throw the intruder out by force, which may include psychological pressure, coercive measures by the family and society on the husband, and legal action;

(iv) to wipe out the joint personal space and revert back to her own personal space and either keep it exclusive or share it again if she contracts a new relaionship.

The woman who is conscious of her rights, and has courage to fight for them, and has faith in her capabilities will, of course, go in either for the third or the fourth option; but if she is not made that way, she would succumb to her lot and accept the other options, and live in misery as a second woman, having lost the personal space which she enjoyed initially.

Every attachment in order to be of a lasting character has to be one that gives happiness to both. It has to be exclusive for each and neither has the liberty to have an attachment with anyone else; dual attachments are never acceptable in intimate relationships. For a happy relationship the parties have to preserve their mutual bonds of attachment, and protect them from all outside encroachment.

Once an outsider intrudes into the common space of a couple, the aggrieved party loses all faith and trust in the other, and the emotional bond comes under severe strain. Trust is the cornerstone of every intimate relationship, and it cannot exist without full faith and complete trust in each other. Lack of faith creates doubt and invokes suspicion, which leads to short-circuiting of the relationship. When the communication breaks, partners draw away from one another, and develop more suspicion, distrust, and fear. Fear of losing love creates the crisis of confidence and the relationship is threatened with a break. Fear may be of any kind, but invariably it torpedoes courage, weakens positive emotions, and develops negative emotions instead. Faith, trust and openness, on the other hand, give stability and blending to intimate relationships.

One of the worst enemies of love in intimate relationships is suspicion. When a person begins to suspect the fidelity of the partner. he/she loses all trust in her/him and their relationship suffers a jolt. The fear of intrusion of an outsider into the common space of the couple creates jealousy and the situation becomes somewhat similar to what happens where there is actual trespass. Once this happens the relationship loses its charm and is soured. Very often, suspicion is based on assumed, imaginary and fictitious grounds and is ultimately found to be without any basis. However, if suspicion continues for long it becomes a belief and generates distrust which undermines love. It is always safer to investigate and end the suspicion as quickly as psossible.

Romance and courting must continue incessantly to keep going the intimacy of a relationship. Love is the most powerful positive emotion, and in intimate relationships it craves for sex, because sex means final acceptance of the partner in one's own personal space, and thereby makes the partners treat their individual personal spaces as common space of both. It is this feeling that gives the relationship its real intimacy, both psychological and biological. when either love or sex is withdrawn, relationship ceases to be intimate and develops negative emotions of hate and revulsion. They induce the aggrieved party to think of inflicting punishment in various forms ranging from protest to violence.

Any tension in a relationship causes pain and agony. All emotional sufferings are generally the resultant of the continuing interaction of conflicting psychic forces, which act and counteract in the subconscious mind without being consciously recognised. This psychological process is the outcome not always of something immediate, or something rational, or something which could be noticed through conscious thinking, but is generally the fall-out of a mass of jumbled-up distressing past memories lying stored in the conscious and the subconscious mind of the partners. They remain unidentified and create tension which can break the emotional cord and even damage their common personal space.

In intimate relationships, even a little misunderstanding can create a lot of trouble. In order to avoid the crisis, one has always to remain conscious of the two determinants of human behaviour, the prevailing psychological environment and the perceptive mood of the partner. The response of the partner may be entirely unexpected if these two basic extemal factors, which always remain unknown and in a state of fluidity, are not correctly gauged and it is always possible to go wrong. One has, therefore, to keep a margin and make an allowance for the error in the expectation of the response.

When two persons form an intimate relationship, they get into a bond of attachment in the sense that they come emotionally close to each other. Emotional attachment involves emotional attraction. When mutual fascination and allurement decreases, and the relationship becomes strained and nauseating, emotional alienation takes place. Emotional detachment causes a break in intimate relationship and the interpersonal responses begin to produce discordant emotions and feelings. Even an offer of love might get a negative response. When response to positive emotions becomes negative, a chain reaction starts leading to intolerance, hatred and even to violence—psychological as well as physical.

Either party tries to shift the blame by resorting to the process of guilt attribution. Even for one's own tension the blame is put on the assumed wrong behaviour of the other. Very often the husband complains that the wife is a psychic case, and she is taken to the psychiatrist or the psychologist for treatment. The wife on the contrary feels that the problem lies with the husband. Sometimes the wife succeeds in taking the husband to the doctor complaining that he had a mental health problem. Both insist that the entire fault is that of the other. Each one tries to show that he/she is the victim and the other one is the wrongdoer. Both in fact suffer psychic aggression and both become victims of the same. Shifting of guilt does not remove the cause, and the malady continues.

When the stress in the relationship becomes unbearable and looks incurable. the aggressor, generally the person in the wrong, gets frustrated gets and resorts to violence. In most cases it is the husband, who resorts to violence as a cover-up of his own frusration. It occurs generally when the man is impulsive, irritable, explosive, and emotionally immature. He is relatively unable to articulate his feelings and thinks he can do so by using violence. He is also a person who does not have an internally integrated social attitude towards violence, and does not consider it wrong to express it.

Wife-beating is not confined to alcoholics, although the incidence is higher when the man is used to consuming high dose of alcohol. It is also not limited to poorer class of people, or to families where wife's educational level is low. Educated young women, even with good job employment, suffer violence; much depends on the cultural level and psychological make-up of the husband. A short-fuse individual fails to adjust himself to the thoughts and feelings of the partner and develops rage and gives vent to it by inflicting physical and psychological suffering on his partner and even on the children.

Inferiority complex also very often leads the man to resort to violence. The man who feels culturally inferior, or socially backward, develops animosity against the wife and unconsciously tries to overcome the feeling by using physical force, thinking it will make good his shortcomings, and make his wife accept his superiority. In such cases the wife suffers for no fault of her own. She may not do or commit any specific provocative act and still get a beating because the husband desires to demonstrate his (male) dominance.

In some cases the husband suffers from a feeling of guilt and shame for some known or unknown reason and in order to overcome it he tries to transfer the guilt on to his wife. By this method he unconsciously tries to attain salvation from the feeling of guilt and shame. He dubs the wife as a guilty person and tries to absolve himself by punishing her. Wife-beating makes the wife feel extremely humiliated, her dignity, honour and self-esteem are shattered and she feels socially degraded. This gives the husband sadistic satisfaction, but does not help him in getting rid of his feeling of guilt, on the other hand it enhances his feeling of shame.

In every case of emotional stress some kind of breach in relationship necessarily occurs, and in case of actual violence, a total break takes place, and produces loneliness, rejection, misery, and alienation. When the detachment becomes complete, restoration of confidence becomes impossible. In such a circumstance, the only remedy against continuing emotional agony may lie in the final severance of the relationship. It all depends on the nature and depth of attachment and its breach.

The emotional cord of an interpersonal relationship can be repaired only so long it is repairable, but when the breach becomes final and irreversible, and the common personal space disappears, the only way to have a happy and peaceful life is to accept the situation, and to replace it by a new relationship.

When the emotional cord breaks and the joint personal space ceases to exist or give happiness, the weaker partner takes the step to wipe off her personal space by obliterating her very existence. Suicide is, however, not a solution for ruptures occuring in intimate relationships, but sometimes that seems to be the only remedy available. A person resorts to suicide in diverse circumstances. Many a time misunderstanding and ill-conceived behaviour of persons living in intimate relationship becomes the cause.

In the course of life, moments come when it becomes impossible for a person to keep one's calm, and 'he', more often 'she', feels that life is not worth living. Generally, such a situation arises when the emotional cord of an intimate relationship reaches or crosses the breaking point, and this happens when the man act in a manner that the woman loses all faith and confidence in him, and feels betrayed. Betrayeal brings not only loss of face, but also makes her suffer humiliation and lose self-esteem.

At times, the woman is made to suffer from physical pain that gives her unbearable psychic trauma. She finds no reason for continuing to live, life becomes a journey without a purpose, and death appears to offer relief from all sufferings.

Love makes the strongest bond in an intimate relationship. When love wanes and disappears, hatred takes its place and then there remains nothing to keep-up the relationship. The woman finds that she is all alone in the world, she has none who may need her love or for whom she should live any longer, and then she takes the extreme step to end her misery.

She becomes desperate when she feels that without any justification she has to lose the love of her husband or her lover. This occurs mostly when the man brings another woman in his life and transfers his love to her, leaving his first love in the lurch. Again, when a woman gets drawn into intimate relationship with a married man and the man ditches her, she finds herself abandoned and life for her loses all purpose; at this stage she thinks of putting an end to her isolation by quitting the world.

Suicide may be the manifestation of an extreme grief reaction. It might also be an aggressive act aimed at self-destruction, or the destruction of something her own life believed by her to be of value to others. In one case it is for self-punishment and in the other for punishment of others, by way of revenge.

Suicide is generally not attempted in a fit of impulsive reaction to some sudden outraging emotional input. It is the final explosion of accumulated tension; when tension grows to such a magnitude that it becomes intolerable, there is a sudden outburst. But there are always exceptions. There can be a specific event which might trigger the action and make the volcano of accumulated stress erupt. It may give the impression that suicide or its attempt was the direct consequence of some unacceptable emotional event, and the person attempting suicide might also think it to be so, though in reality it is the end-product of accumulated tension.

In almost every case of suicide, whether it is the consequence of extreme depression and despondency or of uncontrollable mental agitation, there is always the final rupture of the linking emotional cord which had kept her attached and linked-up to someone she loved. She thinks of leaving the world when she finds that her common personal space with her lover no longer exists and she is all alone.

In a non-nuclear family set-up a woman's personal space remains vulnerable to interference and inter-meddling even by immediate relatives of the husband. The in-law relationships make it incumbent on her to have multiple linking cords with various members of the family. These linking cords can come under stress for various reasons and their cumulative effect can create tension of a very high intensity, it may be of such gravity that the woman may not be able to bear. When the husband himself joins other members of the family, the common personal space of the couple gets wholly destroyed and the emotional linking cord breaks into pieces. The woman finds herself isolated, deserted and unwanted, and feels her life has lost all purpose. Her helplessness drives her to attempt suicide and end her life.

A similar situation occurs when an unmarried boy or girl lives in a family in which the whole atmosphere is full of tension, and the emotional cords of attachment with each other come under severe stress, making intimate relationships disharmonious. A psychological aggression, committed even with good intentions, generally precipitates the situation and makes the young person try to run away from life, and attempt suicide.

Intimate relationships need regular strengthening of emotional cords to keep people connected. This comes naturally from positive emotions like those of love, adoration, compassion and benevolence, and the situation gets reversed when the negative emotions and depressing situations take over. Coping becomes extremely difficult when persons develop negative emotions like scorn, hate and anger, because they create conditions of animosity, and animosity totally destroys an intimate relationship. Once the intimate relationship ceases to exist, the victim becomes isolated and feels her life has become purposeless, and suicide seems to be the only alternative.

Suicide is sometimes wrongly believed by a person to be an act of bravery, but it is not. It does not even help in taking revenge or punishing the guilty. Suicide is attempted only when the person is unable to face emotional turbulence. The cord of intimacy helps a person maintain courage necessary to cope with difficult and adverse situations. Once that cord is snapped, the source that gives strength and incentive to live dries up and the person becomes desperate and finds herself standing alone and helpless in total darkness, then neurotic depression grips the individual's consciousness and suicide alone seems to offer an escape.

Breach of an intimate relationship affects more severely a person who is unable to face and bear the devastating consequences of broken ties of love. Neurotic depression hits hardest when breach and estrangement is caused by someone who had at some stage promised everlasting love. When such a person, for no fault of the woman in love, breaks the promise and demolishes the relationship, it breaks the woman's heart and indirectly forces her to seek solace in death. When a person goes in the state of neurotic depression or in a state of unbearable emotional agitation, the person's mauled consciousness fails to take the decision to live on and face the tragic situation. The taking of such a positive decision requires courage, confidence, and boldness, which the woman whose linking emotional cord has been broken, no longer possesses. She sees vacancy all round and finds that her common personal space has disappeared. She is left with neither the desire nor the vitality to live a lonely life. Intuitively she moves on into an unknown world, which she presumes will be better than the one in which she has suffered betrayal, deception, desertion,...

However happiness can some not by extriguishing the candle but by making the light of love grow brighter and all-embracing of courage is the foundation of life, love is the converstone of intimacy and relationship.

DIANA

When a girl is emotionally involved, then no other factor counts or matters. At that point of time what matters is just the man she is in love with; she can see no further than that, whether he is married or has children is not relevant. When she has given her entire self to him, she expects the same in return. And when she does not get it, it hurts. For her, the rest of the world does not exist or matters, she is prepared to fight the world for her love. That, of course, will depend on her capacity for total involvement with the lover, and indifference to anything beyond this rëlationship. She would at the same time, wish the man to give up his family for her, just as she has given up the world for him. But men fail to respond to the confidence women repose in them, which really amounts to betrayal on their part, and makes women realise that no man is worth all that sacrifice and suffering.

Diagnostic Scan

A very smart,well-groomed, young woman, well-dressed, manicured, wearing well-done make-up and pleasant perfume.

She tries to present a smiling face, but below the mask is the face of a shattered personality.

D. Guess my age.

C. I think, thirty-eight.

D. She gleamed with triumph. I am forty-four. I look younger. I feel younger. I act younger. I think younger.

Diana is a victim of psychic-stagnancy. She has ceased to grow beyond the age of thirty-seven. She feels she is thirty-seven. She thinks she looks thirty-seven, and behaves like a girl of thirty-seven. It was the age when she was in her full bloom, and while in full bloom, lightning had struck and the wind had blown away the petals, and she had become a withered flower. She is clinging to that time in her life and has ceased to move along the stream of life. She had lost the race, could no more continue with her glamorous job of a receptionist in a five-star hotel. Diana, unconsciously, still longs for that life, a life full of glamour and romance. But soon, her dreams vanish and she sinks back into the reality of her devastated life.

D. I love glamour. As a child I went with my mother (who is a teacher) to the U.K. and had my early education in the U.K. We became steeped in western culture. After returning to India. I joined as a receptionist in a five-star hotel. I had to live a posh lifestyle, having to interact with elite foreign visitors. I was married, and I took a divorce.

I married again and lived with my husband. That was the best period of my life. However, while my husband was away for a slightly longer time, I became involved with another man. He promised to marry me. That led me to take divorce from my (second) husband after seven years of happy married life. My paramour invited me to Dubai in order to get married to me. But when I reached Dubai I found he was living with his wife and children. Naturally, I was enraged and came back disappointed, disheartened and shattered. I had already divorced my loving husband and there was none to give me comfort. Then, my elder brother died. I was very attached to him and his death was a still greater shock for me.

Presently Diana suffers from various kinds of obsessive compulsions.

(*a*) Takes three hours to brush her teeth in the morning. During this period, she also cleans her bathroom, sink and does her grooming. Takes bath but does not regard it as a daily routine.

(*b*) If she fails to spend all this time in the toilet, she feels her teeth, etc. are not clean and does not take breakfast or any other meal. The result is that she suffers from anorexia and looks sickly. But she says she eats a lot when she does; probably that is how she manages to avoid acute anorexia.

(*c*) Because of her Obsessional Compulsive Disorders (OCDs) she cannot get ready in time and is always late for every engagement. That was why she lost her job at the hotel.

(*d*) She goes on with her toilet routine so long that she always finds herself short of time for everything. A twenty-four hour day is not enough for her.

Her second divorce coupled with the betrayal by her last lover, has shattered her, and made her what she is.

After the betrayal by her lover, she went to the U.S.A. to settle there and find solace, but returned completely disappointed. On her return, she tried all kinds of treatments including psychiatric, but nothing seemed to do her any good.

She tried to give tuition in conversational English. Only one man responded; however she found that his intention was not to learn English, but only to enjoy her company. She asked him to stop coming. She is without any purposeful engagement since then, and is suffering neglect, insecurity, and frustration.

The test conducted on the Maudsley Obsessional-Compulsive Inventory showed she was having a number of obsessional-compulsive negative disorders;

(*a*) Frequently gets disturbing, nasty and nauseating thoughts, and finds difficulty in getting rid of them.
(*b*) More concerned about other people's honesty (truthfulness).
(*c*) Always gets late for any appointment because cannot get through everything in time.
(*d*) Worries about contamination.
(*e*) Has to check things several times (tap, doors, etc.).
(*f*) Unpleasant thoughts come and upset her.
(*g*) Doubts about simple everyday things.
(*h*) Repeats things over and over again, gets behind schedule.
(*i*) Uses a lot of soap and water for bath.
(*j*) Thinks some numbers are unlucky (four or multiples of four).
(*k*) Takes a long time to get ready in the morning (cannot go to work before 1 p.m.).
(*l*) Excessively concerned about cleanliness.
(*m*) Feels her hands will become dirty on touching money which has passed through many hands.
(*n*) Takes extra long time in the morning ablutions.

Todays, she has been given counselling on three counts:

(*a*) Death of her brother,
(*b*) Honesty of others,
(*c*) Her general behavioural pattern.

She repeatedly goes on adding sadness about her brother's loss to the stock of miseries in her memory, goes on enacting the scenes of her brother's death. She has repeated it so many times that it has become a kind of addiction, she has got entrapped in it.

Counselling

C. Diana, do you not believe that any man who is born must die?

D. I do.

C. Gautam Buddha had emphasised that death of every person is inevitable and certain, and there is no family in which there has not been a death. Your brother was ill and suffering agony. By his death he has been relieved of the pain and torture he was suffering. He could not have become young again and live a healthy life. You don't want your brother to come back and alive an invalid.

D. No. I do not. I have seen his life of agony. I do not wish him to live that over again.

C. *Was it not good for him that he got relief from pain? Think of his gain and not your loss. You loved him, so give up the thought of your own loss. Look at death not as a tragedy but as a deliverance.*

D. I shall try to think of it through his eyes and not mine.

C. *That is right, from negative thought of death you switch on to its positive aspect. Think of life instead of thinking of death. Think of the happy days you spent with your brother. You must feel grateful that you lived with him for forty two years.*

D. I shall try to recall the happy days I had with him and find consolation in them.

C. *Death has many victims and you are one of them. You too have suffered the pain and agony of his death without dying yourself. You were only the shadow-victim and not the real victim. You have continued to die in your sub-consciousness, and are obsessed with the memory of the death of your brother. Reality of an event ceases to exist, but its myth and shadow can continue to exist, because they are not real and can remain embedded in the memory. It is necessary to pluck them out of your mind. If the reality is gone, why should its shadow or its myth be allowed to continue. So, wipe them out of your mind, erase them from your memory.*

D. But how? It is so difficult.

C. *Like any other mourner, you have identified yourself with your brother, and in his death you feel your own. That makes you sad, because unconsciously you feel that you yourself have died along with your brother.*

D. I do not like death. I feel it is a deprivation, it has created a vacuum in my life. Still, it is not possible for me to forget it.

C. *This is because your mind is not willing to accept the reality of death. Just try to realise that death is a reality, and only its memory has remained in your mind. You have to make your sub-conscious mind aware of this reality, and begin to believe that you are alive, and that you are only the shadow victim and not the real victim of death.*

Remember also that death has brought liberation to your brother from the agonising pain he was suffering; so be happy not sad. Don't you regard your brother's liberation more important than your own pain of separation? Don't you think you are doing injustice to your brother who loved you so much?

D. I see.

[These ideas have been injected into her mind through the process of psychic inputs, with the aid of hypnosis.]

Next Session

As a result of counselling, Diana is today a changed person. She is in good shape, she is well-groomed as usual, smiling and charming. During the last eight days, she has had some pleasant experiences.

D. I felt, each day for about two minutes, some type of happiness, a feeling of liberation. Something pleasant happened to me but I cannot explain or define it.

C. *Sometimes things happen for which there is no logical explanation. Why should one worry about the cause of happiness? Even a moment's happiness is better than a million moments of life devoid of happiness.*

D. I no longer feel the agony of death of my brother. The tension caused by his death has disappeared. I am no longer disturbed by looking at his photo. I have finally accepted his death as a fact of life.

C. *Life and death are part of the same process, one is the beginning, the other the end. In between is life. What about your OCDs? Are they not injurious to your health?*

D. I realise my skin is getting not better but worse by use of too much soap. Too much brushing of teeth also is uncalled for. But I have no control over my actions on my unwanted idleness or doing nothing.

Diana has today spoken frankly on her marriages and other relationships.

1. Her first marriage was not successful; there was a significant difference in their cultural backgrounds. She was open minded and modern while he was of consevative views. He did not want even to live independently with her; he insisted on living with his parents, but it was intolerable for Diana. She had a separate house, and wanted to live independently without any interference from his parents.

There was divorce by mutual consent after three years. It had no traumatic effect on her.

2. She married again after a couple of years. This was a very successful marriage and she had a pleasant time with her husband.

Many years later they spent two months in Europe, mostly in Germany. Sometime later, for reasons of their employment they had to stay separately for six months. Diana felt uncomfortable during this period. They patched up, but she agreed to live with him only on the condition that he would not insist on having a child. She did not want a child because of the nature of her employment in the hotel. During this period they did not have sexual relations because she did not feel emotionally or physically attracted to him. During the period of their virtual separation, Diana developed intimacy with another man working in the same hotel.

Diana is by nature romantic, she wants to live a glamorous life. She even loved flirting with young men. In the five-star hotel while working as a receptionist, she had not only the opportunity but, as per job requirement, had to play the role of a glamour girl. There was always an international clientele, mostly from western countries who had fascination for India and Indian girls. She used to come in contact with co-workers also. She fell in love with one of them and had a fling. They came too close and her husband became aware of it. This created a rift between Diana and her husband. She was not ready to leave her paramour. She preferred to break away from her husband. She got a divorce by mutual consent. Thereafter also they continued to be friends. But her ex-husband married another girl and Diana was out of his life.

Even though this divorce was also by mutual consent, it had a devastating effect on Diana because she had always felt secure and happy during this marriage. Diana developed symptoms of depression. She became irregular and developed the syndrome of not getting ready in time. During this period of depression, a hotel colleague, gave her the support she badly needed to overcome the trauma of divorce. The two came closer. They developed an intimate relationship. He promised to marry her and thus gained her love and confidence. He went to Dubai and called her there to get married to him. When she went to Dubai, she found him living with his wife and children .He refused to marry her or leave his family. This brought to an end Diana's relationship with him. Now she was completely shattered.

C. *Diana, how could a woman like you fall into such a trap?*

D. When a girl is emotionally involved, then no other factor counts or matters. At that point of time what matters is just the man she's in love with; she can see no further than that, whether he is married or has children is not relevant. When she has given her entire self to him she also expects the same in return. And when she does not get it, it hurts. For her, the rest of the world does not exist or matter; she is prepared to fight the world for her love. That, of course, will depend on her capacity for total involvement with the lover, and indifference to anything beyond this relationship. She would at the same time wish the man to give up his family for her just as she has given up the world for him. But men fail to respond to the confidence women repose in them, which really amounts to betrayal on their part and makes women realise that no man is worth all that sacrifice and suffering.

Intensive conselling has been given to Diana for tensions caused by her misadventures with her last lover who ditched her.

Counselling made her see the wisdom of forgetting the whole incident because the process was irreversible, and neither the affair nor the faithless lover was worth being retained in her mind. She has completely got over the trauma.

D. I have already thrown him in the dustbin.

C. You have done the right thing.

Next Session

Diana is in good shape, relaxed. Age regression has revealed a hidden cause of Diana's suffering. While she was very young and lived in the U.K. she suffered the trauma of living through the violent quarrels of her parents, who ultimately separated, then Diana was only ten. As a small child she had witnessed her father's cruelty towards her mother and brother. She too was once slapped so violently that she fell down on the heater. Diana never understood why she was beaten.

Her brother used to be regularly beaten by her father. On one occasion, the father very cruelly beat her brother with his belt. This stunned her and made her tremble with fear, its memory still continues to trouble her.

Her mother believed, and Diana never disbelieved her mother, that her husband (Diana's father) was a womaniser. This always created friction and clash between the couple. Diana had witnessed the inhuman and brutal behaviour of her father toward her mother. This too adversely affected Diana's psyche and left a permanent scar on her subconsciousness.

She had no courage to retaliate, and has all along carried the feeling of helplessness, which in turn has made her angry against her own self. She tries to wash off this feeling of guilt and shame by washing her entire body, but without any success.

Ulimately when her patents separated, her mother, brother and Diana returned to India.

There was another important event in her life. While Diana was studying Biology, she had to dissect a frog, and when she touched it, she felt revulsion. This precipitated her hidden feelings of guilt and shame arising out of the cruel treatment of her father toward her brother, mother and herself. It was after this incident that the obsessional compulsion to wash her hands with soap started. The feeling continues concealed in her sub-conscious mind till date in an aggravated form.

The frog metamorphosed the deep sorrow rooted in her heart, into OCD. The frog came to her as the 'prince frog' of the fairy tale, but only to remind her of the incidents when her father had mauled the helpless three by his cruel behaviour. She was reminded by the frog that it was wrongful to injure the feelings of an innocent living being and she must at one for it.

C. Today, it is the same 'prince frog' which has opened the door to your subconsciousness to uncover the real cause of your sufferings. You must be named "frog princess".

D. Yeah! (laughs)

C. Diana, you have a conflict in your mind which remains unexpressed. The inner conflict is between your father's guilt and shame on one side and your innocence and crucification on the other. You have got to get rid of it. Do not carry the guilt of your father, you have in no way wronged your mother or brother, you are completely innocent. You have never done anything to be ashamed of or to feel guilty about. Just realise this, and start on the new road free of the burden of your father's wrong-doings.

Next Session

C. Hello Diana, how is life?

D. Not very good.

C. Speak-up, clear your conscience, what is it now that is weighing on your heart?

D. Human mind is always ready to lay the blame for anything onto someone else. Why we cannot fathom. Why take the blame for anything if it can be pushed onto someone else's shoulders? It is because of this characteristic of the people that all these years I've been suffering from immense pangs of guilt and have remained burdened with the huge weight which had been resting on my tender shoulders. Since my adolescence, when the break up of my parents led to an emotional deficiency of some sort I developed the symptoms of my current situation. All through the next thirty years. I was the butt of ridicule from my entire legion of family and friends, laying it really thick on me as if it was all my fault...

I was deeply scarred by the incessant sniggering and joking at my expense. And my fault was that I was emotionally so sensitive that any and every trauma that I've faced in my life, just pushed me more deeply into this mire of a disorder. When I was faced with the horrendous reality of having lost my job due to my late coming, a job which I loved, I suffered possibly the worst year or two of my life. I was made to feel so directly responsible for this state of affairs and I felt so terribly guilty that at the age of 36, for the first time in my life, I looked up at the ceiling fan and contemplated hanging from it. However, I banished it from my mind as quickly as it had appeared there. It is of course, debatable whether it takes guts to commit suicide, or whether it is the last resort of cowards who can't face the world when the going gets tough. And I've always thought of myself as being strong and resilient enough to face worst situations in life. But having lost my job I was shattered. Still more shattering was the fact that I should have even thought of the absurdity of taking my own life. That was, because of the guilt trap which was being laid on me from every quarter, most heavily and incessantly by my own brother..

Did I enjoy spending hours in the bathroom, being made fun of by all and sundry? Losing my job and being humiliated for that?

C. You are perfectly right, people do not understand the plight of others and not even care to find out the reality and cause of other's sufferings. OCD is a sort of a psychosomatic disease, and no one can be held personally responsible for the same. The adverse circumstances and not you are responsible for this uncontrollable behaviour of yours. There is no reason why you should feel guilty or ashamed. By and by, people will have better understanding and will cease to lay blame on you. In any case, you know the truth, you know that you have not created OCD, then why should you feel sorry or guilty? Better you should pity them for their ignorance. So from now on you shall not feel any guilt for your OCD.

D. Yes there is no cause for my feeling any guilt. I realise what you say is correct, but that will not cure my OCD.

C. This is true, but you will have to try, and by and by they will come under control. You should look into the mirror to see that your hands, face, why the whole body is clean as it ever was. You should look into the mirror to see the purity and innocence of your conscience.

You should start concentrating on other things, and try to give to OCD behaviour as little concern as possible. You should develop a new vision of your future, new ambitions, new hopes, new aspirations, and new dreams.

Write a daily-activity diary, and see how you distribute your time on various activities and non-activities.

Next Session

Diana brought statements of her daily activities and the time she spent in each activity; they show certain aberrations.

1. She does not have proper sleep,
   (*a*) Sleep pattern is not regular,
   (*b*) Sleep timings are not regular,
   (*c*) Sleep hours are not enough,
   (*d*) Sometimes she remains awake the whole night

Remains glued to T.V. till two or three in the night till she falls asleep on the sofa and gets up early in the morning.

2. Her time is very often spent in just lying on the sofa or sitting on the bed with a vacant mind, which she says is the time during which she thinks and plans, but in reality she broods and broods.

3. She does not take regular meals: breakfast, lunch, dinner.

Very often she goes without any food for days together. She cannot eat without cleaning her teeth which takes about three hours, and she does not find that much time. The shortage of time is not because she is doing something, but because she is not doing anything.

Counselling has been directed with objective of:

(*i*) Removal of the feeling of defilement, and the consequential obsession of having more-than-perfect cleanliness meant to erase subconscious memories of contact (body contact) with her lover who ditched her and was responsible for her alienation from her second husband with whom she had spent her life's happiest moments.

(*ii*) Making her realise the need of regular-eight-hour block sleep during night.

(*iii*) Importance of having regular, wholesome meals for her general health and maintaining her glamourous looks and for counteracting depression.

D. I cannot change my routine. I must go on doing what I am doing.

C. Yes you, continue to do what you are doing. However, there is a distinction between two sets of instructions. Dos and Don'ts. It is very difficult to follow negative direction, but it is not too difficult to follow positive directions of Dos. So, you go on doing whatever you like, take as much time in your pet activities as you like. Leave aside the 'don't' instructions but consider the positive ones.

1. Have an eight-hour sleep in one stretch during the night.
2. Eat three regular meals.

D. I know these two things are very essential for health and well-being. I shall try my best to have eight hours sleep and eat regular meals.

Next Session

Diana reported that during the last seventeen or eighteen nights after the counselling she slept for eight hours at a stretch, and also had regular meals. Her appearance has changed. the haggard look has gone, and she looks healthy.

Diana, however, added that she had changed the sleep pattern. Now she sleeps for three to four hours in the night, and compensates it by having a nap in the morning for a few hours. This is because she is unable to get away from the TV till two in the morning as her favourite programmes are telecasted late in the night.

She has started taking regular meals. As advised, she brushes the teeth in addition to her regular cleaning. Diana says she now feels excellent, she has not missed a single meal in the last days. This has done her a lot of good.

Further counselling has been directed to make her reduce the time spent on her obsessive compulsive activities, even as a token; and for reduction and elimination of her negative and non-productive thoughts and for encouraging positive and creative thoughts.

Next Session

D. I do not think my obsessive compulsions are due to any hidden feeling of defilement during the love affair which had left me broken and shattered. I think there must be some other cause, yet to be discovered.

C. Maybe, but let us not worry about the cause, it is their effect that matters. I am more concerned at the moment about your general health and well-being than the number of hours you take for your personal hygiene and cleanliness. After all, you don't do it everyday and the total time taken in the month is not more than what anybody else takes. So, don't worry about it, at least till you regain your lost weight.

Next Session (*on phone*)

C. How are you Diana? Your voice is a bit feeble, what's the matter?

D. There has been a relapse, I have not eaten for three days.

C. Why?

D. I could not manage to brush my teeth.

C. Did you take water?

D. Yes, I do not have to chew and eat water.

C. That's right. So do milk, fruit juice and soup not require chewing and eating. Why can you not have these things too?

D. Of course, I can.

C. So, let's have a compromise. You do not eat solid food till you brush your teeth, but continue to take liquids. In this way you will get at least sufficient nutrition to go on till the stage of taking solid food arrives. You can also take honey and lemon mixed in water.

D. Yes, there should be no problem in that.

C. So, it is agreed that you will not starve on any day. Liquids everyday,solids when OCD permits. And, liquids must be taken in good quantity and as many times as you conveniently can.

D. Agreed.

[Diana has been sticking to this compromise agreement. It has kept her above the starvation level. Sometimes she does complain of feeling hungry, and has to be persuaded to brush her teeth. On the whole the programme is working.]

C. It is also necessary that you get interested in some purposeful activity, any activity in which you may feel interested.

D. I wish I could take up modelling and acting, but I think I cannot do it as my face is not photogenic.

C. How do you know this? Anyway, first go and attend the T.V. shooting session to which you have been invited as one of the audience.

Later (*on phone*)

D. I did go to the TV session. I asked two questions, they were very much appreciated and applauded. I felt very very happy. Even the producer congratulated me.

C. It may mean a big break for you.

Next Session

C. (Diana is in good spirits). You are, I think, twenty per cent cured.

D. No, fifty per cent; I am having food everyday, of course I have solid and liquids sessions.

C. You have to take solids regularly, liquids are meant only to provide for emergency gaps. And what about sleep ?

D. Again, it is the same as with meals; now I have regular sleep every night though I sleep late also get up late in the morning.

C. This is very good; both are directly and basically inter-dependent. You cannot sleep on an empty stomach, and you cannot feel the urge for food if you have sleepless nights.

D. By having regular meals and sleep my health has improved. I no longer have that haggard look, nor do I feel exhausted and distraught. I have gained weight also.

C. Now try and add breakfast to your routine. In the morning, whenever you get up and finish your toilet exercise, wash your mouth and brush your teeth just for five minutes and then take your breakfast. Brushing your teeth in the morning for five minutes is an essential part of normal hygiene, do not avoid it. No harm will come to you by doing this quick brush-the-teeth exercise. It is enough to clean your mouth for breakfast.

D. I shall try from tomorrow. I have already reduced the duration of my teeth-brush exercise, etc., from three hours to one and a half. I have done this during the last two days.

C. Continue to reduce the time further, as much as you can, but don't let it become another cause for your tension. It is better to take more time than to worry about reducing the time for various activities.

D. I shall try.

C. You should not any more submit to the OCD slavery; acquire your freedom, win your liberation.

D. How? I want it desperately, I want freedom from this slavery, I want to be master of my behaviour; I want to behave normally.

C. Then make the determination, declare war and fight to the finish. You are responsible for your own behaviour, don't shirk responsibility. Go bring a pen and paper and pen down your determination that from now on you will never brush your teeth for three hours, and will brush your teeth and do the washing in forty-five minutes.

D. But earlier you had told me to reduce time gradually.

C. Yes, but prophylactic and slow-motion treatment has not worked very well, so now surgery must be performed. There is no time to lose. You must take immediate command of the situation and take determined action.

D. Listen to what I have written. She reads out her determination.

Next Session (*on phone*)

D. Yesterday, I did not brush my teeth at all.

C. But was it deliberate or due to some compulsion?

D. It was deliberate, I did not feel confident that I shall be able to finish in forty-five minutes, so I decided to skip it. However, today I have succeeded. I have taken only forty-five minutes.

There is one thing more I wish to tell you. It is for the first time in so many years that I have a feeling of complete relaxation. Earlier during and after my long bathroom exercises, I always felt tense, vexed, and exercised; I never before felt this kind of relaxation, today I am feeling as if I have done some pleasant act.

C. This is because you have won the battle, you have ended your slavery to your sub-conscious mind. You have got over the feeling of obsessive compulsion. When a slave is made to do a job he does it as if he was carrying a burden and suffers stress and tension; when the same job is done by the master himself it ceases to be forced labour and becomes a pleasant exercise.

Now go and enjoy your dinner. *Bon appetit.*

D. Thank you, I am in a relaxed mood, so today I'll enjoy my dinner.

Next (*on Phone*)

D. During the last three months, I have gained in some respects;

(1) I take food everyday,

(2) I sleep every night/day,

(3) My tensions arising out of broken marriages and death of brother have almost ended.

(4) General feeling of relaxation has come and I no longer just sit and brood.

However, what still trouble me are the compulsive actions, they make me lose all control over time.

C. Whatever is not in your power, and is not the result of your voluntary or conscious act or omission should not be a matter of concern to you. So accept them and don't worry about them.

D. Then I will not be able to do anything positive because I will never be ready in time.

C. You still have twenty hours available, free of OCD. Just spend five minutes every morning after your toilet in brushing your teeth, this is not a substitute for your OCD tooth brushing, and take something even if it be a spoonful of honey. I insist on your doing so because I want to break your OCD.

If I can finish brushing in five minutes, I can very well take my breakfast.

C. This brushing is going to be a conscious exercise free of OCD brushing. You will be doing it voluntarily at the command of your conscious mind, and thereby win the battle against the OCD's unconscious control of your volition.

D. Today I shall positively do it after I finish my toilet which itself will take a long time.

C. Doesn't matter when you do it, but do it. Believe it is a battle we must win without disturbing your O.C. exercises controlled by your sub-conscious mind. I want you to establish a coordination between your conscious and sub-conscious commands, and make your positive conscious commands more powerful than the sub-conscious negative commands.

D. I promise I'll do it today and report to you in the evening.

Evening

D. *(Diana is in a triumphant mood.) After years I have taken both breakfast and lunch and I am ready for dinner. I have made a big breakthrough. I succeeded in brushing my teeth after toilet. Although I took about an hour but I did it and took my breakfast, though rather late, and also my lunch.*

C. It is really a great achievement, three meals in one day!

D. I am going to reduce the brushing time gradually, and also do it a bit earlier. I am feeling so happy I had breakfast and lunch. I don't remember how long back I had three meals in a single day.

C. It will give you energy to pursue your other activities, and also make you gain more weight.

D. Yes, I still am ten kg underweight. With regular food and sleep I shall gain weight and get back my healthy looks.

C. And also regain your fading beauty and charm.

D. How wonderful! Today I am feeling so much relaxed, I never felt like this before, I have no worries, no disturbing, uncomfortable thoughts.

C. By and by you might even get over your OC's but at present don't worry about them, let them be. I am concerned only with your conscious and voluntary thoughts and action and not worried about your OCs over which your conscious mind has no control.

D. I realise it, I must control my thoughts and feelings, and activities other than OCD's and I am determined to go ahead. I have already won the battle against the disturbing and nasty thoughts and depressing feelings which had made my life miserable; in spite of my OCDs I have now a general feeling of well-being.

(***After quite some time***)

C. What's the matter, Diana?

D. I am really feeling disgusted with my OCD. I cannot keep any appointment, and cannot do anything which I wish because I cannot get ready in time.

C. So why worry about it, take things lightly and feel happy with what you can do; and also with what you cannot.

D. I am not a saint, I am not Buddha, I want to enjoy life, to do the things I like. I feel bad and dejected when I fail because of this wretched OCD.

C. Diana, you are perfectly right, most people believe in the "pursuit of pleasure" doctrine, and there is nothing wrong in your searching happiness through fulfilment of your desires. By the way, have you heard the name of Helen Keller?

D. Yes, she was blind, deaf and dumb.

C. And still she achieved a lot.

D. Yes, but I am not a great personality, I am just an ordinary woman.

C. I don't know, you may be wrong. For becoming Helen Keller you have only to reduce yourself and become a zero. Helen Keller gave up thinking about her own disabilities, began concentrating on the effect of such disabilities on the happiness or persons similarly situated. She became a zero so far as her own life mattered, and became infinity with regard to the needs and happiness of everyone else. You too have a commendable quality of self-expression, and you have a treasure of experience and wisdom which can be of immense good to the world. Don't you agree with me?

D. Yes, I know I have a flare for writing, and I can write impressively, but I have no time for that.

C. Your problem is not shortage of time, but lack of will. In a week or a month you are not spending longer time on your OCD activities, than does any other person. You are generally sitting idle or brooding or watching TV for hours together. I do not say you cut your TV time, but I ask you only to write about your own life and problems in the off-time you have.

After some time you might find you have spent your time more purposefully than you had thought. Please try.

D. I can only say I shall try, but I do not promise.

C. I do not ask for a promise, I also do not ask you to fix any time schedule, or even to target any particular topic, I want you just to let your mind wake up and act, and let some ink run on few sheets of paper everyday.

D. O.K. I shall write, but it would be your duty to send it for publication.

C. Agreed. However you will have to send it to me, and will do that only through post.

D. I shall do that.

C. One thing more, you should not expect that it would be published, it might not suit their requirement for one reason or another. Then you will post it elsewhere. Never be afraid of receiving "Rejection slips".

D. I feel so relieved by thinking that my OCD is not a hurdle in every kind of venture. I can go ahead along with my OCD.

C. Of course, you can. But please give up your subordination to it, please treat yourself as the master of the situation and not a slave of OCD. Let it live, accept it as a companion, but only as a part-time and not a whole-time companion.

D. Okay, thank you for allowing my companion to live with me.

C. Let it not create any hindrance in your literary achievements.

D. Very well. I am feeling so much courage that I have began to dream about becoming a great writer.

C. I have no doubt your dream will come true, sooner or later.

SWATI

You should realise the difference between a lover and a husband. Lover is for romance and excitement and, husband is for security, support, care and concern. Once you had a husband, now you have a lover. Then you had no lover, now you have no husband. Ravi has both a wife and a lover. His wife has a husband but no lover.... Ravi will continue to be your rival's husband and your lover... It is mistake to treat a lover also a husband ... The role played by a husband is different from the role played by a lover. The two roles are not the same.

Diagnostic Scan

Swati is madly in love with Ravi, a married man. She has, as she says, fallen in deep deep love with him, and cannot live without his total involvement with her. She wants to have him totally and exclusively. Her love is ecstatic in nature. She feels her love for Ravi is similar to the ecstatic and radiant love Radha had for Krishna, love in which she has devoted her entire body, mind, feelings and emotions to Ravi.

Swati's involvement with Ravi has continued for about five years, both of them are in their thirties. Both are working as executives in the same organisation though in separate establishments. Swati has gone into depression and has stopped going to work without even applying for leave.

In the style of Hindi movies they had married before God, and Ravi had assured Swati's mother that he would always take care of her as a loving husband.

Swati is now sensing Ravi's withdrawal from her, she thinks he has started avoiding her, although Ravi assured her that he still cares for and is as devoted to her as ever.

The doubts in Swati's mind have created in her a fear of losing Ravi and his affection. For his companionship she has staked everything. She refused promotion to avoid being posted elsewhere. She even gave up the opportunity of going abroad. In the office, whispers go round about her involvement with Ravi. This has affected her prestige, respect, and general reputation, but she is prepared to endure it all for Ravi.

The intensity of fear is as deep as her love, both are correlated. Swati is under such a spell of love that she has became blind about the existing situation. Ravi has a wife and two children, he lives with them, and his marriage with Swati was faked only to gain her confidence. She is unable to realise that Ravi can never have full involvment with her, and it is very probable that Ravi is not, like her, ready to take chances with his career, which may be adversely affected by the factum of his amorous involvement with a woman colleague becoming public.

It came out during scanning that there was something very tragic in Swati's life, and that had made her so dependent on Ravi and afraid of losing him. A bit of further probe into Swati's mind, with a little hypnosis, made her burst out, tears began flooding out of her eyes, she was going to disclose what was hidden in her mind:

I was married at the age of thirteen to a man fifteen years older than me. With the family of my husband. I had a very bad and miserable time. I gave birth to two sons. While I was nearing twenty eight, I became ill, I was tortured and turned out, and was not allowed to take my children with me. I filed a suit for divorce, which lingered on for nearly ten years and only recently I have obtained the decree for divorce.

No member of my family supports me. My brother and sisters keep away. My mother also never comes to live with me. My father died last year. I had gone to attend the cremation. There I met my sons, but they too refused to come with me.

I felt completely destroyed, isolated and as lonely as when I was turned out of the house. It was Ravi who gave me support in my time of distress. He filled me with love, made me forget my tragedies, agonies, and gave a new life. My response was equally warm. It was full of emotion, I became completely involved with him and have spent five years of my life in sheer happiness with him.

Swati is a talented woman. She is interested in dance (Bharatnatyam). classical music and also philosophy. She has a collection of works of Vivekananda, Ramakrishna Paramhans and of Krishnamurthi. But nothing has been able to give her peace of mind. She has been going to god-men, attending spiritual discussions, doing puja, meditation, etc. in search of happiness but has failed so far. She is, however, not religious and does not have much faith in God.

After she had narrated her tale of woe and bliss and had received a bit of counselling, she became happy and confident. Her nervousness was gone.All the time she was looking at the watch and feeling restless. She wanted to talk to Ravi whom she had not met the whole day. She tried the phone several times, but it was always engaged. Depression began to appear on her face. After a time she tried again, Ravi was not there, she became disappointed. After a while I asked her to try again. This time Ravi was there, the love parleys began. Her face changed its colour, love was showing itself on her face in full glow.

Counselling

Swati is standing on the precipice, if she falls she will break into pieces. The fall may not be imminent, but the possibility and probability of it cannot be ruled out. She has to prepare herself to meet the more serious tragedy that may befall her by the total withdrawal of Ravi's love. Red alert has been sounded so that Swati may be on her guard.

C. You should realise that Ravi can never belong totally to you. He will never leave his wife and children in order to accept you as his life-partner. He has never come to stay in your flat or to spend the whole night with you. You have been having love-parleys in cinema style outside the home. You have to remain just friends. But even the friendship should not go beyond a point the point of no return. There is already a move for your transfer to another state. You cannot remain on leave for too long to avoid transfer and it may not be in your interest to resign. Once you resign, you will lose all chances of meeting Ravi, you will lose your residence and salary, and even Ravi will not be able or willing to support you.

S. I am ready for any eventuality, except that I can't leave Ravi. I must have him at any cost.

C. Please be more practical and accept that you have no control over the circumstances and things that happen. It was only because of the circumstances that you met Ravi and had the opportunity of getting involved with him. You should be happy that you had five pleasant years, which came like an oasis in the desert of your long dry life of misery.

Swati, you have to learn to accept changes in life. There is no reason for you to fear the future. Nobody knows, it may have greater happiness in store for you. You should be optimistic and live with the hope of a happier future.

S. But, with Ravi's recent behaviour I can only expect despondency, not hope.

C. Maybe, but it does not show love will not grow with time. Even a little distance sometimes helps in kindling the light of love.

Swati, just understand the true import of love. Love means giving of happiness and not craving for it from someone you love. It does not mean attachment to any individual. Love lives inside you, inside your consciousness. Love is divine and brings happiness. Attachment involves desire to possess and acquire, and brings pain. Whenever there is a desire of keeping someone in one's exclusive possession, disappointment results.

S. I do not want him exclusively, but he must continue to love me. I cannot live without loving him.

C. Swati, you continue to love Ravi so long both of you are here and things are favourable, but you have to keep an eye on the future, which you cannot afford to sacrifice for the transient love of Ravi. Ravi can never be your husband or live with you so long as his wife is there. He found you amenable and available for his own pleasure, and in the process you also got pleasure, but that is only a transient phase in your life. Life is like a stream, let it flow on. Enjoy life as it is, it changes from time to time and adopts varied forms and shapes. Sometimes it brings happiness, sometimes unhappiness. One must accept life as it is, If Ravi has to go out of your life, he will, you will not be able to stop it. So remain prepared for every eventuality.

The caravan of life does not take instructions or commands from any single individual, its commands come from millions of uncontrollable factors. It is, hence, contrary to wisdom to stick to anything, let things go on, let life go on, just continue swimming the way you like. You can, to some extent control your own swimming, but you cannot control the stream.

The reason for your fear of losing Ravi is that you do not accept that your role in his life is limited. Like everyone else you too have only small role to play in the drama of life. Ravi's company has to end some day, you must accept it and be prepared for it.

S. I understand, but for me there is nothing else in life except love for Ravi. I want to be his Radha and that is the only role I want to play.

C. You have selected only one star as your object of desire, and you are going on only on a single track. You should have multiple goals and multiple objects for your happiness. Instead of putting all your eggs in one basket, you should find more baskets and more eggs of different varieties.

Counselling has made Swati relaxed. She has begun to see life as a multicoloured picture, a drama with many scenes, acts and performers.

Second Session

Swati came out today disclosing another aspect of her life. Her life in past, before she met Ravi, was not a bed of roses, and the thorns were many and painful. She was living in continuous stress, and nothing gave her relief from distress. It was only when she met Ravi that she saw the dawn of happiness. However, now it seemed that the sun had set, and the night of agony had come back.

S. All the time the thought of Ravi comes and bothers me. I always feel attracted and drawn towards him, but ultimately find I am just chasing a mirage. Even in my sleep I dream of him and wake up only to find he is not there, I feel tense, sad, helpless. My whole life has become a bunch of withered flowers and thorny bushes.

C. Dreams reflect only the unaccomplished wishes and fear of not getting fulfilled.

S. It must be all my fault, Ravi has done me no wrong, he creates no tension, he is full of goodness and I am full of love.

C. But at the end of the dream you get only tension, agony, and distress. This is because of your total and excessive involvement with Ravi, and Ravi's failure to respond.

S. Yes, of course the basic cause is Ravi, his memories, his love and his dropping out from my life.

C. The ultimate misery is always the result of non-fulfilment of one's own desires. In your case it is your failure to get Ravi's love.

S. Yes.

C. Then remove the cause. So long as Ravi is there in your mind, you will continue to unconsciously cultivate more desires to get him and his love, and go on suffering pain and agony; so, kill him, destroy him. Once the object of your desire is destroyed the tempest in your mind will subside and fade away, and finally disappear. Then you will cease to experience pain. Kill him and throw him out of your mind. Deliberately cause his psychological and emotional assassination.Tear away to pieces his photograph, and if you cannot do it, put a floral wreath to indicate his death. He deserves death because he is your tormentor, the cause of your tension, stress and agony. Destroy him the Chanakya way, leaf, stem, root and all.

S. I shall try.

C. No, you kill him just here and now and enjoy a life of peace. Today is Dussehra a good day for burning his effigy. It will bring peace and freedom to your mind. Once the desire is gone, the stream of desire will automatically dry and you will get freedom from pain of unfulfilled desires.

He is now dead. No longer will you talk to him, no longer will you think of meeting or welcoming or dreaming of him. Refrain from talking to the dead man. Avoid the corpse, live only with living beings. For you he is now dead, he has sustained psychological and emotional death. You are now a free person, free from the clutches of Ravi, who is as good as dead for you.

Swati, in this assassination you have nothing to lose except misery, your anxiety, your nerve-breaking stress, and, above all, your fears and nightmares. There are times when you need total annihilation of the root cause of agony.

Are you ready, should we proceed?

S. Yes, I am ready.

Swati has listened to the hypno-sleep stress management tape and has felt relaxed. Input of positive thoughts relating to her problems has made her think more positively. At least temporarily she is consoled and relieved of the heavy burden that was pressing on her heart.

She has taken the tape for listening it daily till she forms the habit of remaining relaxed and having positive thoughts and feelings.

Swati has started looking at higher goals for achievement. She is now thinking of going ahead on the ladder of promotions and progress in her job.

S. I will also try to have more meaningful ambitions, hobbies and extra-curricular activities, such as of Red Cross of which I am also a member. I am interested in the teachings of Krishnamurthi. I will now go to attend the convention being held in Varanasi dealing with his life and teachings. That will give me some interest in matters other than my craving for Ravi. I will try to diversify my thinking.

C. You should, that will make your horizons wider, and your perception of things will change.

Next Session

Swati had a bad day. While riding in the bus, she felt dizzy and fell down. She informed Ravi. He came and both come here together in Ravi's car.

It was a distressing session for both of them, neither wanted to accept the truth and face reality.

Ravi started talking from a high pedestal saying he believed only in God and the teachings of his mother. His mother had taught him to be straight-forward, sincere, and honest. But soon, it became apparent that he did not believe in doing what he professed.

He was deceiving both his wife and Swati, and was truthful to neither. He is not ready to leave Swati, he swears he loves her and will always continue to love her. But it seems, he is interested only in having a nice time, which he gets abundantly in having love and sex with a woman madly in love with him.

He denies Swati's allegation that he was involved with another young woman of doubtful morals, a neighbour of Swati. He says, his relations with her are only those of friendship, no romance is involved.Swati does not accept his version. Swati is sore on this count also but is willing to tolerate it because she does not want to take the risk of losing Ravi.

Ravi admits he was giving much more time, attention and concern to Swati till sometime back, but now it is no longer so. He says that the change is because now his children are growing and he has to have greater concern for them. He has also to look to matters connected with his job.

He admits he does no longer go to her apartment as that may undermine his professional image. Swati does not fear this. So far she is concerned, her love for Ravi overrides all other considerations.

Ravi accepts Swati has no eye on his purse, but dislikes Swati's insistence that he should pay for her food. On the other hand, Swati wants him to pay for her food as she wants to feel she is his wife. They had entered into a marital bond in the presence of God and it is Ravi's obligation as a husband to feed her.

There is no denying that Ravi's concern for Swati has declined, but still he refuses to give her liberation from the bondage of their fake marriage which Swati believed to be real. At the same time he is not ready to withdraw totally from her, he has no will or courage to lose her. In fact, he still loves Swati and fears loss of Swati's love.

According to him, Swati is becoming more possessive and that is the cause of her disappointment. He admits that though he is distancing himself a bit from her, he continues to love her and desires to keep her happy.

C. If you really love her and desire her happpiness, why not release her so that she might find, a husand for herself? Will you help her in finding a husband?

R. No, I cannot let her go.

S. If he leaves me, he will not suffer a big shock, but I shall be broken and shattered.

C. You must realise, he has a wife and children and is not prepared to leave them, he will walk out of your life if his wife gets an inking of your relationship with him.

S. Whatever may come, I don't want to leave him.

C. Okay, then continue.

Next Session (*on phone*)

Swati phoned late in the evening to tell how Ravi felt disturbed during the evening session, and instructed Swati not to get further counselling. He was not prepared for what happened at the session. What he expected from counselling was support for his behaviour rather than censure.

Swati had taken appointment for the next session in the morning, but could not come because of fear of Ravi. He phoned her in the morning to pry if she had gone for counselling. On the phone she told him that she was having tension and stress.

S. I am listening to the stress management tape and trying to get peace.

After a few minutes of counselling on phone she regained confidence (freedom from fear of Ravi's wrath) and became relaxed. She went on:

Your suspicions were well-founded. His wife has become fully aware of my relationship with Ravi. Ravi's behaviour has most probably been influenced by this factor. Sometime back she had even written a letter to the higher officer of the establishment saying that because of my affair with Ravi her family life had become wretched and unhappy. It was on her complaint that orders for my transfer were passed. I did not want to go away from Delhi as I did not want to lose Ravi, so I approached higher-ups and got the transfer order cancelled. Ravi did not do anything to help me.

C. So you know now, he can never be yours, his wife will not leave him, and he will have no courage to let his growing children get aware of his affair with you. It is better to walk out than be rejected and discarded.

Swati goes on talking about her woes and pleasures, the good and bad times they spent together and finally about the decline in Ravi's concern for her. Counselling continued on phone. Ultimately she got fully relaxed and gave a good hearty laugh.

After some time Swati phoned again:

The counselling has brought a massive change in me. I have got over my depression which had made me sit at home. I am going to the office.

She went to work and calmly attended to her duties after one and a half month's absence without leave.

There were mixed reactions and comments from her colleagues. She posed her long absence was due to illness, but did not disclose it was emotional stress that had caused a breakdown. She was now so well composed that no one could guess that there was something emotionally wrong with her.

Next Session (*on phone*)

Ravi again came in the picture, Swati was now again in a flx.

C. You should realise the difference between a lover and a husband. Lover is for romance and excitement while a husband is for security, support, care, and concern. Once you had a husband, now you have a lover. Then you had no lover, now you have no husband. Ravi has both a wife and a lover. His wife has a husband but no lover. It is difficult to find a combination of two in one. But there is greater permanency in the relationship with a husband than with a lover. In your case too, Ravi will continue to be your rival's husband, but sooner or later he will get more involved with his growing family and cease to be your lover A lover who is the husband of someone else, can walk out anytime under mounting pressure from family and social circles. It is a mistake to treat a lover also a husband. So try to find a husband.

S. I have tried, but I find all men come with promises of marriage but with the primary and sole object of having sex and the excitement of romance. They run away when I refuse sex and propose marriage. All men are the same.

C. Try again, but you have first to create a vacancy. So long as Ravi is there, you will be regarded more as an object of sex and romance than a woman available for becoming a wife. Go ahead; think till you come to a final decision.

You are badly in need of a lasting human relationship. Best is a husband, second best is an adopted child. Think again.

S. I shall, I get relaxation, peace and happiness in talking to you, may I have the liberty of talking on phone a few minutes everyday to remain relaxed and composed?

C. You are at liberty to phone whenever you like. Good night, have a nice dinner, a sound sleep and pleasant dreams.

Next Session (*on phone*)

S. I am quite happy. Yesterday I attended the office and did my work in the normal way. Sometimes, however, the thoughts of Ravi did enter my mind and created a little emotional turmoil. I want him always to be with me.

C. You are still trying to find in Ravi a husband. He is your lover and not your husband, his wife is Mrs. X. The roles of husband and lover are different, don't try to mix them. Should I tell a story from Valmiki's *Ramayana*?

S. Yes, please.

C. Once a king had hundred daughters, each one was more beautiful than the other, they were all very charming and their youth was in full bloom. They were frolicking in a garden full of greenery and flowers; a breeze was blowing. The wind god Varun fell in love with them, he became their lover and proposed to be their eternal lover. He said that your youth, charm and beauty will in the normal course of time wane and wither away, and if you marry humans their love too will wither away. But if you accept me I shall make your youth, beauty and charm eternal, you will remain forever full of youth, beauty and charm. The girls reported to the king, their father, about the wind god's proposal.

The king said that the wind was by nature dynamic and remains constantly on the move, kissing one blossom now and another the next moment. He would make a very good lover, but not a permanent lover like a husband, so accept him not. Just let him remain your lover and enjoy its kisses, till you get a husband.

You must see that the role played by a lover is different from the one played by a husband. The two roles are not the same. Think of Radha, the role played by Krishna was that of a lover, the role of husband was played by someone else. The two roles hardly ever get rolled up. You are trying to fuse the two roles. The result will be disappointment, and will bring unhappiness to you. Treat him just as a lover, have as much fun and happiness as you can, and as long as you can, but do not treat him as your husband, do not expect too much from him. Your wedding with Ravi, you know, was just a drama.

May this Diwali bring you more and more love and happiness, more light and more enlightenment.

S. My flat is on the 13th floor, I see a lot of lights all round, however my flat has no Diwali.

C. Why worry, you must be seeing a galaxy of stars in the sky, they are your *deepaks* (lamps), rejoice.

S. No, I cannot. As you said, I see only one star. It is only one star that shines for me in the whole galaxy. And you know who that star is.

C. Yes, I do. But I had asked you to wear broad vision glasses. If you will see the whole sky you will see there are many more stars, and you might like to cast your eyes on more than a single star.

S. But my eyes don't get away from that one star, and my vision does not go round to see any other star.

C. You have to make an effort to discover a new world of stars. The world is very large. It has much to offer and you are aware of what you are missing. Let's think more about it, let's think more about stars that have different hues.

Next Session (*on phone*)

S. I find I am changing. I can think and see things in separate places: love, work, friendship, relationship. I have been able to realise that my job also needs an important place in my scheme of things.

C. Yes, you should have compartmental or departmental thinking. Each matter, each thought and feeling should have a separate compartment, don't mix up things. Each one is important, your love affair has top priority, but it does not mean you should put your work, employment, job in a shelf; they are as relevant for your happiness as having a lover A husband has his own place and you might in course of time find one, though there is not much chance of your getting one so long as your involvement with your present lover continues to be total and all absorbing.

S. I know, but I cannot leave him.

C. Yes, you have become part of him, and he has become part of you. You two are not divisible, so continue to remain one.

S. I am always having some type of fear connected with my relationship with Ravi.

C. Your fear of losing him? But that is a fear about some eventuality that might happen in the future. You do not know your future, and what you fear may never happen, so why bring in future fear to mar your present happiness?

You must train your mind to live in the present and not to worry about the future. You do not and cannot know the future, so you get fears of different kinds. Fear is always born of ignorance of the future, don't try to see it as a reality. The fear of what will happen in future must be kept out of your mind. You must try to live only in the present and never in the future. Otherwise, your present happiness will get diluted, it will become qualitatively down-graded, and your enjoyment will be covered by the shadow of the unknown. Never let one thought interfere with the other. The mixture is not good, and can only cause confusion.

Particularly, never let a positive thought be mixed-up and adulterated with a negative thought. It is very harmful. The two emotions are not only different in character, the two are contradictory. Never let fear come near you. Tell it to wait till the future becomes the present, because you cannot, possibly, live in two time zones at the same time. Please live in the present and enjoy it, and do not spoil it by the fear of losing your lover in future.

S. I shall record this and listen to it again and again, and make it a part of my consciousness. I do wish to have positive thinking, but negative thoughts come to me because ever since childhood, I have seen only misery and I have lived through it. So my thinking pattem has acquired a negative colouring.

C. Now, at least for the last few years you have been living in a different environment; shape of things has changed, everything is good now, so don't worry. Try to forget the dead past, don't recall it again and again; by and by the pattern of your thinking will change, it is already changing, and is becoming more and more positive. Is it not ?

S. Yes, it is, and I hope to get better results.

C. Swati, I want to tell you that during the session when both you had come together, shock therapy had been applied and Ravi was particularly given the shock treatment. You had to receive a bit of it because you are an integral part of the main actor in the drama, and shock could not be given to Ravi without your feeling its tremor. Did it have any positive effect in bringing him closer to you, and making him realise that if he wanted to carry on with you he must make amends, and be more concerned about you?

S. We were both very much shocked, particularly Ravi, but it did have a positive effect. It has brought a change in him. Now he is giving more assurances about caring for me and looking after my well-being and happiness. There is a change in his behaviour towards me, he has started showing more concern for me, he is behaving generally in a more caring way.The message has reached him, "Love me or leave me".

C. This was the theme of the communication sought to be conveyed to him, and to make it really effective, it was done in an unambiguous language.

S. The message has reached him, though he has not relished it. However, the shock treatment has brought the desired result, but something more is still needed to be done.

C. You were both suffering from frustration, fear, suspicion, and concealed anger. The only way to get it all out was to take it out on someone else. I offered myself and both of you, specially Ravi, held me as the object for transferring his own feeling of guilt.It is why a change has come over him and his behaviour towards you has become more loving. He has become afraid of losing you, so he is trying to come nearer.

S. I want him to be not only near and close to me, but to merge in me.

C. Wait, don't be in a hurry.

Next Session

C. What about revival of your interest in your job?

S. Now I am regularly going and working with full concentration. My interest has revived, completely revived.

C. This is because tension and fear have disappeared from your mind. It was the tension in your mind that had made you disinterested in work, now when tension is gone, interest has revived, keep it up.

S. Now I always try to think positive, and remember: what, is and what is not is not. I have accepted life as it is and I feel happy. My tension has gone, I have become more practical.

C. What about 'SWA' relationship?

S. Oh, that too is fine, I have realised I cannot become his wife, I only am and will remain a lover, it is pleasant to love and be loved.

C. If you cannot get the whole, take whatever you can; and then you have the better and the pleasanter part of the wife-lover composition.

S. Yes, if I can't have the whole I should be content with the part, the better part.

C. Oh, Swati, I am happy that wisdom has dawned on you.

S. I have also made some very young friends and have begun enjoying music with them.

Next Session

S. I have written down our tele-conferences in detail, and have started thinking positive. I have also understood the need of taking interest in other matters, particularly my job, and also in activities at home during leisure hours. But, there is something I want to tell you. Recently I had some painful experiences and my grief revived. While I was returning from home after the ceremonies on the death of my father I saw in the eyes of my relatives only crocodile tears for me, this made me cry and weep in the train. A passenger, a boy of seventeen, asked me the cause of my tears. I told him they had come because my sons did not want to come and live with me. The boy became interested and offered himself to be treated as my son. This gave me great relief. We travelled together for more than twentyfour hours and became friendly, he reached me to my house and promised to visit me whenever he was free. I offered to adopt him as my son so that he might live with me. However, having taken a job in the merchant marine he had to go to Bombay and told me he will visit me whenever he came on leave. I felt genuine happiness in the hope that I might get a son.

C. That is very good and encouraging. You have realised that happiness comes even from relationships other than that of a lover or a husband.

S. Some days back a young girl came and stayed with me for sometime, we talked and listened to music, we had a good time.

The counselling had its effect. I have begun to see that persons other than Ravi can also give their love and make me happy.

Of course, I would not go in for marriage with someone else so long as Ravi is in my life. I love him very much, and am also doubtful about getting a suitable man to marry me. I am, however, realising the need of a whole-time permanent companion.

C. Adopt someone.

S. I might adopt someone, but I cannot take care of a child, it requires too much of responsibility and I don't think I can do it.

C. It is not necessary to adopt a very small child, you can adopt someone not so young provided you like him/her, and can treat him/her as your son or daughter.

S. The girl I spoke of is also about seventeen, but soon she may get married and then again I shall be left alone. I feel very lonely.

C. Then try to find a boy for adoption.

S. Yes, I am on the lookout for a suitable person.

C. That is good, but till then make the best of the situation you are living in.

S. I realise this and that is why I have accepted your advice to have a life of multifarious activities, I want to have more stars and more tracks. I have started going regularly to office and taking interest in my work.I feel happy after having got out of my 'sanyas' from work. During those months I thought of nothing but Ravi and of his gradual withdrawal from me; that had made me depressed and emotionally ill, compelling me to come to you. Now I feel much relaxed. I have accepted the reality that he cannot be more than a lover to me.

C. And that too only a rationed and shared lover.

You should learn to practise 'Meditational Love' Love is meditation, meditation is love. Meditation brings happiness, happiness brings meditation. Meditational love means total love, total involvement in love. While you are making and enjoying love, treat it as meditation and get completely involved in it, that will give you maximum happiness. However, meditational love must be in phases and with breaks. Meditation has to end after bliss is achieved, then involvement should cease and there should be complete detachment; it should get out of your mind till the next phase begins. Then start another meditation the "work meditation". Get fully involved in your job, your profession, and completely efface the memory of the earlier meditation, the love meditation. Each meditation should be in a separate compartment.

S. Now, I will try to do things in a meditational way. I have to have a multi-faceted life and multi-faceted meditation.

C. You love music, do you also love dance?

S. I am an accomplished Bharat natyam dancer.

C. Then why don't you get involved in it, you can go abroad and give performances there, you might gain international fame.

S. It would be marvellous, I have cassettes and I can dance with their aid; I know Bharat natyam and also Kuchipudi.

C. Then start immediately.

S. I shall do it from tomorrow. There is a dance school in my neighbourhood, I can go there and practice.

C. Again treat it as a meditation.

S. Should I read what I have written?

C. Please do. (She reads out passages from the diary she had brought with her). They are very good, you write very well.

S. I have written only what you spoke on phone.

C. No no, they are much better because they are charged with your radiant vibes, emotions and pulsating feelings, they have infused life into your writings. Continue to write, ultimately you may produce a book, also try to make audio-cassettes.

S. I am so happy to hear this. I shall continue to write the diary, my diary. Today's discourse will make the next chapter if my diary.

Next Session (*after some time*)

C. Swati, you have a philosophical bent of mind, you have read teaching of Vivekananda, Ramakrishna Paramhans, Krishnamurthi and many other great minds, why not put that wisdom into practice?

S. I have put it all in practice now, I no more feel upset when he is not available. I have understood the meaning of what you had said: love blooms best when it is given and showered on others without expectation of return. My love has now become meditational and devotional. I enjoy just the pure emotion of love and stay happy like Meera.

C. Pure love blooms with its own nectar and produces waves of serene and blissful happiness.

S. Now, I am getting and enjoying that kind of happiness. I feel really happy.

NALINI

A married woman like me, in this bourgeois society, lives under perpetual bondage, her liberation from this marital serfdom is very very difficult as her husband's family and the social environment will not let her leave the home. She has little choice, and has to go on suffering even when her husband is incapable of giving her anything but agony, misery, woe, and torment.

Diagnostic Scan

Nalini phoned to get an appointment for counselling of her husband.

C. What is your name?

N. Mrs. Agarwal.

C. That only shows you are a married woman and the surname of your husband is Agarwal, what is your own name? Don't you have an identity of your own, your individuality?

N. I am Nalini. (Laughs).

When Nalini and her husband Pankaj came for counselling the first thing she said: Today I laughed, I do not know after how long a period. I felt so very light that. I related the incident to my sister-in-law (husband's elder brother's wife), she also laughed. I have never felt so light and relaxed. I realised for the first time that I am, I have an individuality and personality of my own, apart from my husbands.

Nalini, twenty-eight, was married ten years back, has a child of about seven. Nalini is young and healthy but her face is marred with signs of depression, dejection, stress and fear of a gloomy future. She tried in vain to conceal her agony by putting up a mask.

C. What is the problem?

N. I am okay. The problem is with my husband, he is unable to concentrate and remain employed in any job.

C. Alright let me listen to Pankaj.

P. My problem is that I cannot concentrate on any job. I have no confidence. I have done chartered accountant's course, but I have neither courage nor confidence that I shall be able to do the job. At present, I am working in the factory of my father as in-charge of account section, but in fact, I am doing nothing. Nalini will be able to explain better.

Pankaj goes to another room, Nalini takes over.

C. Nalini, why do you look so depressed, are you not happy?

N. I have not known happiness since two years after my marriage. First two years were all right, but thereafter my husband became mentally ill, his job was gone, and it became impossible for him to stay in the joint family. He said he would go to live in some other city and opted for Hyderabad. We went to live there without any roots, his condition became worse from bad, he began to become violent.

C. Did he ever beat you?

N. Yes, several times. Ultimately the neighbours got him admitted into a (lunatic) mental hospital. He was given shocks, etc He became better and for the last two years he has not been violent. Still he is not normal, his behaviour is not congenial.

I want to ask you "Should I leave him ?"

N. Divorce?

N. Yes, my father thinks I should.

C. It may be good for you to get the divorce because from what you have told me about him there is not much chance of his getting completely normal. How is your sex life?

N. There is no such thing in my life, there is neither love nor sex. It is only when in a month or two he wants to have sex, I submit to him.

C. Is he working in the factory?

N. No, he just goes, or is taken to the factory by his father and brothers. I can no more think of living with him alone, away from the family. My life is miserable.

C. Then it is better for you to get freedom from him. You have no happiness in life, and there is not much chance of your having a happy life in future, or at least till he is in the present state of health. You still have a long life to live, your father's advice appears to be right.

However, let us see if anything can be done to bring some happiness in your life while you are together.

(Pankaj is called in and he joins).

C. You are a CA,why don't you take charge of accounts of your family business?

P. I have no confidence, I do not think I am capable of doing the job.

Pankaj is confused in his thinking, he wants to talk about big things tries to give solutions and fails and then tries to change over to something else. He read about misery and happiness in the Institute's brochure and began talking about misery and happiness, then mixed up the ideas with nation's miserable condition. He sees darkness all around and feels miserable. He pleaded he was too tired to talk anymore.

Counselling

Both of them are given counselling about making life happier by developing more love amongst themselves. Pankaj has agreed to make the morning cup of tea and take it with Nalini, and also to have breakfast to-gether.

C. Do you know that the best things you can do with your lips is to kiss, and the second best thing is to smile. Pankaj, try to develop greater love for Nalini, just give her a kiss. It will not be a bad investment, but a very good one, for every kiss of yours she will return five. A very good investment. Try it.

(Nalini feels happy, but doubts if he will keep up his promises).

Both of you need relaxation. Nalini, you must try to give up thoughts of misery and unhappy events, and instead, begin to think and feel happiness, you should develop a positive attitude, and practise the art of remaining happy.

[She is given the audio tape 'stress management' and both of them are asked to listen to it everyday for a week, till the next session.] Remember, misery and happiness are both born in minds of men.

Next Session

Nalini is sad, concerned about her husband's mental health, and worried about her own peace of mind.

Pankaj did not say anything in her presence except saying that she needed to be treated for becoming more practical and coming in harmony with the circumstances in which she is living. When she went out, he continued for a while accusing her of being a non-understanding woman, who does not know how to adjust to circumstances. He feels she has uncontrolled ego, wants things and people (indirectly meaning himself) to improve and come up to the standard which she sets. She should rather learn to live in the way and situation in which she is. They live with the family of his elder brother in one house and his parents with the other brother live in another house. He blames her for expecting too much. He has no work to do and lives on the income coming from the family business. Nalini, he thinks, lives under stress because she is unable to adjust herself to the circumstances in which she is living.

After some time he said he was too tired and Nalini should come and say whatever she liked. However, as soon as she came in he began to say that he had some work and had to go. Instead of leaving Nalini alone, he remained spying from the door and as soon as she started saying something about him, he entered and began insisting that they must go back.

He said that first she should settle down in home and thereafter may come to take counselling.

Nalini wanted to stay and say something, but seeing his mood left with him.

Pankaj is suffering from a concealed sense of guilt, he is afraid of being exposed, hence does not let Nalini talk in his absence. He is probably conscious of his mental condition, and his bad and abnormal behaviour with his wife. He fears Nalini will disclose truth about him.

He tries to show that he is okay and it is Nalini who is not okay.

He is not able to make decisions. He fails to carry on and continue any work, that may be the reason for termination of his job in Calcutta, and cause of his failure to do any work elsewhere.

He suffers from frustration, dejection, depression, and fear of failure. He believes in escapism, that is what made him run to Hyderabad without any pre-planning, and there again he suffered frustration, dejection, and depression leading to violence which ultimately took him to the asylum. Nalini has been the target of his wrath. He tries to find consolation by blaming her in the hope that it will shift his hidden feelings of guilt and shame on to her and he will be able to acquire his lost dignity.

But that cannot bring back his lost self-esteem or remove his hidden feelings of guilt and shame. He has to do penance and learn methods to cope with his fears, frustrations and dejections for which he is not ready.

Next Session (*on phone*)

Nalini said she did not come for counselling because on the last date, immediately after the counselling when they went out, there was a change in her husband's attitude and he expressed regret for the way he left and also made her leave in the middle.

N. He has improved since then and his behaviour has become much better. He has become milder. It has brought hope to me and I have begun to think there may be some way to bring him out of the situation and condition in which he is.

C. Nalini, your options are:

(*a*) To go on nursing him and attempting to get him cured, and in the process continue to suffer misery.

(*b*) To continue to live with him as he is, and get yourself involved in some activity which might bring you economic independence, and keep you engaged.

(*c*) To learn to live happily in the environment of despair, which is very difficult, rather impossible.

(*d*) To get a separation and

(*i*) to remarry

(*ii*) if (*i*) is not possible, then start life new as an independent working woman.

N. I am very sad and unable to take decisions, I do not know what to do.

C. The best option for you is the last one. The condition in which Pankaj is, is not likely to give you any peace of mind, the question of getting happiness does not arise. So take courage, and take the drastic action, follow your father's advice.

N. A married woman like me, in this bourgeois society, lives under perpetual bondage, her liberation from marital serfdom is very very difficult. Her husband's family and the social environment will not let her leave the home. She has little choice, and has to go on suffering even when her husband is incapable of giving her anything but agony, misery, woe, and torment. So I think I have no other option, but for the present I will give some more time to the second option.

C. Please do. There is nothing to get disheartened, it is of course the best option provided it works.A very important psychological constraint which makes a woman helpless is her fear of social condemnation. Still greater is the fear of living alone, a natural consequence of the loss of a spouse. You fear insecurity and hence prefer to suffer agony than to face the hostile world. A woman in your situation needs courage and confidence to take the bold step to push open the gate to a new world.

N. I do want to end the agony, break the chains and get liberation, but I find the chains are too strong to break, and I feel too weak to crush them.

Next Session

Nalini has taken a separate residence and is living there with her husband. She is running a travel agency, her husband is also a nominal participant. She has become independent, but her problems still remain.

Pankaj continues to suffer from depression of the mood—depression with withdrawal symptoms is recurring more frequently. Medicines are continuing, he remains dull and unenthusiastic.

N. I am not happy. I live under tension and stress, feel very insecure about my future, but I have gained some confidence because now I am running my own business, and am no more dependent on my husband or his relatives.

C. That is very encouraging. How is your husband?

N. He is still suffering from depression. He also, at times, gets agitated and violent.

C. What does the physician (Psychiatrist) say?

N. There is some chemical deficiency in his brain which has led to this problem. Medicines are supposed to keep the balance maintained. But it seems the medicines have only a peripheral and temporary effect.

C. So Nalini, you see he is helpless, things are beyond his control. His actions, particularly his behaviour towards you has been reprehensible, but as it is beyond his control you should not hold him guilty for the same.

N. Whatever it be, I am the sufferer.

C. Yes you are, so you should take the necessary action to make yourself free. If the disease cannot be cured, the only remedy is to get a divorce.

N. Yes, I think that is the only way I can get over my sufferings. I hope someday I shall be able to gather sufficient courage to take this bold step.

C. Earlier you do, better would it be for you.

REKHA

Those who are born have got to live till the end comes. So why worry about the purpose? As you have been born, you have got to live this life. Life is a journey from birth to death, continue travelling without worring about it; when the destination will come, you will automatically go away. Life is only a span of time with two terminals, and it is not in your hand either to increase or reduce the time gap between the two terminals, hence live happily so long you are alive.

Diagnostic Scan

Rekha is a well-groomed young woman of twenty-nine. She is a Maharashtrian Brahmin from Mumbai, married to a Sikh from Punjab. She was married six years back and has a daughter about three years old.

Rekha had attempted suicide about two months back by consuming a high dose of pesticide. She has not disclosed what happened which made her take this step, or a specific cause for attempting suicide.

She says she is very unhappy and suffers from depression. Before marriage she was working as a teacher (she has done M.Sc. in Chemistry) but is now living as a housewife. Her husband generally remains out in connection with his employment; he tours in India and also goes abroad.

She feels she is suffering because she is without any friends and lives a lonely life. By moving away to Noida from Mumbai her roots have been cut off. She has also no relationship with her parents mainly due to her inter-religious marriage.

Her childhood was not happy because her mother, a teacher, was too dominating.

Her husband's brother, whose birthday coincided with hers, had committed suicide, and she thinks that people born on that date are prone to committing suicide. The only difference between her and her brother-in-law, she says, was that he succeeded and she failed in the attempt.

C. How are your relations with your husband?

R. Good, he is very caring.

C. What about sex life?

R. It is okay. We have sex about twice a month. We don't have it more often because he remains mostly away and also because by the time I manage to make my daughter go to sleep, he himself goes to sleep.

C. Do you have orgasm?

R. Yes, but he says I am 'cold'. I do not know what he means, and why he says so.

C. Try to discover what he wishes to convey to you by saying 'you are cold'. That might be a cause of your misery, but you know there is nothing wrong with you, so don't worry about it.

R. I wish to have another child.

C. Then go ahead and have one.

R. I have to enquire from the gynaecologist if it is safe to have a child while I am on psychiatric medicines.

C. You may enquire. Maybe, a new child brings you peace of mind and you may not need any further medication. Anyway, tell me why you think you are unhappy. You look quite well. Are you unhappy at this moment or during the short time you have been here with me?

R. No, I have felt no unhappiness while I have been here.

C. Do you weep and cry?

R. Yes, sometimes.

C. Can you tell me any specific circumstances, or particular conditions which make you think you are unhappy or under depression?

R. No, I just feel I am unhappy and depressed.

C. Then give up this feeling. Try to think and feel you are happy. Try to remember happy moments in your life rather than keep thinking of unhappiness. What are your hobbies? Do you paint?

R. No, but I write. These days I am writing on mother-daughter relationship.

C. You have a living toy at home, enjoy playing with her, love her more, treat her as your toy, as your companion and become yourself a child and play with her. That will take away your loneliness and provide you with the most pleasant company. It will help you in writing more authentically about mother-child relationship.

You seem to be suffering from lack of love for your child; you should learn to love her and to love yourself. It is only because of your lack of love for yourself and your daughter, and maybe for your husband, that you attempted suicide. Develop greater love for yourself and your feelings of unhappiness will go.

R. I shall try.

C. Please do not consider yourself lonely, the whole world is there, you are a part of it.

You also have certain obligations towards your child, rather all the children in the world, they expect something from you, they need your love and compassion. You still have a desire for another child, it is a hopeful sign. You have to live to give birth to a new child and then rear it. You should remember you can give only what you have, if you have happiness you will give happiness, if you have unhappiness, you will give unhappiness. So, be happy. You have a loving husband, a loving daughter, a home to live, and sufficient money to spend. You are looking at life, it seems, through dark glasses, just remove them and you will find the world is beautiful, you are beautiful, everything is beautiful.

C. Does your husband ever bring a rose for you?

R. Yes, and he celebrated my birthday in a five-star hotel.

C. So go ahead and enjoy your life. Let everyday be a day of celebration.

R. It is time my daughter will come back from the play school.

C. Go and receive her with open arms, love her, hug her, kiss her, and play with her best friend.

Next Session

Rekha rushed in without prior appointment.

R. "I want to commit suicide, please help me" [She was extremely upset; she placed her hands and head, face down, on the table. Only after a few words of consolation did she get up and began to speak.] "Please help me, I don't want to live, I want to die. I hate my daughter."

C. What has happened?

R. No, I do not want this girl to live with me. Just a little while ago I returned from the gymnasium and wanted to lie down, but she would not let me, she would go on insisting I should get up and talk to her. She would not let the maid feed her, but insist that I should. She wants me to do everything for her, as if I were her servant. I don't like all this, I dislike her, I hate her.

C. You are right that when you come back tired from gymnasium, you should have rest and none should disturb you, you are also right that your daughter should take her feed from the maid and should not insist on your doing all the work for her which the maid can do, but it seems the child is still too young to understand all this. She has no animosity against you, it is her love which makes her act in the way she does. She feels starved of love and badly needs it, she cannot get a mother's love from a maid. You alone can give her the love she longs for. Please try to visualise the whole scene with the child's eyes.

R. Whatever be the cause, I dislike her, I hate her.

C. Rekha, you hate her because you dislike her interfering with your personal comfort. You have certainly the right to have a little time all to yourself, and the child should understand this.

R. Yes, and there is the maid to look after her.

C. Maybe the maid is not a good one, maybe she has no child and is unable to give the child the love and the loving care she needs. Does the maid treat the child affectionately? Is she very strict? Does your daughter feel happy with her?

R. I do not know how the maid treats the child.

C. It appears she does not take good care of the child. However, do you not think this anger in you is giving you more misery than the child was? Is your misery worth it? Remember, your hatred for the child is only momentary because in your sub-conscious mind there is still love for her. Just look back to the moments of happiness you had when your daughter was nothing more than a babe, when you played with her and saw her growing up. They were all moments when you had an exchange of intense love with your little child, who is nothing but a part of your own self.

R. I never got my mother's love, which I always craved and longed for. I never even got my father's love.

C. Rekha, please do not repeat history. Do not try to take revenge on your little daughter, give her all that which you could not get, but would have loved to get from your mother.

R. Whatever it may be, I want to die and I ask you to help me.

C. There is no hurry, and it is no use trying and failing.

R. Don't you agree I have a right to die?

C. Maybe you have, but there is no hurry, enjoy life, make the best of it. When you fix the final date and time for suicide, then we can think about the plan. But till then decide to remain happy. I don't ask you not to die, that may be your right, but till then let no desperation, despondency, or dejection enter your mind. Till then, also accept the love of your daughter, let her give you as much love as she likes, and respond by giving her your own love. It is a matter of only temporary adjustment, only for the period you are alive, so long your heart is throbbing, and your consciousness is feeling and experiencing the various emotions. Till the final date of suicide, please let the emotion of love dominate your life. And one thing more, you will not attempt suicide without informing me. Will it not be an occasion to celebrate?

[Rekha smiles, and goes back happy and relaxed.]

Next Session

R. I am extremely perturbed.

C. Why, has your daughter again tried to play with you and disturb your peace?

R. No, after the counselling I found it was better to love my daughter than hate her. She is very loving and innocent. My parents are responsible for my agony.

C. Why, what has happened?

R. On my daughter's birthday they gave no gifts and presents to me, and not even to their son-in-law as is customary, even when I took so many gifts for both of them. Their behaviour has upset me.

C. Please do not get upset simply because your parents did not give gifts to you or your husband. There may be a hundred reasons for their unsocial behaviour. The main thing is love, affection and concern, did you find any neglect or restraint in their love for you?

R. No.

C. Then be happy, presents are not very relevant, you can afford anything you like. What you needed was their affection and that they gave you, so be happy.

R. Oh, what a pity, I cannot even die. You know my suicide attempt has failed, and you have not told me of any sure method.

C. I hope you did not attempt suicide since you came to me.

R. No, I did not.

C. You have done your post-graduation in Chemistry and you know potassium cyanide is the most deadly chemical. But why do you want to die? Do you still hate your little daughter?

R. No.

C. Probably, you find no purpose in living, life seems to be a meaningless thing, you do not know why should you continue to live.

R. Yes, that is so. From morning till night I have nothing but loneliness. My husband goes in the morning and returns late in the evening. I only see TV along with him and then go to sleep. It is not a life worth living.

C. Yours was a love marriage.

R. Yes, but there is a marked difference in our cultural make up, I am a Maharashtrian and he is a Punjabi.

C. Your marital life does not depend on this difference.

R. That is so, but there is no compatibility between us. He thinks everything is wrong with me because the psychiatrist says there is some chemical imbalance in my brain and that is responsible for my being cold though I am not.

C. Has he made any tests for determining this chemical imbalance?

R. No.

C. Why do you say, you are suffering from depression? Is it unipolar or bipolar?

R. Bipolar, sometimes I get very dejected, and feel running down the drain. It is only occasionally I feel elated.

C. What do you do the whole day, how do you pass your time?

R. I have nothing to do, I spend one hour in the gymnasium and some little time with my daughter.

C. And the remaining time is only a period of sheer vacancy, a time which you spend in brooding over your purposeless life.

R. Yes.

C. Then, let us plan something for this vacant period. Have you any hobby? Do you sing? Can you paint?

R. No, I only do a little writing. I have written two stories, one is about suicide and the other is just a normal one.

C. Have you brought them?

R. I shall bring the suicide story next time.

C. Try to put some paints on a few canvas, without worrying about the result.

R. I have never done painting and I cannot do it.

C. Very well, try sketching. See these sketches, you can copy similar sketches from a drawing book.

R. I can try that.

C. Try spoiling a few canvases too, that will give you lot of pleasure. Do you believe in God?

R. Yes, I do. I also believe in astrology. I feel astrologers can make correct predictions.

C. Then you must be believing that life and death are both in God's hands, and those who are born have got to live till the end comes. So why worry about the purpose? The whole of life is a journey from birth to death, continue travelling without worrying about it, when the destination will come, you will automatically go away. Life is only a span of time with two terminals, and it is not in your hand either to increase or reduce the time gap between the two terminals, hence, live happily so long you are alive. You believe in God, where does God live?

R. He is everywhere, He is also within me.

C. Can you destroy Him ? Can you kill Him by committing suicide? Can you ask Him to go out of your body so that you might destroy it? Can you curtail the period of His dwelling inside your body?

R. No.

C. Then is it not wrong and futile on your part to attempt suicide ? May this not have been the reason for failure in your last attempt ?

R. May have been.

C. Then, let life continue as it is. You are a believer in God, let His will prevail, let Him live peacefully inside you, don't try to destroy His abode.

R. But I told you my life is not a happy one. My husband does not like anything in me. He will even criticise my open hair style and will want me to secure it in a bun, which I do not like. He will find fault with things I do, even things which are of no significance, only to irritate and annoy me and to make me feel humiliated.

C. He is probably suffering from some sort of inferiority complex, maybe sub-consciously he feels you are culturally superior to him.

R. But he always tries to show he is superior to me.

C. Show of superiority by finding fault with everything you do, is indicative of his feeling of inferiority; he tries to overcome it by pulling you down. Take it in a sporting spirit, otherwise it will make you unhappy. Learn tolerance. Don't you want to be happy?

R. Of course, I do.

C. Do you remember the lines "Little deeds of kindness, little words of love, make this earth an Eden and the Heaven above. Tell me how you receive your husband when he comes back late in the evening?

R. It is not an event, I just open the door and he walks in.

C. Okay, let us make a change this evening. Don't you put on any make-up?

R. No, I live as I am.

C. But you must be having materials for a good make-up.

R. Yes, I do have, and also know the art. I do not need to go to a beautician for a make-up.

C. So, this evening you shall have a very good make-up and when your husband rings the bell, you shall welcome him with a broad smile in the same manner as you did for quite some time after your marriage. Let your face show the same loving smile.

R. Why?

C. Only to bring back to you the happiness which you have been missing for so many years. Just try and see. I am sure, your husband will respond with a broader smile on his face, he will take you in his arms, kiss you and love you. Don't you think so?

R. Maybe, I shall try, I earnestly long to get back my lost happiness, and if this can be a way, I shall do my best to look as pretty and loveable as I used to be. I wish to live happily with my husband and my dear little daughter. I wish my life of love might come back.

C. I have no doubt your wish will come true.

ANU

I feel emotional suffocation, my life has come to a standstill, I am moving nowhere... I always carry suicide pills in my bag, even now they are here... I want to end in a tragedy.. My story, my life's drama has already ended...

Diagnostic Scan

Anupama Goel (ANU) is a brilliant girl—lean and thin. She is thirty, but looks to be in her twenties. She is good-looking and attractive, but her spirits have been sapped away by adverse circumstances. Her attempt to commit suicide has failed.

Anu is a working woman with high academic qualifications. She has had a happy past, but her life turned sour and pushed her to the stage of attempting suicide a few months back by consuming sleeping pills. She had fallen in love with Deomani Sharma a colleague, and the love went on growing and turned into infatuation. He is married and has two children. His wife Kalpana came to know of it, and raised a hue and cry. Anu's lover sided with his wife and quarrelled with Anu. This broke her heart and she became very depressed.

Anu feels she has no place in the world as everyone, particularly her father, consider her to be a depraved woman, who has brought disgrace to the family. She is condemned and blamed, and had been forced to feel guilty and ashamed.

Anu is in a state of emotional turbulence. She seems worn out, she has been fasting the whole day and has not even taken water. She undertakes fast for the long life and welfare of her ex-lover whom she treats as her husband. Her condition is pitiable and pathetic. She looks like a fading light, a withering flower, an innocent child, a frightened maiden, a lovelorn damsel, a lonely heart, a lovesick girl, a deprived soul, a suffering Christ, a renunciating monk trying to find salvation through sacrifice, a woman living a meaningless existence. She is living in her own little world made up of her own fancies and fantacies.

She finds herself all alone in this world of artificial morality which offers only misery and promises no happiness. There is everyone to condemn her as a sinner and a depraved person, but none to offer her solace or show her the path to the destination she wishes to reach, the heart of her paramour, the man with whom she had enjoyed the bliss of sacred love. In her mind the memories of ecstatic moments still exist. She pines to get even a wholesome glimpse of her 'god', but all doors are closed, and there is no one to help her reach the sanctum sanctorum.

A. I want to write my will, can you help me ?

C. Why not, but you will have to find two younger persons to witness it.

A. Why, it may not be necessary for younger persons to witness it.

C. Of course, you are right, unless you begin to think of living longer than dying early.

A. I have no interest in living. I shall leave all my assets to my paramour and his two sons.

C. Why?

A. So that after my death he and his wife Kalpana might always feel the pain I suffered and the sacrifice I made.

C. So you want to take revenge and punish them. Why not do it while you are alive? After your death it would be of no value, at least so far you are concerned. Let's think of something more positive. Why do you have a soft corner for his sons?

A. I love them.

C. Do you love them because you see in them your own innocence and the image of your lover?

A. May be.

C. How did his wife come to fight with you?

A. I told her all about my affair with her husband. I specifically told her that I did not want any disruption of their love or marital relations. I only want to love him. But she did not understand my feelings and began to use filthy and abusive language. Since, then there had been break between me and him. Even though he sits in another room in the same building he never talks to me.

C. Why?

A. Probably, he is too timid and afraid of what the people in the office will think.

C. And, why don't you take the initiative?

A. How can I? I do not know how to do it.

C. Just say 'Hello, good morning', offer to have tea together.

A. I shall try.

C. But at the moment you are not in a fit condition. You have allowed your charm to fade and wither away. You have to bloom if you want to attract him, make yourself as charming as you were earlier. Kalpana is your rival, become more charming and attractive. Have you done the make-up?

A. No.

C. Why not ?

A. My spirits have dampened, I have lost all hope, and have no will to live.

B. Don't get dejected, have hope and courage. Do you know you look more exhausted and drained out than you did in the morning? Why, are you on fast today?

A. Today is Karva Chauth and I observe this as the day of fasting for his welfare and long life.

C. Why do you observe Karva Chauth (the festive day on which married Hindu women keep fast for their husbands' welfare and long life), you are not married and have no husband.

A. Yes, I am not legally married but I treat Manu as my husband. I feel I am his wife. We have lived together as husband and wife.

C. More correctly, as "lovers". Don't you see the distinction between a husband and a lover? Krishna was Radha's lover and Rukmani's husband, Radha was also married to someone else, and was only a lover of Krishna. Manu was your lover and Kalpana's husband.

A. That is why I have complaint against God. Why did he assign to my lot a married man? I have grievance against none else.

C. In which god do you have faith?

A. I have faith in the supreme power that has created all life, the sun and the universe. I observe fast on Mondays because it is the day of Shiva and on Thursdays because it is the day of Vishnu and Parvati.

C. Do you not realise the fact that these fasts are sapping off your energy, your health? Be more conscious of your well-being. If for nothing else at least for attracting and winning back your lover. Beetles do not come to a withering or fading flower.

A. For me even a bit of his love is enough. I once told him, he might have a hundred wives, still I shall continue to love him. Once he told me that after the children had arrived, he had developed greater love for them and he cannot leave Kalpana for me. I do not want him to leave Kalpana or to love her any the less. I told Kalpana the same thing, but they don't understand.

C. You should continue to remain his lover. Let not the temple of your love be destroyed, let not your god disappear into oblivion. Hold your courage.

Besides this, counselling was directed to make her feel and believe:

(*a*) She had committed no sin in having a love affair with a married man, and there was nothing of which she should feel guilty or ashamed.

(*b*) She should not feel isolated in the world. Her life was valuable and she should have greater will to live.

(*c*) She needed to develop courage, confidence and faith in her own capabilities to win back her lover.

(*d*) She had to learn to live in the present and not to fear the future.

(*e*) She still had the innocence of a child, and the heart of a young girl, and she needed to grow up to acquire a higher degree of maturity.

Next Session

A. I am very sad and unhappy. I have no desire to live. I want to write my will so that after my death they may live constantly under the emotional trauma of my sacrifice.

C. Anu, you are only a player in the great human drama, your role is of a lover. Even if he draws away from you, you should not quit the stage and walk away.

Please try to counteract your dejection and alienation by writing and singing songs of love like Meera. Instead of losing him totally, make him a part of yourself as a lover and a beloved. Rise above the level of carnal love and try to have the love divine, pure and unsullied.

[Anu has brought her diary and some spare pieces of paper. On one of them are some words of love he had written to her.]

A. He has taken away all except this, but I remember them verbatim and have written them down. This is the letter I wrote to didi after our quarrel. (Anu calls Kalpana didi, elder sister).

B. It is very nice of you to consider her your elder sister, you are great. You are too simple and innocent. How can you expect a wife to share her husband ? No woman, except perhaps you, can agree to let another woman enter the world in which she wants to live alone with her husband. But you have the wisdom of an adult. You can sure become a poet. You are bubbling with the emotion of love, just try to put your love into words, into songs.

[Anu feels happy and elated at the idea of becoming a poetess of love. She has just composed two lines of a song and has set them to tune. It has been recorded on the audio-tape. She promises to write more and sing them. In the poem she offers to give everything for the return of her lover and his love.]

A. Have you seen any other love-lorn girl like me ?

C. Yes, I have. Have you read "Lady Chatterley's Lover"?

A. Yes, I like it very much. I love him no less. I did everything that pleased him, I want him back.

C. Remember, human body doesn't last, but love lasts; it can last forever, it can be a source of eternal joy. All the great poets and artists have been love-lorn, who have suffered the pangs of separation. Their beloved are gone, they themselves have gone, but their creations are still live. You also do the same. Compose poems and songs and sing them, make paintings and see them, give immortality to your love.

A. But what is wrong in Didi's sharing him with me ? I have told her, I do not want him as a husband. I want only a lover, and it is possible for a man to love two girls at the same time. I want to be Radha, let her remain his Rukmani.

C. That may not be possible. The stories of Radha, Krishna and Rukmani are stories about gods and not mortals like you, him and Kalpana.

A. Kalpana is afraid because she is an ignoble woman. Do you know how she fought with me ? Not like a cultured woman but as a wild boar; she used most filthy language. She used similar language also against her husband. Do you want to listen (she spoke some of her dirty sentences) ?

[Anu has a lot of bitterness against Kalpana and considers her the real villain, and guilty of snatching away her lover, and depriving her of his company and love. It was at her instance that she was driven out of the house and left all alone. In spite of it all, Anu continues to treat him as her husband, her lover, her god, the object of her total devotion.

Counselling has been given to make her see the beauty and utility of life and futility of suicide and death.

After her verse of love and longing for love had been replayed, she became calm and began to smile with hope and joy. She promised to write more songs and lyrics.]

Next Session

[Anu has completed the poem (song) which she had begun during the last counselling session. Now it is a three-page lyric. It is a pathetic wailing of a love-lorn damsel begging for love of her lover's response to her own love.]

C. You continue to write. I see in your poems and other writings in your diary, the making of a great poet. Your poems and songs are similar to those written by persons who have suffered as you have. Separation of the lover induces heart-touching literature, it inspires lovers to become poets. Read the lives, poems and songs of Byron, Shelly, Keats, Nirala, and others, all of them suffered like you, you are no exception, and maybe you too become one of them.

A. But why ? I don't want name or fame, I want him and him alone. Bring him back to me, and I shall get all I long for.

B. You are right, I wish to make your poems do the job and induce him to come back to you. You used to exchange poems, songs and spoken words of love to reach each other's heart and to win each other's love. I want you only to make your tools more powerful, more love in your songs will make them more powerful. You can then send them to him. Your poems and songs will act like magnets; more pathos and love they will have, more powerful magnets will they become.

A. I can get them published in papers and let him read them.

C. Of course.

A. I always aspired, and still do, to become a complete woman; no woman is complete without bearing children, I want at least one child, a child from him.

C. Then have it. But you first have to win him back through the charm of your songs. You are the ocean of love, let him be drowned into it, let his heart get filled up with your love.

A. I have lost confidence in myself and always see failure, future looks completely dark and meaningless. Hence I always carry suicide pills in my bag, even now they are here.

C. You can eat them whenever you like, but what is the hurry? A bright light might still be there in your future. Wait a little more, it is not yet too late, you have still a goal to achieve. You have still to get him back, still to have children, still to have a home and a family of your own. There is no hurry, just wait. The future, you don't know, may turn out to be much better than you imagine. Instead of fearing the future, build hopes.

A. I want to end into a tragedy.

C. But death does not mean tragedy. It means nothing to the person who dies, and very little to others. In your case when you will die by committing suicide, Kalpana will rejoice and Manu will feel relieved. Your parents will have to search a 'Rudali' to come and mourn and shed tears as there will be no mourners to weep for you. Suicide is useless. Let your pills sleep and commit suicide.

A. Then get the law changed. Women must get justice. The man who makes a woman fall in love with him and sacrifice the whole of her life, her body, mind, heart, everything, should be compelled by law to wed her and take her as his wife, even though he may be a married man and had to divorce her. This is justice, this is a young woman's right, her basic human right.

C. I totally agree with you, but till such a law is made, you should not walk out of this world, this cruel world which does no emotional justice to women like you, till then your pills should wait. It is always good to have patience and work for a good and noble cause. Take courage, continue the fight and win; do not surrender and die.

A. But my story, my drama has already ended in a tragedy, and the final phase of tragedy is inside my bag.

C. No, only the first part of the play has ended, the second part has just begun. We have still to raise the curtain for the final Act. Be ready to play the new role of a conquering, pushing and aggressive heroine surcharged with love and hope. Life's play is still continuing.

Tragedy befalls not from death, but from life. Life is a continuity of events happy and tragic. Suicide is certainly not such a event. You had a blooming love, then came the tragedy of deprivation. Maybe, now again has come the time for happiness to return with deeper love. You have to get back the love of the one you loved and also the happiness of wifehood and motherhood. Continue the play till the finale is reached. Let the world see the power of love and its ultimate victory.

A. How long have I to wait for this victory of my love ?

C. No one can predict the time, you have to carry on till you succeed.

A. Do you think I have the courage to go on ?

C. Yes, you have, you only need a determination to win. Recollect the moments of ecstasy in your life, the moments of joy and bliss, and believe that you have to enjoy them once again. Keep confident and move on.

Next Session

A. He has no courage to come back to me and give me the happiness I want. Everyone except him, came to console me when I attempted suicide, and till today he has not said a word to console or encourage me, much less the making of promise to undo the wrong.

C. He knows well that it was because of him you had attempted suicide, but had no courage to accept it, he is a coward.

A. Yes, he is a coward, and runs away from me to hide himself behind Kalpana's dirty petticoat. She was in his life even when he promised all heavenly love to me. Why did he show all that concern and love for me ?

Why did he write and speak those words of love to me ? Why did he make me believe he was my husband and I his wife ? Why did he say he did not like Kalpana and would leave her and come to me ?

C. It was all necessary to win your confidence, your love. Would you have surrendered yourself totally if he had not made all these promises ?

A. No. Is this the way men should act ? Is this not a crime against women ? Doesn't it come within your concept of rights of women and crimes against women ?

C. It does, and if it were in my power I would have forced him to love you and live with you.

A. I wish he may sense my feelings and respond.

B. Let's have faith that one day your wishes will come true, it may be only a matter of time.

[Anu laughs, her mood changes, it seems a desire to continue to live is getting rekindled in her heart, and she is ready to put off her date with death.]

Next Session

A. Why do they Manu and Kalpana, and everyone else not realise that I have already married him in my heart and he will always remain my husband ?

C. Like Meera had married Krishna. But for Meera, Krishna existed only as an image in her mind. Krishna lived in a different historical age and Meera accepted him as her husband only figuratively. Listen to her thoughts and feelings in her songs. You become Meera, sing all the songs. Meera composed and sang, add to them your own.

A. There is difference in her case and my case.

C. Of course, your Krishna is living in the same age in which you are living. Your Krishna is a prisoner and a slave of his wife, and cannot come to bestow his love on his Radha. So you have to do something else. Let your talents create a new Krishna, a Krishna who cannot be stolen by Kalpana or anyone else. Let him have an incarnation as your husband in your poems, your songs, your paintings. Let him become impersonal and acquire immortality.

Next Session

A. I feel suffocated.

C. Emotional suffocation ?

A. Yes, I feel emotional suffocation, my life has come to a standstill, I am moving nowhere. I cannot get him, he has shut himself inside the shell of his cowardice. And to add to my agony, everyone tells me and asks me to forget my lover, and find a new husband. I do not want to forget him or to let him walk out of my life, nor do I want to have any other man as my husband. I cannot have two husbands at the same time. I still treat him as my husband.

C. You are right, love is not such a thing, which can be withdrawn from one man and transferred to another. There is nothing wrong in your continuing to treat him as your lover, but if you wish to treat him also as your husband, then do it in the way Meera did, so that he becomes a part of your own personality and ceases to be an outsider. Then you can enjoy his company in the way your mind desires.

[Anu writes a few lines, and sings them.]

A. I want my Dabboo to read this, I want him to read all my poems after they are published.

C. It is a very good idea, write some more and then we can get them published in the form of a book.

A. Am I not a normal person ? Why does everyone condemn me as abnormal, do you also think I am mad ?

[Anu, reads a passage in the book *Personality Disorders*. She reads and smiles].

C. Why do you smile ?

A. This description fits my father, and this D and this me.

C. So you see, everyone has some disorder, hence there is nothing for you to worry. 'Normal' means nothing, everyone has a personality of one's own. There is nothing wrong with your personality. Those who say you are abnormal or mad think they are ideal, and because you are not like them, they call you abnormal and mad. They are ignorant people, forgive them for their ignorance and be happy.

A. But they think I am a misguided woman, a woman who has set wrong and foolish goals for herself, and will achieve nothing.

C. They are wrong, all great geniuses were at some stage considered abnormal. You have a great future. Let your love blossom, let a new light come. Let your oceanic love rise and bring a new tide in your life.

A. I don't know, but I will certainly give your suggestions a trial, I shall try to express my emotions and feelings in musical words and songs.

Next Session

A. He has always been avoiding meeting, talking, even seeing me. Even when I phone he puts the receiver down. Even when he had to hand over the charge of his post to me, he just left the key on the table and ran away like a coward. Why does he act like this, Kalpana does not come to the office to see what he is doing.

C. I think he is afraid more of you than of Kalpana.

A. Me ?

C. Yes, You. He knows that if he comes within the limits and bounds of your love this time, you will not leave him. He is afraid of your captivating smile, your enchanting eyes.

A. I am not so beautiful, Kalpana says she is more beautiful.

C. Does she also say she is more charming, more enchanting, more captivating ?

A. No, she cannot say so, she cannot be such a big liar.

C. He probably thinks your smile and your playful eyes are too powerful for him to resist. Have you heard the couplet about the enchanting eyes of a charming woman:

Amiya halahal madhu bhare, shwet, shyam, ratnar; jiahin, marahin, jhukjhuk parahin, jehin chitwain ekbar.

(eyes) filled with nectar, poison, wine; white, black, red; (make) alive, dead, inebriated, anyone on whom falls their glance.

A. But he does not think so.

C. You are wrong, he has already once been a prey to your charming eyes, and smiling lips. He is afraid of you, and to prevent fresh captivity, he avoids you.

A. I am not a tigress that I will eat him.

C. You are not a tigress but an enchantress. He cannot care to come near you, he will always keep clear of the zone of your influence because of that hidden fear. He knows that if he falls into the trap of your love this time, he will never be able to get out, you will leave open no exit door.

A. Will I be wrong ?

C. No.

A. Earlier I missed the opportunity to have a child, he was afraid.

C. The same fear, I think, still continues.

A. He has given children to Kalpana, Why not to me ?

C. She is his wife. He was afraid of the world and avoided being caught having sex with an unmarried girl like you.

A. Yes, he was afraid of it, he is a coward. I did get arousal and desire for sex, but on one pretext or the other he avoided it and I surrendered to his will. He used to say that he would like to dissolve me in water and drink me so that I become a part of his own self. But he never gave me orgasmic fulfilment.

C. It is this suppressed and unfulfilled desire that has created troubles for you. It has gone deep into your sub-consciousness and got buried therein, and is craving to get released. Non-fulfilment of sex has given you a shock and caused trauma of such a severe nature that you have developed various kinds of abnormal behaviours. You had orgasm but no sex, no fulfilment.

A. Please manage to get him to me and I shall make him have fulfilling sex. I am crazy, I want sex with him, children from him as Kalpana has. I am sure he is still in love with me. Look at this calendar page (she has brought from his office table where she now sits temporarily). He has marked the two dates: one is Valentine's day and the other is my birthday.

C. Both of you are crazy, both of you are suffering agony and pain: you from desertion, and he from guilt, shame, and fear.

A. I wish I could place my head on his shoulder and cry, shed all the tears that are stored in my eyes.

[The probe has made Anu come out with what she had been concealing so long, her craving for sex and pregnancy with her ex-lover and the deep-rooted shock and trauma caused by her not getting fulfilment.]

Next Session

A. I have made a painting (copy) in which Meneka is taking away Shakuntala with her when Dushyant fails to recognise her. I have also written a small poem to be put beneath it. I will have five photo-copies made of this, and so place them at different places that he may not escape viewing it.

C. Now you are positively on the right path. What's the poem ?

Anu reads the poem. English version of which is :

No more my Manu longs for his darling,
No more cares for those moments of love.
But still, the living maiden's tender heart
Whines, wails, weeps, and bleeds.
Alas ! neither has the earth melted, nor ocean frozen,
And his cruel heart has missed not a beat.
When to love no homage is paid, no reverence given,
Living itself loses all meaning, and

Life's lovely petals droop, wither and wane. O' mother,
Take me away from this mirage of illusory love,
Away from these heartless blocks of stone.

C. It is a beautiful poem full of passion and love, and a complaint about the failure of the lover and the whole world to feel the agony of the storm rising in your heart. But why this running away from life ?

A. No woman can bear insult of her love. She wants her love to be accepted, respected and honoured.

C. You are perfectly right. But why do you have grievance against everyone ?

A. Because everyone thinks I have faltered and am a bad girl, no one admires or respects my emotions. No one is ready and willing to acknowledge my devotion to love. I feel really disappointed. That is why I call Mother to take me away from this world of 'heartless blocks of stone'.

C. But, you forget that the whole universe with myriad worlds lies within human consciousness, it lives also within your consciousness. Human consciousness is like a kaleidoscope, it produce innumerable patterns, each representing a particular and a peculiar emotional order. You will, in this kaleidoscope, see all kinds of patterns, some which you will like, some which you will not.

A. My mind does not have a kaleidoscope, it sees only one pattern all round, really the humanity has only one pattern, a pattern in which there is only contempt and scorn for love and the lover if she happens to be a girl. Women in this world are not supposed to fall in love, and men have an inherent right to leave them isolated whenever they like without caring for the sentiments of the woman who has sacrificed all her happiness for the sake of his love.

C. Your thinking is absolutely right, it is based on your personal experience. Don't you think it would be better to write a poem describing the moments of ecstasy and blissful love which you have mentioned in your poem. Please once again ride on cloud nine and see the new patterns made of colourful glittering light of romantic and passionate love. You will find that the world does not really consist of only heartless blocks of stone, but is full of throbbing hearts longing to sing the songs of eternal love.

If I could say a word about your latest poem, it is superb. It shows a transcendence of the emotion of love. Now you have become a lover of love, a worshipper of love, while earlier you were a lover of a lover, worshipper of a worshipper. Love is something which has in it a divinity, it is the highest and best of all emotions, it is far superior to human being for whom it appears in someone's noble heart.

A. But I cannot conceive of love in the abstract, for me it is correlated to the object of my love.

C. Love lives in the consciousness of an individual and gives blissful happiness to the consciousness in which it resides. Every poet, every artist has a beloved, but he/she sings the songs of love and not of the object of love. It is why you have spoken of homage and reverence in relation to your own emotion of love, to the abstract concept of love, than of homage to any individual.

Next Session

C. Hello Anu, your last poem shows that your thinking has now changed, your concern has now gone beyond an individual and covers the bigger zone of love.

A. No, it has changed only so far as my anger is concerned, now it engrosses the whole world. I hate each and every person around me. Whole world is against me, none comes forward to help me, even to understand me. Nothing has changed, I am still a social outcaste. Oh this cruel 'society'.

C. Which society ? There is no society, you are member of no society. They, you call society are only self-appointed guards-of-honour. Don't worry about them. They apply different standards for different persons.

A. They always continue to worry me, they are always there to keep me entrapped in codes of their own wretched morality.

C. You just ignore them, don't hate the world or the entire society or humanity for the fault of these guardians of morality. Hatred is a negative emotion, and negative emotion spells unhappiness.

A. What does it matter ? What is wrong in having negative emotions or being unhappy ? I welcome negative emotions, I wish to live with my unhappiness.

C. Yes, ultimately there is no difference between happiness and unhappiness, both are only states of mental activity: thinking and feeling. That is why it is said that one should experience equanimity both in pleasure and pain, joy and agony. However, don't you think it was better when you had moments of ecstasy and love than what you now have, the unending period of separation and segregation? Is it not giving you unhappiness ?

A. But nobody else feels the pain I am suffering, even he does not feel it; the world is wholly unconcerned about my agony.

C. You cannot change the world, so let it remain as it is. Try to do such activities that bring you positive emotions and happiness.

A. I told you I do not want positive emotion or happiness, I want to suffer and remain unhappy, if this be my lot. What is wrong in being sad and sorrowful ?

C. Nothing, because now it has become part of your life.

A. My greatest mistake was that I got scared of this society when the two of us were together. Had I not hesitated during those moments I would have had his child with me today. He always used to say he wanted a child from me. "Give me a daughter, then ours will become a blood-relationship", he had said. And today, I regret having not taken that step at that moment. Then nobody could have snatched him away from me.

C. Anu, it is not possible to infuse new life into the dead past and make it available to you in the present for being re-lived. It is not possible to go back to the old green valley where you had enjoyed the aroma of sweet flowers of love. Let us be practical and see love in its true perspective, in its broad sense, as an emotion, as a way of enjoying the true beauty and loveliness of life. Then, it will get perpetuity and become available to you whenever you wish, even today.

A. What you are talking is all philosophy. For me love means actual union with my Manu. I want him here with me.

This world, this society has snatched away my life from me. They are least concerned about my happiness. They do not realise what it feels like to lose your precious lover. He is my world.

He has been destroyed completely by Kalpana. He was a gem of a person but he has been reduced to a dumb husband.

C. Anu, you are right that Kalpana has reduced Manu to a vegetable pulp. He has lost all courage and probably all ardour and spirit necessary for romance and love. He is no more the jewel you were fond of, no more the god you had worshipped, or the angel who had given you the happiness you are unable to forget. I fear that even if somehow you manage to get him back, you will not find him the jewel you were searching. He has become dumb and will not be able to give you the joy of life, the nectar of love.

A. I do not agree. I have faith in my own love and am confident that if I get him I shall be able to put in him the same life which Kalpana has made him lose.

C. I do believe your love has that magic.

A. Your experiment of wiping out tears has failed completely in my case, you have not been able to bring him back to me.

C. I don't know, you may be right. You are fighting the battle of love, and love's battle cannot be fought by proxy. No one else can win the heart of your lover for you, you have to win it yourself. Develop more confidence, faith, and trust in your love, and proceed to win him back through the captivating messages in your lovely songs and poems. I hope you will succeed in having your dream materialised.

A. To whom will I send these messages? If they reach Kalpana's hand, she will burst with rage and curse both me and her petticoat husband, and he will begin to shiver and beg for mercy. If I send them to him in the office, he would get scared and conceal them somewhere or destroy them.

C. Whatever happens, the messages will fulfil their mission. Remember, it is a war of love, and you have determined to carry it on till the end, till you get back your Manu.

A. I shall now go on the offensive.

C. And win the war, get Manu back in whatever shape he is. Ultimately, you might discover that, like all wars, the war of love also ends with gain to none, and the booty is not worth the whole sacrifice. Anu, how is your world of art, poems and songs progressing ?

A. I have made a telefilm.

C. That is great. Now you have come on the right track. What is the film about ?

A. It is in respect of a poor child longing for education, and in spite of the father who wants him to earn money for his booze, the teacher manages to give him schooling. The film is, however, lying with the TV people without any response.

C. Doesn't matter, you may remind the person concerned.

Anu has not been able to get back her Manu, and her agony had remained. However, the continued counselling has given Anu a will to live. Now she thinks more of getting back her lover, having sex with him and bearing his children, than of considering death as a better alternative.

RASHMI

Rashmi cannot get out from her mind the memory of beatings she received from her husband; she could stop him only when she brandished the knife, and threatened to kill him. She cannot trust him, and fears he might again resort to his brutal ways. The beatings had a devastating effect on her, and that still persists.

Diagnostic Scan

Rashmi is a well-groomed young lady, twenty-seven.

There seems a lot of tension on her face. She began by saying she had no problem, but on being asked why she then was tension writ large on her face, she narrated her tale of woe.

Rashmi had a serious car accident about two years back, and has still not got over it fully. Her face had been injured, bones of the right arm and leg were broken, and she suffered multiple injuries. She was going in the car when a truck struck it, causing serious damage to the car and injuries to her.

Her right elbow was fixed with a steel plate inside; it has yet to be operated for being removed. Although the doctor had thought it will not move freely, but by regular practice it has begun to move almost normally. Still she cannot do all her work with her right hand; though she can write with it, she cannot paint. However, she can make items of gift and decorate earthen pots.

Rashmi suffered great trauma and pain. Though she has recovered as far as her physical injuries are concerned, her psychic injuries continue to keep her under stress, and tense.

She takes exercises in a gymnasium to keep her limbs moving. She took to aroma therapy. But that hardly did her any good, so she gave it up.

An incident she described as cause of her persisting psychic problems, is that once in the presence of quite a few persons, the aroma therapist in order to show her own importance said that Rashmi was suffering from many problems as she had met with a car accident which left her whole body damaged. This offended Rashmi because she did not want anyone to know of her physical disabilities. She feels her sense of personal dignity and self-esteem had been compromised, and she was made to feel inferior to other women like her.

Counselling

C. Why ? why do you want to conceal this fact from the world ?

R. I do not wish to be viewed as a disabled person, suffering from serious injuries.

C. Why ? You should not be afraid of exposure. You have done no wrong, why do you feel humiliation and shame ? You have developed a feeling of guilt for no reason. You were a victim and not anybody's tormentor. It was the truck driver who had done the wrong thing, he should feel guilty and ashamed, not you. Take this guilt out of your mind, feel no shame for the disabilities or the injuries you suffered. Have courage, let the world know you have suffered for no fault of yours, and you are not guilty. Don't let this feeling continue to pester your mind, otherwise you will always remain in tension. From now on decide that you will never feel guilty or ashamed for anything that happens to you.

R. I shall do so from now on.

C. I think there is something else which is the real cause of your agony and stress. How is your sex life ? Generally the injuries you suffered and the trauma you got would affect sexual functioning. Do you have any problem ?

R. No, it is all right. However, when there is a change of weather and winter sets in, I feel some discomfort in my bones and joints.

C. How are your relations with your husband ? Does he realise this ?

R. No, he does not. My relations with my husband are now better. I was married only one-year back, it was a love marriage, but soon after, my husband began to ill-treat me. He began abusing me with filthy language, particularly in the presence of his relatives, friends and acquaintances. He even occasionally beat me.

C. How ?

R. By slapping.

C. How could you tolerate this ?

R. I could not bear it but had to put up with it. However, once when he attempted to beat me I took up a knife and told him I would kill him if he touched me ever again.

C. What happened then ?

R. Since then he has not abused and beaten me, and has become normal and also more caring.

C. You did the right thing.

R. Did I ?

C. Yes. This was the only way to defend yourself and to stop him. He needed stern action. You should never submit to injustice. Had this violence anything to do with your sex-life ?

R. I do not think so, because it was all very normal during the night. Violence is probably in his blood. He beats his brother, but he is younger, I am elder he should not do this with me.

C. Yes, you are right. Now probably he will not misbehave any more.

R. His parents, ever since he was a child used to have bitter quarrels. Ultimately, his mother was forced out of the house by his father. He married again and brought in a step-mother. I do not know where his mother is. He also doesn't care to know.

C. So he has grown up in an atmosphere of distress and tension.

R. Yes, and after our marriage his father and step-mother turned us out of the house, and also excluded my husband from the business (his father is running an industry). Now he is working with a builder. My husband puts all blame on me for his being turned out of the house and the industry.

C. Were you responsible ?

R. Not at all. I always tried to patch-up their differences. I always tried to bring about conciliation and peace. But he does not accept this and continues to put all blame on me.

C. You know you are not responsible, why then should you feel any guilt ? Forget it, and don't react even if he rakes up the issue. But why is there discord between you two, and why has it developed within such a short time after marriage, particularly when, as you say, he was in love with you and married you in spite of his parents' opposition because you were older than him.

R. It is always an insignificant matter that starts trouble. Argument turns into altercation and then into a quarrel. Then he becomes abusive and violent. I cannot tolerate this and suffer great distress. In my family such things never happened.

C. Think of something which might be the real or more significant bone of contention between you two.

R. The main trouble is that he wants me not to pursue my studies, and live in the house the whole day as a traditional housewife. Alternatively, he wants me to make handsome income. I got work with Rs. 3000 as salary, but he made me give it up because in his view the salary was not high enough. I had ambitions, they have all remained unrealised. But I have now joined M.A. (English) course.

C. What were or are your ambitions ?

R. I wanted to be a doctor, but my accident and illness came in the way. I am however not sorry for that. Then I wanted to go in for export business. I joined an export firm, but there I was taken to be just a sex object, and the owner tried to make advances. I could not tolerate his behaviour and left the job.

C. What next ?

R. I don't know. But I want to do something. I do not want to be always dependent on my husband.

C. Yes, you must try to have your own independent life, but not at the cost of your health or honour. Hasn't your husband sufficient income ?

R. He has, but it is not enough for a life of luxury. We can afford only items of comfort, not luxury.

C. Wait, it takes time to have income that may suffice for luxuries, and unfortunately by that time the person loses all craving for luxury. You cannot do hard work requiring physical labour, so you should go in for an intellectual job like law, teaching.

R. I don't like teaching, I shall think of law. There are opportunities in law. I want a name for myself. I want an identity and distinction.

C. Okay. Let us investigate further about the reason for your husband's remaining cross with you. Normally, a man expects love and sex during marriage, is it because of his not getting full satisfaction that he feels alienated. Does he get fulfilment ?

R. I don't know, but I think we do need marriage counselling. However, he does not, in spite of my asking him, agree to go for marriage counselling. Sometimes of course, pain in my bones interferes, and this causes problems. I do not know when this will occur, however, I try to remain cautious.

C. Avoid tension before sex.

Sex should not be the object of your desire, the objective must always be love. Let love flow in abundance, sex will automatically come as a by-product. If you will crave sex, you will always suffer from fear of non-fulfilment and failure. What causes sexual obstruction, constraint and withdrawal leading to non-fulfilment is generally the fear of failure rather than actual failure. Fear generates tension and tension leads to failure of total happiness and fulfilment. If there is no fear, there will be no tension, and you will have fulfilment. Even if ultimately you do not get satisfying orgasm, don't worry or feel concerned. If you strive for love and love alone, then you shall never experience failure, and sexual fulfilment will come as a bonus, as a reward.

R. What about my husband ? He should also learn this.

C. Teach him also the same thing. He should be more considerate in view of your injuries, which though cured still need caring. Once there is a flow of love, he will get immersed into it and will forget sex, his craving will be for love and love alone. Then sex will come automatically, free of tension and will be fulfilling.

R. I understand.

Second Session

Counselling received by Rashmi during the first session had a good effect. Rashmi reports she is having very little general tension now. She feels she now remains relaxed. Her face today shows no tension, the whole face appears different, it is free of tension.

She says her interest in life is growing, she is now doing the household work normally. Even in studies her interest has been revived. She has started reading books.

He lethargy has gone and she feels quite energetic.

Her family life, including sex life, has improved. Her relations with her husband have also become normal. Rashmi's problem now is that she is still worried about the non-fulfilment of her ambitions.

She, however, says that whatever she wants she always achieves; she has not yet failed to achieve whatever she aspired for.

R. I decided that my right arm should have normal movement, and in spite of doctor's doubts, it has become almost normal.

Everyone said that with my broken bones I should not get married, but I decided I will marry and marry this very man, and in spite of all opposition from his parents, I did.

C. What is your ambition or goal, which you think you now want to achieve ?

R. I don't really know what my present ambition is.

C. Then let us determine it. Let us examine your capabilities.

R. Some years back I had, at the request of a friend, translated a book from French (dealing with women's problems of menstruation) into English. My friend wanted to use it in connection with her thesis. She also paid me Rs. 2,000 just as token remuneration for my efforts. I know French, but have failed to get a translator's job. I do not have sufficient fluency for being an interpreter. I am interested in writing.

C. You had said earlier that your ambition was to get fame, name, and also money. Now take practical steps for the same:

(*a*) get back the manuscript from your friend;

(*b*) get it vetted by your French friend;

(*c*) explore possibilities of publishing it.

R. I shall take steps to publish the English version of the book I had translated from French into English.

C. Write an article on menstruation and send it for publication in journals. But do it without any expectation of publication, otherwise if not published you may feel sorry. Continue to write articles for publication in magazines, do not stop even if you get hundred rejection slips. Ultimately you will succeed.

She has been given a questionnaire to determine her psychological flow.

After sometime Rashmi phoned she was feeling relaxed. She has taken steps to get back her manuscript.

Third Session

Rashmi is not wholly happy. She has answered the questionnaire; the answers have revealed some inner conflicts in her mind. Rashmi has not much trust in her husband. She fears that if his father will ask him to return he will go back, leaving Rashmi to her fate. This has generated in her a sense of insecurity.

Rashmi has revealed more facts about her miserable married life. She had threatened to divorce her husband. That, however, made him change his aggressive, tormenting attitude and he became complacent.

She tried to get some consolation from the fact that some of her friends too were not spared by their husbands, even though they were all earning partners and well-educated. But that has failed to heal the injury caused to her honour, self-respect and self-esteem. This injury has seriously wounded her psyche and has developed in her the feeling of shame and has shaken her self-confidence. It has also meant bringing in her mind the feeling of distrust for her husband and fear of loss of his love. She has begun to doubt if he loves her at all.

The chief cause of her failure to do anything worthwhile after marriage, she thinks, is her husband's uncalled-for interference. She blames him for the frustrations she is suffering.

Analysis of her answers further shows her interest in creative visual art and literature. She made some painted greeting cards, etc., but got disheartened when no one was ready to undertake their marketing.

C. Don't think about commercialising your hobbies at the moment, work only and primarily for your personal satisfaction. That will give you greater happiness and bring you out of the mess in which you presently are. It will end your feeling of frustration. Let your frustration and fear of failure disappear. Just do what gives you pleasure and work-satisfaction.

R. What can I do ?

C. Well,

(*a*) You should take to art painting. Then you can take to making cards for organisations. If any of your paintings or cards is approved, you will get recognition and that will be reward enough.

(*b*) You should try to translate some other book from French to English, and when it is ready, approach publishers. Then you will have greater chance of publishing the book. It is difficult to find a publisher before the book is ready.

(*c*) It will be very good if you will write your biography, rather psychography. You have had a chequered life with many ups and downs, you will find it very interesting to pen down the events in your life with critical insight and understanding. Just make an attempt.

R. I will try.

C. All these are meant to take your mind away from petty disappointments, failures and frustrations from which you are presently suffering. Transform your negative feelings of fear, prejudice, and hatred into positive feelings of hope and achievement through creative activities. You are intellectual by nature, do something to utilise your talents.

R. But all that will not sell.

C. Yes. You need two things—something to give you emotional equilibrium and happiness, and something to bring money. These activities will restore your emotional balance and bring you peace of mind, and also marital happiness. For earning money you will have to do something of the nature of a commercial or professional activity. You can open a boutique because you have done fashion designing. You can take up teaching spoken French. You can take up law as a profession.

R. Law will require four years.

C. Doesn't matter, your other activities will go on, law degree will come in addition. Think of it.

Fourth Session

R. I am still very sore about the behaviour of my in-laws. The step-mother and father of my husband had, while forcing us leave the home and business, made us pay back all that they had spent on his marriage with me. Not only that, they always try to take every month at least a part of his salary. I however, do not think he parts with it, but I am not sure.

C. It has now become an old story. Forget the whole thing and treat the payment to your in-laws as price paid for securing your freedom from them. You are capable of stopping your husband from paying anything more to them out of his salary.

R. An incident has again raked-up my wounded feelings. Recently about a week back I had to attend a function at my husband's cousins place. There I was put to all sorts of humiliation by women as they were not happy with my marriage and were not willing to accept me as part of the family. I am particularly sore because in spite of my requests my husband neither stood up to protect me nor agreed to leave the place and come away.

They criticised me, inter alia, for wearing salwar-kurta suit and not sari. They did not realise that injuries suffered by me during the accident, particularly in the right arm, had made it very difficult for me to wear and manage the sari. They also showed themselves off in heavy gold ornaments and criticised me for not wearing ornaments.

C. Why did you feel irritated ? They were only trying to get over their inferiority. Do you not think they knew you were more highly educated, culturally more advanced, and in every way superior to them ? They were only trying to hide their own inferior intellectual and cultural make up.

R. I know that, although it did not strike me then; now I feel that it was the real reason. But they possess more gold than I do.

C. Do you feel they are superior to you because they have more gold? Don't you think it was a vulgar exhibition of black money ?

R. I do think so, I do not feel gold ornaments enhance anybody's stature or status. I feel no inferiority because of it.

C. Then why did you feel irritated ? Was it because it came as a surprise ? or was it because deep in your heart, you have a hidden dislike for them ? You don't have any malice, but it seems their general hostile behaviour in the past had given rise to a feeling of some type of intolerance in you for their unfriendly behaviour.

R. It may be so to some extent, but the real thing was that I felt let down by my husband.

C. Would it not have been better if you had just kept calm and analysed the reason behind their uncultured, hostile behaviour ? Then you would have realised that it was useless for you to worry about the motivated volley of accusations. Would it not have been better to ignore the same as coming from persons who are not trained to behave in a civilised manner. You only helped them in their nefarious design of humiliating you.

R. Yes, that is so. I should have seen the motive behind their coarse behaviour, and just by ignoring the whole thing I could have defeated and frustrated their plan.

C. That would have saved you from losing your temper and thereby losing your peace of mind. From now on whenever you face adverse situations, just try to keep your cool and give a suitable reply without causing any offence. That will enhance your prestige and at the same time make them realise that their game has not succeeded. Remember that people who suffer from a feeling of inferiority try to do something to pull down those whom they, deep within themselves, regard as superior; the purpose is only to show off their assumed superiority. So, never become a prey to the designs of those who wish to damage your image in order to improve their own.

Your husband could certainly have walked out, but probably he thought it would worsen the situation. Maybe he thought you were capable of overriding the storm; maybe he did not realise you had taken the situation so seriously. Maybe he did not have courage to bear the adverse family reaction. Whatever may have been the reason, it would be better to forgive your husband for his not realising the gravity of the situation. Forget the incident. Get free of its trauma and treat it as a matter unworthy of being kept in the treasure house of your memory.

R. I see the point and hope to cope successfully with adverse situations in future, with courage and better understanding.

Fifth Session

R. I am generally happy.

C. How are your relations with your husband ?

R. He has begun to behave normally, he no longer behaves offensively either by using foul language or resorting to violence. His antagonistic and noxious behaviour has changed into one of concern and consideration for me.

C. That's enough, you have won. He is afraid of losing you and your love. So, you need have no fears any more. He has given good evidence to show he loves you and will never leave you. Is there still the need to go to a marriage counsellor ?

R. I think, not.

C. It is your love and better understanding of human psychology that has brought the much-wanted peace and joy in your life.

R. No, it is your counselling.

C. No, no, credit is all yours, I am only a catalyst.

SHASHI

From outside shashi looks cheerful and happy; however she is full of turbulence, memories of the past make her boil and bitter against her husband.

Diagnostic Scan

Gautam is fiftyfour, a retired army officer, married, has a daughter and a son. The story of Gautam and Shashi is not an unusual story. Many a family live a life of misery for no cause. They lack understanding and concern for the feelings of the partner, and need a little bit of compassion and a little bit of love.

Gautam complains that his wife, Shashi, suspects him all the time. He cannot go out or get engaged in any activity without raising suspicion in his wife's mind. She suspects he will get involved with some woman, and hence restricts his movements and involvement in any activity. He feels very sore and let down. This, along with other tensions has developed in him symptoms of depression and anxiety.

Another grievance of his, real or imaginery, is that she does not even allow him to correspond with or meet his father who lives with his elder brother. Even letters coming from his father, he suspects, are intercepted and not given to him. She does not welcome his relatives in the house, even objects to their coming. But, on the other hand, she welcomes her own relatives.

There is high tension in the family. Nobody talks to the other. There is total lack of communication and understanding.

The wife, according to him, is the master of the house, it is she who controls everything, including the use of car by his son.The son too, is very prone to resentment. His reaction to his mother's commands is often violent. Once he threw away the bouquet he was taking to his girl friend as he was refused the use of the car and broke a few things including the telephone instrument after having phoned his girl friend that he was unable to come.

Gautam is very cross with his wife, thinks of divorcing her, but failing to find any ground for divorce, becomes tense and frustrated. They were married twenty-five years back. They had fallen in love when she was working as a nurse in the hospital attached to his unit in the army. Now they are totally alienated.

Gautam tries to put all blame for all his problems on his wife, considers her a villain. Though he does not say so, he has bitterness and hatred towards her deep down in his mind. He feels he has been reduced to the status of a puppet, the strings of which are manipulated by her. He resents but feels helpless.

Some of his tension is also due to his being unemployed, for this also he puts the blame on the wife. He was suffering from intestinal tuberculosis some years back and is still running low evening temperature. He does not get sound sleep because he lives under constant stress, tension and fear. His ill-health is also a contributory factor.

There are many small and insignificant things that create friction between them and lead to tension and alienation. Some of them are:

(*a*) Shashi feels she is right in checking their son from indiscriminately using the car. On some occasions when the car developed some defect, he left it where it gave trouble and did nothing to get it repaired. She does not have confidence in his driving. She objects to his taking the car out at any time without her permission, as she also needs the car for herself and for her daughter.

Gautam , on the contrary, thinks that the son should have a free hand, and feels that the son should not ever be denied the use of the car. He, however, concedes his wife's right to decide finally.

(*b*) Gautam is in the habit of giving unsought advice to people, he freely gives advice to their daughter and son-in-law, recently married. Shashi insists that they should be allowed to live their life in their own way and Gautam should restrain himself from giving uncalled for advice which is not welcomed by them.

(*c*) Gautam believes Shashi destroys his father's letters and that is why they were having no correspondence. He wants to bring his father home to which Shashi objects as from her past experience she thinks her husband will again begin to find fault with her behaviour towards his father. She has no objection, though, to his going to visit his father.

(*d*) There is a total lack of confidence between the two. Shashi says Gautam always found fault with her way of entertaining the guests, the result is that now they no longer receive any guest.

(*e*) Gautam tolerates no interference by Shashi in his way of functioning or doing things. He tries to be a perfectionist and always remains under tension and fear of non-achievement. Even when people do not turn up in time, he gets upset and tense. The tension is shifted on to his wife on the pretext of her interfering with his way of functioning.

(He was counselled to learn not to be a perfectionist in every matter and not to set unachievable targets if he desired to avoid unnecessary frustration generated by fear of non-achievement).

For not having an employment Gautam tries to put the blame on his wife. It is because, he feels, Shashi does not tolerate and permit him to take employment where he will come in contact with women, particularly young women, that he does not get a job. Shashi feels it is only an alibi for being unemployed.

Gautam tries to shift the blame on to his wife. She is not prepared to accept it. She is willing not to interfere with his functioning, but at the same time she is not willing to giving him a free hand which she fears will result in disruption of family life.

At one stage when Gautam was alone he said Shashi may also be called in from the waiting room so that she may not think there was something he was cooking against her during the counselling. This shows that Gautam lacks self-confidence and has no faith and confidence in his wife.

Counselling

To Gautam has been done with the following objectives:

1. He should realize that everyone is to some extent a puppet in the hands of destiny. He needs to get rid of the negative emotion of hatred and substitute it with the positive emotion of love.

2. He should develop greater confidence in his wife and realise that she is his friend and not his foe. He should develop better understanding of his wife's mind, and develop greater faith in her.

3. And above all, have faith in himself, and not to worry about what his wife thinks.

Shashi, Gautam's wife, looks composed and happy and does not look the villian her husband Gautam made her out to be. She is fifty and has confidence and is apparently cheerful and happy.

Inside, however, she is full of turbulence, memories of the past make her feel bitter against her husband. She says that even at the time she went for honeymoon after marriage he took with him some acquaintance and that spoiled her honeymoon totally. She is very sore about it. It created a sort of hatred (more properly dislike) for her husband. She feels he deliberately created sourness in her honeymoon, and that has continued to be his behaviour all his life. He does not let her have a happy life, he always brings in an intruder. The memory of her spoiled honeymoon lies deep in her sub-conscious mind and always crops up in her conscious mind. It has left a permanent scar on her psyche. She finds it extremely difficult to pardon her husband for this.

It has become difficult for her to forget it because she is unable to believe that it happened just by chance. She believes he never allows her to have the comfort of privacy which is essential in marital life.

The most obnoxious intruder, in her view, whom he brings into her life is his father. Whenever he comes to live with her he creates problems, pretends he is unhappy, and this provokes her husband to nag her. This further intensifies her dislike of the father-in-law. Her father-in-law once brought some 'bhabhut' (ash) from some sadhu (ascetic) and made her put it in all the food she cooked, saying it will drive away evil out of her life and make the family happy. She did it once or twice and then refused. That caused further trouble in the family.

The desire and denial of privacy in her married life has made her averse to her husband's hobnobbing with people and bringing them into their life. Particularly, she has objection to her husband's becoming friendly with women. She feels annoyed whenever she finds her husband enjoying the company of other women. She resents and objects to his meeting women on intimate terms. This makes her husband feel humiliated and insulted.

Not that she suspects any amorous involvement in these relationships, but she cannot tolerate other women entering into the life of her husband.

Counselling to Shashi

Counselling has been directed to make her see that it is necessary for a peaceful life to take things lightly, with greater understanding of human nature and emotions and to take a more charitable view of her husband's behaviour with other women.

C. Shashi, you do the cleaning up of your house everyday with a broom, why should you not do the same with your sub-conscious mind ? Why not broom away the disquieting memories from your sub-conscious mind? Forget the life you have already lived. Fifty years of your life have gone into the dustbin of time, never look back at them, live in the present only. You have to live every minute, bit by bit, as it comes, and then let it disappear in the limbo. No one can live either in the past or in the future. Past is dead and gone, future has not yet come. No one can live except in the present. So try to start life anew, forgetting the painful memories of the past.

Be a new woman, a woman who has just been born. You can even have a new name 'Rosy' because you love roses and flowers. Become one with blooming flowers, love them, see how they grow, just become the flower yourself. That will be a meditation. Just become yourself a flower, feel happy as each flower does.

Counselling to Both

Extensive counselling was given concerning the psychological needs of both

- (*a*) Need to trust each other,
- (*b*) Need of not treating the other as guilty,
- (*c*) Need to love and be loved,
- (*d*) Need to be regarded important and relevant,
- (*e*) Need to end aloofness and become more communicative.

Shashi's response to counselling has been very positive.

S. Counselling has made me realise that the memory of sad events of the past only adds to my misery and serves no purpose. Instead of making me free from stress, it makes me more tense. I very well understand that it is not possible to alter the past and it is futile to dwell perpetually in the past. I have decided to let bygones be bygones.

C. Don't you think it was wrong to interfere with your husband's affairs ? It is for him to choose the way he would like to live; it is his life and he should have the freedom to live as he wishes.

S. I realise he should be left to live as he likes. On my part, I am determined to remain always relaxed, free from worry and tension.

C. That will make your husband also change his attitude and behaviour, and your life will become happier.

Shashi has become completely relaxed and hopeful.

SUKRITI

There was a girl who wanted to marry him but ultimately he was married to me and the other girl was married to some other person. Then a few years back, another woman came into the picture, but she too after some time went out of my husband's life. Now it is Shyama, who is more attractive, has entered his life, and I am afraid of Shyama as she is capable of exploiting her charm.

Diagnostic Scan

Sukriti is a young smart woman in her thirties, a bit fashionable and quite good looking.

She started by saying she is very much confused. Confusion, she thought, was her problem. The term required clarification. Ultimately, it came out that she was suffering from the fear of losing her husband to another woman, Shyama, a divorcee, more beautiful and smarter than Sukriti, also a few years younger to her. The husband is in his forties.

The fear of loss of husband's love led Sukriti to develop jealousy and hatred toward Shyama. She admits that originally it was she (Sukriti) who had introduced Shyama to the family, it was she who had once invited Shyama to come in the kitchen and had let her do the cooking. She lives in the neighbourhood and walks-in whenever she likes. She will enter the kitchen, ask Sukriti to go and have a good time with her husband. Sukriti goes but suspects Shyama's motives; she feels it is only to get some sort of vicarious pleasure of her husband's company, and to win him over that she shows this enthusiasm.

Sukriti desires Shyama to get married to someone so that she might get out of her life, leaving her husband totally to herself.

Sukriti says she is very 'possessive' by nature, cannot tolerate any woman to share her husband. Fear of losing him has become so intense that she repeatedly phones her husband while he is in his business office. It surprises her husband; he fails to understand why she does so.

The fear in Sukriti makes her repeatedly check if her husband is not with Shyama or some other woman. Sukriti's uncalled-for probes not only make her husband feel let down, but also disturb Sukriti; her prying intrusions fail to support her suspicion and make her just restless.

Sukriti begins to feel guilty and frustrated. She feels sorry that she has unjustifiably doubted her husband's fidelity. This has developed in Sukriti the feeling of guilt, which in turn leads to the feeling of shame.

Counselling

C. Can you think of any reason why you suspect your husband?

S. There was a girl who wanted to marry him but ultimately he was married to me and the other girl was married to some other person. Then a few years back, another woman came into the picture, but she too, after some time, went out my husband's life. Now it is Shyama, who is more attractive, has entered his life, and I am afraid of Shyama, as she is capable of exploiting her charm.

C. Your fears seem to be based on suspicion. Tell me of some incidents from which you draw the inference that Shyama has amorous designs.

S. I cannot think of any such incident, and very often I feel there is absolutely nothing between the two, which may be objectionable. My husband is of a very helping nature, and maybe that is why he tries to help Shyama, who has been divorced and is now lonesome.

C. This caring for Shyama seems to be the basis of your suspicion. Does he overdo it?

S. No.

Further probe revealed that there was another reason why Sukriti had developed fear. She suffers from a physical disability. She had a fracture, and a steel bar was fixed, she walks with a limp because of it. It has not been disclosed if this has actually affected her sex life. Though Sukriti mentioned this fact very casually, it seems to be the basic cause of fear in her mind. She feels Shyama is physically superior to her and capable of giving more fulfilling sex; this has caused a crisis of confidence. It has intensified her suspicion and fear of losing her husband. She believes that his relationship with Shyama is not just one of simple friendship, but has emotional overtones.

C. Sukriti, do you think there is an imminent danger to your relationship with your husband?

S. No. I am sure nothing of this kind will happen.

She has been given counselling for strengthening her self-confidence so that she may face the crisis when and if it comes.

C. Your fear seems to be baseless. Your relationship with your husband is under no risk. The danger you fear may never materialise.

S. I am sure of this from what I know of my husband.

C. Coming to the intensity of your fear, tell me where does your fear of Shayma stand on the following scale: (*a*) sex relations (*b*) body contact, hugging, kissing (*c*) platonic love (*d*) spending happy moments together (*e*) unduly pleasant conversation and interaction (*f*) just rendering help to Shyama on humanitarian grounds?

S. I cannot place my suspicion beyond the sixth that is the maximum I suspect.

C. So you see there is no real basis for your fear of losing your husband or even his love.

'Suspicion howsoever great can never amount to proof'. Memorise this and apply it in the case of relations between your husband and Shyama. You should be afraid only if there be some tangible evidence. Suspicion is based on imaginary beliefs and that gives rise to fear. Sukriti, you should learn to be more realistic. By the way, have you yourself ever been involved in any affair?

S. No.

C. You are quite frank and practical-minded, it is surprising that you have developed suspicion against your husband, it is probably because you love him very much. But love and fear don't go together, so don't suspect and don't fear. You should refrain from holding your husband guilty and consider yourself a helpless victim.

(The tears in Sukriti's eyes are gone, she is laughing at herself).

S. A very heavy load has gone off my head. When I had come I was under severe emotional stress, but now I feel totally relieved.

Analysis

Sukriti was very frequently stroking her hair to make them appear more free, more in shape. Probably, she was feeling a little nervous and uneasy because for a woman of substance like Sukriti fear of another woman was hardly dignified, and fear of losing her husband to another woman militated against her self-esteem.

Sukriti's suspicions have created three victims:

(*a*) Ghost woman Shyama who caused fear to grow in Sukriti's mind, suspected of enticing away Sukriti's husband.

(*b*) Sukriti's husband who was being given surprise interventions in order to check if her suspicions were justified.

(*c*) Sukriti is the real victim. Her suspicions about her husband and Shyama having an affair gave rise to the feeling of guilt in her, which in turn created in her the feeling of shameful immaturity. She was no longer in the same old innocent state of mind while facing and talking to her husband

and while dealing with Shyama. She had no explanation to offer to her husband about repeated calls. She may have invented some excuse or her husband may not have asked Sukriti thinking it was because she was feeling lonesome in his absence. People have to resort to make-beliefs and alibis to cover up actions, which they are afraid to make public.

Sukriti was in a state of indecision. She neither wanted to confront Shyama and her husband, nor was happy with what was causing a tumult in her mind. Indecision had created tension, she needed total relief.

Second Session

Sukriti is a bit upset. Shyama and her relations with Sukriti's husband are again at the root of the trouble.

(*a*) The previous evening, when her husband came back she saw and found from his cellular phone that the last call he made was to Shyama. In Sukriti's mind there was an adverse reaction, she felt he was getting too close to Shyama and was flirting with her on phone.

This was a circumstance, which made Sukriti more suspicious about Shyama's intimate relationship with her husband. Sukriti believes that Shyama was not a desirable woman and was in the habit of entrapping men of her liking; this belief is based on information received by her from the maid-servant working in several houses. She had warned Sukriti to be cautious and not to allow Shyama to get friendly with her husband as she was a divorcee living alone and was in search of male company.

(*b*) Another circumstance was that her husband got a new shirt and told Sukriti he had gone to market and purchased it. Sukriti was suspicious, as he never goes marketing alone. Her husband later admitted that it was given to him as a present by Shyama by way of gratitude for helping her in getting the job. Sukriti's resentment is to the secrecy about the receipt of the gift by her husband and making a false story on the issue. In normal course Shyama should have presented him the shirt in Sukriti's presence. Her husband's explanation for telling a lie about the shirt was that he felt Sukriti would dislike his getting the shirt as a present from Shyama, and in order to avoid the embarrassment he told a lie.

Obviously, the husband was suffering from a sense of guilt, and the guilt created fear in his mind. His relationship with Shyama is probably a little more advanced than a man normally has with a woman who is just a friend. He told a lie to Sukriti to conceal the truth about the soft corner he has for Shyama. It was not out of compassion for Sukriti's feelings but because of his feeling of guilt, which had made him tell the lie.

Sukriti is trying to pretend not to mind it because she believed her husband's explanation. She, in fact, does not believe the story, and holds both of them guilty of deceiving her. She thinks they are having a liaison.

She also tries to pretend that she does not mind Shyama's relationship with her husband because she believes he is a good man, and they had eighteen years of happy married life.

Counselling

C. Sukriti, you are in fact suffering from the feeling of jealousy and are afraid of losing your husband at least partially to Shyama. You cannot tolerate Shyama as a rival in love, but lack courage to tell the truth or accept the reality. You need to have more confidence and courage to throw Shyama out of your husband's life in case your suspicion has any basis. However, as yet there is no cause for you to get upset, you should try to treat their relationship as one of friendship posing no threat to your own relationship with your husband.

S. I think you are right.

Third Session

Sukriti has to go to see Shyama today in connection with some work and wanted to know if she should, and how should she behave.

C. You go and congratulate her for getting the new job, and watch her reaction. Try to assess how close the two are to each other. Do not disclose your own feelings or your suspicions. If everything goes well invite her to dinner. At the dinning table open the subject tactfully. I hope you will get good results.

S. I will do as you have advised.

S. (*On phone*): I met Shyama and, as suggested by you, congratulated and invited her to dinner. We met at the dining table. I was simmering inside, but as you suggested, I opened up, I bared my heart. Both of them explained the events, I listened, I felt shy, then burst into laughter in which both of them joined and we had a very pleasant time, full of fun. Now everything has been resolved, I have no suspicion and no tension. I feel so relieved. I am thankful to you for the support you gave me. The anxiety, tension and unhappiness which I had when I came to you first, are all gone and I have returned to normal with full trust in my husband, and with no ill-feelings for Shyama.

Fourth Session

After a few months a more distressed Sukriti reappeared. Her efforts to restore harmony between the trio had failed. Shyama and Sukriti's husband had come closer. Shyama's ex-husband came and took away their thirteen-year-old son; Shyama became more lonely, isolated, and deserted. She was provided employment in the same office in which Sukriti's husband works, and she began to go and return in the same car with Sukriti's husband. More opportunity of interaction in the absence of Sukriti became available to them. Anytime, even at midnight, Shyama's phone would ring and Sukriti's husband would go to her house and stay for about an hour or so to give company and consolation to Shyama. He would tell Sukriti: a friend in need is a friend indeed; and ask her if she would not desire the same response from a friend if she were in Shyama's situation. Sukriti feels let down and cheated, but tolerates his behaviour, finding herself helpless.

C. It has become necessary to give you a bitter warning. Things seem to have gone a little too far. There are three zones in an inter-personal relationship between a man and a woman. In the first zone there is acquaintance and friendship, in the second it is intimacy and emotional relationship, and in the third there is body-relationship: touch, kissing, and sex. Mostly the three zones get mixed-up. In your husband's case the relationship seems to have crossed the first and entered the second zone, about the third you cannot be sure. But entry into the second is by itself sufficiently dangerous and needs more vigilance.

S. What can I do?

C. Keep vigil, and also talk to your husband.

Fifth Session

S. (*On phone*): I have been more vigilant and have also had a word with my husband. He has assured me there was nothing to worry about or get alarmed; his love for me remains as it has always been. He says he cannot afford to lose my love or see me unhappy, and losing me altogether will make his life not worth living. He seems so honest that I believe him.

C. That is very good, but did you ask why is he getting more and more drawn towards Shyama ?

S. Yes, he said the condition of Shyama was pitiable and he was trying to give her the necessary support including emotional support. I also feel Shyama needs support, she is all-alone. Everything seems to be just fine.

C. Then it is okay, your love seems to be very powerful, you can rest assured your husband will not deceive you.

S. I also think, and feel confident, but all the same I will continue to keep an eye on Shyama.

C. But let not doubt or suspicion sour your relationships either with your husband or shyama. Remember the words of Rahi.

Rahiman dhaga prem ka, mat tore chatkay, tute se phir na mile, mile ganth par jaye.

(Rahim says : break not the thread of love; once broken, it unites not, and if it does, a knot intervenes.)

Faith and trust in your husband are essential for your marital happiness, your total happiness.

S. I have and will continue to have full faith and trust in my husband and will never let suspicion spoil our happiness.

C. Yes.

SUDHA

Her tensions cannot be ignored particularly when she firmly believes that her husband has conspired with his parents in planning her ouster and isolation. The situation is volatile and if it explodes it will lead to her direct confrontation with him and his parents. She is very likely to take the extreme step of leaving the house with the children or of doing something more drastic.

Diagnostic Scan

Sudha, thirty-seven, is a married woman with two sons aged thirteen and eleven. She has done M.A. years back. She was a teacher for sometime, now just a housewife.

Home is not yet broken but conditions that threaten a break have come to exist. She says she cannot separate because of social and other pressures, and also does not really want a separation.

Husband-wife live under constant tension as they are not on good terms. He thinks by merely providing money he has done his duty. Wife thinks she needs (more) love and attention and complains that the husband is not even caring for the children. There is no communication between father and sons, husband and wife. They live as separate entities in a family.

Sudha is sad and nervous. There is a flood of tears in her eyes. She cannot give any specific reason for tears, except that she feels her family life is full of tension and misery. Otherwise she is healthy, normal, and pleasant. She thinks her husband has always felt cross with her because she has come from an affluent family and he from a comparatively poor family. The marriage was an arranged one.

She feels ill-adjusted, lacks self-confidence and remains nervous.

Her younger son is not up to the mark, she feels he should do better. This makes her worried and concerned.

She has no specific complaint about her sex life, but is sore because her husband does not agree to have a third child, which she desires. She feels her life which is full of misery, loneliness, and lack of involvement, will become meaningful if she got a third child.

Her relations with her parents-in-law are bitter. They believe in treating Sudha as a traditional Hindu daughter-in-law. She is supposed to maintain a low profile. She is asked not to sit at the table to eat along with others. Her mother-in-law asks her to serve all the five members hot chapatis, and take her meal only after everyone had finished.

This is however, only a manifestation of the deeper malady of making her feel inferior. She is treated in her own home as an inferior person, an outsider in the family circle. Her family (nuclear) has been taken over by her parents-in-law. It may not have mattered to Sudha if all this had not happened, as she believes, with the consent and connivance of her husband. She thinks this is part of his plan to make her insignificant in the family and a non-entity in his life.

This behaviour of her husband and his parents has destroyed her self-esteem. She is not ready to accept it. She wants to live with dignity and to be treated as the mistress of the house or at least equal to other members of the family.

The core of the problem, lies in her husband's withdrawal from her, which has completely isolated her. Day-by-day, things are getting worse. Even in bed they have no communication. He remains withdrawn. She feels neglected, unwanted, thrown out of his life. Her efforts to communicate do not get any response. He never tries to communicate, but smiles contemptuously when she makes an attempt towards it. This led to loss of confidence in each other. They also have no subjects of common interest to talk about.

Sudha's husband feels that Sudha is a psychiatric case, and her behaviour is abnormal. She behaves in an erratic manner. Many years back she left the picture hall and came out because they had reached late and the picture had already run for a few minutes. On another occasion she walked out of the bedroom at about 1.30 in the night complaining of suffocation.

His basic grievance, however, seems to be that she interferes with his management of the family income which he considers as his exclusive prerogative, with the right to spend it as he likes. He also thinks she should have no say in the way his parents spend the money. On the other hand, Sudha believes she has the right to control the purse strings.

He has, Sudha says, no confidence in her, no faith in her ability to look after the children and the home. It is mainly for this reason, Sudha thinks, he has planted his parents in the house on the pretext that they need medical care which is better available in Delhi.

He admits he has completely withdrawn from her life, but tries to put all blame on her. In his view she is guilty for all the troubles in the family. Their younger son has a problem, probably he is retarded. Some psychiatrist has told them it is due partially to parental discord, and her husband feels Sudha is responsible for this too.

It is his lack of faith and confidence in Sudha that, according to him, is the cause for his withdrawal from her life and the consequent breakdown in their relationship.

There has developed a real crisis of confidence in their relationship. He does not accept his responsibility for what has happened to their relationship and wants to put all blame on Sudha for her non-cooperative, rather non-approving behaviour. He is unable to accept his own faults in making Sudha a sad person, a dejected wife.

It is apparent that so far as Sudha is concerned the house has been converted into a prison and the husband has put up his parents as wardens to run its affairs. Sudha is not prepared to accept the situation and is in virtual revolt against the rule of his parents, who are trying to take over not only the management of the house but also the finances. She is not prepared to lose her home and children, and resents being treated as an imbecile incapable of managing her affairs of looking after the children. She does not want to live the life of a prisoner or an inmate of a lunatic asylum with the husband's parents acting as wardens to keep a watch over her. She fears further subordination, loss of independence, and deprivation of her right to act as her children's guardian.

Her tensions cannot be ignored particularly when she firmly believes that her husband has conspired with his parents in planning her ouster and isolation. The situation is volatile and if it explodes it will lead to her direct confrontation with him and his parents. She is very likely to take the extreme step of leaving the house with the children or of doing something more drastic.

Counselling

C. Sudha, you have to play the game more diplomatically. Try to devise a strategy of registering your protest in the strongest terms and at the same time avoiding total rupture. Accept things as they are, and try to communicate with your husband as much as you may without worrying about the response.

[She has been made to learn various coping strategies to face the existing situation]

You should try not to show you feel neglected, and instead act as if everything is normal and you are an integral part of the family. At the same time you should avoid oppressive and negative thoughts that trouble you. You should give up the feeling that you were not a good and worthy wife who could win the confidence and affection of her husband. You should also give up treating your husband as being guilty of neglecting you, rather you should make him believe and feel that he is a caring husband. This will make your husband change his attitude.

You should also not regard yourself as responsible for this unhappy situation. It happened because of circumstances over which you had no control, hence you should not feel guilty or ashamed. Just feel proud that you have saved the home and family from getting completely broken.

Next Session

Sudha phoned she wanted to come today, five days ahead of the date fixed for next session. She came and gave the most unusual feedback.

S. Everything was usual for two days after I had the last counselling, but suddenly on the next day I felt something had happened to me, something I cannot describe, something that had brought a sudden change in me, a change which is very good and pleasant. Tell me what is it due to?

C. It was I think due to the flooding of your sub-conscious mind, your whole consciousness with the light of pure love and self-confidence.

S. I am no longer shedding tears. I am now happy, calm and composed.

C. Sudha, you have now to forget and stop thinking about your failure to get along happily with your husband. You have to pull yourself out of your dead past, and start living in the present with hope and confidence. You have already come on the road to happiness, go on and on and on. Keep enjoying the magical change that has come in your life, which you described just now. You must not allow it to suffer a set-back. happiness once gained must be protected and preserved.

Try to live more and more in the present rather than brooding on the dead past. You become sad and miserable by living in the unhappy past. Create a life of your dreams, a life of overflowing love.

Communicative love-flow strategy has been tried. She has been made to learn and develop communicative love-flow. She has been counselled to believe that it will do her good to generate greater love for her husband, as that in turn will develop in him too a feeling of deeper love for her. She should get more and more involved in her husband's life rather than draw away from him.

Next Session

Sudha has become a fountain of love. Love has begun flowing from Sudha to her husband, but the response is lacking. Sudha complains her husband does not respond to the advances she makes, except to a very limited extent. She has been counselled.

C. Please continue the process of giving more and more of your love to him, and if he returns even 50 per cent or 30 per cent of it, it should be welcome. If by communicating twenty units of love you get back even five units, it is okay. What you relevant is the breaking of the barrier and not the quantum of flow. What you need is only to increase the flow of love so that more may come back. Go on increasing it till your desired quota of love comes back. The communication of love will open the gates of mutual communication of thoughts and, later on, of feelings too.

S. I shall do more on my part and will feel happy to get whatever I get in return. I am already getting some results. Communication between us has started, though it is still very limited.

C. Little things matter a lot in the process of changing people's attitudes and behaviours. Your birthday is coming, celebrate it.

S. My husband does not even remember it, he has never remembered it.

C. You must make him conscious of it, play a positive role and demand a gift from him. If you will demand, you will get it, maybe you get the musical instrument you desire to have. This will give both of you a sense of pride, the pride of giving a gift and the pride of receiving it. It will satisfy your ego and enkindle in him the flame of love which will brighten your lives.

Next Session

S. My birthday was celebrated for the first time in my life. Both of us felt happy and thrilled.

I have once again started making the morning tea for my husband, now we take tea together. Of course, I have always to take the initiative.

No longer do I have to wait till everyone has finished. I join them at the dinner table as soon as I can. I have been accepted in the family. I am no longer an outcast, a stranger, or an intruder in the family. I am trying to give more and more love to my husband, care to my children, and respect to my parents-in-law.

Sudha is completely composed, happy and normal. Her sadness and tears have gone, she has smile on her lips and is cheerful. The wall of alienation and aloofness has cracked and relationship has become sweet and melodious. What they needed was a meaningful dialogue and flow of love. It has brought normalcy, relaxation and revival of faith and confidence in each other.

TARIKA

Remember, you are not going to try sex, but love. Once again fall in love with your husband, treat him as your object of love and yourself become an object of his love. Let sex come as a by-product of love, as a bonus along with your love. The objective should be love not sex, then you will have neither any fear nor any tension. Love is always free of tension and fear disappears when love comes. Love gives only pleasure, no pain, only happiness no fear.

Diagnostic Scan

Tarika is a middle-aged married woman with two children.

T. My grandmother used to curse me and she wished at least one of her grand-daughters should die. It should be me, because my sister Manju was beautiful, a better student, and also a good conversationalist. In the house as well as in school I suffered severe inferiority complex. This complex became more deep rooted as Manju got married stealing a march over me, and went to California. My brother used to scold and beat me even in front of relatives and friends though he was four years younger to me.

I was always treated as inferior, anything that was brought in the house for children was given to the brother and the left-over was divided among the three sisters. I was the least favoured of all children and therefore neglected.

I could not tolerate my ill-treatment by the brother but felt helpless, although Manju could counter him successfully.

At the age of thirteen or fourteen one day I was outside, when from the window I asked my brother Kalloo to open the door, instead of opening the door he took a blade and made a cut on my arm. I bled and went to a neighbour for bandaging.

On another day he threw a knife at me which pierced into my arm when I tried to protect my face. No one came to my rescue or even scolded or punished him for this unprovoked attack. My father used to be away on duty, and mother told me not to complain against him to father who may punish him for his deeds.

For about two years I suffered. I always had fear of injury and death. Psychiatric treatment was given to me instead of giving me protection. A social worker took me for treatment to the C.G.H.S. dispensary.

I was married. After marriage I continued to be ill and could not breast feed the children. Gynaecologist attributed it to my tension.

I dream even now and see myself weeping, terrified, and then wake up suddenly.

I always crave that my children should not suffer from the same fate.

My husband's salary was not sufficient for our needs. Now he is running a factory with aid received from father and Manju. My father had left a house. My brother has grabbed it, it is the subject-matter of some litigation, and at intervals its rent comes through court (Tarika is not sure about all this). I am made to sign the receipts but the money is not paid to me, my brother appropriates it. Mother, as she did earlier, favours the son and concurs in his appropriating the income from the house.

My husband has also given power of attorney to my brother and got his name entered in registration papers concerning the factory, etc. as he thinks the son is entitled to all the money which my father and sister from US had advanced for the business.

Both these things are a source of continuing worry for me. They revive the memory of my sufferings at the hands of my brother when I was a child, and till my marriage.

Counselling

C. The cruel treatment meted out to you by your brother, and the reprehensible support given to him by your mother and grandmother, have left a deep scar on your psyche. They have undermined your self-esteem. Their behaviour is mainly responsible for your psychic ailments and sufferings. Somehow, this has to be wiped off from your consciousness. The present behaviour of the brother, supported by your mother and husband, in regard to the family income, adds to your agony and keeps the wounds alive.

T. Yes.

C. You should take the bold step of refusing to blindly sign the receipt, etc. and insist on getting your due share in the family income and your title to the property. This will help in restoring your self-esteem, self-confidence and give you freedon from the feeling of exploitation and injustice done to you. A little assertion on your part will restore your self-respect.

Have courage, stand up to fight the continuing injustice of which you are a victim. You are entitled to a share (1/5th) in all the assets of your deceased father, including the house, and you must make an effort to get it. Before you sign any receipt or document look at the wound-marks on your arm, and then insist on getting your legal rights. Do not accept your mother's suggestion that everything should go to her son, insist that your husband should not authorise him to take the money he had received from your father or sister. You should also insist on getting back from your brother all that he has taken so far.

T. I shall try and insist on my rights.

C. You should also cease to live in the dead past, and try to forget it. It is no use brooding on the past memories that are unpleasant. Your forty-three years are now dead, start life afresh, a life full of hope, a life free from fear of torture, discrimination and suffering.

T. I shall try.

Second Session

Tarika has been given a wide-spectrum counselling. She feels better and says her tensions have gone and she generally feels quite at ease.

Tarika says she now gets tense only when her children feel unhappy. Her daughter intervened and said that she cries and moans only when the mother is angry and irritated. Both have, on counselling, seen that their discomfort is due to feeling of frustration which arises when they fail to achieve the goals they set for themselves or for others. The mother expects more than the children can render, similarly children plan to do more than they can achieve.

After counselling both mother and daughter realised the importance of setting realistic goals. They agree that hence onward they will go only as far as they can without worrying about or setting standards or goals for achievement in various fields of daily activities. It will save them from suffering failure and frustration.

C. Please try never to get agitated and whenever you do get agitated, write down the circumstances which made you lose your calm.

T. I shall try always to remain calm and whenever I will get agitated in future, if at all, I will write down the circumstances which led to generation of anger in me.

C. This will show that your anger is generally neither called for nor serves any useful purpose. What is needed is to develop more rationality in your own behaviour and the understanding of the behaviour of others.

The exercise of writing down the events will be of great help. You will also continue to listen to the audio-tape on stress management and make relaxation a matter of habit.

T. I also had a gynaecological problem, periods were and still are very heavy and prolonged. According to the gynaecologist it was due to psychic causes. My whole body used to get suddenly swollen, which too was diagnosed to be psychosomatic.

I suffered from unbearable tension for about four or five years. I am at present however free of it.

C. So, now don't worry about it. Forget it. No more will you have any tension and no more any psychosomatic ailment.

Third Session

T. Since the last session nothing exceptional has happened. I have remained normal and composed.

Tarika was made to go through age-regression exercise. She started from the age five and went on to ten.

T. I was always full of fear whenever my mother was ill. Dreadful thoughts came. Even when I went to school I kept on thinking of mother and became worried.

C. Was it fear of death?

U. Probably. When my father was at home, I felt relieved and stopped worrying about my mother thinking that now father is there to take care of her. However, even while he was there, I did not stop fearing as I always thought of the time when my father will go back.

Even today whenever my husband goes to work or takes a flight, fear grips me. I become worried thinking of dreadful possibilities.

C. You are continuously suffering from fear of death of one person or the other. Do not entertain fears for the future. Hope for the best, be ready to face any untoward thing, if it happens.

T. Tears never flow from my eyes. Even when someone near and dear died I never had tears to shed. Other women wept, and asked me also to weep as it was not only traditional and conventional but also good for easing tension but I could never shed tears, probably my tear-glands do not function.

C. Don't you worry about not shedding tears. You are not 'Rudali'. Everyone has her own way of expressing grief.

Tarika, we have had enough of miserable things. Now let's talk of something pleasant, some happy moments in your life. Come on, remember some happy events in your life.

T. I cannot remember any.

C. Okay, tell me about your honeymoon.

U. I had no honeymoon. I did not know anything about sex. It was only when I went back home and a girl of the family came back after her recent marriage and there was a talk that her husband was impotent, and I enquired from my uncle what it all meant and he brought some books for me dealing with sex, that I came to know what it was.

Even then there was complete lack of communication and I did not have any sex with my husband. Then he took me to a gynaecologist for consultation. She found there was nothing wrong with me biologically, it was all psychological. She gave me instructions, and I still remember she said I was missing a heavenly pleasure. Even then sex did not give me any fulfilment.

In the family I was declared frigid, sexually unresponsive and incapable of conceiving. It was only when I became pregnant and Mala was born, that I was deemed and declared normal. During this period I suffered adverse criticism which caused further tension.

C. Was it all okay, thereafter?

T. No, both of us were afraid of second pregnancy; we did not want a second child and took recourse to contraceptives. However, they failed and the second daughter Kanchan was born.

This left me with no option but to avoid sex, which led us to draw further apart.

Questions on sexual adjustment were put to her:

1. Do you regularly have sex with someone? [No]

2. If you are not active sexually, have you been interested in sex, as measured by thought, fantasies, erotic dreams, etc.? [No]

3. How often are you orgasmic in sex with a partner? [Never had orgasm]

4. Have you had problems with painful intercourse? [Sometimes]

5. Have you had problems with vaginal infections, cervical infections, fibroids, etc? [Yes fibroids (not much)]

6. When did you last have sex? [Do not remember, at least not during the last six months. Maybe six months back]

Tarika is forty-two. She still suffers from the same old fear of pregnancy. The fear of pregnancy, aggravated by the failure of the contraceptive which made her pregnant a second time, has made her avoid sex. The fear of pregnancy creates in her high tension and it becomes impossible for her to have enjoyable sex. The gynaecologists have found no physiological defect and believe it is all psychological.

C. Tarika, why do you fear pregnancy? You are now forty-two, at this age conception is not easy and there is no reason to believe that because contraceptives had failed once they will fail again.

Even if you do get pregnant there is nothing to worry, a child at this age will give you additional happiness and will be a source of happiness even after your other children are grown up. Very soon your two children will become adults and independent and the new child, if it is born, will be an asset, then why be afraid of having sex? You said your gynaecologist had told you once that you are missing a 'heavenly pleasure'.

T. Yes, and I never got that 'heavenly pleasure' even at the time when I had got pregnant.

C. It is because you never had a fear-free sex. You became pregnant by accident. Fear of pregnancy, and consequent development of high tension in you prior to and during sex prevented you from having orgasm; it is only when you have orgasm during sex that you can get that 'heavenly pleasure'.

Soon you will have menopause, but it is not necessary to wait till then to enjoy the happiness of orgasmic sex. Do you not want happiness of an intensity you have never experienced? Does your husband ever complain, about your relationship ?

T. He often tells me that his friends talk about their sex life, and the reaction of their wives, but he always tells them that he never had a complaint against me.

C. Does he not indirectly tell you that you are denying him the pleasure which his friends are getting from their wives ?

T. Probably, that is what he means.

C. So what do you decide ?

T. I want happiness, and I shall go ahead with a new honeymoon. But what about my other problems ?

C. They are all related to tension, they are minor matters. Once you get flooded with the high intensity 'heavenly pleasure', all of them will get drowned in the stream of your love-sex happiness and wither away.

Remember, you are not going to try sex, but love. Once again fall in love with your husband, treat him as your object of love and yourself become an object of his love. Let sex come as a by-product of love, as a bonus along with your love. The objective should be love not sex, then you will have neither any fear nor any tension, it will all be love. Love is always free of tension, and fear disappears when love comes. Love gives only pleasure no pain, only happiness no fear.

T. When should I come next?

C. After your new honeymoon.

Fourth Session

T. Since after the last counselling a change has come in my behaviour and in my relationship with my husband. We have come closer, I no longer suffer from the dread and fear of unwanted pregnancy, I am getting into a more pleasant relationship with my husband.

My husband feels much happier, he no longer tells me what his friends tell him about their own family lives.

Our sex and love life has taken a pleasant turn. I am having a beautiful non-ending honeymoon, and enjoying the promised 'heavenly pleasure.'

My husband has given this cheque, kindly accept it as a symbolic donation to the Institute. Please accept this bouquet of flowers from me. It is just a token of gratitude for the happiness that has come to me through your counselling.

C. The honeymoon bouquet?

T. Yes, the HONEYMOON bouquet.

MONA

It is not the matter of history, it is a continuing story. I am still treated as a non-entity. I must not use oil in my hair though I wish to have soft silky hair with oil. I must dress as he wants, do my make-up as he likes, even "bindi" has to be selected by him. I have to live according to his dictates.

Diagnostic Scan

Mona 42, looks okay, in good physical health, but says she is on diet for which obviously she has no need. May be it is one of the multi-facets of low self-esteem with which she is suffering.

Ever since she stepped in and began to speak her eyes are flooded with tears. Tears flow incessantly. Her kerchief is inadequate, so she has been using her 'chunni' to dry her eyes.

She has no obvious reason for this except the reservoir of grief hidden in her mind. She is suffering from a feeling of guilt and shame.

She feels she is an all-round failure. As daughter-in-law, she feels, she was very much harassed, memories of the bad behaviour of her parents-in-law who are now no more, still continue to haunt her. About eighteen years ago when she was about to deliver the second child she was turned out of the house. Neighbours took her to the hospital. Five days after delivery she left Ahmedabad and came to stay with her parents in Delhi. Since then she lived separate from her parents-in-law.

Her husband has two sisters, one elder and the other younger. Both are married with children. She hates them because they make her life hell when they come to stay with her. Even their phone call frightens her. According to Mona they are always finding fault with her behaviour and nag her.

After she was turned out of the house, she suffered a serious psychological set-back.

She was given medicines for depression. With anti-depressant medicines she felt a little elated but not happy. For sometime past she has given up the medicines.

Counselling

M. I get spells of anger, I try to shake it off by beating my pet dog, which has learnt to tolerate my thrashings. On little things I get upset and exasperated.

I always have negative thoughts, I am very pessimistic. Whenever my husband takes a flight. I fear the plane might crash. Even otherwise when he goes out, I fear he may have an accident or meet some other calamity.

My husband tells me daily how his day at work passed. I am not a participant in business except to the extent that I go to the workshop off and on, and look after some business deals. I get no payment for the same. I work free as I think it means helping my husband. I always feel I am worthless and a complete failure in life.

C. You can counter-act this feeling of worthlessness, if you get some payment for the work you do in the office; that will give you the feeling that you are doing something worthwhile, something of value, which can be measured in terms of money. Take some money as compensation for your labour.

M. My husband will have no objection because he pays me as much as I ask, but that does not give me the feeling that I was doing some utility-producing work. I do it with a feeling that it was also my work. I have no courage to ask my husband the wages for my work. I do it with a feeling that it was also my work. I also do some social work by participating in projects carried on by the Lioness Club.

C. And, also the job of looking after your children.

M. Yes, but now I am worried about their marriage, particularly of the daughter.

C. Mona, you feel concerned about the happiness and well being of everyone except yourself. It seems you have made misery your whole-time companion. You suffer from negativity, and think you can give happiness to others by your own sufferings or sacrifices.

M. Yes, you are right.

She has been given intensive counselling for :

(*a*) Developing self-esteem and the feeling that she is also a person who requires care and attention as do her husband and children.

(*b*) Positive thinking and optimism, and stoppage of negative thinking and pessimism.

C. Mona, you need to fall in love with yourself. Love yourself, devote more time towards your grooming and make-up. Spend more time on yourself. Love good food and eat it, enjoy it. Dress a little more glamorously. You are still in the prime of your life, make the best of it.

Try to change yourself, change your attitude towards life, realise your importance, you are loved and needed by your husband, your children and everyone else.

You do not know your future, believe in the goodness of things to come, hope for the best, the best is yet to come. Get ready to welcome it, believe that the miserable Mona is dead and today a new Mona has taken birth, a happy optimistic Mona.

Today you will celebrate this event by preserving the smile and the bloom you have acquired during the course of counselling; you will prepare dishes of your own liking for the dinner, lay the table formally and decoratively, put on a good sari and wear a proper make-up to suit the occasion of your new birth. Today is your birthday, have fun, sing, dance.

[Mona's tears have disappeared, smile has come on her lips].

M. Henceforth whenever I feel tears coming, I will counter-act that feeling with a broad smile, I will laugh. I will never let tears spoil my good looks. I will always be careful about my dress, make-up, etc.

Next Session

Some days later Mona phoned.

M. I gained a lot of self-confidence during the last counselling, but some of my problems still continue. I cannot forget the scene of my being turned out of the house in a pitiable condition. There is something more obnoxious, bad and sad but I am afraid to relate it on phone. Someday I would come and disclose it. It is this rooted sorrow that may be the basic cause of all my psychological problems. Even now my husband plays a very dominating role and does not let me take any decisions. I am still treated by my husband as a baby who needs to be quietened and controlled.

C. Don't worry, have courage. When we meet next we will talk.

[General counselling was given to her to boost her confidence and to give her encouragement and support].

After quite a long time Mona reported on phone that the counselling had done her much good. She has begun to look after her own interests also, and that has given her lot of relief. She has acquired self-esteem and peace of mind.

Next Session

Mona is sad, tears are flowing from her eyes, she tries to speak, feels choked, but speaks:

M. It is only before you I can cry, I can weep, I can shed tears, I can open my heart and tell you what is troubling me most.

C. What's it?

M. I cannot forget the day when I was turned out of the house even though I was in an advanced stage of pregnancy.

C. Was your husband not there ?

M. It was he who had left me on the railway station to board the train. He was under the influence of his elder brother's wife. He is ten years older to me; when I was married I was only eighteen. Very soon after marriage I learnt, he was having a liaison with his sister-in-law who was almost of the same age. I was neglected, abused and tortured. My husband treated me as a stupid child fit only to receive commands and be bossed over by him and his *Bhabhi*. I did not have the freedom to dress as I liked or have a make-up as I wished.

C. Forget it, it has become a matter of history.

M. He thinks I cannot make any right decision, he must purchase everything, and he will always accompany me to the market. Money is totally in his control. I have to ask even for household expenses and that too he decides.

I wish to do something to earn a living, I want financial independence.

C. Then do something, you can open a beautician's clinic.

M. I don't like this profession. I have always been interested in modelling, acting, showbiz. I can dance.

C. Then go ahead and do it, there is ample scope for this at the present moment, talented people are needed. What type of dance do you know?

M. Not classical, but folk dance. I am trying to get training. However, that is to be only an accompaniment to playing a role in TV serials. And alas! My husband is a stumbling block. He will not let me do anything, no modelling, and no acting.

C. Probably, he thinks you will get lost if you get into a profession where males are also acting and predominating.

M. Maybe it is in the back of his mind. I have now developed, thanks to counselling, sufficient self-confidence, and I am going to ask him directly about taking up acting as a career.

C. Try it, he might agree, but chances are bleak.

M. Yes, he even says I do not look beautiful. And recently within a month while he was away, I have become worse because I was always worried about his safety and security. I am always afraid something bad may not befall him.

C. Never fear, try to love yourself, take more care of yourself, of your own happiness. (She has been given counselling on the theme: fall in love with yourself, your life). Find more interests for yourself, do something everyday that gives you happiness, become more end more 'happiness' conscious:

Once you begin to love yourself, you will find everyone loves you.

M. That is so. I find that when I belittle myself and look down upon myself everyone does so. Everyone tries to see shortcomings in me, even in my appearance.

C. So, now you see the importance of loving yourself?

M. Yes.

C. Why do you accept everyone's version that your looks have become worse, or you do not look as good as you used to?

M. I can feel it by looking at myself, even my husband says so. He will not tell it to me if it were not so.

C. To me you look perfectly good. Everyone has to mature, and a matured face does not look bad, maturity has its own grace, its own beauty. At forty-two if you have a face of twenty-eight, you will look ridiculous. It is our Indian culture, which makes people say: You are not as healthy or bright as you were. It is only a way of wishing greater brightness, and happier and healthier looks. So don't think you are not as fine as you should be. Don't worry about what others say. Be yourself, love and like yourself as you are. Avoid developing inferiority complex. Compare yourself neither with others nor with your former image, or the image which you think you should have been having today. Avoid imagining masks for your face. Enjoy yourself.

M. What enjoy? I do not have a life of enjoyment.

C. Why?

M. Even my nights are not enjoyable.

C. Why, do you not have a pleasant married life?

M. No. We have miserable existence in the bed.

C. Why, no fulfilling sex?

M. No.

C. Why, what's the problem?

M. Problem is with him not me. He does not get proper erection, and to boost himself, he just lights a cigarette and begins to smoke.

C. Some special type of cigarette?

M. No, just the normal ones.

C. Is he a heavy smoker?

M. No, he smokes only to arouse sex. I do not like the smoke and get disgusted, many a times the ashes fall on my body, even burning stubs do and I get burnt.

C. Why don't you consult a doctor?

M. I consulted, but the doctor says. He must come, he is not prepared to go. He would just smoke in the hope of getting arousal, but he fails.

C. This has to be so. He fears failure, and to avoid failure resorts too smoking, smoking makes him more conscious of feared failure, he has become conditioned to fear and failure. Fear is worse than failure, it raises the chances of failure. And then it disturbs you too, makes you also conscious of failure, and you also become a victim of fear. You come under tension and tension is the worst enemy of happy sex.

The remedy is to assure him that you will not mind even if he had no erection and no penetration, and he should not worry about achieving something big. He should only love, and not worry about sex. Persuade him to give up smoking in the bed.

M. I am telling him all this, but without any success.

C. Try to feel happy with whatever sex life you have and try to convince him also about it. Tell him what you want is love, not sex. Love is the real solution. Love and get loved.

M. I am feeling so happy and relaxed. Whenever I come to you I feel I am okay and there is nothing wrong with my life.

C. This is true, there is nothing wrong with your life.

Mona no longer has tears, nor a miserable, sad appearance. She has begun to look happy. She smiles.

M. The happiness, which I now have, will last for a few weeks, and then again…

C. No, no, now it will last, believe me, it will last the entire life. Just remain calm and relaxed, and let your husband be drowned in the flood of your love. Love never loses.

SARITA

Sarita, life is nothing but a play, we are all playing our roles in the drama of life. In the drama of your marital life, there were scenes of a tragedy which still disturb you. Your husband, your sister and some other women were the real actors in that drama, you had only a spectator's role. And you were never on stage but always behind the screen.

Sarita is thirty-five, married with two children—daughter, thirteen and son, three. She is an M.A. in economics and working as a teacher. She is healthy and good looking, though not very attractive.

Sarita posed to be happy and said she had come because her daughter had some problem.

C. Sarita, are you really as happy as you pose to be? I feel your happiness is only skin-deep, and there is some rooted sorrow lying hidden in your sub-conscious mind. Come on, speak out, open yourself, it will give you relief.

Sarita's throat choked and she began to speak with her tears flowing.

How is your family life? How are your relations with your husband?

S. I was married fourteen years back, he is eleven years elder to me. For the last ten years I am having a miserable life. My husband is having affairs with other women.

C. Why are you not giving him full sexual satisfaction?

S. I am, there is no problem. I have asked him if there is any shortcoming in me, I am educated, good-looking and am always ready and willing to give him whatever he wants, but he does not respond. He says womanising is in his blood, and he cannot give up the enjoyment he gets from other women.

C. Do you know the women with whom he had or has affairs?

S. Yes, one of them was my own sister, she is two years younger to me. I am morally very conventional, I do not look at any man amorously, my husband is the only man in my life. I want my husband also to be like me, I cannot tolerate his being unfaithful.

C. How is your sister?

S. She has a different temperament, but she too began to dislike my husband's unacceptable lustful behaviour and ultimately there was a rupture. Now neither she nor her husband comes to our house, although I do communicate with them on phone. All our relatives have come to know of it, and I feel ashamed because of him.

C. Did he have affairs with other women too?

S. Yes, my friends have told me, and we had serious quarrels. Our relations have not been formally severed, though a stage had come for my seeking divorce. Then I thought of the children and restrained myself. Then I decided to live on my own, I took to higher studies, and have become a teacher. Now, I have my own income and my independence. But, there is no happiness, no peace of mind.

C. Does he live with you?

S. Not presently. His employment is also not very good. Now he has gone to Lucknow and taken a job there. We hope to join him after the school closes for the vacation. I do not know if he still has woman in his life.

C. Sarita, believe, that whatever happens is good. You should try to look a little deeper into human psychology. Every person has a unique personality of his own. Some aspects of a man's personality are controlled by his genes, some by long family traditions, some by upbringing, some by social company, and some by the type of opportunities one gets in his life. Maybe all these factors are responsible for his unsavoury behaviour.

S. His father is a widower, but he too was having affairs with some women, and probably has some even now, though he is now in his seventies.

C. It would be better if you begin to live in the present and forget the past. What has happened has happened, you cannot wipe it off, you cannot efface history. Can you undo the past behaviour of your husband? No, you cannot, so it should be treated as a dream and forgotten.

Sarita, life is nothing but a play, we are all playing our roles in the drama of life. In the drama of your marital life, there were scenes of a tragedy which still disturbs you. Your husband, your sister and some other women were the real actors in that drama, you had only a spectator's role in it. Not even that; you were never on the stage but always behind the screen. If you were not a party, and you played no part in the drama, why worry about it, forget it. It has nothing to do with you, you were a shadow victim, you were only vicariously affected by what the other actors did, so just treat it as a play on the stage of life, and forget it. Do not continue to worry about what happened in the past. When it was live on the stage, you had heard the background sounds and visualised in your imagination the tragic scenes. That made you feel cheated and you had traumatic suffering. You are still getting its tremors. Maybe, now that drama has finally ended. It is no use making it live perpetually in your memory. Hope your husband will henceforth play his role differently.

Does not the constant remembrance of these tragic scenes make you feel unhappy, sad, angry, and revengeful?

S. It brings me misery and agony, and a feeling of disgust and disappointment.

C. Do you want your life to be full of misery or filled with happiness?

S. Of course, I want happiness.

C. Then do not burden your mind by continually reminding it of such events that bring you nothing but misery. If you will think of miserable events, you will remain miserable. But if you will remember the events that brought you happiness, you will get contentment. Think of the happiness you got from your husband, think of the pleasures, the positive pleasures he brought into your life, and do not think of the wrongs which he committed, particularly when they were meant to be kept secret from you, and you were never directly, even indirectly, involved in them. Maybe he was himself a victim of circumstances and was unable to resist the temptation of getting clandestine pleasure with other women. Maybe now with the passage of time and change of circumstances he has acquired a new personality.

S. How can I be sure he will not behave similarly in future?

C. You cannot be sure, nobody can be sure of what will happen in future. But wisdom lies in thinking positive, in believing that future will be good and bring happiness. Hope for the best. At least today you are not aware that he is having an affair, maybe today he is having no affair. You say you want happiness and not misery, then go on believing that future will bring you happiness, let no negative thoughts enter your mind.

S. I think I should develop more optimism and look at brighter sides of things. It would be better for me to think that with the passing of years my husband has acquired greater maturity and will act with greater concern for me and children. He loves them.

C. That is the way you should think, and believe in what you think. That will give you peace of mind.

S. I am already feeling greatly relieved, relaxed, and happy. It seems a burden has been lifted off my head.

C. One thing more, only by way of a post-script. You should never let your mind be pestered with negative emotions like anger, hatred and revenge, but develop instead the positive emotions of mercy, compassion and love. This will take away the bitterness out of your marital life and bring sweetness into it. Take this as your mantra.

MANJIT KAUR

I am no more a married woman, I am a widow as you have put it. Where is the question of my having the happiness which is due to a married woman with a husband alive and living in the same house? He hates me, and I do not love him, I wish to punish him for his misdeeds and bad behaviour, for deserting me and making my children virtual orphans.

Diagnostic Scan

Manjit is a middle-aged smart, good-looking woman with a broad smile on her face,which soon begins to fade with the trickling of tears from her eyes. She appears to be in her forties and feels elated when told that she looked much younger than her real-age fifty. She has a daughter, twenty-two, and a son, nineteen. Son has gone for training as a merchant marine cadet; the daughter is doing B.A. degree course, final year.

M. Lately my daughter has developed symptoms of withdrawal, she has begun to show disinterest in everything including studies, she is otherwise very intelligent, was always very good at studies, knows dancing and is interested in debating.

C. Then what is the problem, what is it that disturbs you?

M. My daughter feels very disturbed, suffers born inferiority and shows symptoms of withdrawal. She feels like a fish out of water. But she loves me all right.

C. Did she ever have a broken love affair?

M. Not exactly, but she did have a sort of an affair with a man who was married. It did not last long. She felt hurt, and got so much disturbed that she gave up her job. She has begun to feel that all men are bad and has developed a general hatred for men as a class.

C. What about your son?

M. He is all right, he has a loving nature and keeps clinging to me. Even emotionally he is very much attached to me.

C. You have not said anything about your husband, how is your matrimonial life?

M. I have a husband living with me, that is all. He eats the food I cook, I look after his other needs too. In the evening he drinks, dines, and goes to sleep in his room.

C. Oh, so you are a widow with a live husband staying in the same house and eating the same food that you eat?

M. Yes, you have described it very well, I am the widow of a living husband. I have no concern with him, so haven't the children. He makes no contribution to the running of the house; even the huge amount needed for my son's training in marine engineering had to be arranged by me single-handed. I work to run the family.

C. Why, what's the matter with your husband? Did he never work or earn?

M. No, it is not so. He was in the film line, he worked as a financier and a producer, and we had a pleasant life. But he suffered a serious setback, he was broken and we had to leave Bombay. Since then my life has become miserable. I do not know what he does, but he earns enough to purchase his drinks. Luckily the house is in our joint name and so he cannot deprive me of my abode.

C. Don't think negative, think positive, think of happiness, the happiness which is your right as a married woman.

M. But I have accepted the challenge, I have courage to face all situations. Can't you see the happiness on my face?

C. Yes, but this happiness seems to be just a show. You may not be unhappy, but you do not have that positive happiness which you enjoyed while you were having a loving husband. There is no reason for you to deprive yourself of that inner happiness which one gets out of love, the happiness which comes from being loved by someone you love.

M. That is now all out of question. He deserves nothing but punishment, and I am giving him the punishment by refusing to treat him as my husband.

C. Do you know that by inflicting this punishment on him you are really punishing yourself? By trying to make him miserable, you are in effect bringing misery to yourself as well. And, that is more severe than you realise; it is affecting your sub-conscious mind, it is having its effect on your son and a bad impact on your daughter. Your son's behaviour towards you indicates he wants to fill in the blank in your life, he tries to play the role of his father, of course, he is doing it unconsciously. Similarly your daughter is trying to punish your husband by drawing away from him. Her aborted affair with the married man, has made her find a parallel with your relationship with your husband. She has begun to hate all men, and has unconsciously joined you in the battle against your husband and wants to punish him for bringing unhappiness in your life.

M. She wants me to leave my husband and marry someone else who might make me happy. But I cannot get separation, my son is against breaking of the home.

C. But, yours is already a broken home. A broken home comes into being not only by judicial separation or divorce, but by the breaking of emotional ties between a couple. Even though you have a husband, you are really a widow and a divorcee. End this situation. It is very necessary for your happiness as also for the happiness of your children that this illusion should end. You should get a divorce.

M. But I do not know if I want to throw him out.

C. Then the alternative is to forgive him and end his alienation, and to bring him back into the family. Maybe his financial break-down has made him an emotionally wreck; your support might bring him back to you, and you might get back your lost happiness.

M. I would like to give him a chance. But I do not know how he will react.

C. Then, from today, try to reverse the process, just give him a red flower this evening and see the reaction.

M. No, I cannot do this.

C. Please try, and see the change that comes in your relationship.

M. Okey. I shall give him a yellow rose.

C. That does not matter, give him yellow, white, black, any colour. What is necessary is to convert your own hatred into love. That will have a wonderful effect on him. Even if he does not respond, don't worry, try again tomorrow, and the day after, and the day after... Love can never go waste, it will bring good dividend, dividend of love. They say it is better to light a candle than curse the darkness. Please, try to break the ice, do it for the sake of your daughter who is passing through a critical phase.

M. I feel it is an experiment worth attempting.

C. It is. Let not your ego come in the way, just go ahead, take the initiative, take the big leap. You are today in a stage where marital happiness can be enjoyed to the full. Do not let this time slip away. Start the new journey tonight.

M. I shall gather courage to take this bold step. I hope I shall succeed.

C. I am confident you will.

Next Session

M. Things are as they were, but I have learnt to enjoy them, rather to accept them. Still at times, however, when he talks offensively I do lose my cool.

C. Is it necessary to lose your cool?

M. Then should I become a statue?

C. Yes, what is wrong in it, every God in temple has become a statue.

M. But I am not a God, I want to live, walk, play, and talk, I cannot be a God, I am full of emotions and feelings.

C. Then, don't become a statue, but accept your agitated state as something natural, something enjoyable. You are a human being, and it is natural to have feelings and emotions, and it is also natural to react to inputs of thoughts even when they come from your husband.Treat your reaction as a natural outcome of your mental functioning. Behave as naturally and normally as you can, don't think of it as something unusual.

Only thing I want is that you do not take things to your heart, try to remain happy even in the state when you are not cool, and secondly not to let this state continue beyond the period that is absolutely necessary.

M. How can I limit its duration? When I lose my cool I become tense and unhappy.

C. There is nothing wrong in becoming a little bit tense if it is only a reaction to an unpleasant input of unpalatable thought. Don't you feel bitterness in your mouth when you eat something bitter ? However,very soon your good taste is restored, and the process gets quickened by eating some sweet. Try the same thing with the thoughts that come to your mind, just try to think of something pleasant. All you need is to become your own self once again, as quickly as possible; do it consciously and you will find your cool will come back immediately.

M. I do realize my reactions are the natural outcome of the inputs I get.

C. I only want you to always remain the happy go-lucky Manjit you are. You look natural and normal when you are smiling and laughing. Let the real Manjit, never put a mask to hide her inner happiness. Even if you lose your cool, take it sportingly.

M. I shall henceforth try this mantra.

C. One thing more Manjit, put on the wall of your room an enlarged photograph of yourself, with a pleasant broad smile illumining your face. Near it also hang a mirror and look at your image, particularly when you may be losing your cool, compare the two, and let your mirror-image become a copy of your face in the photograph. Will you do it?

M. Certainly, I shall.

DIMPLE

There is nothing wrong for a growing girl to get attracted to a young woman and develop a special liking for her, particularly if she is attractive, beautiful, charming, smart and intelligent. That can also be lesbian love, something uncommon, though not a rarity.

Diagnostic Scan

Dimple is a young girl of twenty, not very good-looking or girlish, but a little lacking is girlish delicacy, she is otherwise smart and alert.

D. Since the age of thirteen when I was in class VIII I have been having a liking for my teacher, and even till date I am too fond of her.

has taken exception to your behaviour. However, it seems obvious that you had a special liking for her, verging on infatuation and even now you have a very keen desire to be near her and enjoy her company. Sex has many phases and finds manifestation in different forms. A special liking for a charming young woman which makes a girl in her teens to send greetings and good wishes to her is really an indication of her having a concealed love of the variety of amorous love. This desire was born in your sub-conscious mind, but failed to get fulfilled as the lady did not favourably respond to your overtures of love, rather she rejected your offers. This made your hidden desire of *affaire d'amour* more keen, and more desirous of getting fulfilment. Even till date when you have become twenty, that desire has not died, and you still wish to give up your higher career for the sake of coming nearer to the lady in the hope of having the pleasure of her company. Your inherent desire still remains the same, the winning of her love and fulfilment thereof. You still have admiration, attraction, and infatuation for her, you are still craving for her company. All this indicates you have a lesbian love for her. You think lesbianism is bad and have therefore, developed a feeling of guilt. You should realise that you have committed no wrong for which you should feel ashamed or guilty. Did you ever tell your parents about this, or talked it over with your friends?

D. Yes, my father said it was not right and my mother gave me a warning that I might have to repent for this. As regards friends, I have not discussed all this with them but they know about it. I have never considered this as a manifestation of lesbian love.

C. But your parents did think it was not normal behaviour for a young girl to get so fascinated with a charming young woman and to send her messages of good-will. You probably do not realise that they were really your love letters carrying messages of love to the young lady.

D. But is it not common that sisters love each other?

C. It is, but they do not send messages of love, particularly when the elder sister resents and deems it objectionable and complains about it, and disciplinary action is taken for that behaviour.

Love has of course different forms. There is love between mother and daughter, sister and sister, friend and friend, teacher and student, but the love you had for that lady was not of any of these types. It was a case of typical romantic love, which was prompted by your fascination for a beautiful young lady, and had deep roots in your sub-conscious mind and has persisted for years together, and still compels you to find a way to come close to her and become her companion. There is absolutely nothing wrong in having romantic love and attraction for another person of the same sex. You should not treat it as something ignoble and feel guilt or shame for having it.

D. I do feel guilt, but not shame.

C. You should not feel even guilt. You are feeling guilty because you have come to believe that you had committed a sin in sending love messages to that young lady. That is due to your ignorance of the true nature of love. Love is never bad, it is immaterial whom you love. It is also not abnormal for a young girl to become highly impressed by a charming, smart, educated, and attractive young woman who happens to be her teacher. You wished in your heart to emulate her, to become like her, to come closer to her, and you thought the best way was to send greetings and good wishes to her; she did not like it and everyone condemned you, so you began to believe that you had committed an unpardonable wrong. You have since been feeling guilty. If you were a coward you would have succumbed to the pressure and repented. But you are a brave girl, you decided to continue the adventure and you decided to get the lady's love by becoming her colleague. What's her name?

D. I will not tell you her name.

C. Is it because you think it would bring a bad name to your lover?

D. No, I do not wish her to know that she has been the object of my desire, and I still desire to be close to her.

C. That is good on your part to think like that. She must now be in her early thirties, is she married? Anyway, this is not relevant. What is important is that in case you join the same school as a teacher, that lady will be left with no option but to accept your company whether she likes it or not. That will make you feel guilty in case she has to accept you under force of circumstances.

Even supposing she accepts you willingly as a friend, will it help you in any way? She will not accept you as a lover and that will fail to satisfy your inner desire of winning her love and that will create further agony for you. Do you think all this is worth it?

D. I don't know, my mind is in a state of confusion, I do not know what to do.

C. You have taken the past events too seriously and you are finding it difficult to get out to that situation. It is time when you should see the whole episode in its true perspective. All that you did was what you thought or rather felt was right. Did it not give you happiness at that time?

D. It did. I felt happy in sending card-messages to her, but I am unable to get over the feeling of guilt.

C. You have the feeling of guilt for what you did years back when you were too young to understand its implications. That chapter is now over. Presently you are doing nothing to annoy her, so there is nothing today for which you should feel sorry or guilty. Look at the whole incident as a fairy tale. It was a happy experience, you enjoyed it. Treat it as a comedy, a happy dream, and not as a tragedy to feel sorry for. Carry happy memories of what you did and not of the failure in getting the desired response. Everything is now over, it is all dead and gone. Past cannot he relived, so forget it. Now you are a grown-up girl going forward to build a happier future; let not those little things mar your happiness,either today or tomorrow.

Why not send a new card now to her and watch her response. This should be a UNICEF card, address her as Didi and sign it as 'your loving sister'. I think she will respond. That will give you lot of strength and make you see that your feeling of guilt is baseless; even if she does not respond, it will give you a fresh inning and make you forget the old ones. It is better to face the problem squarely by taking a positive action than spinning imaginary stories about the consequences of a past event. Your feeling of guilt is continuing because you believe that the lady is still carrying on a grievance in her heart for what you did in the past. You will get over this feeling of guilt once you come to know that she is no longer harbouring grievance against you, and is no longer holding you guilty for what you did when you were only thirteen. You can even go and meet her, that will again cure you of your feelings of guilt. All you need is to open a new channel of communication. That is exactly what you are trying to do by planning to become a teacher in the same school. That is a long process and is likely to stop you from achieving your ambition of going higher up.

Analysing differently, you seem to be still carrying in your sub-consciousness a sort of hatred for that lady for her negative response to your overtures of love, and you wish to take revenge. Your purpose in becoming her colleague is only to impress on her that you are no longer inferior to her, and were of the same status as she was. You also have a hidden desire of getting what you failed to get when she was a teacher and you were a student—a favourable response to your messages of love.

It may also be that you had sent the cards very innocently, and her reaction was abnormal. Normally, a teacher will appreciate a student sending good-wishes cards to her, and will respond with love. Maybe she had some unhappy experience and that made her react in such a strange manner. Anyway, today everything is over and you can forget the whole thing as a pleasant adventure with no definite destination.

D. It seems it was all a drama, a real-life drama which has became a part of my life.

C. Yes, but there is nothing wrong in it. If you just let the dead past sink into oblivion, and decide to live in the present, free from the shadow of the past, there will be no problem. Look at the present as it is, think how best you can utilise it, and then act accordingly. You have enjoyed the first part of life's drama, now put the curtain down. It is intermission. Now again lift the curtain and play your role in the second part of the drama with a new theme unconnected with the first part.

D. That means I should give up the plan of becoming a teacher, and go ahead with my plan of joining the university.

C. Yes, and go with a clear conscience and a firm belief that you had committed no wrong as a young girl of thirteen, and that the whole event was only a 'Mid-summer Night's Dream'.

RAGINI

But he always continued to live in my mind. It was only his presence in my mind, the memory of happy moments spent in his company, and his selfless love that made me retreat my steps and not commit suicide. Really it was he and not my husband who saved me.

Ragini is miserable, sad, and unhappy, tears flow continuously from her eyes, and she goes on wiping them.

C. What's the matter Ragini? Why do tears come in your beautiful eyes?

R. My problem is that I am smart and people say I am beautiful, but what is the good of it when I am despised and ill-treated by the one man in my life, my husband?

C. Are you not loved by your husband?

R. Loved ? I am abused, there is not a single filthy word of abuse which my husband has not hurled on me. l am insulted, cursed, maligned.

C. Not beaten?

R. I have always been beaten. He hurts, abuses and becomes violent. I have suffered more than any woman I know.Now I have learnt to tolerate, I become silent and get beyond the range of his hand and thus avoid his wrath. That alone calms him down, at least for the moment.

C. Why have you suffered humiliation, degradation and violence for so long?

R. This is a man's world and he has greater physical power.I have no option but to suffer. Moreover, now my daughter has grown up, she is seventeen and I feel domestic violence will have an adverse effect on her. So. I exercise discretion and accept suffering in silence.

C. Does your daughter behave appropriately?

R. No, she too is a little abnormal like her father, off and on she threatens she will commit suicide.

C. Have you never thought of separation?

R. I have, quite often.But I find it extremely difficult.I have no one to support me, even my father does not support the idea. I have no place to go, no financial source to maintain myself. Here at least I have some income from the factory which is on rent.

C. What do you think is the main cause of your husband's abnormal behaviour? Is it his failure to have a proper job?

R. Yes, but the more serious is his inability to get his share in the properties left by his father which have all been grabbed by his brothers. Whenever I talk about it, he goes into rage.

C. It seems it is because of his frustration that he behaves abnormally. He has failed to get his share, is too weak to fight, is unable to accept the injustice done to him, and that makes him frustrated. As a result of frustration he has ingrained in himself a lot of anger and takes it out on you. You will do good not to take up the issue because he is too weak to face it without being disturbed.

R. I have already given up talking about it. But I am suffering tension and agony all the same. [Tears again appear in her eyes]

C. Don't weep, have courage and confidence and hope for a better furture. You have talked a lot about your miseries, now tell me something about the happy moments in your life.

R. I cannot remember any.

C. Well, think of your honeymoon and tell me about it.

R. Even my honeymoon was a moment of misery, it was not something pleasant which I may describe.

C. How about your sex life?

R. I have no sex life. There can be no happiness in sex when both partners live under tension, dislike each other, and have no mutual understanding.

C. Were you not happy when your daughter was born?

R. No, for various reasons.

C. Did you not have happy moments with your friends?

R. Yes, with my friends I did have some happy moments. Should I recall them? But that will mean living in the past and you have asked me to treat the past as dead and not to remember it.

C. Yes, I do not want you to live in the past. I want you only to open gates of your memory lanes so that I might go through them and pluck out the pieces, pleasant and unpleasant, that obstruct your experiencing the blissful happiness you are entitled to enjoy.

R. I shall have to think, and find the right key to open all the locks of the gates leading to my memory lanes.

C. Very well, let us look only at your problems which have come in the open.

R. My basic problem is that I want to do some income-generating work. But he will not permit me to do anything, he always suspects I will lose my chastity, my character, and begin flirting with young men. He always accuses me of being immoral and of lose character.

Because I am good-looking, he thinks, people will necessarily entice me away.

C. Do you also fear it might happen? Did you ever have an affair?

R. I have no fears. I never had an affair, not even a boy friend. I am confident I can protect myself, no man can touch me or play with my honour.

Then why are you afraid, you go ahead and do whatever you think would be a good job to do. Why do you fear your husband, you have already borne his wrath and suffered his violence. And, you had suffered all that because you had no courage to resist and no confidence in your ability to strike back and win. A man who is in the wrong, generally lacks courage to face any person who is in the right, even if she be his wife. You have only to stand up and proceed to take the job you want. If your husband objects, ignore his objection and go ahead with your mission. Once he knows you are determined to move, he will withdraw. And once you begin to work he will see that you are doing the right thing, and may even support you.

R. It really seems I myself lack the courage and confidence. Lack of financial support and backing is also a factor that unnerves me and prevents my going ahead.

C. Give up your fears and proceed; you cannot do anything unless you are prepared to take a little risk.You are healthy, young, intelligent, educated, you should go ahead and do what you plan.

R. You seem to have brought a complete change in me. I had become so depressed that I had begun to imagine I have become too old to do anything, that my life had come to an end and I had no future. Now, I have begun to feel young once again, capable of doing whatever I want.

I have begun to feel I am a fearless woman with confidence and have gathered sufficient faith in my abilities and capabilities to march ahead.

C. You are now a new woman; the weak, and weeping Ragini has gone and in her place has appeared a new Ragini full of confidence and courage. Go ahead, start just now and report your progress. Do not procrastinate, this is the opportune moment, success is waiting to welcome you.

[Ragini is all smiles]

R. I am going to start working from this moment.

Next Session

Ragini is very happy.

R. Last counselling has done me a lot of good. Now I remain fully relaxed. For the next two days I was turning my thoughts up and down but thereafter light came and I became stabilised. I have now accepted him (my husband) as he is, a man with a little streak of insanity. Only recently he abused Neera our daughter, in the most filthy language, thrashed her and bumped her head against the wall.

C. Why?

R. For no reason, she only asked him to bring something from the market where he was going to make some purchases.

C. He seems to have a split personality, sometimes he becomes a devil and sometimes divine.

R. No, he never becomes divine, at best he only becomes normal, which means he ceases to be abusive and violent.

C. He is suffering from frustration.

R. Yes, the main cause of his frustration is his inability to earn a living or do anything fruitful.

C. Was your marriage a love-marriage?

R. No, it was an arranged marriage; very distantly we are related and his father liked me and got me married to his son.

C. Did your husband approve of the marriage?

R. No, he never liked me because I wear spectacles, my eyesight was weak and I had no option.

C. That cannot be the real cause, there must be something else.

R. It was his inherent eccentricity. I never knew he was not of sound mind and was not normal. He was always finding some fault with me, *eg.*, that I was not wearing the sari elegantly, or that my make-up was not good, although I was always better groomed and dressed than any of his relatives including his sister.

C. When did the trouble really start, was it soon after marriage? Did anything particular happen? If so how did you respond?

R. Within a few months of our marriage things had gone so bad that I went to the river to commit suicide, but changed my mind and came back.

C. Why did you try to attempt suicide?

R. My husband had behaved so badly that I thought of committing suicide.

C. Did you attempt it ever again?

R. I attempted twice again, but during the next two occasions, he followed me and stopped me. All this happened during the first three years. Once when I was in the family way and the third time when my daughter was about two years old. Every time I took the step only to escape from his callous and cruel conduct. It made me lose all interest in life, it was so disgusting to live with him that I decided to commit suicide.

C. How is your sex life? Why didn't you have a second child?

R. My sex life is miserable. How can anyone have sex with a man with whom she has no emotional attachment? I never could have any emotional involvement with him, I always detested his inhuman behaviour. That is also the reason for my not having a second child. I had only occasional sex, and that too was never orgasmic. It was always a matter of routine job.

C. Don't you think it would improve your relations with your husband if you try a little bit of a romance, love and sex?

R. It may.

C. Then try, let it be one-sided, and if you feel it gives you some pleasure continue it. Also see if his attitude becomes a little better towards you and your daughter. Start with a kiss.

R. I do not understand why he becomes a beast as soon as either of us speaks to him, he gets enraged by the very look of us. Anyway, I shall try to start a new life.

C. But you don't look ugly or unattractive, what makes your husband behave like this?

R. I don't know, my daughter is still better and looks quite innocent.

C. Does he feel you are corrupt or immoral or something like that?

R. I think, he does. But it is all baseless, I never had an affair with anyone.

C. Just try to go back to your younger days, to your days in the college, you must have been looking pretty good at that time, were not boys attracted towards you?

R. Yes, that is right. One boy was very much fond of me, but I had no emotional involvement with him.

C. After your marriage, was there anyone who came in your life, and you got emotionally involved with him.

R. I have never spoken about this matter to anyone. It has remained a secret all my life.

C. But why? There is nothing wrong in having a friend or even a lover. Love always gives happiness, it is a positive emotion and no one should be shy of speaking about it.

R. Okay, I will tell you. There was a man in my life before my marriage, he had proposed to me, but I could not accept his proposal and marry him because he belonged to a different caste and I had no courage to go against the will of my father or the society. He, however, continued to remain interested in me even after my marriage and very frequently phoned my sister only to keep in touch with me. This continued for quite sometime, then he stopped.

C. Come on, tell me something about your feelings concerning him; it is necessary for you to tell me everything so that your conscience might be rid of the hidden feelings and subdued emotions that appear to be the hidden cause of your agony and stress. Yes, come on, don't hide anything. Once you have agreed to open up, then open up completely.

R. I always regretted refusing his proposal and not taking courage to revolt and marry him. I have never been able to pardon myself for that.

C. You were too young at that time, and you never expected your husband would not be a normal man. So do not feel any sort of guilt, regret is all right.

R. Yes, that is so. But he always continued to live in my mind. It was only his presence in my mind, the memory of happy moments spent in his company, and his selfless love that made me retreat my steps and not commit suicide. Really it was he and not my husband who saved me.

C. He came as an angel in your life when you needed him most. Have you not continued to get him in your mind off and on, specially when your husband treats you cruelly?

R. I don't know whether I should tell you everything.

C. You should, that will give you relief. He is, I am sure, still living in your sub-conscious mind; let him come out.

R. I remember him everyday till today. He lives in Delhi. I have not contacted him so far.

C. Because you fear you may not once again get emotionally involved with him.

R. It seems so, though I had never thought like this. However, now I see, I really fear emotional involvement. I fear sex, my daughter is now seventeen, I fear my coming too near him will mean emotional involvement and that will surely lead to sexual contact, for which I am not prepared.

C. But you said that because of gynaecological problem, you cannot have pregnancy now, then what is the fear about?

R. I don't know, but the fear is there.

C. It is wrong to live with fear. He may be having a wife with whom he may be having fulfilling sex and may not want to have sex with you. Your relationship may not even reach that stage. It is better that you establish contact with him and go as far as you like. Now you are quite mature, and so must be he, there is thus no risk of your getting sexually involved with him. And, suppose you do have sex with him, what is wrong? You will not be committing any sin if sex will come only as a by-product of love. In any case the chance of having sex is almost nil. But your opening of friendly dialogue will give you unlimited psychological relief, your lost happiness will come back.

R. Then I will have a husband who does not love, and a lover who is not a husband. I will start living with two beings at the same time.

C. Rather three. Your husband has split personality, with the addition of your lover you will have the third, the man who has in the past acted as an angel and saved you thrice from the clutches of death.

R. That is right, without him in my memory I would not have been alive today.

C. So go ahead. I don't want you to have sex with anyone other than your husband, but I want you to rekindle your friendship without having any kind of fear. If you will go in search of love with your mind loaded with fear, you will fail and not be able to get back your angel, and your search for happiness will remain a mirage. That young man has continued to remain with you throughout your life and is still the object of your unfulfilled desire. Once that desire gets fulfilled your happiness will acquire the magnificence of Radha's ecstasy, and your relations with your husband will also improve.

R. I am going to make the experiment and hope to succeed and acquire a new brand of happiness.

C. The wonder-brand.

However, I feel your longing for your lover has by now acquired the same nature as was that of Radha or Meera. You had desired sex when both of you were in your teens or early twenties, since then much water of ecstasy and agony has flown through the stream of your emotions, and your longing is now only for platonic love, and even when now you will meet him you will not desire to have sex with him, and I am sure that will be his reaction too.

R. Yes, now as I reflect more deeply I feel I really long for his love and not sex; I will probably feel satisfied if I meet him and have a purely emotional involvement.

C. Maybe, when you meet him you do not even get into an emotional involvement, what you are really craving for is love, you wish he may also be carrying in his heart the same craving for love which you are having. You wish to go back into the past and relive it so that you might make him your dream-husband. Your desire to get married to him could not be accomplished at that time, and it has remained buried in your subconscious mind, and you still wish the fulfilment of that hidden desire. However, if you will reflect further, you will see that it was the craving of youth, and with the passage of long years, both of you have acquired maturity and now your mind's demand is of pure love and not of erotic involvement. As the whole thing is still in your subconscious mind you are unable to think beyond the stage in which you were when you were only twenty. You still believe that he has also not changed, and would still wish to take you as his wife. This belief might come out to be just an illusion.

You see, when both of you were young, your love was full of passion and that invigorated your longing for sex, but you could not get fulfilment because you were unmarried. Now that stage is over and neither of you will like to go in for that type of romance. What you desire today is pure love which has in it more of concern for each other, than passion and eroticism.

R. I feel you are right. Today when I look back, it appears we were living in a world of make-beliefs, a world of imaginations fancies and fantasies. It was all very exhilarating, it gave us intense joy; we thought there could be nothing beyond it, we were really living in a heaven of our own making.

C. And, suddenly all your dreams shattered, you got married, and after sometime your lover also gave up and stopped communicating with you . You do not know he too may have been married and may be having a happy family life. With the passing of time things change, lives change, we travel from the world of emotions to another world with new patterns. However, there is no doubt that it would give you great happiness if you would meet him. It would remove the pressure your frustration is causing in your mind. The unfulfilled yearning has got to be fulfilled to whatever extent it may be possible in the changed circumstances.

R. I wish to meet him and have a word of love with him. I understand we are no more the same young couple. With the passage of time our expectations have also changed. I think your guess is correct. If we meet the same emotions and feelings may not revive. Most probably, we shall only enquire about one another, smile and feel happy and wish happiness to each other. My only desire is that he be happy.

C. Your curiosity will be satisfied and that will give you happiness. As yet, everything has remained a mystery, it all looks like a fairy tale where the princess is still waiting to meet her Prince Charming. You have remained emotionally in a fix for about twenty years, now you are aspiring return to the same world and to the same time when you had to part with your lover and live a life of emotional duality. Go and meet your Prince

Charming and have the emotional unity with your lover. That will make you get over your subconscious craving to make love with your lover. And, at the same time see the existing reality with your young daughter standing by your side.

R. And, then I shall find that I am no more that Princess, my young daughter has taken my place and it is time for her to get a Prince Charming. Probably, that will bring fulfilment of my unrealised and shattered dream of having love and sex with my young-age lover.

C. Yes, your sub-conscious mind and also your conscious mind will find fulfilment of your dream. You shall then begin to enjoy your present life.

R. I am feeling great relief and relaxation, it seems my craving for emotional involvement with my lover is melting away. Now I feel I shall be content to have him only as a friend, just a friend and not a lover.

C. That will improve your relations with your husband also. You will no more consider him a villain or a rival of your lover. You could never have fulfilling sex with your husband because your young-age lover was always living with you in your mind, and his image always made you consider your husband a villain and an intruder in your private world. In intimate relationships there is space only for one.

R. I think that this revolutionary change in me will bring a big change in my relationship with my husband, and in his relationship with me.

C. Even his abnormality, which you call insanity, might undergo a change, and he might start behaving more sensibly and lovingly. His attitude towards your daughter might also change. The change in your emotional set-up might even bring in to his disturbed mind a new light of love and make him a loving husband.

R. It seems a new life of happiness is waiting for me.

C. When are you going to meet your ex-lover?

R. Never, it is no longer necessary. I have already met him and have bid him adieu.

KADAMBINI

While Kadambini was talking about her husband him and was asked if he also beats her, she burst out. Suddenly a gush of tears came, her eyes became red and flooded with incessant flow of tears. She mumbled that she was systematically and regularly abused, and beaten if she said anything in protest. Again and again tears flooded her eyes; she had been given a thrashing this morning also.

Diagnostic Scan

Kadambini 32—with two kids, lives with her husband. Kadambini looks a smart woman with a broken heart, rather she is an embodiment of a broken personality—sad, wretched, crushed, miserable, a woman whose whole self has been shattered.

She complains she has lost all self-confidence, and is unable to take and make decisions. Her husband has reduced her to a pulp.

Before her marriage, ten years ago, she was employed in an Embassy, was a self-confident woman and she is a university graduate. Recently she has done a course in film production and management.

However, ever since her marriage she has remained an unemployed woman. Her husband will not permit her to work. He will not let her go out or meet anyone saying that she will get corrupt. He already accuses her falsely that she is a corrupt, immoral woman.

He himself is uneducated, having studied only up to class VIII. In Chennai before their marriage, he used to do some work as an interior decorator. Now he poses to be working but apparently has no source of income. He has sold away Kadambini's flat for more that one million rupees and alleged that he had purchased a shop worth Rs. 1,00,000 or so in his own name. Rest of the money, he said, he had invested in his so-called business and spent in meeting household expenses. He neither earns himself nor permits his wife to work. He has incurred debts. Only a few days ago some of his creditors came and took away the TV set, etc. from the house.

He has told Kadambini that since before marriage, he used to have pain in his spine and was taking some drug to which he has become addicted. He had taken de-addiction treatment in a hospital and spent about Rs. 20,000 with no result. He continues to take the drug.

He has a very bad temper and is a terror in the house.

She appears to be a woman who is oppressed and suppressed, and is a victim of her husband's cruelty, and that has made her lose all her courage and confidence. She is completely broken, and is unable to take any step to make herself financially independent. Her husband will not permit her to do anything worth-while which might make her feel independent. He wants to keep her in absolute subjugation.

She is mortally afraid of her husband. He has threatened her of dire consequences if she approached the police, and that he has contracts with high-ups and nothing can injure him.

Counselling

Kadambini was put under a very mild hypnotic spell and communicative therapy was applied to make her calm, composed, and relaxed. Slowly she gained courage and confidence and became normal. Her tears dried-up and smile began to appear on her lips.

C. Let your past not mar your present and block your future. You should give up the fear you are suffering from, and be ready to fight back. Aggression, not surrender is what is needed to save you from the torture and cruelties of your husband.

[She has begun to see the birth of a new woman in herself, a woman with courage to stand up and fight back against her husband's oppression and inhuman treatment. A new spirit of courage and confidence has come to her].

K. I have decided to go ahead, and will no more accept subjugation; I will no more surrender to the restrictions and constraints put on my freedom of movement and meeting people, or taking up a job to earn a living; I will no more tolerate and accept beatings by my husband but will fight back.

C. Determine finally that you will remain happy hereafter. Today is the day of a new birth for you. In you has today born a new woman with maturity and courage to face life alone, if necessary. Have courage and go ahead.

Remember that both misery and happiness are products of one's own consciousness. You had formed the habit of remaining miserable, from now onwards you will change and feel liberated and get into the habit of remaining happy.

K. There was a time when I was full of courage and confidence, now I have nothing.

C. You are wrong, you still have courage but have lost confidence. Courage and confidence have to be seen in relation to some tangible action. Courage and confidence are needed to do some act, hence they have to be considered in relation to some activity and never in a vacuum as a general disposition or condition of mind. Once it is viewed and considered in relation to a particular activity, it comes to be received by the mind as a practical tool to guide the action for which courage and confidence are needed, otherwise it remains just a vague and aimless desire.

K. I understand, I need confidence and courage to take appropriate action, I hope and believe I will succeed. I feel I am bold and brave. I feel elated, delighted, and roused up. I had come with tears in my eyes, I am going back with smile of courage on my face.

Second Session

Kadambini has no tears in her eyes, she has a pleasant face with a broad smile. She is, as she says, a changed woman. Previous counselling has changed her personality and outlook towards everything. She has taken steps to get employment, has approached a few places and is hopeful of getting a job very soon. She wants to take up a media job. She is fully determined to be financially independent. She needs a source of income and is determined to have a job, more particularly because of what happened a day before.

The previous day morning she had a devastating experience. One woman with two men entered her house while she was cleaning the floor, and the woman began abusing and beating her. She slapped her repeatedly. The man also did a bit of their job and tried to push her into the kitchen to lock her. Two men standing in the lane outside the house, who were seeing this came to save her and the intruders walked away abusing her with filthy language even from the street. They claimed her husband owed them Rs. 2000, they had a cheque with them, which had been dishonoured. They belonged to a nearby electric shop.

Kadambini was taken wholly by surprise. The woman without asking for money or anything just began to abuse and beat her. Her children hid themselves in fear.

Her husband had gone out only a few minutes before for a shave or something and returned a few minutes after the assailants had left. He told her that he was sorry, and that the ugly incident may not have happened had he been there.

Kadambini was too much agitated, she called her parents and went to the Police Station and lodged a written report, but the police neither gave her the copy of the report nor took any action. Her husband did not make any effort to mobilise police action, or even to get the copy of the report.

Kadambini was terrified and deeply hurt by the sudden attack on her in her own house, but she managed to become calm, she had successfully applied the strategies to cope with stress of an unwanted assault which she had learnt during the previous session, and regained confidence.

In the evening one of those persons who had beaten her came along with a man named Raju (name changed) who is believed to have a say with the police and asked Kadambini to compromise. Her husband was present and indirectly supported them. They wanted Kadambini to withdraw the report. The woman who had given her the thrashing in the morning, they said, will come to her to apologise and Kadambini may by way of retaliation beat her and abuse her if she liked, and her husband will not be required to pay Rs. 2000 which he owed to the woman.

Kadambini who had by now developed sufficient courage to meet the situation refused the offer. No compromise or retaliation could bring solace to her. She was no more the old human pulp, but a woman of action with a fighting spirit to vindicate her honour.

Taking courage, she went in the late evening to the Police Station to enquire about what action was being taken on her report, but was given a vague reply that proper action would be taken in due course.

Her report to the police, she believes, had not been officially recorded, as no copy of the same had been given to her. The police, however, called the woman who had beaten her to the Police Station and asked her to apologise and warned her to severe action if she misbehaved in future. The woman apologised. Kadambini was not satisfied, but feels helpless. She, however, feels that now she has gained sufficient moral strength to face any such situation in future.

While abusing and beating her, the woman had snubbed her for trying to get a job in television or film production. Kadambini is surprised not only by the timing of the attack made on her in the morning, but also as to how that woman got aware of the fact that she was trying to get into film production. Except her husband, none could have told her of it.

Kadambini's suspicion against her husband's involvement in the incident became stronger due to the circumstance that he was absent only during the short period the assailants were in the house. She smelt a rat and saw a game in his absence during the crucial moment.

Kadambini suspects that this incident was part of a conspiracy engineered by her husband to stop her from proceeding further in her effort to get employment, particularly in the media world where she had to report on the day of the assault. She doubts if her husband was innocent and was not involved in getting her humiliated and beaten.

[General counselling has been given to restore her self-confidence and to make her overcome the trauma and also to be prepared to meet successfully anything worse that may come in future].

Kadambini is now determined to go ahead. Whatever may happen, she will not retrace her steps. To achieve economic independence she will move on to seek and get a job.

Kadambini is not interested in living any longer with her husband in conditions of virtual slavery and deprivation, with a constant feeling of insecurity for her life and honour. She wants to live with dignity and is prepared to face and overcome whatever hurdles may come in her way. This incident has given her more courage and firm determination to move forward.

Third Session

Kadambini seems to be stable, more confident and less emotional. Her husband has also begun to recognise her identity as a human being. During this period she only once received a slap, and that to, she thinks, was not really intended. There is, she says, a general improvement in their relationship. She has now become more assertive and commands and gets sufficient money for household expenses. She is no longer required to beg and take whatever her husband gives. However, she is still not totally able to prevent his violent behaviour.

K. I get into high temper when I have confrontations with my husband, particularly when he says that I shall get exposed to sexual exploitation and will become immoral and lose my character if I work along with men.

C. This is not the correct thing to do. Your getting into rage makes your husband believe that his was the best stick with which he could give you a thrashing and accordingly uses it to oppress and humiliate you. His sub-conscious mind has become so conditioned that it makes him act violently more as an automatic machine than as a thinking human being with a sensitive conscience. And so far you are concerned, as soon as he opens his artillery, a pre-recorded memory of past events comes in your mind and you become disturbed, agitated and enraged. It is like a mental tape-recorder that begins operating automatically on getting the input from your husband. Prevent this.

K. How?

C. Please do not mind what he says, and do not react to the volley of abuses and accusations he hurls on you, ignore his words regarding your becoming an object of sexual exploitation, and behave as if you have not heard him. Go ahead with your plans with courage to face all consequences. You are quite capable of coping with adverse situations and creating a tension-free psychological environment. You are a woman of steel, you are Durga, you are Shakti, you are a woman who knows no fear now.

The counselling has brought a change in Kadambini's outlook, it has made her see the basic problem in its true perspective. She has understood that it is a case where the husband in order to atone his own guilt, seeks to inflict punishment on the wife. By this process he hopes to shift his own guilt on to her.

Kadambini informs that the change in her attitude had a positive impact on her husband's behaviour. He realised that battering her would no longer serve his purpose. He also understood that the fault lay really in his own thinking and behaviour, and his hostile attitude towards Kadambini was not conducive to family's emotional well-being.

Both have come closer, the communication-gap has shrunk, mutual understanding has grown, and the former love relationship is getting restored.

MANJU

I never had an immoral life; the guilt was in his own mind, and he looked at me through the dirty glasses of his own past.

Manju has just left her husband's house in Delhi and come to stay in her parents' house with her three children. She is an M.A. (Political Science) and has been working as a teacher in a private school.

Her husband is working as a salesman. He is eight years older than Manju. They were married thirteen years ago when she was twenty-five. It was an arranged marriage. From the very beginning the relationship has been running through troubled waters. Finally now she was getting out for good. She has come on the pretext of attending someone's birthday party, with no intentions of going back.

C. You look pretty, youthful, healthy, with a broad smile on your face, why is it you have a strained relationship with your husband?

M. It is my beautiful face and my good looks that are the cause of all trouble. My husband suspects, and has been suspecting ever since the marriage, that I have lovers and am corrupt.

C. Did you ever have an affair? Tell me truthfully, it is necessary that you conceal nothing from me.

M. No, I never had an affair.

C. What is it that makes him suspect your character? Does he know anything about your private life?

M. Neither there is, nor there ever was any cause for his suspicion, but he has always been telling me that I was a woman of loose character. When he pestered me too much, I told him a cooked-up story about my love affair with a boy when I was young and unmarried, and to avoid further recriminations I told him that the boy was already dead.

C. Did it satisfy him?

M. No, he has never given up suspecting me of having affairs.

In fact I discovered he had affairs with some young women. I found many love letters among his belongings and when confronted he acknowledged he was having affairs, but now they were all over. On this, I tore off all the letters and said the matter is now closed for both of us. We are quits, let us forget the past, and live with trust in each other.

I never raked up the matter again, but he has continued to accuse me of being a woman of loose character and of going about with different men. It is all false, I never had any affair with any man.

C. Then why this suspicion?

M. He has some mental problem. His suspicions are not confined to my character, he even suspects that I, along with my relatives, am planning to kill him. He had some cysts on his back, I brought him for treatment to my brother's house and he was operated upon in the hospital and cysts were removed. He, however, suspects that cysts have not been removed and something has been done, with the doctor's connivance, to kill him.

C. Does he make his feelings public?

M. Yes, he talks about my being of immoral character before everyone. This causes great embarrassment and I am looked down upon by everyone. My dignity is compromised. Now he has been publicly accusing me of conspiring to kill him.

C. Does he beat you?

M. He tries to, raises a his, but before he can hit I move away. It is only by avoiding the crisis scene that I have prevented being beaten and he does all this even in the presence of our relatives.

C. Can't you patch up?

M. It is not possible.

C. Is your decision to live separate and alone final and irrevocable? If it is not, then don't make too much of it and go back to him because you have not yet told him that you were leaving him finally.

M. My decision is final, it is irrevocable.

C. Then be prepared for all consequences, he might come and entreat and beg your pardon and request you to go back, he might come with some people to force you to go back, try to snatch away the children, make a police report and go to court accusing you of many misdeeds and seek civil and criminal action against you. Are you ready to take all these risks and face the consequences?

M. Yes, I am.

C. You seem to have suffered a lot of tension and are grief-stricken.

M. Yes, I have since my marriage been suffering mental stress and tension. I had developed ulcers in my stomach and they still continue.

C. What did the doctors say?

M. That they are the result of my tension.

C. If it is so, then release the tension.

M. How? That is why I have come.

C. You have accumulated a stockpile of suppressed anger. If you had fought with your husband, or even allowed him to beat you, which of course, would have been wrong and would have greatly injured your dignity and self-esteem, you would not have accumulated this stress, and allowed it to fester your system and caused those ulcers. However, it is now a matter of history and has to be dumped into oblivion. It is not going to happen again.

Try to think of your goodness in avoiding violent conflict and suffering the consequences of the bad behaviour of someone else. It was only because he was your husband you tolerated this humiliation. It was your regard for peace in the family that you underwent the suffering, so you have no reasons to feel ashamed; rather you should feel proud of yourself. This will help you getting the tension out of your sub-conscious mind.

Did you not get bouts of anger, and did you not try to suppress them?

M. Yes, I did get very angry when he accused me of unchastity, particularly in the presence of those who mattered in our family and social life. I was always extremely upset when he tried to be violent.

C. Anger is a negative and damaging emotion, you had not till then learnt to keep your temper under control, so you did have its damaging effect and it went into your subconscious mind and still continues to be there in the form of suppressed anger and sorrow. It has created in you a feeling of retaliation and revenge which again lies hidden in your mind. Your husband has always been trying to hurt your feelings, downgrade you and disgrace you, and succeeded in making you feel ashamed and guilty. That has made you suffer agony. But it was not due to any wrong act of yours. So there is no cause for you to feel sorrow. It was all done by your husband, because he did not possess a balanced mind, you cannot hold yourself responsible for his wrongs. There was really no reason for you to get upset because you should have known that your husband was mentally sick.

Anyway, you cannot undo the past but you can certainly stop it from spoiling your present. You have never done any wrong, you were really the victim of an unsound mind. You have no reason to feel guilt or shame for anything done by him. Don't you think you did no wrong, but have been suffering because your husband has a guilt-laden and suspicious mind? He tries to pass his own guilt on to you.

M. I never had an immoral life, the guilt was in his own mind, and he looked at me through the dirty glasses of his own past.

C. So from now on, you will not let your mind be pestered by thoughts of the past, you will forget his accusations as nonsense. The past is dead, don't look at it.

M. Well I shall forget the past but what should I do now, when I have left him finally?

C. You have the freedom to live alone, you are not under any obligation to live with a husband who is guilty of cruelty towards you. Even if you can avoid being physically assaulted, mauled and tortured, you have the right to refuse to live in perpetual misery.

However, you should remain ready to face all consequences, nothing serious may happen, and if it does happen then think of what to do, and do it without fear. Once you are ready to face the situation life will become normal and peaceful. Try to remain relaxed and calm; never get agitated, never let feelings of anger, hatred, or revenge enter your mind.

M. I realise I have all along been suffering from the feeling of guilt and shame; but now I have got rid of it. I wish to remain free and live with honour and dignity.

C. Go ahead.

Analysis

Suspicion and distrust are the genesis of emotional imbalance. They produce hatred, anger and bring about alienation of love. This is exactly what happened in this case. Finally finding herself unable to bear the tension any more she left her husband with determination never to return.

From the very beginning both suspected each other, and believed the other to have had affairs prior to marriage. Manju foolishly made a false confession of her love affair. Her husband never believed that it was a story cooked-up by her only to save herself from his unfounded accusations. She discovered love letters of her husband and had full justification to develop distrust in her husband. Her expectation that her husband's suspicions will end after she told him that her boyfriend was dead proved to be wrong. He continued to charge her with continuing unchastity.

Naturally, Manju suffered severe mental tension and emotional stress leading to psychosomatic problems. The growing tension in her husband's mind through continued suspicion and distrust made him more and more miserable and sceptical about the innocence of his wife. As a consequence, Manju suffered more and more frustration, suppressed anger and deep-rooted sorrow. It developed in her intense hatred and revulsion against her husband. The suspicion and distrust in the mind of the husband made it impossible for them to get any marital happiness, and made their lives intolerable. Living together became impossible for Manju. No wonder she has run away to escape from the misery of living together.

ANAMIKA

He is full of suspicion, suspicion has got ingrained in every cell of his polluted brain. My wings have been cut, and I have been put in a cage.

Young smart woman, with the look of a responsible woman.

A. I live with my two daughters: sixteen and thirteen.

C. Are you kidding? A mother of a girl of sixteen has got to be thirty-eight and not twenty-eight.

A. I am thirty-eight. I know I look much younger than my age.

C. Does the credit go to your beautician or the health club?

A. To none, I am as I am. I always had a good form and worked in various jobs-dress-designing, Television, Citi Bank.

C. What are you doing now?

A. Nothing. For two years I have done nothing. Ever since I was married we had financial difficulties. I always took the job to supplement my husband's earnings, and had always to give up because of opposition. That is why I had to jump from one job to another.

C. Why did he create hindrances?

A. His plea was that I would become corrupt and will be enticed away by unscrupulous males. He does not realise that if I would have been so inclined, I would have more time and opportunity if I am free at home than when I am on job.

I am very much concerned and worried about my daughters. The younger one has some speech disability and had to be taken to a special school. I had to spend a lot of money and had to run from one doctor to another for her treatment. I had to do it all alone. She was not cured and is still suffering from the disability.

My other daughter suffers from tension and depression and is not able to cope with her studies, she had to continue in class X as the Principal was not ready to let her take the Board exam.

C. Are all of you happy otherwise?

A. Not at all. Our house is a den of 'humanimals' where the adult male (my husband) continuously howls using abusive, filthy language from the time he comes back late in the evening, and the rest of us have to suffer. There is continuous quarrelling between two of us. Now the elder daughter has also begun to show some resistance. She says: at the most he will kill me, let him kill me.

C. So, all of you are living in distress and high tension and this explains why your daughters do not have normal growth. So long as tension and stress remains in the house, one will suffer speech disability and the other will fail to progress in her studies, and you will remain the worst victim and suffer misery and agony.

What about your sleep? Do you get sound sleep during the night?

A. No, my husband goes on increasing my dose of sleeping pills (now the dose has gone to ten tablets). I sleep at about two or three and wake up late in the morning. I do not want to wake up early, I do not want to see him, I wake up only after he has left the house.

C. Since when are you having this kind of troubled life?

A. Ever since I was married eighteen years ago. My husband is of a quarrel some nature. His father had a big business, there was a quarrel in the family and he was turned out and given no financial support. He had struggled and failed in business, now he has taken employment. The income is not enough and there is need to supplement it, but he will not let me do or stick to any job. Since my mother died two years back I have no support; my husband has made my father also to distance himself from me.

C. All right, you have talked enough of your miseries, let us talk about your happier moments. Tell me about your honeymoon.

A. I had no honeymoon, I was totally ignorant of sex. When I went back and was talking to my father, my mother over-heard me and said my husband was suffering from impotency. He never had erection. My father took him to the doctor and he was given treatment, but it did not help. I have all along lived a miserable life. Somehow our two daughters were born.

C. So how is your love-sex life in the present? When did you last have fulfilling sex ?

A. I never had orgasmic sex, and no fulfilling sex since the birth of my second child. For the last ten years we are sleeping in separate rooms. We have no body contact, we don't even like sitting together or near each other. That is the only way to avoid the brawl, rather attempt to avoid it, because shouting match, we have every night. This has become a normal routine in our house.

C. It is creditable for you to live in such an environment.

A. His younger brother is also like that, but his wife escaped by getting a separation; she had support from her parents. I have none to support me. I also fear financial difficulty if I separate.

C. That is no problem because you and your children can claim maintenance allowance. However, let us not worry about it at this stage.

A. But why is there such a hell in my family?

C. It is clear, his impotency and your sex-relations, are you also frigid?

A. No, I am not frigid, I am sexually responsive, but he is not. Sometimes I do feel I need sex. I need love, but I get only despair and frustration. Absence of intimate relationship is of course, the greatest cause of my miseries, it is the worst curse on me. I am suffering stress every moment of my life.

C. A life without love is of course a curse. But you know you cannot change the circumstances, you cannot turn your husband's impotency into potency simply by sleeping in a separate room and playing shouting match every night in which you get nothing but volleys of abuses and foul words, and in consequence lose you sleep. Just accept the circumstances, and until and unless you decide to separate, try to have a peaceful life.

A. How?

C. You can reduce your tension by bringing a little change in your thinking, and accepting the world as it is.

A. I am longing to get happiness, freedom from this life which is full of agony and stress.

[Anamika is given counselling for developing a positive attitude and becoming optimistic].

C. Try to feel happy even though you might be living in the midst of miseries. Forget what is not avoidable and make the best of a bad situation. You know it is not possible to mend him, so it is better not to argue with him. Silence is generally a very powerful weapon to counteract the rage of the adversary. Whenever you find yourself in an adverse situation, just get relaxed and start flowing towards psychic silence through your mantra: CALM CALM CALM... That will bring you peace of mind, and make him give up his rage. Play this cassette, and you will feel relaxed.

A. I am already feeling happy and relaxed. What am I to pay for this cassette?

C. A few broad smiles filled with joy and happiness.

A. I knew you will say some such things. See I am already smiling, and having the feeling of joy.

Second Session

A. I am really in distress, what is this life in which there is nothing but tension, disgust and no love. I want to get out of this hell.

C. Then get separation, live independently, have courage and confidence to do something to be financially well off.

Anyway, why does your husband suspect that you are prone to getting involved with other men, and losing your chastity?

A. I don't know, maybe it is because of an old incident. About ten years ago I was living a very miserable life, my husband was giving me no love and happiness. I was extremely sad and dejected. My husband provided me not even adequate financial support, I felt insecure, I became involved with a friend of his and undertook various kinds of jobs including modelling. Once my interview was published in a newspaper; I had entered the world of glamour, the world of show-biz, and was getting name and fame. That made my husband feel jealous of me. He began to bear a grudge against me, and in order to take revenge started accusing me of improper and unacceptable conduct. He also made my friend leave me.

C. How long did that relationship last? Was sex involved?

A. There was no sex, but there was certainly emotional involvement, we had become good friend. The relationship lasted for about a year.

C. Anything else?

A. He was himself having an affair and felt guilty. He was involved with an unmarried girl, and the affair continued till she was married, and went out of his reach.

C. So, you were quits.

A. No, there was a big difference in my affair and his affair, my affair was open, his was clandestine, he always told lies about his relationship and tried to conceal guilt. He wanted to put on a mask of high morality and chastity, but it could never hide his true face, and in order to overcome his own guilt, he began playing the morality card against me.

C. That seems to have led to your virtual separation. Such a separation is worse than divorce or judicial separation, because then you can live apart and escape the daily tussle and disgracing humiliation. You are really brave that you can face all this and live with so much of suffering. But at the same time it shows you are a coward, you completely lack courage and confidence to take the right action. But why?

A. Because now I am without a friend and a well-wisher. My mother is dead, and my husband has by his malicious disinformation campaign made my father believe that I am a depraved girl, and deserve no sympathy or support. He had earlier given me permission to occupy his Ghaziabad house, but on my husband's intervention he has backed out. My husband says the key of that house is with him, and I cannot be allowed to live in that house except under his direct control and along with him. I want to get away from him, I want to live and work as an independent person.

C. Anamika, always remain conscious of the fact that you are not guilty of any degrading behaviour. Your conduct was graceful and upright. You did what the circumstances demanded, there is nothing wrong in a woman's doing the jobs you did. Even in your involvement with a friend there was nothing wrong. You are innocent and are suffering along with your children only because of the reprehensible conduct of your husband. Take courage, and live with your head high. Go ahead and take up some job. Without that you can never be happy.

A. I also think so.

Third Session

A. I feel I am too weak to act, I lack courage to take any bold step.

C. How do you test your ability or disability to act?

A. Whenever I attempt to do any work or take up any physical activity. I feel weakness and pain in my body.

C. It is all because you do not feel you are doing the right thing. Courage to act lies in the belief that you are doing the right thing and weakness comes when you feel you are doing something wrong. Courage, strength, weakness, fear, they are all correlated; weakness and fear are opposite of courage and strength, the two groups are the products of different thinking patterns and feelings. Just think you are doing the right thing, and you will have no difficulty, in succeeding in your effort.

A. Besides keeping me economically dependent on himself, he does everything to make every one of us unhappy.

C. Can you give any instance?

A. About two months back I planned to give the children some good time. We went to the cinema, he was all along showing he did not enjoy. Then we went to a restaurant, there he became so tense that we were in a fix what to do. We could not just get up and walk out, nor could we place an order. So, after waiting for some time I ordered the cheapest menu and somehow finished the dinner and came out. My elder daughter is no more a child and silently felt choked by the unbecoming and insulting behaviour of her father.

My mother's sister lived nearby, we went to her house. When she enquired about us, my throat choked and I wept and wept. My husband who was full of rage began to complain about me, saying I was a bad woman who loves to enjoy life with young men, go to pictures and eat in restaurants. My aunt believed him and without giving me any chance to explain the situation, reported against me to my father. My husband always makes me feel I am a depraved woman and deserve to be denied all respect.

C. I think you are suffering from severe frustration. You want to work and live well, but are forced not to work and earn, that makes you frustrated and depressed. It is the cause of your agony and distress. It also leads to the feeling of shame and guilt.

A. I have done nothing to be ashamed of or to feel guilty about.

C. It is not the shame and guilt of doing something wrong, but of not doing something which you consciously and subconsciously consider you should do for a proper living. You have a feeling that you are doing wrong, at any rate not acting correctly, in sitting at home and not working to have independent income. There was nothing wrong in your appearing on the T.V. or doing modelling or giving interviews, or running a boutique or working in the Citi Bank. They are all noble things to do, and all girls like you are doing these jobs. You still feel and honestly believe that there is nothing wrong in doing these jobs and as a consequence you feel guilty of not doing anything to keep yourself purposefully engaged. You feel ashamed of yourself for remaining idle and living like a cabbage. That is the real cause of your misery.

A. I have lost all courage. I feel ashamed that I cannot manage even my children, my elder daughter no longer listens to me, and his inhuman behaviour makes her feel worse.

C. It is your own tension and frustration that makes you feel weak and unable to manage your daughter. How can you expect a girl of sixteen to take instructions from a mother who is not able to manage her own affairs and suffers from frustration and sense of failure, and lives under tension and suffers misery, and on top of it all is continuously scolded by her own husband every night?

Please try to get over your own tensions, and your daughter will begin to accept your commands, suggestions and directions.

A. I shall try, and hope things will become better.

After Some Time (*on phone*)

C. Yes, Anamika, how are you?

A. Well I am still in a bad shape. My husband is as much a problem as he ever was, and my daughter has become worse.

C. What about your getting some job? Did you not try to get a prosaic type of job which has no shine or glamour in it, nothing that might make your husband feel jealous?

A. I have not yet been able to get one, really I could not make any earnest effort. My self-esteem has gone down. I know if I get into a job I shall regain my lost self-esteem, but I feel I have no courage. I generally remain unhappy, sad and dejected.

My husband is not willing to come for counselling, and does not seem to be in any mood to change his behaviour.

C. He seems to have become a victim of his own guilt, self-detestation with ill-will and hate towards you, and above all his unfounded suspicion.

A. He is full of suspicion, suspicion has got ingrained in every cell of his polluted brain. My wings have been cut, and I have been put in a cage.

C. A broken cage. Your house has become a broken home, you are in shatters your children are love-starved, and your husband has himself become a prey to his own craziness.

A. I feel helpless, I have no courage to take divorce. I have no option but to suffer in silence and continue to let the world believe: *and they lived happily ever after*.

SWETA

But I cannot live with him so long that woman is there with him. Why not? Accept your Malaysian rival as an unavoidable evil. Let her live with him in absentia. You forget her. As long as you will carry her in your mind you will feel disturbed, she will go to bed along with you and it will not be possible for you to have marital happiness with her being constantly occupying a place in your mind. Turn her out of your mind. Just let her get lost, give her back to your husband, wash your hands.

Sweta is a smart young woman of thirty-eight. She looks healthy but morose. She was married when she was twenty-three, her elder daughter is thirteen and younger, five. She is well-educated, was a teacher for sometime, then took a job in Malaysia where her husband was working. She came back and did computer training courses, her husband has also returned, but has not been able to get any employment.

Their married life has seen many ups and downs. They still continue bound together in matrimonial alliance, but she enjoys no marital happiness, and has thought of judicial separation. Her husband wants non-judicial separation. For all practical purposes the home is broken but they still continue to live together in the same house.

S. I am not happy and I know I cannot be happy with him, but still I have some soft corner for him, I still feel some emotional attachment to him.

C. Do you mean emotion of love?

S. Yes, not exactly love, but something like that. I wish to get away from him but sometime become hesitant. I fear he may take away my daughters; the elder daughter has already developed some kind of dislike for me, and does not wish to obey me.

C. That is natural, your home is already broken, there is no emotional coherence, and your daughter probably holds you subconsciously responsible for it. She is living in a broken home where the mother is not permitted to exercise the authority, she is entitled in her relationship with her husband; that makes the child feel her mother need not be obeyed. But as you have not brought about this situation, you should not hold yourself responsible or guilty for what has happened. You should also give up worrying about the behaviour of your daughter, you cannot change her attitude towards you till you regain your position in the family, so accept it as it is.

S. Everyone thinks I am a failure as a wife and as a mother and that makes me uneasy and depressed.

C. That really makes you feel guilty and you feel ashamed.

S. Yes.

C. But why? Have you done anything wrong to bring about this situation? Can you tell me what it is that has brought about this situation?

S. He had an extra-marital affair in Malaysia, and he has made no secret of it. He contemptuously tells me that I was responsible for it because I did not give him as much happiness as that other woman did. Even now he is in touch with her, everyday he has long telephonic conversations with her. That upsets me.

C. It is natural, any respectable woman in your position will feel let down, betrayed and will get upset.

S. He drinks heavily but does not become noticeably drunk.

C. Do you also drink?

S. Yes, sometimes, but that is never more than one peg. He also smokes heavily, I feel disgusted. This has all become worse since he lost his job.

C. How can he get a job with his heavy drinking? He seems to have become an addict.

S. Yes, he has become an addict. I live under great stress. When we lived with his parents, their treatment towards me was bad, we moved on to our own and felt happy, but his affair with the Malaysian woman has spoiled our life. I went to a spiritual (Pranik) healer, he advised me to do meditation, and gave me a mantra. But that has not worked, I am unable to feel happiness; all the time nightmarish thoughts come and disturb me.

I wish to have a separation. We have already divided equally our earnings and finances, and I am getting a house built independently for myself. It would be my house.

C. Why do you want only a separation, it is no use going half way. If you want to separate, separate for good, get a divorce. Ask your husband to agree to divorce by mutual consent.

S. If he agrees it is well and good, but if he does not, can I get it on the basis of his affair with the Malaysian woman?

C. Have you any evidence?

S. No, except one bill of his mobile phone showing long calls to her in Malaysia.

C. That may not be good enough. Try to obtain his consent. From what you have said it seems he will not resist very much. He is probably suffering from some sort of inferiority complex. You seem to be culturally quite high-up, and maybe superior to him; you are interested in literature, you sing very well (Sweta had sung a Bengali song a little while back), you have had good employments, and look bright. Maybe it is to show his superiority that he wants to pull you down. He carries on an affair with a Malaysian woman, who is in no way a match to you, he has taken to excessive drinking and smoking, and tries to find fault with you whenever he gets a chance and nags you whenever he can; he blames you for every short-coming of his own and also for the bad development of the elder daughter. He has given you financial separation, agrees to have a mutual separation, and maybe he will feel that he will gain greater heights and happiness by giving you a divorce. You should at least try to probe into his thoughts.

S. I shall, I know he has always been suffering from inferiority complex and always tries to make me feel inferior and worthless. His effort is always to disparage me and make me feel small.

C. Your greatest problem is your lack of decision. When a person fails to reach a decision, she suffers frustration, and frustration causes stress and tension. So you must take a decision. Decide whether you would like to continue to live as his wife or like to take a divorce. Once you take a decision, much of your tension will go.

Please do not feel you will be doing anything wrong in taking a decision to take Jworce. You can talk the matter over with your friends without feeling any guilt or shame in doing so. It is no offence to think of divorce if your married life is full of agony, misery, sadness, and stress. Your talking with your friends will by itself give you relief.

S. I understand and will try to take some final decision very soon.

C. It is immaterial what decision you take. What is essential for your happiness is to get rid of this uncertainty, this state of vacillation and doubts. You are living a miserable life, so think and take a final decision, a final resolve to continue or end your married life.

In case you decide to continue, then change your life-style, change your thought pattern, and try to enjoy life as it is. Do not feel offended but enjoy your husband's relationship with the Malaysian woman. What does it matter if he talks to her on phone, he cannot have an affair on phone. Take things lightly, that might make your husband also to look at things differently. You will feel happier.

S. Maybe, but I cannot tolerate all that, he has made my life miserable and unhappy, I cannot even move in society with my head up, I always feel guilty and ashamed, because unlike everyone else, I am unable to have a comfortable marital life. My whole life is full of distress and tension, even my children have no love and respect for me. My house is hell, and I am burning in it.

C. Don't be disheartened, feel composed and proceed to take a decision, a final decision. Please relax and think that the future may have pleasantness and happiness in store for you. You do not know your future so live with hope, and everything will turn out well. Dark nights come only to welcome the new down.

Next Day (*on phone*)

S. After I talked to you I felt very relaxed, my confidence and self-esteem came back, my feelings of guilt and shame disappeared and I went to talk the whole thing over with a friend. She thought I had to take some positive action, and wondered why I had kept silent so long, all along suffering pain, agony and distress. My fear disappeared and courage came to me, I talked to my husband today and asked him to agree to have divorce by mutual consent. He said he had no objection, but proceeded to tell me of difficulties in the process. He took coffee and breakfast with me, and asked if I had talked with my parents on this matter. He also said that I should keep this matter in a shelf till I had given interviews for the two jobs for which I had received the call.

Now I feel very relaxed, but again his consoling behaviour is coming in the way.

C. It is good, you have given him shock-treatment, and wait to see its effect.

S. I know it will not change him. He will not change, he cannot change. He will not give up his Malaysian lover, his drinking, smoking and all that nasty behaviour towards me. I want a divorce.

C. Then behave more calmly and secure his consent.

S. He has already given his consent orally, now I shall prepare the divorce papers and then ask him to give his consent in writing.

C. That is okay, don't be in a great hurry. First give your interviews for the jobs, and then take up the matter of divorce. Go step by step.

Next Session

Sweta's with husband.

C. When I see both of you, I feel you are fit for the "Made For Each Other" contest, both of you look young, smart, jovial, loving.

R. But we never felt that way. Our married life had only short spells of happiness and long ones of misery. I think we are not made for each other, we have no compatibility. I am a perfectionist and have a very logical mind. I am an engineer and have passion for things to go methodically and remain orderly. Sweta does not even like my desire of punctuality, she will give up an appointment or programme rather than stick to the time schedule.

C. The schedule framed by you?

R. Yes, because I insist on punctuality and she does not. May I proceed with my story?

C. Yes, please.

R. After our marriage fifteen years ago, we had a happy life for a couple of years and then our elder daughter was born and we got a common purpose to work for.

My parents are old, my elder brother is blind, one sister is a widow and the other is married and has her own family. I feel I have obligations to care for my parents, brother and sister. Sweta does not tolerate my parents, and that always created problems whenever they came to live with us.

Again, when we got our second daughter, five years back, there was a period of happiness. I got a good job in Malaysia, we went abroad and lived comfortably with a high income at our disposal. Sweta also took appointment as a teacher. This period too, though it was peaceful, cannot be termed as a period of marital happiness. We always had the last word. I had to accept and suffer defeat, failure and unhappiness.

C. And probably that made you look out for someone who might give you solace.

R. Maybe it was so. There was a Malaysian woman who was supplying material which I was purchasing for my company. She was always good to me.

C. You are still having contact with her?

R. I sometimes talk to her on phone. There has never been any physical contact.

C. What is important for generating love and affection is emotional contact and that seems to be there between you and her. Talking to her gives you happiness. There is nothing wrong in getting happiness from wherever it is available. Sweta is not giving the happiness you want and that lady is giving you emotional satisfaction.

R. I cannot say so, but I do not want to leave Sweta in the lurch.

C. Why? She is unhappy with you and wants separation, you too get no happiness in your relationship, then why not separate?

R. She has always been demanding separation. She does not want to live with me.

C. And you did partition all your financial assets?

R. Yes, because I wanted that she should not be in a disadvantageous position while negotiating for a separation. I want to be fair.

C. If neither of you is happy, and both of you have for a long time lived in agony why not have a divorce? I think she will not like to live with you unless you cut off your relationship with the other woman, no wife can tolerate a rival, no woman can agree to share her husband's love with a mistress, even if the husband has no physical contact with her. What is important is the emotional attachment between you and the Malaysian woman. Can you leave her finally?

R. I can stop phoning her for a month, two months, and six months…After all, I cannot break her heart, I am concerned about her emotions too. Whenever I think of leaving her, I begin to feel compassion for her. I am not a hard-hearted man and cannot do anything that might bring unhappiness to her or to Sweta.

C. But why do you want to continue the relationship with Sweta when you get only anguish, distress, and wretchedness. Will it not be better to give her divorce and become a free man? Then you shall be able to get from your Malaysian friend the happiness you desire. You must be forty-four or forty-five, and have still a long life to look forward to.

R. I am forty-two.

C. Then why become your own enemy and keep shut the door for greater happiness coming to you? After giving divorce to Sweta, you can marry your friend.

A glow of happiness is already showing on your face. If only the thought and vision of coming nearer and closer to your friend brings the sunshine of joy on your face, what will happen if she comes to you, and you get her as your rightful companion?

R. I have never asked her about it. However, I think she may have no objection coming over to India.

C. Even you can go to Malaysia.

R. I will not like to go, as I want to stay near my parents so that I might be with them whenever need be.

C. That is right. But here the question at the moment is whether your chances of getting the happiness you desire, will be enhanced by giving divorce to Sweta or not it. You have two options, continue to live in the situation and circumstances you are, or to start a new life.

R. I would like to think more and then decide.

C. Certainly, such an important decision must be taken after full deliberation, you might even consult your Malaysian friend. Divorce would be painful if you will act without due deliberation, but will be enjoyable if you will act after full deliberation. Your objective is to live a happy and harmonious life.

Sweta (*on Phone*)

S. What has been the upshot of your talk with my husband?

C. He does not seem to be averse to the idea of accepting your proposal; however, he is still not sure if he would become happier by giving you divorce.

S. What about that woman? Don't you think he is deeply involved with her?

C. Yes, he is, and may not be able to cut off his emotional relationship with her. He wants time to think and deliberate, probably he wants to know what the other woman's reaction will be, whether that would bring her nearer and marry him.

S. He has not talked to me since then, probably I will have to initiate the talk. I am sure he cannot give up that woman and I cannot live with him so long that woman is in the picture. I am determined to go ahead and will get divorce papers prepared and ask him to sign.

C. Okay.

Next Session (Husband)

R. We cannot live together, we have no option but to separate.

C. Then give Sweta a divorce, she wants it.

R. I just want to live separately, and not have divorce. I want to have a fresh trial to see how things go.

C. But that will not solve the problem; if you want to separate, then burn all the bridges.

R. My problem at the moment is concerning the children. Sweta insists that because I am walking out of the house I should break the news to the children, and also take them along. I cannot do this, but she insists.

C. Well, what is relevant is not the breaking of the news, but the breaking of the home. One girl is fifteen and the other five, hence it would be better that they live with their mother.

R. I am willing.

C. Then, send Sweta, I shall talk to her.

Sweta

S. I do not want divorce.

C. Why this sudden change?

S. I feel I still have some emotional attachment with my husband…

C. And, you have no boyfriend to marry after divorce.

S. Yes, I feel I shall get lost without him.

C. Then live with him.

S. But I cannot live with him so long that woman is there with him.

C. Why not? Accept your Malaysian rival as an unavoidable evil. Let her live with him in absentia. You forget her. As long as you will carry her in your mind you will feel disturbed, she will go to bed along with you and it will not be possible for you to have marital happiness. So far as you are concerned, you have no emotional attachment with her, she is nothing to you. If your husband wants to keep her in his mind, let him preserve her, if he wants to talk to her, let him do it. Why should you worry about it, feel depressed and spoil your spirits? By thinking about her you get only annoyance, hatred and agony, so do not think of her, and enjoy your happiness by mentally obliterating her existence.

S. But I cannot keep her out of my mind.

C. Do not ever try that, because whenever you will try to push her out of your mind you will necessarily have to first bring her into your mind. The only way is to leave her to live with your husband, and you live as a free woman, never allowing her to bother you. Whenever she may try to enter your mind just divert your mind to something else. It will take some time, but very soon you will get rid of her.

S. I shall try not to think of her.

C. This is what I mean by your accepting her. Tell your mind that she belongs to your husband and you have nothing to do with her. She is his lover, not yours. Do not feel concerned about their affair. Don't even enquire about her, let them live in each other's mind. You have a hundred things to think to make yourself happy. You need freedom from her and that will come automatically as soon as you will get your mind occupied in something positive. After all, she is not worth remembering, she does not deserve a place in your mind. Don't you think so?

S. I agree.

C. Then let us start from the time she was not there is your life. Let us take this entire period as a time of eclipse, now the eclipse is over and the moon has come out. This evening when you go back, take with you a beautiful red rose and present it to your husband with a smile on your lips, let your face glow and bloom like the rose, let your lips extend an invitation. I am sure he will respond.

S. It will look very artificial.

C. Maybe, but it will convey a big message.

S. (Sweta smiles broadly) I shall do this, and see how it works.

C. Send him here tomorrow.

Next Morning

R. Sweta told me you wanted to talk to me.

C. Yes, I wanted to tell you what Sweta wishes to tell you, but is unable to do it. Did she give you a red rose last evening?

R. Yes, she did, but she said nothing. I thanked her for the rose.

C. Through this rose she wanted to convey to you her love. She is still in love with you, she still has emotional attachment with you, and she wants you to give her the same love, which you had been giving her before the rift.

R. But I cannot forget my friend, and she cannot tolerate her.

C. You can keep your lover with you in your mind, talk to her on phone if you like; however, you will not thrust her on Sweta nor let her come in between you and Sweta.

R. For that I am ready, but Sweta will never agree.

C. Sweta has agreed, she will no more talk to you about her and you will not talk to her about your paramour. Your relations with her are your personal matters, and you will not bring her in to interfere with your life with your wife and the children.

R. I am agreeable to this.

C. Very well, then respond by presenting her a red rose, a beautiful half-open bud. Do it with a smile and loving kiss. You should also request her to sing a love song.

R. She never sings.

C. You have never asked her. I have heard her, she sang beautifully a song from *Geetanjali*. Please make a request, and when she sings, show your appreciation. Of course, if you like it.

R. I know she had learnt music. I shall do it all as you have said, but I do not think she will respond.

C. Let's hope this will be the beginning of a new love affair between two old lovers.

Sweta (*on phone*)

S. What happened?

C. Did you get the rose and a request for the song?

S. No, nothing.

Husband (*on phone*)

R. We are still living as before, there is no change in our lives.

C. Why don't you take a decision, that will make both of you get out of this mess of doubts and uncertainties.

R. I shall try, but I do not know what decision I should take.

C. It seems both of you are suffering from a fear of the future, and also unable to accept the present as it has come to be.

Next Session (Sweta)

C. How is life? You look quite cheerful.

S. Nothing has changed except me. I have learnt to control anger. Trivial things do not worry me any more. I have triumphed over the feelings of jealousy and envy. I feel relaxed, relieved and contented.

C. That is great. But does it mean you do not get worked up or you have learnt to suppress your anger?

S. I think it is more of the second variety. He is nagging me all the time. He will object to everything though it may be quite insignificant. He just tries to find some excuse to nag, and that annoys me, but I do not now enter into arguments and thus avoid confrontation and dissipate my anger.

C. His idea probably is to make you feel guilty and thus lower your morale and weaken your resistance to his own feeling of inferiority and defeat.

S. I also think so, now he feels he has lost the battle because I show no concern to his relationship with his Malaysian paramour.

C That has taken the wind out of his sails and he feels frustrated, and attempts to fight you on some other issue.

S. He has now found a new issue, all the time he tells me that I have received unearned money, his money, in the process of partition. His sole attempt is to get it back. He shows repentance for making me share the earnings, but I am determined not to give it back to him. After all, nothing could have been earned without my active cooperation, and I also earned and put my earnings in the common pool.

C. You are doing the right thing. If you will part with money it will break your backbone and you will lose all your strength. Don't let your money be siphoned off. He too got an equal share, so why feel worried?

S. Yes, I know that, and it is for this purpose that he is making all efforts to impoverish me. He wants me to arrange for his journey to Calcutta to meet his parents. I have agreed to purchase one way ticket so that he might go and I might get the opportunity of calling my parents to discuss the situation with them. I have already informed them of it. Although through the control of my anger I remain calm and relaxed, I feel unhappy whenever he nags, and that he does all the time. I also loe my composure and feel agitated. He will not leave the house even though I have told him a number of times to go away. The house is mine.

C. So long you are living together, you should manage to remain calm and happy. Instead of suppressing your anger, learn to keep your cool. You should feel bad only if you do something wrong, and not if someone else acts wrongly; otherwise you will suffer agony for the fault of someone else. When he nags you, he is guilty of misbehaviour, and not you, you are only the victim. It is not necessary for you to punish yourself for the wrong behaviour of your husband. It is his deed, let him suffer for it. At the most you can feel sorry for him. Just ignore the nagging and feel as if nothing has happened. That will not only save you from getting angry but also make him realise that his nagging is a useless and ineffective weapon and is too blunt to cause actual injury to you. Maybe that realisation makes him behave better, and he may give up nagging.

S. Sometimes I feel afraid that he may become violent. He drinks even during the day and smokes all day.

C. And you, being his only known enemy, might become the victim of his violence. Now as that Malaysian woman no more comes in between you and him, and you have encouraged him to go to Malaysia for some time, he might calm down and give up excessive drinking and smoking.

S. I have told him to adopt her, but that has made him develop fear of being rejected by her. He is not sure if she will like to marry him or even live with him. Still, he cannot turn her out of his mind and be at peace. He will neither live in peace nor let me have peace.

C. But now, as you said, nothing bothers you.

S. Yes, but it is very difficult to live with a man who is always nagging you and will not let you live as you like. He will not let me practice on the computer even though he knows that I need to do so as I am taking the course. As soon as I will sit, he will come and take over.

My husband always asks me not to meet my boyfriend, if any, without consulting my parents. He neither wants to live with me nor tolerates a rival, even the internet boyfriend.

C. Life is very interesting, full of joys and sorrows, otherwise it will not be worth living.

S. But in my life now the sorrows are in abundance and joys only rare. At times I think of leaving everything, even my children, and going away to take a job in the Middle East. I have an offer of a teacher's job, but I do not want to be a teacher, I want to complete the computer course and take up some suitable job.

C. You should not think of leaving the children and escaping. You are not an escapist, and also not a defeatist, just go on living till the light appears on the horizon.

S. I must ask him for a consent divorce.

C. I don't think he will agree, he is too weak and afraid of leaving you. He is too dependent on you.

S. That is there but I help him not out of love, but only on humanitarian grounds. I cannot bear a man living in my house to suffer, so I tolerate and support him. I always try to remain happy and cheerful.

C. That is the essence of life; you don't have to try any longer, you have already achieved it all.

Next Session

S. Things are as they were. No change, except that I have learnt to live with the circumstances as they are.

C. And what about your new adventure, your date on the Internet?

S. Oh, it is wonderful! I have regular chit-chat. With one I have become a little bit romantically attached, he seems to have really fallen in love with me. I have responded favourably. Oh, it is real fun, and I am enjoying it to the full.

C. Is love-making fun? What stage have you reached?

S. Oh, it is fun to make love on the internet. I have become thirty-two again, I have given my age as thirty-two and have begun to behave as if I were only twenty-eight. Oh, it is a great thrill. He says he is twenty-eight and looks his age. When he talks with me he gets emotional as if I were his Date, young and beautiful, full of gusto and passion for love. We have exchanged our photos and talked on phone, one call from USA lasted half-an-hour. Oh, whenever I remember all this I feel very happy!

C. So, you are having real happiness. Continue to have happiness as much as you can, as long as you can.

S. But sometimes I fear I may not get so impulsively involved that I may not be able to come out. I am still not divorced, and he has even proposed marriage.

C. What did you say in reply?

S. I said yes, I know it is all fun. I am getting messages of love and I reciprocate.

C. Does your husband know about all this?

S. He only knows that I chat on the internet. Once he himself opened the web, and also over heard our conversation on the phone. He does not like this. However, he is not aware that we are making love parleys. Generally I operate when he is not there, or in the night when children are asleep. However, I feel no fear or regret. Why should I when I do not get any happiness from him? He is always drinking and nagging and making me unhappy, so what is wrong in my having a little fun and romance. I am afraid only of too-much involvement.

C. Don't fear, otherwise all your fun will go, you will not be able to communicate with the freedom you need in making romantic parleys. Go on doing what your heart prompts; don't worry till the stage of no return is reached.

S. He is ready to fly to India to meet me.

C. Delay that, otherwise the romance will come to an end. Better to continue moving ahead on the journey singing and dancing in love than reaching the terminus for which you are not yet ready.

S. Yes, I also think so. I do not want to interfere with the great happiness I am experiencing in this adventure of love-making, I wish to continue it as long as possible.

C. That is the right spirit. After such a long spell of darkness, light has come in your life, make the best of it, have as much happiness as you can. After all, it is not real but only an internet romance.

S. No, for me it is becoming more and more real, I am really getting involved.

C. I don't think you are reaching a point of no return. You are only getting the love of someone who is ready to give it. Your heart is vacant because your husband had been denying you the love you need. It is not a case of unwanted involvement of sexual character, it is only a play which involves fun, love and romance. So do not worry about its becoming unmanageable, just go on and on so long it is enjoyable and gives you happiness. Now you are quite mature and you need not be afraid of the drama in which you are acting as a romantic heroine and nothing more.

S. I feel there is nothing to fear and I can go on receiving and sending the words of romantic love on the internet.

C. Do one thing more, get print out of all the messages you send and receive, they will make a beautiful story and a drama.

S. Some have been wiped off, but I shall get out the prints of all that are still in the computer and continue to take prints of all the beautiful messages that I send or receive. I am also playing a little mysterious trick, I have given neither my correct name nor correct age.

C. Maybe your fiance is also doing the same.

S. Maybe, but he looks quite young, handsome and also innocent.

C. You are great. I admire your courage to face life with all its odds and to enjoy it to the full. Please go on, your objective is to get maximum happiness and you are getting it.

S. Yes, certainly I am.

Next Session

S. I have written a poem.

C. That is real progress, real achievement. Please let me see it.

S. Here it is:

Sensible Friend

Like attracts like
and Friendship strikes,
Sweetness prevails
As it blooms and sails.

But alas! expectation soars
The devil appears and roars
The lovely flower of friendship withers.
Leaving you in tatters.

It makes you wonder
Why did I blunder
You realise your mistake
And shudder at your fate.

But the story may not end
If you have a sensible friend,
Who helps you mend the broken chain
Friendship is cherished again

One learns a lesson
Never to lose a friend again!

C. That is wonderful, Sweta. Now you have become a poet, a poet of love and friendship. I am sure this little bud will soon bloom into a beautiful flower and spread its fragrance all round.

S. Thank you. Have you been able to get on to the internet?

C. No, I don't know yet how to reach the web site, but I have read the print-outs you gave me about the meaning of love.

S. Today I have got a very good poem; I have taken a print-out and shall give it to you.

C. Please. And then you act as my medium and go on passing print-outs to me. Anyway how is your love affair going with your internet boyfriend?

S. Oh, it is fine! It is so exhilarating that I forget everything and become really happy.

C. So now it has become your meditation, continue getting this blissful happiness.

S. I am having a perfect holiday and I do not want it to be spoiled. Thank you for bringing all this happiness into my life.

Next Session

S. He has come back from Calcutta.

C. How is he?

S. There is very little change. But now he does not rush out of the room in the night for a drink. He was also become a little milder, maybe because of my attitude of 'no concern'. I have begun just to disregard his presence as a husband. For me he is just an individual in the family. My parents had come for a short while, they also suggested that I should treat him just like this.

C. What about his attitude towards the children?

S. He loves the children, and I used that concern of his for getting back a small portion of the money I gave him for purchasing the house in Calcutta. I told him I have no liquid cash, and I needed it for an emergency and education of the children. He is not prepared to return the balance.

C. That I had told you even earlier.

S. He says he would go back to Calcutta after the repairs in the house are completed. I wish he might not return and stay in Calcutta.

C. What about the Malaysian woman?

S. I do not now let her enter my mind, so far I am concerned she is a non-entity. He tried a few times to phone her in my presence so that I might get a feel of her existence and presence. I resisted and told him not to do it, and my strict attitude has worked.

C. How are your Internet friends.

S. Oh, fine! Now I chat with a few of them and do not stick to only one.

C. To avoid involvement?

S. Yes, that gentleman from Egypt had really become too emotional and fell deeply in love with me. So I gave up, I want just fun and entertainment and nothing more.

C. You need diversion. You need someone you may feel concerned about, someone you may care for, someone who may care for you.

S. I think you are right, it is so relaxing and comforting to talk about one's emotions, feelings and problems to someone who is ready and willing to listen and feel concerned about you.

C. Your face shows a sort of glow of contentment fulfilment.

S. I look contented probably because now I suffer from no tension and always maintain my cool. I no more feel any guilt. I feel neither any guilt nor shame in chatting with friends on the Internet in the presence of my husband.

C. So you have conquered fear, your worst enemy. Fear is responsible for most of human tensions. Once you conquer fear, there will remain nothing to stop you from getting peace of mind and blissful serenity. Your friends on the internet have filled the vacancy that was created by your husband's retreat and unfriendly behaviour. Now you are again having the feeling of fullness you were missing.

Is it not a case of paradise lost and paradise regained?

S. He has agreed to sign the divorce papers. However, he goes on vexing me day and night. He has purchased a lap-top computer and is always trying to come to the chat site I am in and complains I am talking to wrong persons. I have told him it is none of his business, but that has made no difference. Now he has gone to Calcutta, and from there he goes on making calls only to psy if I am at home or not, or if I am chatting on the line.

C. It must be very annoying?

S. It disturbs my peace of mind and I get irritated in spite of my determination to keep calm. Even during the night he rings and I wake up, and when I sleep again he rings again. I am feeling disgusted and also helpless.

C. It seems he is trying to make pin-pricks with the intention of breaking your nerves. Probably, he thinks by this method he can bring you down on your knees, and make you give up your attempt to get divorce and agree to live as a subjugated wife.

S. I also think so, but I do not take a stiff line as I do not desire unpleasantness. I try to avoid distressing confrontation.

C. You have to strike a balance between the two situations: suffering the agony of unwanted interference with your life and your inherent goodness which does not permit hurting the feelings of others.

S. The difficulty with me is that my temperament and my upbringing do not let me take a stiff attitude. I cannot think of hurting him even if he does not behave in the manner he should.

C. This is a very noble thought, it shows the magnanimity of your heart. It is probably also the reason why you are able to maintain your calm in the midst of all turbulence.

S. A good news. I have got an appointment as a teacher, I am expected to join after a week. So now I can feel more independent and take a more stiff attitude.

C. It will make your life more enjoyable as you will get not only diversion but also adult company.

S. That will release some of my tension.

C. Of course, it will. Sweta, today looking at you I see a double picture of yours. Beneath your smiles I see a stream of tears. You look rather sad at heart.

S. I am. I try to keep up my composure, but then comes his call and I get agitated, irritated, worked-up, and finally feel dejected and sad. My smile becomes artificial, and my desire to get independence becomes more acute.

Finally, Sweta succeeded in getting a decree of divorce.

ARUNA

Forget suicide. Death does not depend on your timings. You can neither lengthen nor shorten life's span, you cannot postpone or advance the time of death's arrival. When death comes, welcome it, but do not run after it, you cannot catch it

A young smart woman of twenty-six, with a face that shows desperation, dejection, gloom, and fear of failure.

Her father died many years back, mother is suffering from cardiac problems. She has three brothers and five sisters and barring a sister and a brother all are married. One brother lives abroad and he supports the family consisting of the mother and the unmarried ones.

Aruna is the worst of the lot as she has no source of income. She has done M.A in Political Science. She lacks self-confidence, and the level of her self-esteem is very low.

C. Come on Aruna, let us talk.

A. It is only here, before you, that I feel I can talk openly and without any constraint. Everyone thinks and tells me that I am not fit to undertake any responsible job. That makes me lose all courage and confidence. I feel defeated, disappointed and consider myself an all-round failure. I feel I am worthless. I do not want to live at all.

C. Then why are you living?

A. I did attempt suicide twice, but failed.

C. Try some better method. Anyway, did you ever have a love affair?

A. Yes, but now I have no friends. What to say of boyfriends, I do not have even a girl friend.

C. Tell me something about your love affair.

A. I had a boyfriend, we had a pleasant romance, but then he ditched me. I still do not know why, he always praised me and promised ever-lasting love but then suddenly backed out.

C. Any other?

A. Yes, one more. While the boy was having an affair with me, I found there was another girl in his life. She was more beautiful and of fair complexion, while my colour is dark. I loved the man and hence thought of coming out of his life so that he might get the more attractive girl.

C. You are of a sacrificing nature and that seems to be hindering your ultimate success.

Now all these incidents have become matters of history. You treat them as dreams that came in your life, gave you pleasure and pain and disappeared. It is wrong to live in the past. Look forward with hope, may be you are destined to have a better partner in life. Why do you feel hopeless? There is no reason for you to think that your life is over, you have a charming face, a healthy body, and colour of the skin really does not matter.

A. It does matter in the matrimonial market, I have no one who can take the initiative of finding a husband for me. My mother remains ill and none else cares. It is very difficult for a young girl like me to search a husband. The world is full of men who win your confidence, make you trust them, then exploit your youth, have romance and walk out without marrying you. I went to a marriage bureau and the woman running the bureau introduced me to a divorcee. I do not want to marry a divorcee.

C. Yes, you are right but you should not worry about it. Worry does not help. Just wait, maybe once you begin to earn, you get a good offer. Do not lose heart, think positive with hope of success.

Do you believe in luck, fate and God?

A. I used to believe in God and used to do regular puja, but I found God does not help people like me. So I have almost lost faith in God, but still I cannot take the risk of giving Him up, maybe He exists.

Of course, I believe in fate and luck. Circumstances have forced me to believe in fate; but I see no reason why God should write such a fate for me.

C. Why do you think like this, don't you see you are one of a million in India who has the good fortune of having higher education and getting a master's degree? You are lucky to have a brother who supports your family. Of course, you need an employment to feel independent and gain confidence and higher self-esteem. Why not think of some self-employing job? You can give tuition to children, it is very paying and you can make good money even while remaining in your own house. Which grade students, you think can you coach?

A. I can teach students upto class VII.

C. Then you try this, explore the possibility.

Second Session

A. I am very upset the boy with whom I was having an affair has married the other girl. I am now all alone with no boyfriend.

C. You had neither given him the offer to marry nor made any real advance in that direction, why should you feel sorry if he has married another girl? How far had your affair gone?

A. We used to have friendly meeting. I don't know if we were in real love. We never had physical contact, but in my heart I wished he may become mine.

C. Now it is time to forget him. He has already married another girl. There is no use crying over spilled milk. Maybe he was not made for you. If he could select another girl, then he was not a person who could have given you the happiness you would have desired to get as a wife. Everything that happens is always for good. Maybe there is someone still in hiding who will make a good husband and give you the happiness you long for.

Aruna, I think your basic problem is that of lack of physical and financial security. A husband is, of course, the best choice for providing all-round security. A good employment may also be a good option. You should try to find both a husband and an employment and don't be very fastidious.

A. I am trying my best, but see no ray of hope.

C. Don't get disheartened. Keep up hope and go on trying.

A. That is exactly what I am doing.

C. No, not exactly so. You are suffering too badly from the fear of failure and that dislodges your confidence, and weakens your efforts. This fear seems to be baseless because you are still very young, attractive and well-educated, there is no reason why you will not, sooner or later, find a loving husband and a remunerative job. So go ahead without letting fear affect your self-confidence.

A. I shall make renewed effort with greater hope and confidence.

C. Yes, that is the right spirit. go ahead.

Third Session

A. I have started taking tuition, feel a little happier.

C. That is very good.

A. But still no lover no boyfriend and no husband !

C. Oh, don't worry! Wait a little longer. Try Internet, you may find someone.

A. That is a good idea, I shall work on it.

C. Yes, go ahead with hope and confidence. Keep interested in life. It is important to remember that life is a continuing journey and the road is full of hurdles. Sometimes one walks on the soft green grass with a loving companion, and sometimes alone on the sands of a desert. Very often, one sees an oasis, but finds it was only a mirage. But sooner or later the desert always ends and the oasis comes as a reality. You should always go ahead with hope of a brighter future; the darkness of night is never permanent, the dawn of happiness will also come to illumine your life, just have patience and wait for your Prince Charming.

A. But how long ? How long can I wait for my Prince Charming to come!

C. Have you read the fairing tale Sleeping Beauty? Princess Aurora there waited and waited for years. There must be some good fairy watching you too, and will send to you your Prince Charming. Don't be impatient. You are only twenty-six, give your fairy a little more time. She sent to you two Princes, but they were not the right ones, so she must be waiting to find a right Prince for you. Just give her some more time. Live with cheer and joy because no Prince likes a sad, sorrowful or dejected girl.

A. (Laughs) Okay. I shall live happily till my Prince Charming arrives and continue to live happily ever after.

I am still very disappointed but am feeling better. I have got two tuitions but that is not enough. I have to earn more to get going.

C. I know, but be happy that you have made a start. A plant always takes time to grow.

A. But my plant is growing in slow motion, and the fruits are not yet to be seen.

Well there is a good news. I was wrongly informed that my boyfriend had married some other girl.

C. Then proceed.

A. No, it is useless. I once phoned him but his response was not of love, he did not even behave courteously, but rudely, put down the receiver.

C. Doesn't matter. Try again, he may not have been in good mood when you phoned. Please do not let him feel that you are desperate, otherwise you will not get a good response. Let him develop more attraction for you. Do not give up.

A. I shall try. I am very upset. Whatever I do goes wrong, even for doing good I get condemnation and abuses.

C. Why, what has happened?

A. In response to my request, the matrimonial bureau offered me the proposal of a man thirty-eight years old. He was too old for me, so I informed my elder sister, who is thirty-two to meet him. Then my brother-in-law and my unmarried sister met him, but things did not materialise. My sister, as usual, talked to my mother and she was angry. Both of them accused me of being a bad sort of girl who goes about places and meets undesirable persons. No one helps, but everyone is ready to accuse me, when I am doing no wrong except trying to find a husband for myself.

C. Don't get upset, probably that man was not a good man.

A. But why should everyone accuse me and abuse me, even when I try to do something to help them? My mother is always having some grievance against me and is always cross with me. There is none in the world to speak a kind word to me, to help me solve my problems. I wish to put an end to all this, I wish to commit suicide.

B. You have already attempted twice.

A. Yes, I am not getting potassium cyanide, and I do not wish to fail again.

C. Forget suicide. Death does not depend on your timings. You can neither lengthen nor shorten life's span, you cannot postpone or advance the time of death's arrival. When death comes welcome it, but do not run after it, you cannot catch it. Instead of chasing death, enjoy living, be happy and make merry while you are alive. If you will continue to think of death, you will not be able to live away from the shadow of death. So give up the idea of suicide, and learn to live.

A. I want to live and not die, but I want to live like other girls with a loving husband and a peaceful home.

C. You are right, however it would be better if you will first stand on your own feet. Remember the saying,: marry in haste and repent at leisure. Once you are able to earn a living, you will get good offers of marriage.

A. I have not phoned that boy a second time.

C. You have done well, your cultural background is entirely different from his and then he is not responding favourably, so it is better you give him up. It will be best for you to forget marriage till you get a good job.

A. I have been called for an interview tomorrow for the post of a teacher in a school, I am feeling very nervous. I was very upset and despondent, however, after talking to you I feel I am normal,my depression seems to be melting away. I am still feeling so bad about the behaviour of my sister and mother that I feel I shall blunder in the interview.

C. Forget it all, otherwise you will not be able to do well in tomorrow's interview. Feel happy, your confrontation with your mother is now over. Do not try to re-live the past, come out of it and live in the present. Prepare yourself for tomorrow's interview. Do not go there with a grim face or a broken heart. Develop courage and confidence and show it on your face. Laugh and be happy. Come on, give a laugh Aruna.

A. (Laughs) Thank you for giving me a new life of hope and confidence.

C. Be a good actor, and play your role successfully during the interview tomorrow.

A. Thank you. I will do my best.

Next Session

A. I am feeling better.

C. Why?

A. Accepting your suggestion. I have given up the search for a husband.

C. That has taken a load off your head. It is always better to throw away things that give headache, just wait for the opportune moment.

A. My mother and sister have still not become quite reconciled, and always view my activities with suspicion, although there is no reason for that.

C. Slowly they will understand that you were only going out to matrimonial bureau because you were in search of a proper match and for no other purpose. Now that you have given up that search, they will come round and begin to feel you are a well behaved girl.

A. They did not let me have the teacher's job because the salary was not high enough.

C. How much did they offer?

A. Two thousand two hundred.

C. Something was better than nothing, that would have removed your feeling of worthlessness, and restored your self-esteem.

A. I did not refuse but my mother and sister phoned that I could not join on this salary.

C. Probably they want you to stay at home.

A. Maybe, however I do not want imprisonment. I want to live in the open world with an independent income of my own.

C. That is right, take courage and join the teacher's job in any school, at any salary. It will give you experience and exposure, and would help you in taking a jump on to a better job. Then your income from tutorials is there to supplement it.

A. I shall surely take-up a job. I think that is a pre-requisite for my happiness.

C. Certainly. But don't forget that all these are necessary supplement to make you have an enjoyable life. You must realise that life is a stream and you a swimmer, go on swimming and never think of quitting. Be sure that life holds for you happiness in store and one day you will find your fairy coming to bestow on you all the happiness you are dreaming of. So let the thought of suicide no more enter your mind.

A. Yes, I have decided to live on, and face the world with courage and confidence. I am no longer thinking of quitting the arena.

C. Good, Aruna.

GUILT SHAME AND FEAR

— Subjective awareness
— Victims of rape and violence
— Rehabilitation

2
Guilt Shame and Fear

"He that knows no guilt can know no fear".
(*Phillip Massinger*)

Guilt and shame are the cancers of human consciousness; they make the mind suffer agonising pain, and also cause terrifying fear. Fear as a matter of fact, is an unfailing, unavoidable, and inescapable fall-out of the feeling of guilt and shame. That in turn creates panic and makes fight against the feeling of guilt more difficult, and lets it take a very heavy toll of human happiness. Its continuance makes the individual sink deep down into the abyss of despair.

Guilt is the subjective awareness of having violated some personal, familial, societal. and even religious norm, which may be real or imaginary. Guilt involves the feeling of culpability, or moral responsibility for some conduct contrary to the norms of good behaviour. In every case it is non-objective in character and depends on the individual's personal concept of norms of behaviour.

The feeling of guilt generates symptoms of 'self-blaming', with focus on self-accusation and self-deprecation, which automatically gives rise to the feeling of shame and helplessness.

The feeling of guilt develops in multitude of situations:

(*i*) when there is a failure to achieve what one desires, plans, or promises to achieve;

(*ii*) when there is a failure to prevent the happening of something one desires, plans, or promises to prevent;

(*iii*) when one does something which he/she desires, plans, or promises not to do;

(*iv*) when one omits to do something one desires, plans, or promises to do.

In every one of these contingencies the desired or undesired happening is regarded by the person concerned as socially or morally adorable or condemnable. It is this special character and feature of the event that makes the person condemn himself/herself for having failed to accomplish or to prevent its happening.

Self-condemnation is the genesis of the feeling of guilt and shame. Even events which do not have very serious social or ethical consequences may create the feeling of guilt and shame depending on the accompanying circumstances and the personality of the individual.

The fear of condemnation by others aggravates the feelings of guilt and shame. Although this fear very often turns out to be baseless, it succeeds in causing agony much greater than might be caused by the feared condemnation itself. Fear of being censured is ten thousand times more terrifying than censure itself, and gives rise to traumatic feeling of guilt and shame.

Worst kind of guilt and shame grip consciousness when a woman suffers sexual assault. Young women are excessively vulnerable and more than often suffer its grave and devastating consequences.

"I have never been free of the fear of rape", says Susan Griffin:

There is hardly a woman who has not suffered a "mini-rape" in her life, or who is not under the risk of being actually raped. Diana Herman thinks a woman suffers `mini-rape' when she receives an obscene phone call, or a pinch in the crowded bus, the wolf-whistle from a person walking on the road, or a stare of a man looking at her bust with lustful eyes when she goes shopping...

Whatever may be the nature of rape, the woman suffers psychological trauma. The trauma of mini-rape may not be as severe as that of actual rape, but she does suffer the feeling of guilt and shame and injury to her psyche. Even when a woman escapes rape, she gets most of the traumatic sufferings that result from actual rape.

The woman who is raped gets a severe psychological shock, she develops a false feeling of guilt and shame and suffers loss of self-esteem and begins to believe she is a depraved woman entitled to no respect, reverence, honour or dignity. A rape victim, immediately after rape passes through a critical period, a period of serious crisis. Invariably, the woman suffers life-and-death type of crisis, her entire emotional framework gets shaken and broken, and she loses her self-esteem and self-confidence. She becomes either highly excited, agitated and furious or becomes totally benumbed and silent.

Rape, and similar offences against a person has a peculiar reaction, it makes the victim brand herself as guilty, condemn herself as blameworthy and feel the worst kind of shame and humiliation. She begins to consider herself as the tormentor, and forgets that she is the victim entitled to love and support of everyone.

The feeling of guilt is, however, not confined to the person who is assaulted, but sometimes gets developed even in the person who makes the assault. In various situations the aggressor himself/herself becomes the victim of his/her own assault and suffers the agony of guilt. This is because 'guilt' is a subjective awareness of violating a social or moral behavioural norm.

In common parlance, a victim is one against whom an assault is actually made. Psychologically considered, even the aggressor is a victim of the misdemeanour. Victims can be divided into three categories. In the first category come those who suffer physical or 'psychic injury as a direct consequence of the act of some other person. Speaking more widely, even a surgical operation performed by a doctor may cause psychic trauma, and place the patient into the category of an emotional victim. Similar may be the case of persons who suffer deformity and disfigurement by injury in an accident. In the second category come those who make the assault and cause injury to someone else and make them suffer trauma. Third category of victims include persons who are deeply concerned with the health and happiness of victims of the first two categories. Persons falling in the first category may be called the 'Mauled victims', those coming in the second the 'Guilt victims', and those of third category, the 'Shadow victims'.

We are concerned here only with psychic injury suffered by a victim which makes him/her feel guilt and shame.

Lady Macbeth was a Guilt victim. After the murder, she could neither sleep nor live in peace. She cried: "What, will these hands never be clean?" And, when Macbeth asked the Doctor about her health he replied: "Not so sick, my Lord. As she is troubled with thick-coming fancies, that keep her from her rest". And in desperation Macbeth entreated:

"Cure her of that:
Canst thou not minister to a mind diseas'd;
Pluck from the memory a rooted sorrow;
Raze out the written troubles of the brain;
And with some sweet oblivious antidote
Cleanse the stuff'd bosom of that perilous stuff
Which weighs upon the heart?"

Both Macbeth and Lady Macbeth became victims of their own deeds. They too suffered the agonising consequences of guilt and shame. They too needed psychic rehabilitation, the uprooting of the cause, the erasing of its consequences, and calming down of their troubled psyche.

Leaving Macbeth aside, the common human being of today who commits a heinous crime or even a crime of lesser degree, or makes an assault causing personal injury to some individual, also becomes a victim and suffers trauma. His inner conscience is troubled by a feeling of guilt. Her tries to overcome it by a process of rationalisation; he tries to find a justification for his act which the society condemns. There is a revolt in his sub-conscious and the conscious mind, and that creates in him tension and stress. He feels shame and becomes unhappy. Even though he may proclaim he is happy, his mind is tormented by the feeling of guilt and shame. Many a time he tries to drown the feeling in the artificial psychic pond of intoxicating liquors and drugs with false pretensions of merry-making.

The remedy lies not in fake self-deception but in undertaking some sort of penance. The mechanism of conscious or subconscious penitence helps in releasing the tension. Penance requires acceptance of guilt and making of confession to someone whom he values and trusts, or to his own consciousness. He needs to unburden his conscience. He has got to atone for the wrong which he committed and which continues to weigh upon his heart. The feeling of guilt, deeply rooted in his sub-conscious and the conscious mind cannot leave him till it is plucked from his memory.

Punishment is another way of washing away the feeling of guilt and cleansing the conscience. Punishment very often acts as an antidote to the curse of guilt, it reduces the pressure of the feeling of guilt and acts as an eraser to 'raze out the written troubles of the brain'. So long the guilt remains unatoned, 'the mind' remains in the state of turbulence. The vision of the sufferings of the offended person, the mauled victim, continues to haunt the guilty mind, and makes it suffer the consequences of the psychological rebound action. The punishment may make him feel liberated.

Much graver, of course, is the agony and suffering in the consciousness of the mauled, the real victim of assault. In most cases it is a woman who is the mauled victim. Amongst all crimes and assaults against women rape is the worst. She suffers much greater anguish, misery, pain, and torment than Lady Macbeth or her like ever did. Her psyche is not only injured but shattered, her emotions are mauled, her honour is compromised. She needs sustained effort for removing her feeling of guilt and shame. In most cases one is reminded of Cleopatra when she said:

"................., and I have nothing
Of woman in me: now from head to foot
I am marble-constant; now the fleeting moon
No planet is of mine."

In many cases, the woman gets so stunned and benumbed by the feeling of humiliation that she is unable to speak. She becomes dumb. That creates a very tough situation as the feeling of guilt prevents her from opening up.

Trauma caused by rape, and for that matter, by any violent crime against a person, creates a complicated and multi-dimensional emotional upheaval. All assaults, physical or psychic, cause some kind of post traumatic stress disorder (PTSD). Generally, PTSD symptoms are anxiety, depression and feeling of guilt, shame and fear. The result of PTSD is that the person loses self-confidence, develops low self-esteem and lack of assertiveness. PTSD, resulting from rape or murderous assault or excessive emotional pressure creates multifarious fears that often cause crying spells, nervous breakdowns, sleeplessness, eating disorders and withdrawal from social interaction. These symptoms interact and have a chain reaction giving support to each other. The chain reaction continues unless psychological hammer is applied to break the chain.

Sexual dysfunctioning is another symptom generated by the feeling of guilt and shame attached to forced sex. The victim begins to regard herself as responsible for the acts of her own tormentor and becomes dispirited and suffers from symptoms of withdrawal.

In many cases of personal assault, the victim takes on blame herself, thinking she could have prevented the incident if she had acted more prudently. Such a feeling developed by retrospective introspection makes her believe that she herself is the offender and that makes her assume the role of Lady Macbeth. She begins to worry if her hands will ever be clean. As a result, she goes into a peculiar type of depression—the depression of helplessness. This is nothing peculiar with women, similar feelings can develop in a man if he is physically assaulted.

Even in a case of domestic violence, the woman suffers from the feeling of shame in spite of her knowing she was not guilty. Feeling of shame can arise even in cases of uncontrolled emotional stress. The severity of PTSD wiresponds to the emotional impact the offensive act had on the victim. That in turn, depends on the emotional health and the state of consciousness of the victim at the time of assault and the fear that was developed in her by the threat and dread which the victim was forced into by the vandal. The nature and extent of fear depends also on the age of the victim and the gravity of helplessness in which she was plunged.

There are various other factors, personal and circumstantial, on which the intensity of PTSD depends. But in all cases it has a direct correlation to the nature, type and intensity of the fear the victim experiences perior to and during the assault, and the character of the trauma that follows the assault.

The fear of recurrence of the assault and the threat of further torture held out by the criminal or his associates to the victim to force her keep her mouth shut, very often unnerves the mauled victim and puts her into horrifying agony of silence. These situations retard the process of overcoming the damage done by the assault, and prolong the pangs of trauma. The fear and threat of a repeat assault forces the victim to keep the poison inside when it should be spilled out to get relief.

"Sorrow concealed, like an oven stopp'd
Doth burn the heart to cinders where it is."
(Titus Andronicus, Act II, Scene III)

The experience of the event gets into the memory of the victim and remains lodged in the subconscious and the conscious mind for a long time. Whenever the memory gets an opportunity, it re-enacts the incident, causing revival of the traumatic experience. However, it goes on decreasing with the instinctual and reflex action of the victim to overcome the trauma. The practice of coping strategies makes the memory of the incident wither away more quickly and finally, to become almost non-existent.

The third category of victims, the shadow victims, consists of the near and dear ones of the 'mauled' as well as the guilt victim. It might also include those who consider themselves responsible for the conduct of guilt victims, and the protection of the mauled victims. Their suffering is the echo of the real victim's sufferings. For instance, when a person is killed or injured or otherwise assaulted, her children, parents and other near and dear ones suffer a shock. The shock is really the echo of the mauled victim's trauma but, at the same time, is also independent of the shock suffered by the mauled victim. Their emotions are afflicted, their sense of justice is hurt, their love for the victim makes them identify themselves with the mauled victim, and they suffer the same kind of agony and trauma as does the mauled victim.

Sometimes the victim feels she can get relief and reduce her feeling of guilt and shame through revenge. But revenge being a negative emotion, cannot effectively heal the wound, it can only camouflage the reality of the suffering. However, in some situations it does act like a healing balm by satisfying the victim's sense of justice.

All kinds of assault create turmoil and turbulence in the mind of the victim, and the quietening of this storm involves essentially a process that brings maximum peace, courage, hope and confidence, and gives her freedom from fear. And, this can best be achieved by the victim's accepting as true the words of Oberon in *A Midsummer Night's Dream*: Act IV, Scene I.

> "And think no more of this night's accidents
> But as the fierce vexation of a dream".

Physical assault is, however, not the only thing that generates the feeling of guilt and shame. It may arise in different situations and in innumerable ways.

The feeling of guilt can develop in the consciousness of a person even when there is a psychological or emotional attack. Acute psychological affliction creates more quickly and effectively the feeling of shame and also of guilt than does physical assault. Even in intimate relationships situations arise when one is made to suffer humiliation and feel ashamed, as when a woman is proclaimed responsible for somebody else's misery of unhappiness. The creation of the subjective belief that one has acted against some moral or societal norm of interpersonal behaviour is sufficient to make a person feel guilt and shame. This unwanted and emotionally disturbing feeling can arise even though it may be based on a wholly erroneous picture of the entire situation. At times, one is made to suffer inferiority complex through systematic nagging and fault finding. This makes the mauled victim feel a peculiar type of suppressed guilt and a lot of unexpressed shame. The guilt victim, on the other hand, feels victorious, but remains subconsciously unhappy, and sometimes also ashamed of having done a wrong to someone innocent. The mauled victim feels helpless in the situation and makes all effort to keep her agony concealed in order to preserve her honour and dignity.

It is not uncommon for a guilty person to transfer his own guilt to an innocent person, and thus to feel free of the effect and consequences of his own wrong-doings. In such a case the person to whom the guilt is transferred suffers all the painful consequences thereof for no fault of one's own. This transference becomes easy when the innocent person mistakenly thinks that she is responsible for the partner's blameworthy behaviour. In this way she herself becomes the guilt victim and suffers the agony for the conduct of someone else.

The personality make-up of a person is a significant factor in the generation of the feeling of guilt and shame. Some people who are able to analyse, understand and evaluate the events more rationally succeed in avoiding the trauma, while others, who are emotional and sensitive by nature become an easy prey to the feeling of guilt and shame. It all depends on an individual's capacity to face and resolutely confront awkward and embarrassing situations and emotional upheavals, which in turn is itself conditioned by the person's own attitude towards life.

Much depends on the person's placing emphasis on living in the present or making the past control one's life. In order to cope with such situations, it is necessary to forget the past and accept the reality of the present, and to recognise that the feelings of guilt and shame arise only out of something which has become a thing of the past. "Guilt and sin are only a fear of the past". (Charles P.Curtis) Guilt and shame have no reality when considered in the context of the present, they are nothing but products of memory, mythical and forgettable. Love, compassion, and a bit of understanding, coupled with a dose of self-confidence and a higher sense of self-esteem provide a good antidote to clear the mind of the feelings of guilt, shame, and fear.

POOJA

The psychic injury has the tendency to take different forms; it may develop fears and create various types of tensions. In the memory the picture of the traumatic event goes on repeating itself. It creates fears of recurrence, of loss of love of near and dear ones, and of dignity and honour in social life. The feeling of being a depraved person has devaluing effect on the victim's entire personality. She begins to feel she is no longer as she was, and is not similar and equal to everyone else in her social and family circles.

First Session

History

Pooja was a student of B.A. Four years have lapsed since she dropped out.

Young girl - Average looking - Full of fear and tension.

Suffers from obsessive compulsions, washes her hands a hundred times, takes long baths, uses a lot of Lux soap and Pepsodent toothpaste. Always has a feeling of uncleanliness, goes to latrine only after it is cleaned by her father. Does not participate in doing domestic chores.

Has been treated in hospitals and by private psychiatrists—no success.

Has been beaten several times by her parents for her abnormal behaviour, particularly for taking long baths and washing hands very frequently.

Diagnostic Scan

Four years back while she was standing in a queue at a bus stand, an elderly man (75) posing to be a god-man (Tantrik) with power to cure all illnesses, approached her and inquired if she was suffering from any illness. Pooja told him that she was suffering from constipation. He invited her to his house for therapy. She along with her elder brother went to his house. He took her into a room and asked her to bare herself. She took off all her clothes except panties and bra. (subsequently it came out that she had put off her bra too).

The man fondled Pooja's whole body. He did everything short of rape.

She was asked to come again which she did. The whole thing was repeated. Even then she did not realise that she was being used by the man for his self-indulgence and he was not giving her any treatment. Finally, after four meetings, she stopped going.

These incidents have left a permanent scar on the psyche of Pooja. It has produced a condition similar to the one caused by rape. The trauma at the time of the incident was not serious but PTSD (post trauma syndrome disorder) has been very serious. It has left her shattered. She has developed the feeling of shame, guilt, and fear. She feels her whole body has been defiled. She tries to clean it by repeated soap washings and baths, but fails to get over the feeling of defilement.

This had also meant her dropping out from the college for four years; which too has added to her feeling of inferiority; she is unable to face her relatives and friends. It has meant loss of confidence and engendered fear of the future. She is still unmarried and her parents have begun to believe her marriage may not be possible, which intensifies her agony.

She has developed obsessive compulsions and needs psychic rehabilitation. She fears that her body defiled by the man will never be clean again. She thinks she has been permanently defiled, and will ever remain an outcast and suffer ostracism all her life. What is needed is to unburden her mind of the feeling of shame and guilt.

Counselling

She has been counselled to make her realise that she was innocent and was a victim of crime and confidence trick.

C. You have not committed any wrong for which you should feel sorry or repentant. You were a victim and need a clearer understanding of the situation for the healing of your wounds. It was because you were made to believe, through the confidence trick, that you were receiving therapy for your constipation, so you succumbed to his nefarious designs; therefore you cannot be deemed guilty of any wrong act. You should realise that you have been a victim of a confidence trick, of fraud and unwanted molestation. You should shed your feelings of guilt and shame because you have done nothing wrong. You do not need cleaning of your hands or body with soap and water. The dirt lies inside your consciousness and not on your skin. Regard the entire episode to be just a dream and forget it.

Nothing has happened to your body, it remains as pure and innocent as it was. Baring of body before a man and even its being touched does not defile it. Your body has not in any way been defiled. It has not been soiled and remains as clean as ever, it requires no washing In any case, you are not what you were four years back, your skin has totally changed by now in four years, your present skin is completely new and untouched by the man. You should forget the past.

She has started feeling better, her looks have changed, and no longer show apparent signs of guilt. She is relaxed and has begun to hope she will be able to get over the trauma and the PTSD.

Pooja, please remember that 'time' by itself is not a healer of psychic wounds. The psychic injury caused by an assault on the honour, dignity, chastity and purity of a woman through molestation of her body, cannot disappear just by passage of time. The emotional injury, the psychic wound continues to stay in the victim's consciousness unless removed by some kind of therapy.

The psychic injury has the tendency to take different forms; it may develop fears and create various types of tensions. In memory the picture of the traumatic event goes on repeating itself. It creates fears of recurrence, of loss of love of near and dear ones, and of dignity and honour in social life. The feeling of being a depraved person has devaluing effect on the victim's entire personality. She begins to feel, she is no longer as she was, and is not similar and equal to everyone else in her social and family circles. Much of it depends on and varies according to the victim's cultural background and the reaction of her immediate associates. Pooja, you follow the instructions and soon your troubles will go, and you will again become normal.

Second Session

Pooja says that the memory of the incident still troubles her and she still goes on washing her hands a number of times and taking long baths. She cannot take bath everyday for want of sufficient water and availability of vacant bathroom. She no longer, however, uses the kitchen as a bathroom as she used to do earlier. She continues to wash her clothes with soap and does not use the washing machine. In the process they get faded and damaged.

Pooja's father has been advised to adopt a more positive and sympathetic attitude towards her and try to accept her as she is. That will give her the much needed support to become normal. He should encourage other members of the family to adopt a similar attitude. Pooja feels her parents are helpful but her brothers are not; they are fed up with her behaviour.

Pooja promises she will try her best to improve; she says she makes the effort but fails.

Counselling

Pooja was made to listen to the tape on hypno-sleep, she slipped into hypno-sleep. She was made to look back into the past and speak out.

C. Please recall the incident in as much detail as you can. She narrated the incident now more elaborately. She said she was taken into a room in the house, it was full of pictures of different gods, the man posed to be a *Tantrik* and went muttering mantras. She was hypnotised so that she felt unable to resist his advances. She accepted his statement that she had been possessed by evil spirits and will be freed of all evils that were responsible for her ill-health (constipation).

He forcibly bared her body, taking away all the clothes except her panty, he removed even her bra. He was not loving or caressing her but pressing and pawing her breasts and all parts of her body. She was in pain. He used his mouth and hand to molest her. She was forced to drink what the man said was cow's urine. Her brother was sent out to bring a bit of earth from a road crossing and that was put under her feet. It was veritable torture. Her brother was not admitted into the room.

She was then allowed to go and directed to return after two days. She did not inform her mother and went again. This time again, the drama of torture and molestation was repeated.

She was asked to come again. This time she informed her mother who asked her not to go, but Pooja was so infatuated that she did go again. This time he intended to go further, but on being told that she was having menses, he let her off and asked her to go back and come later. Pooja says her menses saved her, otherwise she would have been actually raped this time.

Third Session

She was again put under hypno-sleep. While she was still in hypno-sleep, suggestions were given to make her believe that she was still as pure and chaste as ever. You were saved from being defiled by your own body function. Your body is as virgin as it was. Dont's you think so?

P. I can of course, see nothing wrong with my body, but my mind is restless all the same.

On phone a young woman was asked to tell Pooja her own story in which she said she was a victim like Pooja. She spoke; "I had suffered more than you. I also got trauma and for many years suffered from obsessive compulsions of the same type as you are having. However, I got over the trauma and succeeded in bringing to an end the obsessive compulsions by seeing the whole thing in its true perspective. I could see that I was not guilty and my body was as clean and innocent as ever, there was no need to wash my hands or body or clothes. There was no stain of sin on my body which needed to be removed."

This phone had a good impact on Pooja, her hope of a cure got a boost. Positive inputs have made her believe at least for the time being that she is innocent and not guilty. She has been asked to maintain a daily activity and thought chart and try to reduce the time of bath and tooth-brushing by one minute per day. She now takes thirty minutes only to brush her teeth and clean her mouth, a significant reduction.

Fourth Session

Pooja brought the paper on which she had written an account of her daily activities and obsessive thoughts as she was directed The salient points appearing from her statement of daily routine of thoughts and activities are given below:

1. Daily routine of activities

(*a*) Teeth-brushing takes too long. Repeats the whole process of brush movement sixteen times. If someone interrupts, she start afresh.

(*b*) Washes the tea cup again before drinking tea from it.

(*c*) Washes her hands several times at a stretch and at intervals.

(*d*) Always fears her hands are not clean.

(*e*) If she does not get the opportunity to wash her hands or is interrupted by someone, she gets headache and a feeling of fear in her mind, and feels serious uneasiness in limbs and fear in general.

(*f*) Washes her clothes with soap, rubbing them repeatedly eight times and takes all precautions to have them washed clean. Dries her clothes separately and does not permit them to come in contact with other persons' clothes.

(*g*) Takes bath with Lux soap, applying the soap twenty times and uses lot of water kept in separate buckets. Does not take bath everyday like others in the family, bathes at intervals of three or four days.

(*h*) Sees T.V. from 3 to 5 p.m.

(*i*) Cooks evening food and washes the utensils.

2. Study

Believes she cannot grasp what she reads, or remember what she studies. Has lost faith in her capability to study feels she has deteriorated a lot, lacks confidence. and thinks she is comparatively inferior to others in studies.

3. Thoughts and feelings

(*a*) Sits alone in her room brooding about her plight. She imagines and feels she has become worthless, she has lost everything, everyone dislikes and hates her, thinks she is insane with no chance of becoming normal again, and that every member of the family has disowned her. She compares herself with others and feels inferior and becomes sad and dejected.

(*b*) She sees no hope for herself, is despondent and fears the future; she feels she is lonely; there is darkness all around her.

(*c*) She is always worried about why she has been condemned by God to a life of misery when she has done no wrong to anyone.

(*d*) She has lost all interest in life, is tired of living like this. Often she gets so depressed that she thinks of committing suicide. She sees no purpose in living, remains sitting alone, weeping and crying.

Pooja was again made to go into the first stage of hypn–sleep and was asked to describe her own role in the tragic episodes. This time she elaborated how she felt compelled to go to the designated house, where she was told by an old woman to get her treatment from the *tantrik*, otherwise she would go to hell. Next day she went again and suffered molestation.

P. I neither raised alarm, nor cried for help from persons in the house or from my brother who was in the other room. Even though I felt pain I did not scream. In a way, yes, I permitted things to go on.

When I came out I did not tell my brother or the friend who had accompanied me that my clothes were taken off, and I was molested. I did not tell them of kissing, fondling, pawing , etc. and the pain I suffered. Not only did I conceal the truth but told the lie that he had caressed my body by touching only the clothes.

I also did not disclose the truth to my mother and continued to lie about the real facts.

Next day again I went voluntarily, taking my brother along. I did not offer any resistance to the *tantrik's* offensive actions as I was under some sort of hypnotic spell, and his eyes were so terrifying that I allowed him without protest to fondle my body as he liked.

I cannot give any explanation for my abnormal behaviour of not shrieking at the painful mauling of my body. I did not resist my being alone in a closed room.

I continued going there for the same purpose, ignoring my mother's suggestion not to go, on the plea that I shall get cured of my chronic constipation.

It was only on the last occasion (maybe the fourth or fifth) that I escaped being raped because I was having menses. If I were not having menses I would have probably allowed sexual intercourse, but now I feel I had been saved by my menses.

The inferences which can be drawn from her revelations are:

(*i*) During the process of molestation she was getting sexual arousal. It is normal that when a young girl is fondled with sexual overtones, there will be arousal of sexual desire in her. She was, on the last day, it seems, desirous of having actual sex, but was disappointed. This again could have given rise to symptoms she has developed.

(*ii*) Sense of guilt for having participated without protest in the whole drama, not speaking the truth and telling lies about what happened, and the development of the sense of shame as a consequence of the same.

(*iii*) *Tantrik's* actions showed he was suffering from sex-perversion.

C. Pooja, what you are going through your unwanted activities is nothing but an attempt to undo what had actually happened during your meetings with the *tantrik*. The whole series of episodes has gone into your subconscious mind and has become a part of your consciousness. Because you cannot go back into the past and get the whole scene re-enacted and erased, your subconsciousness takes you back and presents before you an invisible picture, so that you might wipe off its ill-effect and cleanse your mind. You are obeying only the commands of your sub-conscious mind.

You are washing your entire body because the *tantrik* had touched it with his hands. Your subconscious mind makes you see an invisible picture of the whole scene and you do the same exercises that were done by the *tantrik* in a reverse manner so that you might get rid of their effect. You were kissed violently by him and that has led to your brushing the teeth and cleaning your mouth several times to wipe off the kiss. But at the same time, this reminds you of the feeling of his kiss; you should, therefore, stop all this because that constantly reminds you of the traumatic event and you continue to suffer the agony. You are re-enacting the scene, and at the same time trying to wipe off its effect; the two will stay or go together. So, stop trying to wipe off the memory of the incident.

It may be difficult for you to suddenly give it up, because it has unconsciously got linked to the non-fulfilment of your desire to get actual sex. Your desire was of utmost intensity, particularly because it was going to be your first experience of sex. You had already been surcharged with deep emotion and uncontrolled passion for sex, and that has left a very strong impact on your psyche.

If you were craving for sex, please accept the truth. That will bring relief to your mind and give you freedom from continuing agony.

P. No, I was not a consenting party, I was under the hypnotic spell of the *tantrik* and my role was only that of a controlled robot.

C. But why did you keep everything secret?

She accepts her guilt about concealing information from her brother, friend and mother. She admits that she did realise at the moment that what was happening was not right, the disclosure of which was almost certain to degrade her in the eyes of everyone.

P. I concealed everything lest they object and I maybe prevented from continuing my visits to the *tantrik*.

As a consequence after the entire epsode ended, you began to feel guilty, ashamed, and defiled. Your whole thought pattern got polluted and made you perform the cleaning rituals.

C. Pooja, the way the Tantrik acted establishes that he was suffering from a mental illness, sex perversion. He was acting under the influence of a mental disease. There is thus no reason to take the incident very seriously; it would be wise to forget it as being the act of a mad man.

Intensive counselling was given on the following :

(*a*) Pooja's case was not an exceptional one, but one of the many that occur every day. She should get over the feeling of shame and guilt by realising that it was a case where she became a victim in an event perpetrated by the perverted sex instinct of a mentally sick person.

(*b*) The clothes she was wearing on the fateful days have, by now, worn out and thrown away. The clothes she was now wearring have no association with the shameful incident and do not require special washing.

(*c*) Brushing of teeth for too long or washing hands too often, or taking bath with too much soap and water could cause more harm than good, and that it was all a consequence of and connected with item (*a*).

(*d*) Her washing of the cup in which tea is offered before drinking from it, was only because her sub-consious mind always revived her memory of the cup in which she was offered and made to drink something, which the *tantrik* had said was cow's urine. Her subconscious mind was trying to make her avoid it and drink tea after the cup cleaned of the urine. It was necessary to disassociate the *tantrik's* cup from the family cup.

Fifth Session

New line of counselling was adopted with the changed objective. Instead of attempting to support her plea of innocence, it was diverted to focus on her positive role in the episode. It was changed with a view to make her see the reality, and not to conceal and run away from the truth. If she was a willing party in the whole episode, then she should admit it. Self-deception and lying is never helpful. Only through this method could she get rid of her feeling of (hidden) guilt.

Finally Pooja spoke:

(*a*) I did have the feeling of enjoyment and arousal of sex during the time he had been fondling my body. He was doing everything that a husband would do in the process of love-making, and I did not protest either verbally or by resistance, or shrieking even though I felt some pain at times.

(*b*) I concealed everything from my mother, brother, and friend, I never told anyone that I was enjoying the whole thing.

(*c*) I repeatedly went to him of my own free will, probably because I was enjoying the whole thing and getting a pleasure I had never experienced before.

(*d*) Had I not been in menses I would have probably indulged in actual sex without protest. The question of being in menses came up only for sexual intercourse, it was not relevant for other acts of love - making.

(*e*) I was throughout an un-protesting participant in the whole episode and was going to him without any compulsion, I was going of my free will. It was only later that I felt I had done the wrong thing, something which is not done by good girls and had not been done by anybody else in my family.

Slowly and slowly, through prolonged counselling Pooja came to realise that it all happened in the normal, natural way.

C. You were eighteen and fully ready for sexual enjoyment as it is a normal function of the human body. It is the nature's call that makes one at this age and stage of growth, ready for sex, it is a natural urge in every girl and you were no exception. Once you were subjected to the process of love-making, it was natural for you to enjoy the advances. You did nothing wrong for which you should feel guilty.

P. I understand. I know that a large number of young girls of my age in the west and also here, have some experience of sex.

(Observation)

Pooja no longer sees any abnormality in the way she behaved, but feels it was bad as it is not deemed proper by the society.

C. But in the circumstances, you did not have much of a choice. You were a victim of circumstances. So there is no cause for you to feel guilty.

(Observation)

Her problem is that she has all along tried to conceal the truth by pretending innocence. She has been trying to conceal the truth (her voluntary participation and experience of pleasure and happiness she got during the encounters, and her desire to have actual sex). By putting on the veil of falsehood she could only deceive and befool herself. Her sub-conscious mind was making all effort through her obsessive compulsions to make her appear innocent according to established norms of morality. She has really been a victim of false and unnatural moral codes about young women's conduct.

She is conscious of the fact that in her mind there was a desire for actual sex, but it remained unfulfilled because of her menses (although she now fears that actual sex might have been more damaging). Her hidden desire might still be persisting.

Through the counselling she has begun to realise that by washing her body and clothes she was not washing away the defilement, if any, of her body and clothes, but she was doing so only (as a veil) to hide the truth about her being a willing party to the very deplorable and degrading episode, and that it will serve no purpose.

Sixth Session

Pooja is generally happy and relaxed. Her tension has almost disappeared. But she is still not able to get rid of her obsessive actions. She lacks faith and confidence in her capability to give up the habits. She is afraid of the consequence of behaving normally. However, she does not know what she fears. It appears she will be deemed abnormal by everyone.

She has been given intensive communicative counselling for:

1. Strengthening the will to get rid of the obsessive compulsive behaviour by making her realise that it is necessary if she wanted to get

married, because no one will marry a girl who suffers from such disorders; and even if she is married and carries these disorders along, her husband will not accept her and she may be thrown out.

Pooja is keen to get married and now believes more compellingly that the change in her behaviour is necessary. This has created in her a stronger will to free herself of the obsessions.

2. *Confidence building:*

C. (*a*) You still have a beautiful face and body but it is likely to become unacceptable to a prospective groom if it is subjected to deterioration by excessive use of soap. Do not spoil it, preserve it, it is your most valuable asset.

(*b*) You have great courage, confidence and will-power as exhibited by your conduct in coming for counselling and disclosing all that is regarded as degrading for a young girl like you. It requires immense courage to tell the truth in matters like this. Telling the truth which in effect means acceptance of guilt about a conduct which brings shame to a young woman, is not an easy thing. This is indicative of the fact that you are a woman who possesses confidence, courage, strength of will, and desire to get rid of undesirable habits. Just try a little harder and you will become a woman of normal habits.

(*c*) She is asked to sing. She cannot sing but has recited some couplets. It has made her open up and utter poetic words, perhaps, after a gap of four years.

Pooja has begun to feel more confident in her capabilities. She no longer thinks she is a good for nothing girl.

P. But I have no courage to face any situation; I am afraid I shall not be able to bear the tension I will get by changing my long standing habit of washing mybody and my clothes in the way I do.

C. Don't worry, just give up. I shall take care of the consequences. You are coming next week. If in the meantime you feel anything unbearable you just phone me and I will take care of it. Don't fear anything. Have faith and confidence.

All obsessive compulsions, and the ones you have, create the urge to continue, it is similar to the urge felt on the withdrawal from alcohol or drugs by a person addicted to them. The addiction becomes part of one's life and controls her/his behaviour, it generates a fear of consequences and that prevents the addict from giving up the drug. There is no doubt that when you will give up your addictions (compulsive actions) you will suffer the pain of deprivation, but that will not be unbearable, except for a day or two. Bear it, and in a few days it will go. Don't have fear of suffering on that account. Every achievement requires sacrifice, it involves suffering, but the reward is much greater than the suffering, and it is always worthwhile. In your case the expected reward is very great. Just think of the reward—marriage, and the pleasures and happiness of married life.

P. But, I have no courage to act differently.

C. You have. Give up this negative thinking, it unnerves you, takes away your courage and confidence and makes you too weak to undertake the required step. It is better to attempt and fail than to accept defeat without making the attempt.

So far as you are concerned, the chances of failure are very meagre, so go ahead and you will surely succeed. You know how much agony you have suffered during the last four years. Will a few days of suffering be any match to that prolonged agony? It makes you feel slighted in the family and social circles. Every day it means loss of honour, dignity, faith, courage and confidence. Your getting de-addicted will bring you back your lost honour, dignity, faith, courage and confidence, and above all the reward of a loving husband. Believe it, you have the courage to throw away the obsessive habits. Your fear is ill-founded. Will you do it?

P. Yes, I will try.

C. No 'try', do it.

P. I shall.

Pooja says she can make paper flowers, and did make them, but always destroyed them, finding no tangible use for them.

C. You continue to make flowers as you had been doing.

P. I have been making only buds, no flowers, and then I tear them up.

C. It is because you still feel you have not blossomed, you still consider yourself a bud who has been mauled and destroyed. What you have been doing is the manifestation of what is happening in your sub-conscious mind.

Now that stage is over, you are no longer the human bud of eighteen, whom any man can maul and destroy. You are past the stage of budding, you are now a blossomed flower. Open up your petals, feel the bloom in yourself, feel the maturity, the confidence, the courage to face all the weathers—mild as well as rough.

Go and make some good flowers in full bloom, bring them as a gift for me.

P. I will surely do it, I shall make flowers and bring them for you.

Seventh Session

Pooja says she feels a lot of improvement. When asked how she felt generally about herself, she replied: "I am much-much better. My feeling of guilt and shame has almost gone with my acceptance of the truth that I was a consenting participant in the whole episode, and the realisation that I had committed no sin or crime in doing so. The counselling has done me much good, it has made me a changed person. I have come back to my normal stage."

Pooja is no longer suffering from those effects of trauma for which she originally came for counselling. Her feeling of defilement has gone.

She, however, continues to wash and bathe for long periods and clean her own clothes as she did before; she says it has become an automatic process with her. She fears she will get cracked if she leaves this as she is doing it automatically like a machine.

Eighth Session

P. I constantly remain churning the thought in my mind and remain worried, hence I am unable to concentrate on my studies, I am really unable to do anything. I cannot get away from that single thought, it has become an obsession.

C. Come on; describe that thought which still worries you.

P. (With much hesitation she spoke) I cannot forget that incident. I wish I could kill that man.

C. But why? He was a *tantrik*, *tantra* is not invented by him, it is a science or a system of spiritual healing practised in India for the last 5,000 years. It is practised also in other countries such as China and several African countries in different forms. He had told you he was a *tantrik* and he will cure you by *tantrik* system.

P. Yes, he did.

C. So he did not act dishonestly. Anybody who is not completely ignorant of *tantrik* system, knows that *tantriks* rely on sex energy, they arouse sexual instinct in young women and finally their procedure ends in copulation. They believe in Shiva-Shakti concept, where Shiva is treated as a passive male and Shakti as active and possessed of all powers. Only when Shiva comes in actual sexual contact with Shakti that spiritual powers are born in both, and Shiva becomes Rudra and Shakti becomes Durga.

The *tantrik* concept of Shiva-Shakti is expressed in the form of 'Linga' in every temple. There, Shivas male sex organ is shown inside Parwati's female sex organ, it manifests Shiva's acquiring supreme divine power through sex. It is only through this process that the passive Shiva is believed to become 'Rudra', the terrible warrior.

P. I did not know it then when he had met me.

C. But you did come to know about the system when you visited him, and consented to go on with the treatment.

P. Yes, I did. I have already said I went there again and again, of my own accord.

C. Why do you want to kill him, he is just like any other doctor who claims to cure people? There are hundreds of systems of spiritual healing being practised in India, such as 'Kundali Jagaran' and 'Reki'. *Tantra* is a known way of awakening spiritual power in people through the medium of sex. They believe that sex energy is of the highest intensity and can cure every disease. *Tantriks* are, you know, very popular with politicians and big personalities who wish to realise their ambitions. I do not mean to say that *tantriks* are good or the system is good; or is capable of achieving results; but it is claimed to be a healing system all the same.

P. I am aware of this, but I have suffered so much because of it.

C. After all what did he do, nothing except seeing you naked and touching your body amorously. You have suffered no injury. Even doctors, particularly gynaecologists and surgeons bare the woman and touch her body. You have conservative views, just go to the West and you will find people taking sun-bath almost nude, you can go to beaches and swimming pools and see bare human bodies. No harm is done to a woman if her naked body is seen by a man or even touched, particularly when he is doing so in a process of spiritual healing. Have you heard of *Bhagwan* Rajneesh, (Osho); he believed and preached that great things can be achieved through love and sex.

P. He was bad.

C. Have you read any book of Rajneesh or heard his tapes?

P. No; but my friend said so.

C. That is too much, just see these few books of Rajneesh, and if you wish to listen I can play his tapes for you.

Pooja looks at one of the books and on seeing Rajneesh's photo said 'he also looked like this'.

C. Osho too was a sort of *tantrik*, and something more. Of course, he belonged to a different class.

P. That man also had a room with pictures of gods, and looked like a god-man.

C. Then why are you so much against him that you want him killed? He was just doing what his healing system required him to do. He had learnt from books, and was doing only what has been practised in India for the last 5,000 years. All the doctors do what they have learnt.

P. But I have suffered so much as a result of what he did.

C. Don't you know of serious reactions caused by many medicines given by doctors, or operations performed by them?

P. Yes, I do. Then why have you such a feeling against him? He was doing only what his system of healing required him to do.

(Pooja smiles, her face shows she has understood the implications, and she has begun to shed her feeling of hatred and revenge against him. She felt relaxed and comfortable. Her anger against her tormentor disappeared and so did her desire to kill him).

C. Now tell me, have not your psychological troubles been reduced by 80 per cent ?

P. (she gives a smile saying 'yes').

On phone after some time

Pooja says she is feeling very relaxed, but is not yet able to do all as instructed. She means she has not been able to get rid of compulsive activities.

She is very soon going to take her B.A. Examinations after a gap of four years.

She says she has forgiven the *tantrik* and has no grievance against him and no desire to see him dead or punished. She has got over her feeling of hatred, and the wish to take revenge.

That has brought her peace of mind. It has also taken the sting out of the episode; instead of its continuing to be a story of hell, torture, and the devil, it has become a play, a drama with many actors including herself. As a consequence, the feelings of guilt and shame, and also of fear of social and family ostracism have disappeared. Her agitated mind has regained peace and happiness.

Pooja suffered from both obsessive thoughts and compulsive actions. Her obsessive thoughts have almost come to an end. They arose out of her feelings of guilt and shame, hatred and revenge, and fear of social ostracism. They had disturbed her emotional balance. Now, with the disappearance of negative feelings her emotional balance has been restored and she is now perfectly relaxed and happy.

Ninth Session

Pooja is quite composed and is once again happy. There is a marked change in her attitude. Though obsessional thoughts about the event still linger in her memory, they do not cause fear and trauma. With every counselling session fear and trauma went on decreasing, and by now they have almost disappeared. Counselling has made her realise that no irreparable injury had been caused to her during the entire episode, and there was nothing for which she had to feel guilty or ashamed. She has understood that it was all like a dream and was just a normal thing that happened during a session with a *tantrik*. She did not suffer any somatic injury as sexual act did not take place. She got real relief by understanding the *tantrik* concept of healing through sexual rituals.

Pooja appears to have got over the feeling of bitterness she was having against the *tantrik*, and also the feeling of self-blame and guilt she had developed, which she was trying to shift over to the *tantrik*. During an earlier session she had said that she had pardoned him, today she had become more positive and says she no longer holds him guilty. Her feeling of hatred and desire to liquidate him have gone. By accepting him as a practitioner of a faith based on Tantra, has removed she has been able to remove from her mind the impression and conviction that he was a devil who should be punished, killed and eliminated.

P. Even if he was not a devil, and was only practising Tantra, I should not have allowed myself to be exploited. I feel guilty for being a party to the whole drama which has brought shame in my life.

C. But you did not know anything about Tantra at that time, and you were just eighteen; an innocent girl. Can you not pardon that innocent girl for whatever happened? Imagine she is here, sitting by your side, begging for pardon: Excause me, pardon me for what I did in total ignorance. I was too young and innocent, I have not done anything purposely to bring shame or unhappiness, so pardon me, you can even punish me if you like, impose any punishment you wish. You have already been punishing me severely for the last four years. Do you think my fault was so grave that four years of punishment is not enough? If you think that punishment was not sufficient give me any other punishment, that you consider adequate. You may even give me physical thrashing if you like.

"Pooja, please accept her apology, don't be too hard-hearted. After all she was only eighteen and perfectly innocent, and nothing really hurtful has happened to you, be merciful and pardon her. Pooja, do please pardon her."

(Pooja smiles, feels relaxed)

C. So you have pardoned the eighteen year old Pooja who had not acted wisely?

P. Yes, I have.

C. So, now you cannot punish her any more. You have to give up your tirade against her. No more anger, no more bitterness, no more imposition of any kind of punishment.

P. I shall try.

C. No trying, you have pardoned her already, you cannot punish her any more.

P. Okay, I shall no more carry any grievance against her; I mean against myself.

After some days

Pooja phoned: "I am very happy and have completely overcome my obsessive thoughts, and ended my self-imposed isolation and alienation. Once again, I have started laughing and conversing with everyone, something I had missed for years. I no longer feel I am out of tune with anyone. I have become exactly as I was, four years back.

I can now concentrate on my studies, and am preparing to appear at the B.A. Examinations after having skipped it for so many years."

C. That is the right attitude. Be full of hope and self-confidence. A bright future is assured for you.

GEETANJALI AND MEERA

General analysis of Meera's dreams and ordeals show a deep-rooted fear in her mind about her ex-stepfather. It appears that she is forced to have sex, and its trauma has gone deep in her mind. She feels she is treated by him as a substitute for his former ex-wife who, though divorced, still lives with him. Meera feels she is treated as a replacement of that woman. In the dream she enters Meera's body and Meera becomes Sheshank's sexual partner. She feels pregnancy and the growth of a human foetus inside her womb and it grows and grows like a plant. Its coming out of her body is indicative of the fear of the foetus growing into a child and coming out of her womb.

Diagnostic Scan

Geetanjali

Geetanjali forty-five is a woman of substance. Quite alert and physically in good health, she is well employed and gets good salary. She is highly educated and works as a teacher. But her face shows signs of stress, mental tension and anguish. She is sad and morose. She says she has lost interest in everything including going to the job, driving the car, in short, doing any activity. Living itself has become devoid of any interest or purpose.

Geetanjali insists that she hates Meera, her daughter and detests her. Geetanjali is sore with Meera because she lives with Sheshank, her ex-husband, the husband of one night. Geetanjali believes (mainly on the basis of information received from Sheshank) that Meera had illicit relations with Sheshank even before her own marriage to Sheshank which had taken place about four years ago. She also believes that now they are living as husband and wife. Geetanjali dislikes Meera's coming to her only when she is in some trouble which requires help, specially when she is sick and needs her mother's nursing and care. As soon as Meera's purpose is served, she goes back.

Geetanjali asserts she has been left with no emotional involvement with Meera and could not care less even if she had illicit relations with Sheshank. She says she feels no shame on that score. However, observation and deeper probe gave lie to this and revealed that things were otherwise.

Geetanjali's first marriage was an arranged marriage. She was married because her father insisted. Her married life was not happy, it was full of discord and tension. It lasted seven years. She had one daughter from that marriage Meera and a son, who are now twenty and eighteen. Her husband had died when Meera was only five and the son three years old. She reared her children all alone as a single parent. Meera is now studying in B.A.

It was only about five years back that Geetanjali came in contact with Sheshank, a prosperous industrialist having a luxurious farm-house with a swimming pool and other amenities in Jalandhar in Punjab where she is working.

Geetanjali never realised that Sheshank was really interested in Meera, and that Sheshank gave all attention to Geetanjali only to win her confidence so that she should not be an obstruction in his satisfying his lust with Meera. In fact Sheshank had married Geetanjali only as a ploy.

Geetanjali saw the game and just a day after her marriage took steps for divorce. Divorce proceedings continued for three years. She could get divorce only on filing in court a statement in writing stating that Sheshank was innocent and she and Meera were guilty parties.

On being further molested Geetanjali went to police and also filed a complaint in the Magistrate's court. But it all boomeranged, she had to withdraw the complaint under threat. Both mother and daughter are living in severe fear because Sheshank has obtained from them some writing saying that they were never molested by him, rather reverse was the fact and the two women were trying to blackmail him. They were made to state in this document that the complaint filed against him in the Magistrate's court and the statements given before him were false. On their advocate's advice, who according to them had been won over by Sheshank, the complaint had been withdrawn. This document in which both mother and daughter were made to admit that they were of loose character, is always used by Sheshank to blackmail both of them.

Meera

Meera comes in and joins. She looked sickly and tense, as if stricken by terror and fear, she seemed to be unhappy and altogether disinterested in life, unable to find solace anywhere.

She was very reserved and appeared almost dumb. All she said was, she is not happy, but did not exactly know why. She insisted there was nothing particular for her to say.

She was dishevelled and shabbily dressed. She was taciturn and uncommunicative. Her whole appearance and demeanour showed that she was under some sort of threat and was having deep-rooted fear.

Counselling

M. I get love from my mother and have nothing to complain. Ten days back when I had come from the house of Sheshank to stay with my mother, I got a telephone call from him, my stepfather and I went back after a short time.

She was not willing to disclose what was she told on the phone, which compelled her to go back to her stepfather's home.

Geetanjali, her mother, at this stage, said that Meera was very good at palm-reading.

C. What is your reading of your own palm, Meera?

M. I will soon become mad.

C. Yes, if you remain like this, but what makes you predict this? (She shows me her palm, I hold it and look at it.)

M. This line is the brain line and it is going down curbing leftwards. That is the indication of impending insanity.

C. No, there is no such indication in it. All palms have such lines. Lines take the shape from the way the hand was inside the mother's womb. Have you studied palmistry?

M. Not particularly, but everyone knows this much. I have read some books.

[Earlier she was shown two paintings hanging on the wall and she was asked what she saw there. She said she saw an 'eye' and..., but did not proceed any further.]

C. The make-up of your hand shows you could be interested in art and painting, you could be more emotional and sentimental than practical. You easily succumb to pressure from others. You have little power to resist, and no courage to say 'No'.

Why does your face show so much tension? Your eyes are not relaxed, you seem to be living under terror of something that you fear may seize you, what is it?

You are loved by your mother, she is very much concerned about you. Her protective hand is always sheltering you. You should have no fear. Have faith in mother's love, that will give you courage and confidence.

[Something unexpected happened. While I was still holding her hand she felt some vibes, a sudden change came in her attitude and she said: "I like you, I will tell you everything." As this happened she became relaxed, tension disappeared from her face, and she began getting out of her state of fear and dread.]

She admitted she was always haunted by fear and terror, she was not free to act according to her own will. Then she went on to describe her nightmarish dreams.

Meera remembers bits of some of her terrifying dreams.

She describes her dreams:

1. Someone was forcibly pulling me. I was chained.

2. Snakes.

3. Killings.

4. Bloodshed, flowing blood—stream.

5. Something was growing out from my body, from the right side abdomen area, like a plant.

6. Pipe, blood and flesh.

Mother dresses and bandages the wound.

7. Some woman with long hair entered my body. Former ex-wife of my stepfather whom he had married and divorced before his marriage and involvement with my mother, and who still lives with him, was also sitting there, she came near and finally entered my body. These images become more and more prominent, and persistent. The scene then changed. Stepmother had disappeared.

8. It seemed I was wandering in the sky, then suddenly I was falling down to earth. Wandering on the slope, I came down falling.

9. Stepfather is always present.

10. Me and my mother are also there in the scene of my dream, both crying and weeping.

[Geetanjali intervened and said she too had a dream.] She describes the dream:

G. I along with Meera enter the house. Meera is to take bath. We close all doors and windows. A big Octopus creeps in the window and pushes in one of its legs through the window, I take a pair of scissors and cut the tentacle. We go outside, son also joins. There we see big buffaloes.

Interpretation : Octopus- buffaloes represent Sheshank who is trying to intrude and take away Meera. Geetanjali has fear and acts to defend her daughter.

Interrogation of Meera

C. Has anyone ever tried to make you have sexual relations against your will ?

M. Yes.

C. Only attempt or actual rape?

M. My stepfather tried but could not succeed, he stripped himself completely and made attempts. He was always trying to molest me and also cajole me into submission.

C. Have you ever had any other experience in which someone tried to assault you sexually, that is, he made serious unwanted sexual advances but did not attempt rape?

M. A boy once tried to force me to be physically close to him. He was my friend, I was emotionally attached and was about to get married to him. I avoided physical contact. This was before I was taken away by my stepfather.

I believe in superstitions, occult and super-natural things; such is my state of mind, it is not normal. Somebody has done something to my mind by occult. Someone wants to destroy me. Sheshank, the stepfather, and his family (his ex-wife, sons, daughter-in-law, daughter and her boyfriend, all of whom live together with Sheshank) want to destroy me.

The former ex-wife of Sheshank threatened to beat me. Stopped only at my threat of becoming aggressive.

Stepfather pulled my hair once, Called me bloody bastard woman. He held my head as if to crush it, but gave up. They beat me many times, one day he gave milk to drink, it contained some drug. I became almost unconscious.

Whenever I want to get away from his house, I am pulled back inside the house and forcibly kept in. For last one year, I was kept in a separate house like a paying guest. Sometimes, four young man came and actually beat me. One of them had bad intentions. I have developed a feeling of revenge, but I am helpless.

I know my stepfather has committed many offenses and is a bad man, I wish to punish my stepfather and his relatives but he is rich and resourceful.

Stepfather blackmails me in order to force me to submission.

He got some papers signed by mother to silence and blackmail her.

Conclusions

General analysis of her dreams and ordeals shows a deep-rooted fear in her mind about her ex-stepfather. It appears that she is forced to have sex, and its trauma has gone deep in her mind. She feels she is treated by him as a substitute for his former ex-wife who, though divorced, still lives with him. Meera feels she is treated as a replacement of that woman. In the dream, she enters Meera's body and Meera becomes Sheshank's sexual partner. She feels pregnancy and the growth of a human foetus inside her womb and it grows like a plant. Its coming out of her body in indicative of the fear of the foetus growing into a child and coming out of her womb.

The pipe, blood and flesh, bloodshed, and the dressing and bandaging of the wound are indicative of fear of the birth of the child.

Her falling down from the sky on to the slope refers to her fear of consequential degradation and loss of honour, prestige and status in social life and the family.

Meera is living in wrongful confinement, is abused, threatened, beaten, cruelly dealt with and sexually abused and assaulted by her ex-stepfather. She is in a hopeless, helpless condition. She is living like a sex-slave under constant fear of getting pregnant and becoming an unmarried mother.

The inhuman treatment meted out to her in Sheshank's house has so conditioned her that she is unable to escape from the environment. She has developed hatred for him, but is still infatuated by him.

It was only when Meera fell ill and became very weak and sickly that the stepfather did not stop her from going to her mother for nursing. She has come to live with her mother and does not wish to return to Sheshank's house.

There is severe tension in Meera's mind caused by the deep-rooted fear of further molestation and sexual abuse, she even fears death. She has these fears not only from Sheshank but also from his relatives and associates.

At the same time she is infatuated with Sheshank. She also seems to carry in her mind the memories of some pleasant sexual relationship that she might have had with Sheshank, which exercise on her a competing pull towards him and make it difficult for her to part from him. It is impossible for her to resist compliance to his telephone calls probably because of the threats he holds out to her from time to time.

She also has a sense of defilement which makes her feel guilty and ashamed and scared of meeting her relatives and friends.

Her attitude towards Sheshank is ambivalent, oscilating from hatred to affection, and that accounts for her mental instability.

At the same time, she has love and regard for her mother and brother, with an insistent desire to live with them. She gets a feeling of security and protection when she is with her, but ultimately finds herself too weak to face the wrath of Sheshank, and with his cunningness and resourcefulness he is able to counteract her mother's efforts to get her back through the aid of police or the court.

These conflicts in Meera's mind make her emotionally vulnerable and bring about confusion in her thoughts, emotions and actions.

[Intensive and wide-spectrum counselling, however, has at least temporarily enabled Meera to resolve these conflicts; she has chosen to live with her mother and feel secure rather than go to Sheshank and suffer disgrace and humiliation. This change has brought stability into her mind and she has become calm, her tension has disappeared and she has developed a feeling of security.]

Next Session

Meera looks fine, her appearance has changed.

Her appetite has improved, she has gained weight, and no longer does she have a sickly appearance; she now looks healthy and cheerful. She has started taking interest in her studies and resumed attendance in college.

Her mother said: "You have given a new birth to Meera. I am overjoyed to get back my daughter. She is no more tense and sickly, thanks to the counselling, she is now a normal healthy girl, full of interest in life and her surroundings."

Geetanjali's hatred for Meera too has disappeared, and motherly love for her daughter has grown full-fledged in her heart.

Next Session : (*after some time*)

Geetanjali came and reported that many incidents occurred in between affecting the life of her daughter. Ultimately, Sheshank succeeded in whisking away Meera; all efforts of Geetanjali to get her back failed.

Extensive counselling was given to Geetanjali to make her stabilise and cope with the new situation.

Geetanjali has come to believe that Meera will not return, and it is no use worrying about what happens to her. Meera has chosen to live with Sheshank and whatever consequences follows she must bear them.

She is now ready to live without her. But if Meera returns she will forgive her and take her back into her arms.

She has accepted the reality, it has given her consolation and peace of mind.

Geetanjali feels relaxed and happy.

Geetanjali came again after sometime; she is perfectly normal, with no tensions, no worries.

Final Session : (*after a long time*)

After a very long time Geetanjali dropped in, she is all smiles, full of life and gusto.

C. How are you, Geetanjali ?

G. You can see, guess.

C. It seems you have won a victory. You seem to have attained peace of mind, joy and contentment.

G. You have guessed right, I am now quite peaceful. Thanks to you, I have solved all problems. I have accepted the inevitable as inevitable, and achieved what is achievable.

C. That is excellent, how is your son?

G. He has grown-up very well, and is now doing a five year course in Japanese language.

C. That will assure a bright future for him.

G. Sure.

C. Oh, what about the great young lady, Meera?

G. We made a compromise. I have accepted the inevitable and allowed her the liberty to live wherever she liked, and howsoever she liked. It is her personal life, and I gave up worrying about it. But I made her agree to continue her studies, I devoted hours, days, weeks, and months in teaching her. Now she has a Master's degree, and is a teacher in a school. She is quite happy.

C. Congratulations Geetanjali, you have achieved what I could not even foresee.

G. It is all due to you. I learnt from you the basics of living, living without tension, attaining peace of mind, accepting the inevitable and never giving up the hope. I moved forward always looking the light of the lamp of love for my daughter, which you had lighted during our first meeting. That bright glow of love gave me unfailing strength and courage to move on and on.

C. You have become, I find, more poetic than you were. Have you written some more poems?

G. Yes, quite a few, but they have not yet been published.

C. That does not matter, please recite your poem. I am keen to see the glow of the light of love illuminating your heart.

[Geetanjali recites a couple of her poems.]

C. Emotions within you have become more sophisticated and poetic, and you have given them a language to fly and make everyone happy. Heartiest congratulations.

G. I am now enjoying the peace of mind and the bliss that makes a person happy.

C. It is wonderful. From tears you have become smiles. That is all what is needed.

After quite some time, Geetanjali reported that Meera had come back and was living with her, and soon she will get married to a going man.

The whole episode seems to be a sort of psychodrama in which Manisha was the centre-piece, and Surabhi the main player. Manisha's husband was a supporting actor. Informants played the role of instigators and the 'friend' acted as the villain who remained behind the curtain and never appeared on the open stage. Someday, he may appear and clarify that Surabhi had spent the night in his house, but not with him.

Diagnostic Scan and Counselling

All members of the family came. Parents of Surabhi said that the problem concerned the daughter.

Surabhi

Surabhi is a healthy girl of twenty-two, confident looking. There is, however, tension visible on her face; her eye-brows twist when she speaks. After a few minutes of conversation she became relaxed. Her mother said, Surabhi had put on weight and needed slimming.

Surabhi is neither so fair nor so good-looking as her mother Manisha. This may have some relevance in the making of Surabhi's unwelcome attitude towards her mother.

Surabhi was a good student till she did her 10+2. Later, she could not succeed in any competition for admission in a recognised engineering college. She then got admitted in a private engineering college in Calcutta. She had difficulty in her studies and could not complete her semesters in time. As a result, she lost one year, and will take one more year to appear in final B.E. (Eng.) examination.

She lives with some other girls in an apartment in Calcutta as a paying guest. Her hostess provides food, which is not to her liking, and she supplements it by eating outside.

She has gastro-intestinal problem and sometimes gets headache also. She was suspected of having T.B., but chest X-ray was normal.

She admitted that she remained under tension even in Calcutta and her gastro-intestinal problem gets aggravated when she is under tension.

Surabhi had suffered insomnia in the last couple of months, but now she says she is okay.

Surabhi says she has no problem of her own, but remains tense only because her parents remain under tension.

She fears failure in the examination. She is more afraid of condemnation by parents than of failure at the examination.

She is interested in painting, dance and music, but has not been able to acquire any proficiency in any of them.

Ganeshan

Ganeshan, her father is suffering from hypertension. He is repentant about reposing his faith and confidence in Surabhi, and spending a lot of money on her education in Calcutta which, he thinks had been misused by her.

G. I believe in truth and transparency and expect the same from every member of the family. Surabhi is not a truthful girl, she does not show transparency. She never informed me of her bad performance in the Calcutta college. I used to send her considerable amount of money. She has misused it, this amounts to breach of trust. She has taken undue advantage of our love and affection.

I have begun to hate her. I wish her to become a good girl, a good student, and truthful person and hide nothing from me or her mother, but my wishes remain only dreams.

Manisha

Manisha is more calm and balanced. She too has a severe disliking of Surabhi, mostly for the same reasons. On further probe she spoke about one particular incident which had made her very sad and also averse to Surabhi.

M. Surabhi has spread the rumour that I am a woman of loose character, and had an affair with a man who was a student of my husband. Surabhi told this lie to my husband's brother and wife, and also to some other persons in Calcutta.

C. Did anybody believe this accusation?

M. Nobody has believed it, and I know it is totally false and baseless.

C. Then do not worry about it. This accusation is unbelievable and has been treated as such by all to whom it was conveyed; so you should forget it and forgive Surabhi because she did not understand its implications.

[Counselling has made Manisha feel relaxed and relieved]

This information, however, is of significance in understanding the subconscious and conscious thinking of Surabhi. Following determinants may be at the back of this unusual conduct of Surabhi:

1. *Envy* : Surabhi's mother remains well-dressed, well-groomed, and is much better-looking than her. This may have created in her feeling of jealousy which may have prompted her to malign her character and spoil her image. According to her mother, Surabhi always said that she should not wear nice clothes and should not look as smart as she does. Her attempts seem to be directed towards tarnishing the image of her mother in order to boost her own.

2. *Defence* : Surabhi may have some illicit affair and on being confronted by her uncle and aunt, may have resorted to frontal attack on her mother by involving her mother with the same gentleman. This could has been so because they had threatened to report the matter to her parents, specially the mother.

3. *Revenge* : Surabhi may be harbouring some grievance against her mother, resulting in some form of hidden anger.

4. *Psychological problem* : Something might be emotionally wrong with Surabhi.

Surabhi as well as her parents have been given counselling and have been motivated to think more positive, forget the past and start living in the present with the hope of a brighter future.

Second Session

Surabhi seems to be depressed and suffering from some sort of fear, appears to be afraid of her parents.

S. My parents consider me a 'misfit'.

C. Misfit in family?

S. No, misfit everywhere; misfit in life itself.

C. Do you also feel insecure? Do you feel you need protection ?

S. Yes, I live in fear because my parents believe I am a bad girl and need to be punished.

Surabhi belives, and rightly to some extent, that her parents (and even brother) consider her guilty of reprehensible conduct. This has made her harbour feeling of guilt and defiance. They accuse her of not putting enough effort in her studies, of being a spendthrift, becoming fat and bad-looking, making her unsuitable for marriage. They also accuse her of being corrupt, because she spent a night in the house of a person who is unmarrieds and thirty-eight years old. It was with him she was alleged to have accused her mother of having a liaison. Her father (whom she had informed on phone of her stay with the man) thinks that she had more than permissible familiarity with him. He draws this inference only from the fact that instead of calling him uncle, she called him by name.

Surabhi denies all allegations and comes out with a new story. Maybe she is concealing the truth, she says she had spent a night at the house of a woman (middle-aged) of the same village and community to which her father belonged, who had invited her to attend a religious function. She has a son of about twenty-seven. Surabhi alleges that it was this woman who had spread rumour against her and told one of her friends that Surabhi was not a good girl as she did no cooking and offered no help in doing household chores while she was there. This had affected her reputation to some extent. However, she denied that this woman had accused her of immorality or any compromising behaviour with her son.

[She related all this only after she was put under hypnotic spell. It is possible that she made subconscious interchange of personalities.]

She is very suspicious about her parents and feels they are against her, they do not like her, and consider her a depraved person.

Manisha has a different story to tell. She believes that Surabhi is jealous of her, because she is no match to her in looks and also in elegance, and her style of living. She considers herself to be a beauty and in every way superior to Surabhi. Surabhi, she says, wants her to live like ordinary lower-middle class woman, somewhat like a nanny, and not like the fashionable mistress, Manisha feels that Surabhi has no right to criticise her. Manisha objects to Surabhi's suggestion (as she says) that she (Manisha) should wear less attractive, less expensive, ordinary clothes. The insinuation is that Surabhi indirectly wishes to suggest that Manisha is a woman interested in attracting young persons. According to Manisha she never behaved in a manner which was not in conformity with the decency and decorum required of the wife of a senior army officer.

Manisha complains that Surabhi remains untidy and unkept, she does not observe dignity, decency and propriety in her habits and daily conduct.

She does not admit the accusation that she wears expensive clothes. According to her, Surabhi does not wish to remain smartly dressed, she likes remaining dishevelled.

Manisha says that because she receives greater concern and attention from her husband than Surabhi, Surabhi feels jealous of her.

Surabhi does not accept these allegations. She says she has no complaint against her mother and never made any accusations or held any grudge against her as alleged by her mother.

However, she does feel unhappy with her parents.

C. Manisha, as an experiment you should change your attitude temporarily and give friendly and motherly treatment to your daughter. At least for six weeks you should refrain from treating her as a bad, spoiled, worthless girl, and give her love and affection, so that she may not feel she is unwanted in the family.

Surabhi could not have deliberately meant to injure the feelings or reputation of her mother. If she really did say anything about that man's relationship with you, it must have been either in self-defence or because of something being wrong with her. In either case she deserves sympathy and not condemnation, she must be loved and not punished for it. You are her mother, you should be more charitable and pardon her.

M. I am unable to believe that the people in Calcutta had misinterpreted Surabhi's words. I do believe that Surabhi did accuse me to infidelity.

Both my husband and I have felt greatly grieved by Surabhi's spending the night at an ummarried person's house, and this has brought bad name to the family. No wonder we have developed a sort of ill-feeling towards her.

(Slowly through counselling, however, Manisha became inclined to agree that Surabhi may not really be a bad or despisable girl.)

M. Surabhi believes in birth after death and thinks that in her previous life she was born and lived in Tamil Nadu, and had a Ph.D.

C. Maybe this is so because Surabhi has infatuation for a man who has a Ph.D. and has begun to identify herself with him, thinking this was so in her previous life.

M. I also think so.

C. It is all a matter of fancy and imagination, don't give any importance to it.

S. I accept that I had spent one night at his house, but it was because it had become late for returning home, and I did not think there was anything wrong in accepting his suggestion to stay in his house as he was well-known to the family. I had gone to his house for consultation in connection with a project I was doing. I had informed my father about the night's stay.

C. However, it did cause some misunderstanding in the minds of your parents. Why don't you try to show greater love and affection towards your parents ?

S. I never meant to cause any pain to my parents. I agree to show positively my love for them by doing even such little deeds as wishing my father and mother goodmorning and good-night.

[Counselling has been given to make Surabhi believe that nothing very injurious or wrong had happened and even if she had spent the night with that person she should not feel guilty because she had not done anything which was wrong or condemnable.]

C. Surabhi have courage and face the situation with confidence. You are now twenty-two and capable of meeting adverse situations. In any case nothing had happened which may have caused any permanent injury to you; you should not, therefore, harbour in your mind any sense of shame and guilt. Such feelings of guilt and shame, even if they are wild, create-psychological problems.

S. But I know that nothing wrong or blame-worthy had happened, and there was nothing of which I should be ashamed of or feel guilty about.

C. There was thus no reason for you to develop hatred against your mother because of the wild allegations made against you. You had the right and freedom to meet him, you did nothing wrong in staying over-night in his house, hence you should not suffer from any sense of fear, shame or guilt.

S. I do have a lurking memory about my previous birth but it has no connection with this man. I believe that in my life I was myself a Ph.D. It may all be just a dream.

I love my mother; I respect her, honour her. I do not wish that my mother should live like a nanny and not as an officer's wife with good make-up and rich clothes.

C. Then why all this blame on you?

S. Once one of my father's relations in Calcutta had told me that my mother was unfaithful to my father. Maybe, he had conveyed his own feelings to my mother putting his thoughts in my mouth.

C. Why do you look depressed and sad?

S. My parents and my brother think that I am jealous of my mother. Every now and then I am condemned and made to feel that I am inferior. It is this hostile treatment that makes me feel sick and depressed.

[Extensive counselling made her feel relaxed and her self-esteem was restored. The feeling of being considered a condemned person vanished and she began to feel happy and innocent.]

Third Session

Surabhi is quite calm. Her mother is also happy.

M. Counselling has done a lot of good to Surabhi, and she has returned to almost normal, rather she has become fully normal; and that gives me happiness. My happiness depended on the happiness of my daughter, and now when she is happy, I too feel happy. However, that horrid accusation still continues to put me to shame. I am unable to get that thorn out of my mind.

C. Manisha, you are still suffering from distress because you are unable to accept.

(*a*) Surabhi was not guilty of any such behaviour during her stay in the house of that gentleman which was condemnable. You subconsciously believe that Surabhi had sex with him. You are not willing to accept the statement of Surabhi that nothing of the kind had happened.

(*b*) That your informants from Calcutta may not have correctly comprehended Surabhi's version and may have wrongly reported that Surabhi had accused you of having erotic relations with that gentleman.

M. Probably that is so. I always considered him a good man, and I really cannot believe that he had misbehaved with Surabhi or taken advantage of the situation.

C. Knowing him as you do, why do you not believe your daughter?

M. Yes, I should, but they reported like that.

C. Don't believe them, they might be trying to blackmail you and Surabhi.

M. Maybe.

C. Manisha, let us accept for a moment that Surabhi had made the wild accusation against you, which you very well know to be nothing but pure imagination, should you carry it permanently in your mind? Will it do you or Surabhi any good?

M. No.

C. Then the wiser course is to forget it. And, if you do not wish to forget it or even pardon Surabhi for this, then punish her. What punishment will you wish to give Surabhi? Has she not suffered enough because of loss of mother's love and her father's contempt for such a long period? So, mercy and pardon are called for, and that is the course you should adopt. You will find her reformed by this attitude of yours.

On the other hand, by continuing to hate her you shall become more and more miserable. It is better to get over the feeling of hatred and enjoy happiness. Even for the sake of happiness, of your husband your son, your daughter and also yourself it is necessary that you pardon her. After all, you are her mother and it is your duty to correct your daughter and teach her to be sensible. Everyone can falter, she has also faltered, so take a broad view. No real injury has been caused to your reputation because no one has believed these allegations.

It is best for you to forget and forgive. It will do good to both of you, and bring back faith, trust and love between mother and daughter, so essental for filial happiness.

Accusations of infidelity had generated in you a fear that you will be discarded by your husband, this has not happened, so your fear is baseless.

Your unconscious fear that it will make you stand disgraced in the eyes of your relations, too, was baseless as no one has thought you to be of loose character; the story has not been believed by anyone, and deserves to be forgotten. Now come out of it; you are innocent and the accusation has not affected your image, so relax and feel as if nothing had ever happened.

M. I here and now pardon Surabhi. By forgiving and pardoning her, I am feeling relieved and relaxed. I no more feel vexed, annoyed, or agitated. I am so happy. I cannot describe the joy and the love. I am feeling for my dear daughter Surabhi. I wish she may always be happy.

The whole episode seems to be a sort of psychodrama in which Manisha was the centre-piece, and Surabhi the main player. Manisha's husband was a supporting actor. Informants played the role of instigators and the friend acted as the villain who remained behind the curtain and never appeared on the open stage. Some day he may appear and clarify that Surabhi had spent the night in his house, but not with him.

In this drama Surabhi had developed a truncated personality to face the complicated situations arising in her life. She began to believe in the myth of reincarnation. She assumed a fictitious personality of a woman who had a cruel father, an ambitious mother, a friend with covetable academic degrees, and accepting everything as real, she began treating herself a victim of circumstances. She was too weak to face the overburdening situations and therefore unconsciously took recourse to her assumed life in a previous birth. On her getting over the disturbing situations, her fears disappeared and she regained her normal self.

Manisha was the victim of suspicion and suffered from the fear of loss of love, honour and prestige. In her effort to fight this fear, she developed stress, her entire consciousness got obsessed with fear, she developed hatred for Surabhi, whom she considered guilty of making the worst attack on her honour and fidelity to her husband. She desired to take revenge by making Surabhi acknowledge her guilt and repent for the same. Her psychic vision became blurred and she was unable to see reality and assess the situation without bias. The accusation became almost a nightmare for her, it made her lose self-confidence and strength to face the situation. Even though she knew and believed that the accusation was false, she suffered the shock.

However, the maternal love got the better of everything, and she became totally reconciled to her daughter and regained peace and composure.

Once Manisha accepted Surabhi, Ganeshan lost no time in embracing and loving her as ever.

PREMAWATI

Premawati's thoughts, desires and actions seem to be for the purpose of atoning for some unknown sins. She is suffering from some hidden feeling of having done something very wrong and sinful.

Age sixty-two, had education only upto primary level in school.

Premawati is suffering from O.C.Ds. She fears going to latrine as after every time she passes stool she takes a complete bath with soap and water. This has created a fear in her, she remains under tension for the fear of having to go to toilet, still she goes to toilet a number of times.

The tension creates a very uneasy feeling in her, and she suffers from what she calls *ghabrahat* uneasiness. She is taking medicines for this and also for getting comfortable sleep at night.

She constantly desires to give away to someone her bangles, her nose tab and other gold ornaments in the hope of getting peace. Whenever she sees a dead body going she wishes to give clothes to it. She does *pooja*, and worships all the deities, performs *katha* and distributes alms to beggers.

Premawati's thoughts, desires and actions seem to be for the purpose of atoning for some unkonwn sins. She is suffering form some hidden feeling of having done something very wrong and sinful.

Diagnostic Scan and Counselling

C. Are you afraid of something? Do you always try to wash away some sin which you feel you are guilty of?

P. Yes, it seems it is so, but I have never knowingly committed anything to displease the gods. However, it seems I have unknowingly and unconsciously displeased the gods.

C. You have really done nothing, and should not have any such feeling in your mind. Anyway, it would he better for you to do some positive acts to please your gods, and get rid of this curse. I suggest that on every full-moon day you perform *Katha of Satya Narain* in the traditional way.

P. I have been doing it already, I make *prasad* offerings to the God, and then share it with those who participate, and also distribute some money among the poor at the temple.

C. Then remain sure that god's curse will never fall on you.

P. Why then do I have *ghabrahat* and have to take bath repeatedly ?

C. Don't worry about the baths, now it has become part of your nature and will continue, so let it be as it is; after all there is nothing wrong in taking bath three or four time a day.

P. Everyone says it is wrong, even though normally I do not go more than twice.

C. From now on they will not say so. It is because you are worrying about it that you are suffering, it creates in you the feeling of shame and guilt.

P. Yes, it does.

C. If you take it as nothing bad or wrongful, you will get rid of the feeling of guilt and shame, then you will not have any tension. Your *ghabrahat* is nothing but feeling of tension; it will automatically go once you will begin to feel there is nothing wrong in taking bath more than once or twice, number of baths is immaterial, it does you no harm. Try to take it as something normal and all your tension will disappear.

Instead, enjoy it, feel happy about it, it is invigorating to take a bath, it refreshes your body and gives relaxation. You have only to change your attitude. Just do it and you will be happy.

P. I think you are right. I am doing nothing wrong in taking bath a number of times.

C. Your baths are correlated to your urge to pass stool several times. This again is due to tension. Once you remain under tension, your whole system gets disturbed and you get relief by passing stool. So the remedy lies not in worrying about the number of baths but the avoidance of tension. You are suffering from fear of passing stool and that fear prevents the full clearance of your bowels at a single go. The cause of all your tensions lies in something that creates the feeling of guilt in your mind. And, that is due to something deep-rooted in your subconscious mind. You should believe that gods have no intention of punishing you. You have always lived a pious life, you have never done any such thing which might have displeased any of your gods. Have you?

P. No, I have never done anything which could be called sinful. I am always doing good and virtuous deeds.

C. Then remove this feeling of guilt from your mind. You are good, pious, and virtuous, so gods cannot be displeased with you. You are doing wrong in blaming gods.

P. Yes, I know Gods are all good and merciful, they cannot have grievance against anyone, or curse them who are their devotees.

C. Are you not a devotee?

P. I am, and I have never defaulted in serving my gods.

C. There is thus no reason for your gods to be displeased with you, hence give up this feeling that gods are against you. Going to latrine a number of times or taking bath several times does not mean you are under the curse of gods. It is a matter of habit, a long-standing habit. Do not worry about it.

P. So there is nothing wrong in my going to toilet or taking bath a number of times ? I have, therefore no reason to blame my gods or feel I am under a curse ?

C. Not at all. However, I believe that now with your changed attitude your tension will go and you will not need to go to toilet so many times in the day. Moreover, as it is not due to any divine curse, it is not necessary for you to take bath everytime you go to toilet. It is all a question of personal hygiene, do as you think suitable, keeping in mind your age and general health. If you find it is not necessary, give up. Anyway, do not feel concerned about it.

P. I am now feeling relaxed, you have given me great relief.

BELA

Ultimately, Bela did succeed in getting over her bitterness against intimacy with men, and relished the experience which every young woman needs to get fulfilment and bliss. Love, adulation, affection, and infatuation succeeded in making her overcome her fears and complexes. It was the love of Bela's lover and her own total surrender that gave her the feeling not only of security but also of being cared for, being treated as a human being and as someone who deserved the love of a very desirable person. Her ego was fully satisfied. She saw her conquest in being conquered by Cupid. From the 'Beast' she became the 'Beauty', a woman full of compassion and love. The 'Woman of Hate' became the 'Woman of Love.'

Bela is a smart young woman in her thirties. She is a graduate and has done diploma courses in secretarial, computer and other connected professional disciplines. Working as a Secretary in a commercial undertaking with responsible duties. Married at the age of twenty three. Unsuccessful marriage, non-adjustment, separated after five months. Divorced after seven years.

Her grandmother was very conservative—died two years back. Father-mother, lived together but not without discords. There was always bitterness in the family, quarrels—punishments—conflicts.

Complaints and Diagnostic Scan

B. I am very irritable, always cross, no person is an exception. I scream, beat, bite. The whole world knows and says so—my parents, sister, relatives, acquaintances, and colleagues in the office where I work know what I am. I am easily provoked, always remain tense, strike and scream at the least provocation.

I alway offer resignation from the job whenever provoked.

I never smile, always frown, have no friends, everyone keeps avoiding me. I too avoid everyone. I say hello not even to my boss for whom I work as private secretary.

I am friendly only with one girl, whom too I seldon meet. I just eat boiled rice and curd, I do not take normal meals. I have a maid servant. I live in a two-room flat all alone.

I befriend no neighbour, do not like to play with children and I have no hobbies.

In spite of being warned to be punctual, I fail to reach office in time. I do wish to reach in time, but fail to make it.

C. What do you consider is the cause of your behaviour as a tense person?

B. Can´t say.

C. Being unfriendly with colleagues, neighbours?

B. Can't say.

C. What do you think is the reason for your losing temper?

B. Intolerance.

C. Why do you think you are so intolerant?

B. Don't know.

C. What makes you scream?

B. To make others accept what I say.

C. What do you expect from this behaviour: Subduing others? Defeating others? Conquering others?

B. All of these.

C. Do you want the life-style you are leading or you want to change?

B. I want to change.

C. What is the kind of girl you would like to be: Always confident?

B. Yes.

C. Always smiling ?

B. Yes.

C. Always loving ?

B. Yes.

C. Do you think punishment is better than pardoning or the vice versa?

B. Punishment is more desirable than pardoning.

C. Do you think tolerance is better than revenge?

B. No, I want to take revenge.

C. Will you feel ashmed if you become the model girl of your choice?

B. No.

[One very relevant thing disclosed during further scanning was her hidden urge to get married and have her own children.]

Bela was given counselling to make her behave more positively in dealing with others.

Next Session

There has been good response to the counselling.

She did say good morning to her boss. Felt better when she greeted him and he responded with a smile.

Could not find any names whom she could send greetings as advised, as she has no friends.

Further Scanning

Abhors anyone entering her house. Wants no guests.

Advised to mix with people over a cup of tea.

She is very sad because she lives alone. Even her parents do not like to stay with her as she becomes violent. Such an incident happened a few weeks before she came here.

She is dejected, full of animosity for everyone, she feels everyone knows and believes she is a quarrelsome, screaming, fighting woman, unable to behave normally.

In her childhood too she was always a fighter. She could not tolerate denial of her demands. She was used as a tool by other members of the family to make her father do whatever they wanted. She could scream and fight and get things done.

Her parents did not have a peaceful life. They also had inter-se quarrels and fights.

Counselling

She is counselled to develop greater interest in other matters and try to feel compassion and concern for other people.

She always reaches office late, because after she gets up in the morning, she again goes to sleep and gets late. Every night she determines not to be late, writes it down on paper and repeats it a hundred times, but to no avail.

C. Take this tape on stress management and listen to it in the morning after waking up. This will give you relaxation and you will not require a second nap.

B. I shall try.

Next Session

B. When I played the cassette in the morning I fell asleep on reaching the stage of deep hypno-sleep.

C. Omit the first part and proceed directly to the suggestion part of the tape. Better play the tape while sitting and not lying down.

B. I had a bad week, I quarrelled with a junior and a peon. I realise that it is not right to be intolerant, but I am unable to control myself.

C. It is a case of obsessive compulsive action. You are obsessed with the idea that you are a bad girl and have been so for the last thirty-three years. That does not mean you cannot change.

Please be optimistic and not pessimistic.

B. I have a feeling of inferiority.

C. This is probably the cause of your aggressive attitude. Your aggressive behaviour is not generally offensive, but is often used as a tool for preventing the attack.

B. I am a fighter and aggressor, it is in my blood.

Next Session

Bela describes the dreams she had some time back:

Maternal grandmother gives me mental torture, I experience agony. Everyone tortures the other in my dream.

Bela is too much concerned about everyone, her relatives in particular. She always thinks her father will be in a pitiable condition after her mother died. Her dreams indicate:

1. Her obsession about her agony and suffering, considers all members of the family responsible.

It may be just a dream version of what she constantly thinks in her waking state. The dreams are acting as an outlet of the suffering her mind is undergoing. Her subconsciousness may have attempted to cleanse itself of the great obsession under which it is living. Her mind is attempting to bring them into readable state in order to get rid of them.

2. She is not happy with her actions and doings, and regrets her behaviour because she is basically a compassionate person, a person who cares for others, It is only because of fear of torture that she takes to violence as a defensive measure. She fears her own future, she fears that in future her entire family will, like her, suffer torture from each other because they do not have sufficient control over their behaviour or necessary defense mechanism to avoid torturing each other.

The inference that she is full of fear is also evident from what happened last week. There was a matrimonial advertisement. Bela contacted him on phone. He responded, and at his suggestion went to meet him at a particular restaurant. It was a cheap restaurant in a rather bad locality. As she met the man and talked to him, she felt she had been trapped. When she said such a restaurant was no place to meet, he offered to take her to the nearby flat where he claimed to live alone. Bela became all the more suspicious and felt great fear. Somehow, she managed to escape on an auto-ricksaw and returned home, trembling with fear and terror. She narrated the whole incident. She was afraid that he might pursue her. She had, however, not given him her home address, but feared he might get it from her office. She received a phone call from him the next day but refused to go to see him even in a good hotel. She was still full of terror and fear. She was counselled that there was nothing so unusual to make her so terrified, and there was nothing to fear; and in any case she was herself of an aggressive type and could tear the man to pieces if he tried to harass her, so there was no cause for her to fear. She became consoled, gathered courage and became calm.

This episode reveals that basically she is a woman suffering from fear, she uses violence only as a defence mechanism.

She suffers from what may be termed Human phobia. She is afraid of human beings because from her early childhood she has been a victim of domestic tyranny. Her husband also gave her nothing but misery. She has lost confidence in people. Society does not offer her security, the security every person needs, especially a lonely young woman.

She is all alone, she is afraid of living alone, she desires to have company, but because of her loss of faith and confidence in individuals, she is unable to socialise and make friends.

C. You should build faith in the basic goodness of all human beings. You are good so is everyone else. Just develop greater confidence in yourself, your colleagues and neighbours and everyone else, you will find a new world has opened up to welcome you.

Next Session

Bela was extremely tense. She had received a letter from her parents asking her to remarry her divorced husband. This had made her lose control of herself, and she made a bedlam and flurry in her house, wept and cried so much and so loud that it attracted all the neighbours. She frantically went to the flat upstairs to phone but could not get the line and continued boiling inside.

B. I had also quarrelled with a person working in the office. It was the first time in my life, that I had let a challenging person go unhurt.

The incident had upset her balance of mind and she was bursting with rage when she came back home, and on receiving the letter from her parents she got out of control. Her complaint was that though her parents knew the man is suffering from a disease, and there was a divorce because it was impossible for them to live together, still they were insisting on her marrying him again only because he is of their caste. Her parents, however, feel he is the only man who can accept her, no one else will.

C. Calm down Bela, now everything is over, you have given vent to your rage.

B. I am convinced that I can never improve or change and my place is only in the mental hospital.

C. Every cloud has a silver lining. Don't you see that today you did let the man escape your wrath. Is it not something strange and commendable?

B. (Bela smiles). I don't know how and why I behaved so strangely, this may have been due to the counselling.

C. And this may not be the end but the beginning of a life of normal behaviour. Today is your birthday, and the day's good behaviour (free of violence) is a good sign. You are improving, you are changing, one day you will be as normal in your behaviour as any other girl.

[Her problem is connected with her father's annoying behaviour and also with her inability to find a husband. She is very keen to have a husband and her own children. But still she seems to have no intention to cultivate the emotion of love, probably because the emotion of hatred has gone so deep in her sub-conscious mind that she feels unable to permit any positive emotion enter her consciousness. The process of counselling has to go on.]

C. Try to change your pattern of life. Believe that Bela of the past is dead and gone, a new Bela has come into existence, a Bela who wants to be happy, non-excitable, friendly.

B. But, if I will behave like a good girl, say hello to my colleagues or wish good morning to my boss, everyone will think something has gone wrong with me, and that I have become abnormal, my changed behaviour will be taken as abnormal. I am afraid to change.

C. I don't think everyone will react like this, the reaction generally may be something different, one of approval and appreciation. You have come here to change. So you should start behaving like the girl you want to be. Instead of feeling ashamed, you should feel proud to have developed into a new woman, having the kind of personality you wish to have. You should hope for a better response from everyone; behave like a friend, and give up the fear of being misunderstood, and then see the result.

B. I shall try.

C. Give it a week's trial.

Here is some home work for you: write an essay on such a topic as:

(*a*) Violence is the weapon of the coward.

(*b*) Violence is always the result of frustration.

(*c*) Use colours for making paintings, just put colours on a canvas.

(*d*) Show your love to children by offering them toffees, make friendship with children in your neighbourhood.

(*e*) Bring flowers and keep them in your room.

(*f*) Try mixing with people.

Next Session

B. My dictionary does not contain the word 'Politeness'. I am by nature rude. Recently someone high-up phoned and asked me to connect the phone to my boss, the General Manager. I was too busy with the work already in hand, and directed the caller to contact another phone number as I was busy, and slammed the phone. The gentleman complained of my impolite and rude behaviour. I was warned by my senior not to behave rudely in future.

It is impossible for me to be polite, I had done nothing wrong in asking the caller to contact another secretary. I was rude only in saying so and slamming the phone; was there anything wrong I did?

C. You were, of course, right, but courtesy is a norm of good behaviour. In future try to be polite.

B. I shall keep this in mind.

[Bela, as advised, tried to make her room more lively.

She brought some sketches she had made earlier; they had only thorns. She was asked to avoid thorns and think of flowers and paint them with bright colours without worrying about their shape and to continue her sketching programme. Her new sketches show not only thorns but also flowers.

She has been asked to buy a canvas, a few paints and brushes and start painting on the canvas. This will provide her the happiness of creativity and make her vision of the world more lively and colourful.]

Next Session

B. I still frown and do not keep a smiling face in the office because that will look artificial and forced. It will not correctly show my inner feelings which contain nothing but anger. Everyone believes I am a bad girl, not open to correction; my father also says so. I know everyone considers me an incorrigible villain.

C. Do not think like that. Try to change your behaviour, just try.

B. I remain aloof because my mixing-up will make everyone around discover that I am a devil with a capital "D". That will lead them to hate and fear me more. The consequence will be that no one will like to be my friend or talk to me. I therefore, think I should wear a mask and let everyone see a wrong image of myself in which I should appear as a mute Goddess, a nice, decent, well-behaved woman who loves silence and aloofness.

[In this process she attempts to make everyone see a masked picture of hers and not her real self.]

C. No one likes a dumb woman, one who shuns company and wants to live in a closed crucible, it makes people feel suspicious.

Cultivate positive, healthy emotions, and maintain consistent good temper. Do something which might give you happiness, and then enjoy it, and continue doing it for at least thirty minutes at a time. Do some painting, or reading of novels, short-stories and other books.

You have to change your beliefs about yourself. You have in you the virtues which only exceptional people possess. You have donated one kidney to save the life of your sister. You did it voluntarily and for no gain. But if no one, not even the recipient of the kidney, has a good word for you, it is not your fault but the meanness of others. Everyone your father, sister, relatives instead of praising you, has tried to belittle its value and branded you as an evil person. This has left a permanent scar on your psyche, just remove it. By donating the kidney you had done something praiseworthy and not to be decried. See the whole thing in its correct perspective and you will see the inner goodness of yourself.

B. I have started wishing good morning to my G.M.

C. Become more cordial with your colleagues, chat and laugh with them.

B. But I fear if I will talk and laugh with them, they will respond in a way I would not wish, and that would make me tense and (maybe) even violent. So I think it is better to keep aloof and avoid trouble.

C. Have faith in the effectiveness of good behaviour.
Behave like other girls in the office.

B. I am not normal like other girls, I cannot talk and behave like them.

C. Try to copy them. Be courteous and polite like them, be happy and smiling like them. All this is necessary because you feel you are not normal. Give up the idea that you are different and not like the other girls. Try to make friends and you will find everyone is just as you are. All you need is to cut short the distance, if you will take one step they will take two steps to feel oneness with you.

B. How can I do all that, I am totally upset. Very recently I had got angry at my father when he visited me. I have not yet been able to forget the same. He had condemned and cursed me and had said I would never be blessed and happy and will always remain a cursed woman, I may marry again and again, but will never be able to live as a married woman. His curse made me lose my temper. I cannot get over my father's curse, I am doomed.

C. Any woman in your position would have got enraged on receiving curses from her own father. Your behaviour was quite normal, abnormality was not in you, but in your father's behaviour. So, don't get upset, forget the event. A father can never curse his own daughter from his heart, so the curse will not be effective. He only meant that you should remarry your ex-husband. Try to analyse and see the real intent and meaning of your father's words. Learn to forget and forgive. Remember, a curse is only a thought, it has no substance, no potential, no power to enforce itself or effect the life of anyone, not even of the person cursed. So, do not worry. Enjoy the meal tonight with music classical or light, as might suit your taste.

Next Session

Bela reported she was feeling better, she did not have anything unpleasant during her holiday trip with a friend to Haridwar, as she had feared.

During the last four weeks she did not have any trouble in the office either. Things appeared to be going on a little more smoothly.

But still, she is suffering from a severe fear of the future. She is always afraid of losing her job because no sooner the officer says anything unpalatable, she thinks of resigning and if she does, she loses the job. She 1might also be forced to give her resignation by circumstances not under her control.

She is also very much against her parents, particularly her mother, for their suggestion (and insistence) to remarry the same man she had divorced because she thinks it would be impossible for her to live with him. They also threaten to withdraw all facilities (residential house) if she refuses to remarry him.

She is suffering from various fears like:

1. Fear of losing employment. It is based on her own intolerance and reaction to some recent remarks of her boss. Her past experience makes her fear that any day may see her tendering her resignation and becoming jobless. This fear makes her apprehensive of everyone in the office, and has generated high tension in her mind. She has lost peace of mind and suffers from all the traumatic consequences of stress and distress.

2. Fear of not getting a new man to marry her and the pressure to

remarry her divorced husband.

Counselling : Given on the following lines:

(*i*) Hope for the best and do not think that the worst will happen. Pandora's - fairy of HOPE is designated your God fairy. Fairy of hope will always remain with you and you will not take any action under apprehension or fear without consulting her.

(*ii*) No incident may ever occur which may make you tender resignation, and remember that since you have begun taking counselling you have never even attempted to submit your resignation. So give up this fear as a thing of the past.

(*iii*) You should accept that your boss and other seniors have the right to think and take such decisions as they deem proper, and to ask you to act in a particular manner. You can reason out, but not take offence and resign.

(*iv*) You should become more tolerant, more polite, and good humoured. If you are happy and tolerant, your thoughts will generate similar feelings in others, and you might get better response.

(*v*) Instead of being ready with a resignation letter, you determine not to resign and to continue in the job, and that you shall not resign without consulting me.

(*vi*) Freedom from fear can come only by your living in and thinking of only the present and not worrying about the future till it becomes the present.

C. Regarding your problem, don't you think that everyone, including your mother, has the right to have a particular opinion; and that your parents too have a right to give suggestions about your marriage? It is, of course, not right for them to suggest that you should marry again the man whom you have divorced. but you cannot enter their mind and change their thinking. No doubt it is open to you not to accept their suggestion. Let them think as they like and you should not get disturbed by their suggestions. You know it is not possible for you to live with that particular person and you have the right to stick to your decision not to marry him. Go ahead to find another man. There is no reason why you should not get a desirable match, you have only to widen your area of choice.

B. I am making efforts, but with passage of time, chances are getting bleak.

Counselling given for ego-strengthening on following lines:

1. Basically you are a good girl. You are a woman with compassion and love, love and concern for others is demonstrated by your act of donating one kidney to your sister without expecting any

return.

2. Adverse circumstances during childhood made you prone to be too apprehensive, too afraid of everyone, and you resorted to aggressiveness as a defence mechanism. As a consequence you lost faith in every individual. That led to more and more loss of faith in yourself ; more and more aggressive attitude in you.

3. This lack of confidence in others and in yourself has developed in you fear of the future, fear of poverty and loss of job. This fear leads to your becoming frustrated and aggressive, which you wrongly treat as your weapon of strength, although it is only an expression of fear and fright.

4. The failure and breakdown of your marriage has led to your developing distrust in every man. It has meant loss of love for everyone, including children. You have a longing for a husband and children but by being deprived of either, you have become averse to coming in contact even with children. You cannot tolerate others' children because you have none of your own. You are finding yourself to be an abnormal woman as everyone of your age has a husband and children. This is absurd thinking, there are thousands of people whose marriages have failed, but they have no courage to get divorce; you are a brave girl, you cannot tolerate unhappiness, so don't get disheartened. Instead of developing aversion, develop love for all.

She was put under a little bit of hypnosis and given following suggestions to strengthen her ego, and advised to remember and repeat them:

I am a good, normal, loving person. I'll no longer harbour distrust for any person. I'll trust all. If I'll trust everyone and have a good feeling for everyone, everyone in turn will have trust in me and have good feelings towards me.

I know I am basically a good person, and I harbour malice towards none, I am pure and loving at heart and have full faith that I shall be able to act like a very normal person. I shall frown at none but give a smile to everyone. I know if I smile I shall feel happier. My smile will travel around, everyone else's face will also begin to glow with my smile.

I decide, henceforth. I shall never carry this grim face which shows I am ill at heart, I will always carry a broad smile on my face. It will change my outlook on life. It will kindle the flame of happiness in my heart. I'll feel happier, it will give me a new look, a new face, a new confidence. I'll cease to be afraid of others, and become much more confident.

Smile on my face will not look something odd, but only reveal the goodness that is lying hidden in my heart. It will bring out my true nature and help me become more friendly with my colleagues and with everyone I meet, my neighbours will also begin to feel better.

I really love every child, how innocent they are! But I am afraid of showing my love to them because I had an unhappy childhood. Now, however, things have changed. I am no longer that little child who had suffered the abuses and curses of all including my parents. I am now a grown-up woman, a mature person, capable of protecting every child including the ADULT little Bela if she is made to suffer now. I can console her, protect her.

Now I am an adult, fully confident of living a happy life. I have my own individuality, my own personality; neither can I live the life of anybody else nor can I permit anybody else to live my life for me. Today, I am independent, confident, happy, capable of looking after myself and protecting my interests.

I have been a little impulsive in my behaviour, I am moved more by my excitement, sentiment and feelings than considered reason. No longer shall I act like that; before taking any decision or action I shall cool down and reason out. I shall always act on the basis of reasoned thoughts and not impulses.

I am not afraid of the future as I do not know what it is. It may be better, my fairy friend HOPE tells me my future will be brighter than today. I am hopeful of the future, I believe everything will turn out well. I am happy, confident. I love the plants, their green leaves, I love flowers, they give me pleasure they give me joy, happiness, love, peace, pleasure, I am happy, I am happy.

Next Session

Bela is much more calm and composed today.

B. I have succeeded in restraining myself from quarrelling with my co-worker who tried to irritate me after one week's truce. But today, though I had started boiling up, I managed to keep the temper under control. I did not adopt the aggressive attitude. I always recalled in my mind the word CALM and the suggestions received during counselling.

C. It was very good you remained calm and quiet.

B. But everyone thinks I am an insane devil.

C. How do you know that? You cannot read what is in somebody else's mind. If you remain relaxed and then talk, no one will think of you as a mad woman or a ferocious tigress. In fact you behave aggressively only because you think you need security. Ever since you were an infant, you did not get security the parental security, and you started wearing the mask of a ferocious tigress. You want everyone to remain warned that you are a ferocious tigress who will tear off any person who comes near her. By wearing the mask of abnormality you are only trying to conceal your weakness. Take off this mask of a mad ferocious tigress; become a woman who is neither afraid of anyone nor is a threat to anyone.

B. It seems I have been wearing a mask, now I will put it off and behave like a normal good woman.

Next Session

Bela seemed to be in a pleasant mood.

B. I am happy at my latest conquest. I had received a lashing from a manager a week back, I was taken unawares, and hence could not fight even a verbal battle. I had done nothing to provoke him. I was shocked and felt disgraced. For one week I suffered the torment. Everyday, every minute I had been thinking of how to take revenge. I have never accepted defeat. This time, as I was taken unaware, I could not strike back, even though I was innocent and had nothing to do with him. I became upset and shaken and went on brooding and planning how to take revenge, how to humiliate him. I lost my sleep, my peace of mind. I started telling everyone I met in the office or elsewhere how I planned to retaliate, and humiliate him.

Three days later I found the opportunity. The same man was withholding my application of 'No objection certificate' for getting a passport. I had got the information that orders had been passed and it was this man who was sitting over the file for the past six months. I went to the general manager's room where this man was also present and burst out. The general manager sent him out of the room, calmed me by assuring that he would not abuse me any more, and, if he did it again, disciplinary action will be taken against him. He made me drink a glass of water which cooled me down. Next day, I received the no-objection certificate.

C. So you won the battle, the guilty has been punished. But there was no reason for you to suffer agony for the interim period. As you had done no wrong, you should have talked to him directly. He might have apologised because he was only passing on his own humiliation on to you, it was a case of transference of guilt. It was very good that you did not react violently and allowed the attack to pass off.

B. Even now I feel surprised how it happened. Maybe the repetitive counselling has conditioned my mind.

Next Session

Finally, one day Bela suddenly got married to an NRI from the USA. Marriage did not last two days. There was a fight and separation with bad blood on both sides.

The astrologer's prediction about her marriage being happy and long had proved to be worng.

The man filed a suit for divorce in the USA. He sent nasty letters to her, and copies to the Managing Director in her office, and to her parents. She also retorted and wrote back but did not contest the divorce action. This meant a serious loss of face for her and she went on three month's leave, as she became too depressed and upset.

She took long journeys to religious places in the Himalayas. But it brought her no consolation.

She is mighty afraid of her American husband. She still gets threatening letters from him saying he would come to India and enforce his right as her husband. Sometimes she thinks it was good, but generally is unhappy as once again she had to suffer the loss of matrimonial solace.

She also went to Mumbai to investigate how his first wife had died. She met members of her family and found that she was tortured by this man and forced to commit suicide. She wants to take revenge not only for his bad treatment towards her but also for torturing his first wife.

The court in the U.S.A. has decreed divorce. She is afraid of her ex-husband as she believes that even after the US decree of divorce he will come to India and exercise his marital rights because the marriage was performed in India. She is suffering from immense fear, but still desires to take revenge by humiliating him.

B. I am so upset that I would commit suicide.

C. You may, but wait till you have taken revenge.

Now you have nothing to fear, you are now a free woman. Divorce decree passed by the U.S. court is as good as passed by an Indian court. You should now live without fear, he is no more your husband and can do nothing to injure you.

B. So he can do nothing?

C. Absolutely nothing, feel happy.

[Bela has tears in her eyes, and wipes them]

Go ahead and find another husband.

[Bela laughs, she is completely relaxed.]

She is badly in search of company; a husband. She feels deprived as she feels particularly bad when she finds that everyone except her has a husband and a family. She still wishes the American may return, although she hates him and fears him. Various types of thoughts make her confused and unhappy. Sometimes she thinks of her first husband. He is willing to come back; but she is not ready to accept him again because she thinks it will mean her defeat.

She lives under an illusion. In matters of intimate relationships, she believes, she is someone like a goddess whom the husband must worship as a devotee and serve as a slave.

Prolonged and sustained counselling has been given to her to make her realise the wisdom of being realistic, practical and looking at things in their true perspective.

Next Session

Bela has been generally well. She got a new house and a phone. Her pessimism is changing into optimism, her negativity is moving towards positivity, and introvertion towards extrovertion. But she is still far away from being just normal. She has come down from the pedestal of goddesses and become human enough to have happy relationships with men. Her fear of men has gone, she is feeling relaxed and happy.

Next Session

B. I am suffering from extreme fear, I am very afraid.

C. Of what?

B. I was having an affair with a handsome young friend. I became pregnant. My life became hell as everyone in the neighbourhood was passing remarks on his visits and my spending nights with him. I was afraid also of my colleagues in the office. The criticism and condemnation I feared would be too horrible to bear. I could think of no option but to have abortion, and I did have it.

C. You should have had the courage to tell everyone the truth. So much did you need and long for a human companion, and when one came, you threw him away. Did not your boyfriend intervene?

B. He did ask me not to get abortion, and was ready to give his name to the child. He was, however, too young to force his will on me. I had extremely nice time with him, now he is getting married to some other girl.

And, now my problem has become more serious.

C. What ?

B. My desire to get married and have a child has become more intense. I have given advertisement for the same. How will I be able to have a husband if the man comes to know of the pregnancy and abortion. No one will now marry me, and even if he does he will throw me out on getting to know about my affair. I am terrified to think of the consequences. My father will also be enraged on knowing about my affair. I have no courage. I feel I do not have even the physical strength to bear the child. Oh, I am so afraid of delivery, it is so painful, I shall never be able to face it.

C. Calm down. Today you do not have any man ready and willing to marry you, so don't worry about your future husband; let him appear on the scene, then we will talk about it. Don't be too terrified, even on being informed of your pregnancy he may happily accept you and marry you. Wait till the occasion arises.

Your second fear that you will not be able to bear the child is also baseless. Did you have any difficulty during your first pregnancy? How long after did you get abortion ?

B. Six weeks; during this period I had no problem in harbouring the foetus in my womb.

C. Then why are you afraid? If there was no problem during six weeks, there will be no problem during nine months. Was it all not a pleasant experience after such a long, lone waiting ?

B. Yes, it was. But the pain of delivery, Oh I cannot bear it, I have seen in movies how women suffer with labour pain.

C. Firstly, it is a bearable pain, and every woman can and does bear it; however, now it is not necessary to go through it as the operation can be performed to get the child delivered without unbearable labour pain. Anyway, there is no reason at the moment to worry about this fear. You are not pregnant, so why think of that pain. Postpone it till you become pregnant. Do you have any other boyfriend?

B. Yes, I have a boyfriend, a lover. If I get pregnant with him the same situation will arise again, and my neighbours will throw me out and I shall face trouble in office. All that will be impossible to bear a second time.

C. Don't be afraid, have courage to face the world. You are already thirty-seven, there is not much time for you to wait. You have already given advertisement and you might find a husband, then there will be no problem. It has become common in the West for women to have children without getting married.

B. Yes, I have read about unmarried mothers, but that is not the case here except in hi-fi social circles.

C. Maybe, but you need not worry about this fear till you become pregnant. And this time you will not go for abortion, and bear the child whatever may happen.

So live without fear, carry on with your boyfriend if you fail to get a husband. You have longed for and suffered for more than fifteen years, do not suffer any more. If you get a child, all your problems will disappear.

B. I also think so, but I can't face my neighbours, relatives and colleagues.

C. Have courage and ignore them. In any case do not feel scared till the occasion arises.

[Bela looks happy, her fears have gone, she is no more afraid of pregnancy or delivery pain.]

B. There are no marks of any type on my body from which anyone might guess or know I had pregnancy and abortion.

C. So, forget it. Take it as if it were all a dream. Just go on with life without any kind of fear in your mind.

B. I feel relaxed and happy. I am no more afraid of pregnancy and the pain of delivery. I wish I had carried the child and faced the world with courage.

C. You are a brave woman, never be afraid of public criticism. Learn to face the world. Truth is supreme. Fear is only the outcome of the feeling of guilt. In making love you commit no wrong. Neither love is ignoble, nor is a love-child.

B. I agree, but I felt terrified when I thought everyone will brand me guilty. Guilt and fear came together.

C. Very well, let us forget it for the present. Tell me, was it is not for the first time in your life that you had felt real happiness when you spent a few moments with your boyfriend?

B. Yes, it was a heavenly pleasure. I got real happiness in his company, and sex with him was very fulfilling. I also enjoyed conception but had to get abortion as I was unable to face the fear of social onslaught. I really never had any happiness in my life. The moments I spent with my boyfriend were movements of bliss, which I can never forget, even their thought gives me unfathomable happiness.

C. This great experience of love and sex has made a great impact on your life, and now you are a changed woman. From a woman who had known only bitterness you have changed into a women who has enjoyed real love and happiness. The foetus has no doubt gone out of your body, the happiness it gave you continues to live in your memory. It is a psychic treasure, do not lose it; enjoy it, preserve it, let your whole personality grow with the memory of that happiness.

B. I do feel happiness and wish I may never lose it.

Ultimately, Bela did succeed in getting over her bitterness against intimacy with men and relished the experience which every young woman needs to get fulfilment and bliss. Love, adulation, affection, and infatuation succeeded in making her overcome her fears and complexes. It was the love of Bela's lover and her own total surrender that gave her the feeling not only of security but also of being cared for, being treated as a human being and as someone who deserved the love of a very desirable person. Her ego was fully satisfied. She saw her conquest in being conquered by Cupid. From the 'Beast' she became the 'Beauty' a woman full of compassion and love. The 'Woman of Hate' has become the 'Woman of Love'.

MEENA

I am miserable, I am always suffering from some sort of fear.

Diagnostic Scan

Meena is middle-aged. she is forty-five, and has entered the stage of menopause. Ever since her menopause she feels more tense and gets bouts of anger more frequently. She feels nervous and worries very often about the future of her two sons.

About five years back her husband had a serious accident in which he suffered multiple injuries. Since then he has become more irritable and gets angry at the least excuse. His irritants consist of everything, however insignificant it may be, which is not to his liking, e.g. non-removal of some thing from the place he did not want it to be. He even criticises and condemns his wife for conversation with guests and visitors if he considers it was not appropriate, and he always finds it was not so. He thinks he is the wisest of all and expects everyone should act and behave in the way he would have liked them to. His sons remain afraid of him. Whenever she does even a little thing, argument develops and he gets agitated; as a consequence she becomes upset.

Meena suffer from depression and body pain. Her right arm and right hand become numb. She fears she might get paralysed and become disabled.

She often weeps and cries. Even here, her tears began to flow. There is some hidden sorrow in her mind which makes her shed tears without her knowing the cause.

Counselling

M. I am miserable, nervous, always suffering from some sort of fear.

C. What kind of fear, please speak more specifically.

M. I do not really know, but I think my fear is about the future of my sons, I wish they may be able to earn and live well.

C. But, they are already doing well, and the chances are that they will succeed in life, and make your dreams come true. So there is no reason for you to worry or have fear on that account. Anyway, can you control their fate of destiny?

M. No, I cannot.

C. Then let them grow with freedom, let things happen as they happen. If you cannot know or control their future, forget about it, think only about the present.

Do you have financial constraints.

M. No, there was a time when my husband's business had failed, and also when he had suffered the accident; now there is no such problem, though I cannot say I am very well-off. My husband hands over all his earnings to me, and I have to manage the household. Sometimes I find a little crunch, but generally I manage to save something.

C. So, you should have no cause for fear of the future. (General counselling was given to bring her out of the fear complex.)

The cause of your fears and tears seems to be something different. How is your relationship with your husband?

M. It is so so.

C. Be specific. Do you have normal sex. You have happy nights ?

M. Yes, in a way. I go to bed at 11.00, he continues watching T.V. till 1.00 and then comes and sleeps.

C. So, he tries to get vicarious romance and sex through movies.

M. Probably.

C. Why don't you insist or at least try to take him along when you retire? If necessary, you can have a T.V. in your bedroom.

M. We do have a T.V. in the bedroom, but he is never in a mood to come to bed till he is tired enough to fall asleep.

C. It seems the main cause of his remaining cross with you is lack of emotional and physical communication. It would be better if you take a positive step toward establishing this communication. The cause of your tension and distress and their psychosomatic effects on your limbs, etc. may also be due to the blockade of your emotions and desires, and lack of your emotional and physical communication with your husband. This may be causing some sort of disappointment and dejection in your life. So you should try to move forward.

Do you wish him goodbye when he goes to the factory and welcome him when he comes back? Do you normally give him a kiss?

M. No.

C. Please do. And why are you not putting on proper make-up on your face?

M. This is how I remain.

C. You need to have a change. From today, you wear proper make-up, dress more elegantly and give him a good welcome with a broad smile when he returns in the evening.

M. He would say I have become mad, and would laugh scornfully.

C. Try it. Doesn't matter even if he calls you mad, madness is better than depression which makes you suffer misery. Please do not live like a tree with leaves falling off, leaving it bare, instead bloom, as it does in the spring, let there always be happiness in your life, let your face, your whole body bloom like a blossom. Develop the emotion of love, it will give fragrance to your entire life, it will change your misery into gaiety and joy. Let everyday of your life be a day of joy, and every night a night of honeymoon. I do not mean you have sex every night, but you should make love every night. Be as happy as you were during your honeymoon.

M. I understand, I shall try.

C. Love yourself, fall in love with yourself, try to make yourself as happy as possible. Fall in love with someone, that will rejuvenate you, and the best person to fall in love with is your husband.

M. I have never in my life fallen in love with anyone, including my husband.

C. Doesn't matter, the past is past; try to live in the present. Both of you are in your forties; it is the best age to generate love, to fall in love with each other. Once you will take the initiative, he will surely respond, and both of you will get a beautiful emotional experience which you have missed so long.

M. It seems I am going to live in a new world, a world of love and romance.

C. Yes, that is precisely my intention. Please do give this experiment a chance, and you shall find a new spring coming into your life; all your woes and problems will disappear.

M. I am already feeling relaxed, happy, and thrilled. I wish I could get immediately and for ever into this new world, the world of happiness and joy.

C. The gates are open, just walk in.

After Quite Some Time

C. How are you Meena?

M. I am fine. I have tried the experiment, it has yielded good result. I feel relaxed and comfortable.

SAMISHTA

No more does she regard herself the little thief...

M. (Samishta's mother) Samishta has the bad habit of stealing money from my purse. I fear leaving even my ornaments in the open. Only yesterday, I discovered she had stolen a Rs. 500. currency note from my purse.

S. But, I did not know it was a Rs. 500 note, I thought it was a hundred rupee note.

C. But that does not make any difference, what did you do with that money?

S. It was only yesterday that Mummy discovered it, I had taken it sometime back to purchase snacks for my friends for lunch in school, and the canteen man returned only Rs. 30.

C. So he cheated you. Do you think it was good? After all, whether it belonged to you or your mummy, that man got the benefit because you never told your mummy. If you had asked for it, your family would not have lost this money.

M. I never refuse, and give her money whenever she asks. Of course I cannot afford Rs. 100 everyday. I am only a teacher, still I try to satisfy all her needs.

C. Samishta, why do you need all that money?

S. My friends always eat their lunch in the school canteen, and they decry the home-made lunch I take to school. I have to join them and have to pay occasionally.

C. To keep up your prestige?

S. Yes.

C. Do they not bring their lunch?

S. No, they live in the boarding house. One of them is from Mumbai and she gets Rs. 1000 every month and spends lavishly.

C. They are rich girls. How are they in their studies?

S. Not good, just like me.

C. That means you do not have company of girls who are good students.

S. I do not like them, they are always busy with their books, they have no spirits, no fun.

C. You know your mother is a teacher and has a limited income, she has to live within her means. Anyway, how much money do you need in a month?.

S. 100.

C. Suppose your mother gives you Rs. 100 will you then not pick it stealthily from her purse?

S. Yes, I will not.

C. Then it is agreed. Why not you manage the family finances? Let us appoint you the finance minister. You will be paid Rs. 400 and you shall give to your mother whatever she needs for household expenses; you will be free to withdraw whatever you think necessary for yourself, but it will not exceed Rs. 100 in the month. You will maintain regular account of all the expenses and show them to your mother everyday.

S. I am willing.

M. Then she will spend the whole amount in one day on herself.

C. No, she will not, because she is the finance minister in charge of the finances and has to spend the money as you do to run the house.

M. Will she give me Rs. 200 ? I need for Tuesday market.

C. Yes she will. You will examine the account everyday, and replenish the fund when it is finished.

Samishta, I hope you would always remember that the money is your money, and as finance minister you have to consult your mother, who is the chief minister, about the budget and the expenditure.

S. I shall. I am agreeable to this arrangement.

C. Samishta looks quite intelligent. Does she remain under some tension?

M. Maybe, but there does not seem to be any apparent reason for her stress or tension. I look to all her needs.

C. Very well, let us forget it for the moment and try the experiment.

M. I doubt it will succeed.

C. I think otherwise. I hope she will change. But there is greater need for you to change, Madam, you seem to be a negative thinker and a pessimist. Become an optimist and think positive. It would not only bring happiness to you but also bring a change in Samishta; she will become the girl of your dream.

M. I wish it may be so.

Next Session

Samishta is very happy and relaxed. Her mother also feels happy and peaceful. It did not become necessary to give a lumpsum money to

Samishta, she thought it was better to ask her mother for money whenever she needed. She has been asking for reasonable amounts and her mother is happy to give it whenever she asks.

Samishta no more feels the need of stealing money. Her feeling of guilt has gone, no more does she regard herself a little thief, a person who could not face her loving mother like an innocent girl. A sense of dignity and self-esteem has developed in her.

Her hidden tension has also gone and she has begun taking interest in her studies, and feels confident that she will do well in the examinations and will pass.

ANURADHA

Anuradha is suffering from the feeling of guilt and shame. She admits she feels shame because her daughter-in-law has made three suicide attempts, but denies she has a feeling of guilt, although her feeling of shame has arisen only out of the suicide attempts made by her daughter-in-law.

Diagnostic Scan

Anuradha is in her fifties. Raja is her son and Reema, his wife, they have a three-year-old daughter.

Reema has attempted suicide three times.

She refuses to take psychiatric medicine. Raja is under psychiatric treatment for depression (withdrawal).

They (all) used to live together, the grand-daughter is very much attached to grandparents. Now Reema and Raja live on the upper floor in the house of Raja's parents. Left to herself, she would shift to an independent house.

Reema has a young maid whom she treats as her friend and confidante. She is made incharge of the child during the time Reema goes to work. She keeps the door shut and does not let the child come down to spend her time with grandparents. This has created a lot of tension for the grandparents, particularly Anuradha. Anuradha says she is happy, though she is not, and is feeling greatly distressed because of the loss of the child's company.

Reema thinks that it is Raja's depression that is the cause of her misery and was responsible for her attempts to commit suicide. She feels upset because she thinks she will have to live all her life in this state of misery.

After a long session it has come out:

(*a*) Anuradha is suffering from the feeling of guilt and shame. She admits she feels shame because her daughter-in-law has made three suicide attempts, but denies she has a feeling of guilt, although her feeling of shame has arisen out of the suicide attempts made by her daughter-in-law.

(*b*) Anuradha has a latent fear of losing her son, she has already lost her grand-daughter.

(*c*) Anuradha tries to show that she considers Reema a very good woman and loves her and wants always to live with her. This is a case of self-deception. She really believes Reema to be guilty of separating the grandchild from her, and making Raja go into depression. She is not ready to admit the truth that she does not consider Reema to be a good and innocent woman. Deep in her heart she has hatred for Reema, and wishes to punish her.

(*d*) Raja has gone into depression apparently because he has no courage to face the demand of Reema to have a home independent of his parents. He loves his parents and has told Reema he cannot leave them, and if Reema liked she could move to some other place.

(*e*) Reema is grieved because she believes her mother-in-law is trying to deprive her of her daughter and her husband. It is this conflict which has created animosity in her against her mother-in-law, and made her prefer her maid to her mother-in-law for being incharge of the child during her absence.

(*f*) Anuradha has already suffered a heart attack and this is another reason why Raja does not want to live away from his parents. This has led to severe conflict between him and his wife and to her repeated suicide attempts.

(*g*) Anuradha does not get enough sleep since the daughter-in-law has established a separate kitchen.

(*h*) Reema seems to be not much worried about the impact of her behaviour on her husband, his parents, and the child. Her grief arising from her strained relationship with her mother-in-law is too much for her to bear, she prefers death to a life of mental agony with a husband suffering from depression and the mother-in-law putting all blame on her.

Counselling

C. Anuradha, you are trying only to deceive yourself and everyone else by putting on a mask to show that you consider Reema a good and innocent woman who loves you and desires to live with you, and that in your heart you do not feel guilty, but only ashamed, for the attempts of suicide made by Reema. You must face the truth, accept things as they are. You have done no such wrong for which you may feel guilty or ashamed. There is nothing wrong in loving your son or the granddaughter. You have only to be a little more considerate towards Reema. She also needs your love and affection, try to treat her as your daughter, as a young woman dependent on your compassion. All you need is to change your attitude towards Reema.

Your only fault is that you basically hate and dislike Reema. You have to give this up. Hatred is a negative emotion and causes agony, substitute it with love which is a positive emotion and brings happiness.

You should open dialogue with Reema concerning the child so that the feeling of deprivation may go, and Reema may realise her mistake and correct her attitude.

A. It is easier said than done. I cannot bear being deprived of the company of the child. Only yesterday after Reema went away the child came rushing to me, but was immediately called back by the maid. Even the child felt sad, but was helpless.

C. You directly talk to Reema in regard to the child and explain to her that you have no intention of snatching away the child from her, and on the other hand, the child's withdrawal is likely to adversely affect the emotional health of the child. The child needs love, which in the absence of mother, can be given by the grandparents. Promise to be good to both. Tell her you love the child and have nothing against Reema.

A. I will talk to Reema directly and explain my feelings to her. I understand, it may be possible to reach Reema's heart through the child. I shall try my best.

C. Try to have a common dinner. Be courteous at the table and show to Reema through your behaviour, that you love her.

A. Tomorrow we will dine together, and I shall do my best to make Reema feel happy.

C. Treat Reema with greater consideration, she needs your love. I am sure if you will show mercy, you will get mercy. It is only mutual regard and love that makes life happy. Even in the interest of your son it is necessary for you to see that Reema remains and attempts no more suicide.

A. I shall do my best to bring peace and happiness in the family.

C. You have also to realise and accept the truth that Reema feels unhappy because you do not give her love she craves for, and that she is living in agony because her husband suffers from depression. Please relax, and give up your concealed feelings of guilt and shame caused by Reema's attempts to commit suicide. The suicide attempts have caused feeling of guilt in you because you think she may not have taken such steps if you had been more caring and loving. However, it has become a matter of history so forget it and start a new chapter of happier relationship. Love is a person's strongest weapon, and you can easily conquer Reema by your love. It is necessary to make her happy, as on her happiness depends the happiness of your son, and ultimately your own happiness.

A. Can I forget Reema's unsavoury past behaviour?

C. Yes, you can, you should. It is no use remembering the past and going on suffering agony. Start today the new chapter of life. That will bring you happiness. All you need is to forget and forgive. Be magnanimous, pardon her, and feel the greatness of being a person who can give pardon to others, and love even one's enemy. Then, Reema is not your enemy, she is your son's wife and mother of your granddaughter.

A. I realise I am missing happiness and living in agony because of my harbouring in my heart a feeling of hatred against Reema. I am now determined to change myself, change my attitude and behaviour towards Reema, and start loving her. After all she is my daughter-in-law. From now on I shall treat her as my daughter and myself as her 'mother'.

C. It is great, your happiness is now a sure thing.

(After quite sometime, on phone.)

How are you Anuradha? How are your son and daughter-in-law?

A. Everything has changed, our relations are now quite normal. In the meantime, however, Reema changed her job and both of them have shifted to another house. They come to visit us almost every week. The magic of love has worked.

C. This is very good. How is your grand-daughter?

A. She is fine and Reema even permits her to stay with us. However, when she stays for more than a week with us, Reema gets suspicious.

C. Why ?

A. She thinks that her daughter's attachment to me will make her drawn away from her.

C. You can explain to Reema that you have no intention of taking away her daughter, and you are only giving her additional love. You are quite a tactful lady and, I am sure, you will be able to allay her fears. To win Reema's confidence, it may be better not to keep your granddaughter with you for long periods at a stretch.

A. I think, that would be ideal, and will remove from Reema's mind the little doubt that still remains lingering in her mind. But, on the whole, all problems have eased out and our life has become normal and happy.

KANTA

You have unconsciously taken yourself to be responsible for the misdeeds of your husband. It is this that generates in you the feeling of shame and guilt. You are simply not responsible for the actions of your husband. His misbehaviour cannot be deemed your misbehaviour. You have no reason to feel or harbour in your mind the feeling of guilt and shame. You are not even vicariously responsible for the reprehensible conduct of your husband.

Kanta is fifty-two, healthy but not fat. By appearance she looks morose and tense. She poses to be having no tension though she does not look so. She wants her husband a retired army officer to be psychologically treated.

K. He is a womaniser and this activity of his brings shame to me and my family. He drinks from morning till night. He also smokes a lot. His womanising habit had resulted in disputes even while he was in service. I have become particularly disturbed because of his recent misbehaviour with the maid of our married daughter who had come to visit us. It has become difficult for me to engage any maid, as my husband casts an amorous eye on every young woman, and makes advances. I have to remain constantly with the maids to give them protection. Word has gone round about his behaviour and I face contempt everywhere. My social life has been badly affected.

He squanders away all his income and makes no contribution to the running of the household. I was a working woman, but now retired and receive pension with which I somehow manage the household.

C. Bring him for counselling.

K. My husband is not willing to come for therapy probably because he does not consider himself a sick person. He feels what he does is his right and his privilege.

C. Kanta, you should then accept the fact that your husband is suffering from an incurable psychological malady and you should put up with his disgusting behaviour as part of his and your life. You must accept him as he is and live without tension. The tension you have developed and the agony you are suffering is due to your feeling that you are a part of your husband and his wrong deeds are your wrong deeds. It is this identifying yourself with your husband and his obnoxious behaviour that makes you feel sad and miserable.

You have unconsciously taken yourself to be responsible for the misdeeds of your husband. It is this that generates in you the feeling of shame and guilt. You are simply not responsible for the action of your husband. You have no reason to feel or harbour in your mind the feeling of guilt and shame. You are not even vicariously responsible for the reprehensible conduct of your husband.

Both the daughters are grown-up who know and understand the reality of the situation, same must be the case with persons in your social circle. Once you get rid of this feeling of guilt and shame, everyone will see and understand that you are innocent. This can happen only when you refuse do feel guilty or ashamed for the fault of your husband, and openly deny your responsibility.

K. I am feeling relieved of a burden. I think I have no reason for having the feeling of shame and guilt. [Tension has disappeared from her face, she looks completely relaxed].

C. You are, 'you you' are not 'he'; he is 'he', he is not 'you'. You are innocent, you are not guilty of any bad behaviour. He is guilty and responsible for what he does.

K. Yes, I am 'I', I am not 'he'. I am not guilty and have no reason to feel ashamed for his misdemeanours. I repudiate all responsibility for his abhorrent activities, and will no more feel ashamed for what he does. He, and not I, is guilty; it is he and not I who should feel ashamed.

C. You know things with your husband are beyond remedy. Your husband is suffering from a psychological aberration which you cannot cure, and for which your husband will not take necessary psychological support. There is no reason for you to let his guilt be transferred to you. From now on, you must feel exonerated and live a new life free of the feeling of guilt and shame.

[Acceptance of reality has helped Kanta free her mind of the feeling of shame and guilt. She has succeeded in stopping the transference of shame and guilt from her husband to herself. She is now a new individual with an identity of her own, independent of her husband.]

K. Oh, I am so relaxed, now I can live in peace.

Next Session (*on phone*)

K. Thank you, I have no more any problems. I no longer worry about the behaviour or conduct of my husband. I feel no remorse for his actions.

I find that seeing innocence on my face, everyone thinks there is nothing wrong with me. I am now quite happy and have no tension.

C. Good.

MIRICHIKA

Yes I cannot die again and again, night after night. If during the first nightmare I had died I would not be alive the next night or today. Anyway, now I am alive, I have a new life. In every way now I am a new woman.

First Session

Diagnostic Scan

Mirichika twenty-six, married, one child. Good natured, happy, smiling, a little shy, clings to her husband as if she was seeking his protection, wants him to stay with her during the counselling session. Tries to explain this by saying, she needs him because she is not fluent in speaking English or even Hindi, can speak only Telugu. She appears very nervous.

Mirichika looks ill and to be in agony.

Her husband says she is a psychic patient, she is under psychiatric treatment and takes heavy doses of tranquilisers for getting sleep at night. But the dose fails to bring full-night's sleep. Doctor threatens to increase the dose further. Other psychiatric medicines are also being administered.

She suffers from nervous breakdowns. Her whole body becomes numb, her nerves get tense and she feels numbness all over; first her fingers become numb and then gradually numbness spreads and the whole body gets affected. She feels energy sapping out of her entire body.

In the night her condition becomes worse. She does not get sound sleep. At times she wakes up, and once she is awake, she is unable to get sleep. Then she feels extremely nervous, frightened and panicky.

Once she had a nightmare recently, she dreamt she was dead. She woke up, felt very nervous and clung to her husband and daughter. She suffered great agony and fear. Fear of death now haunts her. She often gets the same nightmare.

Mirichika's husband thinks all her troubles, particularly the nightmare and fear of death, is the result of her taking some drink offered to her during Holi. He thinks it contained "Bhang" or something which made both of them unconscious for a while. Mirichika was not used to Holi in Andhra Pradesh. It was probably her first experience of being drenched with coloured water.

The explanation appears to be just a måke-belief excuse. There does not seem to be any nexus between the two events, either in proximity of time or nature of things.

Her looks, her way of talking and general behaviour, all reveal that she is suffering from intense emotional tension and stress.

Mirichika is a normal housewife, interested only in household chores. She does not want to take up any job beyond what is needed to run the house. After marriage she came to Noida. Her husband has a feeling of inferiority because most young women in Noida and Delhi speak fluent English and many work and earn a good salary. Mirichika complains that her husband vexes and coerces her by insisting that she should speak fluent English like other girls, and should learn computer operation. He has purchased a computer and insists that Mirichika should learn to operate it and thereby earn good money.

Mirichika says that her husband scolds her and repeatedly says he had dreamt of marrying a girl who could speak fluent English and work to support his plan of establishing a computer-cum-management institute. However, he had to marry Mirichika because of his father.

This is a constant source of anxiety and tension for Mirichika. Her problems seem to be the result of stress caused by her inability to acquire fluency in English and fear of loss of love of her husband.

That seems to have created in her a sense of shame and guilt, which in turn brought psychosomatic illnesses.

Mirichika comes from a rural background. She has done B.Com. With Telugu medium. She had learnt Hindi and also English. She speaks Hindi, and English but is not very fluent, and does not have an anglicized accent.

A little bit of pleasant conversation in which she gradually began to participate, brought a change in her appearance. From tense looks on her face she began to look relaxed. She in now in a mood to respond to the input of positive suggestions.

Counselling : Counselling is given on the following points:

1. It was not necessary for her to learn speaking fluent English. English, which she knew and spoke was sufficient for her purpose. She should make no effort to acquire proficiency in English like Delhi girls who are educated in English medium schools.

2. She should take pride in speaking Telugu, her mother-tongue, and Hindi which is the national language. Her knowledge of Hindi was good enough and she should not suffer from any complexes on that account.

3. She should also not attempt to learn computer operation for which she has no taste and which creates tension in her mind. Nothing should be done which may produce uneasiness in one's mind.

4. Mirichika wants to live as a normal housewife. Taking up of any activity for making independent income was likely to result in creating tension. She should not worry about earning extra money because her husband's salary was enough to maintain the family. She is in a position, as she says, to run the household with her husband's income, and there was no financial problem or need for additional income.

The counselling brought a marked change in Mirichika, she began to smile and feel as if a burden had been lifted off her head. She became fully calm and relaxed.

When the session was about to come to a close, she felt her fingers with the other hand to discover if they were numb, but to her surprise and amazement there was no numbness in her fingers. She touched other parts of her body, but there was no numbness anywhere. She smiled, but feared that she might get it again during the night.

Ultimately, however, she began to believe she may not get it even during the night.

Conclusions

The nervousness and numbness that Mirichika felt were really the rebound actions, or reflex actions to resist the pressure exerted by her husband's insistence on her acquiring proficiency in speaking English and learning computer operation. This pressure had created high tension in her mind and unconsciously she had been trying to fight back the stress by developing subconsciously the feeling of numbness all over. The same tension is the cause of her nightmare. She would prefer numbness and death to the torture of learning English and operating the computer.

Her newly acquired belief that she has the right and freedom not to do what she does not like gives her immense relief. Her original self has been restored.

After a little more of pleasant and encouraging conversation she began to see there was nothing so serious in the dream of death she had, and there was nothing she should be afraid of. Finally she came out of the mess.

M. Yes, I cannot die again and again, night after night. If during the first nightmare I had died I would not be alive the next night or today. Anyway, now I am alive, I have a new life. In every way now I am a new woman.

Second Session

Mirichika looks quite composed and happy.

M. After the last session I felt fully cured. For two days I had no numbness either in hands or any other parts of my body. But I am feeling a little bit of it since yesterday.

I have reduced the dose of medicines to half and still I am having nice sleep.

C. It is very good, gradually you will become free from all your problems.

M. I am no longer having the feeling of numbness; I am feeling quite normal.

C. Your tension has melted away. With the release of tension you have regained your self-confidence leading to freedom from psychosomatic effect of high-voltage tension you were having.

M. The terror created by my dreams of death has also begun to wither away.

C. It was due to your fear of losing the love of your husband. You feared that your failure to acquire fluency in English and not working at the computer will make your husband withdraw his love. The fear in your mind was caused by the feeling that you will be discarded by your husband. This fear became over-burdening because of the feeling of helplessness to overcome the situation. Now you have overcome that fear.

There is no reason for you to fear because you are doing nothing wrong. You will be justified even in refusing to talk in English with anyone who could speak and understand Telugu or the national language Hindi. That will help you overcome the feeling of inferiority and make you feel equal to others. It is a matter of shame not for you but for them who cannot or do not speak the mother-tongue or the national language.

[Intensive counselling was given to reinforce the earlier inputs for removing her inferiority complex, and this brought a noticeable change in her mood.]

Third Session

Mirichika is quite happy. She has given up all medicines.

M. Now I have no problem except for the pinpricks caused by threats given by my husband in a veiled manner that one day there will be the eruption of his volcano of hidden hatred and anger, and that will make me suffer real agony. My husband still occasionally flings at me the charge of my being worthless, and holds out the threat that he will go into an angry outburst in the presence of my parents when they come next.

C. Mirichika, you should overlook and ignore his threats. Behave as if you have not heard his words, but do not behave in a manner that he may feel ignored. You are a good actress, play your role with a smile. At the same time remain prepared to bear the heat of the lava with the calmness of Buddha. However, I am confident the volcano will never erupt. He loves you, he will never do anything to hurt your feelings and make you unhappy. It is unwise to fear the future. In ninety-nine per cent of cases the feared event never happens. So live fearlessly, live happily, have faith in your husband's goodness, in his love for you.

M. I know he loves me and may not create a scene in the presence of my parents.

But the fear and tension caused by my disturbing nightmares and dreams of death still continue, though in a much milder form. I fear death because it will mean the loss of my husband and daughter. I am afraid of becoming lonely.

C. But this is a thinking in a reverse order. You dream your own death but believe in your survival and the death of your husband and child. You really fear separation from them, you fear your husband's withdrawing his love from you. That is the basic cause of your tension. It was this that had created and generated the first nightmare and had made your sub-conscious mind repeat your dreams of death.

M. I also had some dreams in which I experienced electric shocks.

C. This too is the dramatization in sleep of the sub-conscious fear of punishment your husband threatens to impose on you. It is the result of the psychological shock you have been receiving from your husband. Just develop more faith and trust in your husband, and all your dreams of horror will disappear.

To Mirichika's husband: You have to make a choice: You may have a Telugu-speaking wife and a happy home, or a benumbed, tense wife and a miserable home.

H. I choose the first option I assure you (Mirichika) I love you very much, and even if you remain the Telegu-speaking Mirichika and do not become the girl of my pre-marital dream, my love for you will continue to be the same. I assure you that my love will never be less, but will continue to grow with time.

With the assurance given by her husband she has totally got rid of the fear created by her nightmarish dreams. She has become completely relaxed. Her husband's changed attitude has helped her in regaining the lost confidence. Love and faith given by her husband have rekindled in her a new hope and expectation of a happier future.

Mirichika's husband had so far failed to realize that his behaviour towards Mirichika was not correct. He is now determined not to bring any unpleasantness in her life and not to do anything that may injure her feelings.

Concluding Session

After some days Mirichika's husband telephoned to express his gratitude for bringing happiness in his home. He said that Mirichika was very relaxed and happy.

Perhaps, his own tension has melted away, his unconscious desire of revenge and punishment has gone, he has seen the wisdom of accepting Mirichika as she is and not as he would have liked her to be.

Mirichika joins her husband in expressing the feeling of joy and happiness.

KANAK

How can I feel the pride of victory and be happy when I constantly feel I have ceased to be a complete woman, I have become dishaped? Everyone will look at me and see my deformed contours. Breasts are what make the woman a thing of beauty, they are the essential components of her body a woman ceases to be woman without a breast. I am not yet married, and now who....

Diagnostic Scan and Counselling

Kanak is in her early forties, she is working as a teacher. She was diagnosed to have cancer, and recently one of her breasts was removed. She is suffering from shock, trauma and fear. She has not yet been able to get over the shock of the operation, and in spite of the doctor's assurance, she fears her second breast will also get affected. In addition, she is suffering from strong feeling of shame.

C. Kanak, please remember that darkness of the night is never a permanent feature, not only the light of the moon goes on brightening with the growing moon, but the sun rises every morning. There is always a new dawn waiting for the end of the night. In your life too, the dark night of cancer has now come to an end, the day is bound to follow. Your other breast is perfectly healthy and the medical report confirms that all malignant cells have been removed and none exists any more. So, please feel hopeful, and believe that your other breast will not be affected.

K. I wish the doctor be right.

C. There is no reason for you to doubt, and now you can always get yourself checked and take preventive treatment. You should feel happy that your other breast has not been affected. Think positive. Is there any rational, scientific reason for your fearing that your other breast will be affected?

K. No.

C. Then, why fear? It is the age in which medical science is progressing by leaps and bounds, and very soon you will find women getting freedom from this disease. So shed your fear and feel relaxed and happy. Fear of the future is just like fear of a ghost, and it is better not to expect a ghost, but to hope that the ghost will never appear.

K. Whenever I think of the agony I have suffered, I begin to shudder.

C. It is natural, but you have already faced the agonishing moments and have won the battle. In a war what matters is not the suffering caused by the bullets but the ultimate victory. You have won the battle, defeated your worst enemy, the cancer. It is an occasion to feel delighted and not to mourn. Celebrate your victory.

K. How can I feel the pride of victory and be happy when I constantly feel I have ceased to be a complete woman, I have become de-shaped ? Everyone will look at me and see my deformed contours. Breasts are what make the woman a thing of beauty, they are the essential components of her body, a woman ceases to be woman without a breast. I am not yet married, and now who...

C. What is wrong if a cancerous breast has been removed? It is not something unknown in the present world, you are not an exception, there are thousands of women who have undergone this surgery. Moreover, you need not worry about what others think, particularly those who do not have an understanding mind, who do not know what real beauty means. Real beauty lies not in the shape or size of a woman's breast but in the contents of her thoughts, beliefs, feelings and emotions, in her attitude towards life and the whole world.

Kanak, you are a talented person, don't you write or paint, or sing?

K. I do write sometimes, I have composed some poems.

C. Please recite one.

(Kanak recites a poem)

Oh it is very good: but do you write only such poems that depict a sad and depressed mood?

K. No, I also write poems with a happy mood.

C. Please recite one of them.

[Kanak recites another poem]

It is really very good. Have you published any poems? How many have you written?

K. I have not yet published any. I have written quite a few.

C. Then collect them and give them to me, I shall see if they can be published in the form of a book. I am sure they will make a very good anthology.

K. I shall try to collect them.

C. Go on writing. More you write, better you will feel. You know real poetry is born out of a distressed heart. Your time of distress can be easily converted into a gift. I see a great future for you. Please look-up and see the new horizons, they are full of the glow of a new sunrise, a new dawn.

Next Session

K. I am feeling better, but still I am not out of the mess. I still have the fear of the future. The doctor has asked me to take rest for one month more, and not to join the school.

(She is given general counselling to make her feel happier by accepting the present as it is and being hopeful of a better future).

C. Maybe life has something exceptionally good in store for you.

K. That is what the astrologers said. If they were right, today I would have been a happily married woman with children in my lap.

C. Maybe they were wrong, but that does not mean you should not enjoy your present as it is. All married women are not happy, marriage does not necessarily mean happiness. Happiness lies within one's consciousness, it depends on the acceptance of the situation as it is, and in making the best of what is and not worrying about what is not. Please do not let dejection enter your mind. You have won the battle against the most dreaded disease of the day. Feel the greatness of your achievement. Just feel relaxed.

K. I am trying to accept the situation and hope to go forward with greater courage.

C. Take the lamp of hope in your hand, and like Florence Nightingale move on to show to the millions of women suffering from breast-cancer the road to a contented future, show to them, through your example, the ways and means of successfully facing the situation with confidence and courage. Do this great job.

Next Session

K. Today the doctor has given me clearance, now I can go to school. He said it was for the first time he had seen me as a woman and not as a cancer-patient and thought I was beautiful.

C. It is very encouraging, I am very happy; now from tomorrow you join the school with full confidence, thinking as if nothing had happened. People get ill and have surgery, that is all part of life. All you need is to get over the feeling of shame. You do not look bad, and at least one man, your doctor, has said you look beautiful as a person, as a woman.

K. He had not seen me when I was young, then I was really beautiful.

C. Yes, you must have been from the point of view of vital statistics.

But do you not know that real beauty comes with maturity ? Cleopatra and Helen of Troy were both in their mid-forties, like you, when they were considered beauties of the world. Even today Miss World and Miss Universe are not selected on the basis only of their vital statistics, it is talent that is more important; a woman's real beauty lies in her graceful behaviour, and emotional content. And, measured by all these standards, in spite of your losing one breast, you are entitled to be placed in the category of world's most beautiful women.

K. Oh, you are pulling my leg.

C. Not at all, am I wrong in what I have said?

K. No, you have said only what is true, I understand this. Further, now they make such dresses that the removed breast can be concealed.

C. I know that, and you can hide what you consider as your shame. But what I am trying to impress on you is that surgical removal of a breast is not a matter of shame, it is necessary surgery to cure a disease. One should feel shame only for a wrong or ignoble act she does, and not for the happening of something she is not responsible for. You are not responsible for the disease, you did not cause cancer in your breast, why then should you feel ashamed?

K. I know I am not responsible for my cancer, and I feel there is nothing I should be ashamed of.

C. Then take this out of your mind, go out in the world with your head high. I wish you to set an example for your sisters the world over and not to let them think this disease to be a cause of woman's shame. You were a victim of an illness, and you have emerged victorious. Go to school, to your friends, and everywhere without the feeling of any kind of inferiority, appear in the world as if there is nothing wrong with you.

Will you go to school tomorrow?

K. I think I should.

C. No, tell me that you will.

K. Yes, I will.

Next Session

K. I went to school, nothing untoward happened. I have begun to feel normal. I went also to cinema with a friend.

C. That is great. Now write a poem, describe how happy you feel.

K. Well, last time the doctor had asked me to write about myself and my disease, and that he will assist me, edit it and get it published as a thesis on cancer. But, whenever I attempt it, I feel depressed

C. I had asked you to write poems of love and happiness, and not about your disease and suffering. Your doctor knows about cancer, but not about the delicate emotions of a young woman, please give it up. If you be keen about writing your, health biography, then wait for a few years, or let me do this task for you. In no case will you delve on this subject till you get clearance from me. I want you to inhale happiness, drink happiness, experience happiness.

K. I don't think I can ever be really happy, the thought of being single always pricks my conscience.

C. Then get married.

K. When I was young and beautiful, I had a line of suitors, and I rejected everyone. My near ones, including my mother, always pampered me by saying I deserved a much better match. Now I realise what a fool I was.

C. Forget the past, find one now. Even today you are sufficiently good looking to attract a suitable man.

K. I have one still hanging on with a proposal, but I do not like him.

C. Why ?

K. He has beard and mustache.

C. That is not enough ground for rejection.

K. He has two children. I could have tolerated even that but he is a bore. After a few minutes of conversation, I feel disgusted, I cannot stand him. My mother also thinks so.

C. How long will you continue to remain your mother's baby ? Anyway, leave him. Give a matrimonial advertisement in the newspaper, and also on the Internet.

K. But, as soon as anyone will read about my having only one breast, he will not respond.

C. It is not necessary for you to give it in the advertisement. You can disclose it after you get a suitable proposal. And then you told me here is at least one gentlemen begging your hand even when he knows you do not have two breasts. This is not such a deformity which will deter a suitable man from falling in love with you.

K. That is certainly so, love does not depend on the shape of a woman's body but on the beauty of her thoughts and emotions, particularly the emotion of love.

C. Then, you should proceed immediately to give an advertisement. When will you?

K. Within two days.

C. Okay.

I understand but I do have fear of God. I give offerings lest I get God's curse. I fear they may not become unkind to me and as a consequence I may suffer.

Diagnostic Scan

Mala is a student of B.Com. and is also preparing for ICWA examinations. She is fair, good-looking, apparently having no problem.

It took quite some time to make Mala open up.

M. I have no friends. I feel my head gets blank, I get confused and I am unable to make decisions, I change my mind quickly.

I do not do certain things such as dusting and cleaning with as much competence as I would like to, I make mistakes. I cannot concentrate. I fear I might forget the bus route while returning from school. I lack confidence.

[She complained she was having severe headache, but got immediate relief after acupressure was applied to her temples.]

[She denies she ever feels sad or weeps. Her mother reminded her that she had cried even yesterday. Mala said she did not remember if she had shed tears yesterday or ever before. Soon, however, after her mother had been sent to another room, she began to weep profusely. She was finding it difficult to control the flood of tears in her eyes. After a little bit of confidence-building she regained her composure.

While she was a child, she was often slapped by her mother, but Mala tries not to remember any scolding or thrashing. Maybe, she wants to present a contented and happy image of herself, or she is afraid of remembering the unpleasant past. The second reason seems to be the real reason, her general feeling of fear which she tries to conceal.

Her mother once fell ill and while she was ill, Mala felt very upset as she always feared she might die.

Once Mala's mother got her horoscope examined by an astrologer who told her that Mala was under the evil eye of God Saturn (*Shanideva*), and in order to escape his wrath she should, on every Saturday, go to the temple and offer water to the Peepal tree. Ever since, Mala has been doing it regularly in order to gain the goodwill of *Shanischar Devata* and to avoid his wrath, which was supposed to be responsible for her supposedly bad health and luck.

C. Why do you think 'Saturn' is a God and offering water oblation to him via the Peepal tree will keep all evils away from you?

M. The Pandit has told me so, after seeing my horoscope.

C. Do you know Saturn is only one of the planets like earth? Saturday has been named after Saturn. There is nothing to make it a god. Giving of water oblations to the Peepal tree on Saturday cannot have anything to do with Saturn, or what you call *Shani Devata*. Think more scientifically, don't believe in superstitions. Interested persons have created these superstitions to keep the common people under the threat of divine displeasure, so that they may succeed in exploiting them. So long as you remain under fear and subscribe to this superstition, it will be possible to extort money from you. Be on your guard, shake off this superstition, and get rid of the fear of divine curse and divine displeasure.

M. I understand but I do have fear of God. I give offerings lest I get Gods curses. I fear Gods may not become unkind to me and as a consequence make me suffer.

C. So this is the reason of your fear of God, or more correctly, of various gods and goddesses.

M. Yes.

C. If you do believe in gods and goddesses, remember they are benefactors of men, women and children, and of every living thing on earth. They are embodiments of love and compassion and give *Vardans* (benevolences) and not *Shraps* (curses). That is why they are called gods, otherwise they will become their opposities the devils. They do not expect from you oblations or offerings, they are above human wants. God is said to be *antaryami* (one who knows what is inside the consciousness of individuals) he knows everything. Gods need nothing, not even your oblations.

Be more rational, that will remove from your mind the fear of god's displeasure.

Second Sessions

M. I have got over the superstitions, and no more do I fear the wrath of Gods.

But I have no interest in the study of course books. I do not study at all and fear I will fail.

C. You want to study and still you fear studying. Anyway, why do you want to study?

M. My ambition is to become a big boss, a top accountant, for that I have to pass exams and that requires study of books.

C. In the meantim, begin to read books which you like, thereafter you will get inclination to study course books. Just get into the habit of reading books, any book, that you find interesting. Forget everything about passing exams. That will remove tension from your mind, and gradually you will begin to comprehend and grasp even your course books.

M. I always feel guilty because I am not studying course books, instead only watching T.V., listening to radio and indulging in idle chats. I know it is a criminal waste of time and I feel guilty about it. That creates tension and that makes it difficult for me to comprehend and grasp my course books.

C. Reading course books seems to be a punishment for you and results in a dislike for all reading. If you change your objective, reading will become a pleasure and you will get attracted even to your course books. Do try it. Anyway, who do you think it is criminal waste of time to watch T.V. or listen music or chat with frends ?

M. There is no reason, I just think.

C. Then get rid of this thought and cure yourself of the feeling of guilt.

Third Session

Mala has given up all puja, etc. and has gained freedom from superstitions.

Her aversion to books is gone and she has started working on her course books. Mala's mother says there is a lot of change in Mala, the change is all for the good. Change is not marginal but substantial.

Mala is quite happy, and has started paying more attention to her studies, so that she may not fail. She has even begun to feel that she should work with the idea of getting high standard of success in exams. Her negative attitude has changed into a positive attitude.

Mala is interested in dance, music, and painting. She is counselled to devote more time to develop these hobbies. She will now take proper coaching for dancing in classical style. This will remove the feeling of vacancy in her mind of which she complains.

M. I no more have the fear of failure and am sure I will shed tears no more.

C. But you have the freedom to shed them if you like.

M. She laughs.

After some time Mala phoned that she was concentrating on her course books, but sometimes felt she was not able to grasp what she read. At intervals she phones whenever she feels the need.

She is given simple counselling and she feels her problems were resolved. Finally, she did appear in the Exam (B.Com.) and passed. She felt she had won the battle.

M. I have become a graduate, and have also done two semesters in computer management course.

C. Congratulations.

M. All my friends say I am too simple, and it is not good that I do not get exercised and become angry. They say it shows I am not fit for going ahead.

C. They are absolutely wrong. Remaining calm and not getting angry is a virtue, and everyone should cultivate it. You have learnt, let them also try to remain unagitated.

M. Does it mean I lack self-esteem?

C. No, self-esteem means having good or correct opinion about oneself. It is connected with self-confidence. Lack of anger shows you have self-confidence, and so long you do not feel you are inferior or bad, you cannot be deemed to be lacking self-esteem.

M. So, I must not feel inferiority complex because I remain unperturbed and do not get angry and fight.

C. No, you should rather feel proud.

M. They say I am inferior as I do not have sufficient ego, and pride, but I do have self-respect. I honour the values I have. What is the distinction between self-respect, ego and pride? Is there anything wrong in my behaving the way I do?

C. No. Have you read Jane Austen's *Pride and Prejudice* ?

M. I once had, but now I do not remember.

C. You read it again and also read some other good novels, it will give you an understanding of the emotional life of a growing young woman. You have crossed your teens.

M. I have, now I am twenty. Does it make any difference?

C. Certainly it does. Now you are having a transformation, from adolescence you are entering adulthood, from girlhood you are entering womanhood. The whole world is changing for you.

M. My mother says I am changing, and complains that I am not behaving the way I did. I even take a period off when it is possible and spend the time in some restaurant with friends, just chatting. My mother thinks I am going stray.

C. She is not realising that you are now twenty and entering her world, probably she has forgotten that period of her life. She is afraid you may not take a wrong step and land yourself in difficulty. She wants you to exercise caution, and she is right.

M. I just spend time with my friends and have a little enjoyment.

C. Are your friends girls or boys?

M. Girls only. We are a group of nine, and discuss our problems but find no answer. Many questions arise in my mind, and I find no answer to them, and get worried.

C. What sort of question?

M. Like; what is life? What is the purpose of life? What should be the principles and ideals in life?

C. Oh, Mala, don't let this rubbish pester your mind. Leave these questions for philosophers, you are still a young girl, it is time for you to play, frolic and enjoy, sing and dance. That is life, that is the purpose of life, that is the ideal you should have.

M. I do not know what I want from life, I do not know what my right image should be. I keep on worrying about such things.

C. Forget everything. Live the life as it is, it will go on unfolding itself on its own, you need not worry about it. Give up thinking about your future.

All your dilemmas are the outcome of the transcendence you are having in your life. You are leaving adolescence and entering womanhood and all your problems are the problems of growth and transformation. You do not need to think about them, just ignore them. From a bud you are becoming a blossom, all you have to do is to forget yourself, and bloom.

M. I feel so relieved and happy that I wish I could dance with joy.

C. Do.

SUNITA

There is something I wanted to disclose, but my husband has always prevented me from coming out with it on the pretext that it would make his family's private matters become public, and this he would not tolerate. Today I got the chance to come alone as he is out on professional work...

Diagnostic Scan

Only in the last (sixth) session did her mind really get unlocked and she regained peace and freedom after the volcano had erupted.

Sunita is a middle-aged woman, looks healthy but her eyes are full of tears.

Her husband is an accounts officer in some firm.

Sunita is a housewife but gives tuition to some children.

She has attempted suicide once, and occasionally threatens she would commit suicide.

Her mother-in-law has come to live with them and has become a source of tension for Sunita. Sunita says that all money is in her husband's control, and whenever she is given money for household expenses the mother-in-law comes to check how much is she getting. She also finds fault in whatever purchases Sunita makes. She tries to accompany Sunita whenever she goes out with her husband. Even for day-to-day purchases she accompanies Sunita and thus deprives her of the freedom to spend any money as she may wish.

Mother-in-law has taken control of the kitchen and Sunita has been virtually ousted by her. Though over eighty-five, she is stout and insists on doing all cooking for the family, specially for her son. She insists on serving and feeding her son, ignoring his wife. Sunita feels insulted and ignored. She wants to remain in control of the kitchen and serve meals to her husband.

Whenever there is a festival she will not let Sunita even enter the kitchen or touch anything. She is treated as an untouchable.

Her husband supports his mother, and says it will be better if she is allowed to take complete charge of the kitchen, including cooking of food for Sunita. Sunita is being persuaded by her husband to agree to this proposal on the pretext that it will give her plenty of leisure to enjoy.

Sunita, he knows, cannot agree to this proposal, which will reduce her to a non-entity.

Sunita is asked by her husband to accept his mother as the mistress of the house, and tolerate her whims.

Sunita wants to have her legitimate place in the family. She does not want to lose her home, her kitchen, or her husband.

Mother and son often engage in chit-chat, but whenever Sunita appears they abruptly stop the conversation or change it. She is never permitted or tolerated in the mother-son relationship.

Sunita begins to suspect them of conspiring or planning something against her.

Counselling

During the counselling session, the husband realised the validity of some of Sunita's complaints and agreed to give some money to Sunita to spend as she liked. She will, of course, spend it on household needs and will maintain an account of the same.

Sunita has, during counselling been trained to learn some coping mechanisms.

Sunita's tears have gone and her face has become pleasant.

Second Session

Sunita is in much better mental health today. She has received Rs. 5000 from her husband and feels happy about getting a little economic freedom. She said she had felt happy the whole day and night since she went back after counselling, but this morning at ten she again fell into depression. Neither she nor her husband is able or willing to disclose the situation which led to her depression. She is in high tension and is suffering from concealed agony as she is unable to speak out what happened in the morning.

Sunita is made to lie down and listen to the audio tape on hypno-sleep. She went into hypno-sleep. After twenty minutes, when she got up she said that while listening to the tape she felt she was getting out of mental confusion. She will like to experience relaxation by listening to the tape more often, and will even practice meditation if so advised.

C. You need to see things in their true perspective and learn to accept life as it is. Avoid living in the past or the future, live only in the present.

S. Since I have taken counselling I am trying to live in the present and not to brood over the past or live under fear of the future. I am trying to accept life as it is. That gives me peace of mind.

After a few days Sunita informed on phone that she has changed. She is no longer in the same sorry state in which she earlier was and was now in a happy and cheerful mood. It was, she said, a rare experience of happiness that she got through counselling, and was enjoying it.

Sunita said that though she was happy, she wanted to tell me something which she could not say during the earlier counselling sessions as her husband was always watching her, and would have later taken her to task for disclosing something he wanted to hide. She wants to come alone.

Third Session

Sunita and her husband took special time as Sunita was too depressed and could even resort to committing suicide; they came late in the night.

She wanted to go to her father's house for a few months to escape her mother-in-law. She was being subjected to non-stop nagging by her mother-in-law. Only yesterday when her husband was away and Sunita took the copy of *Bhagavad Gita* to read, her mother-in-law began scolding her for touching her book without having taken bath immediately before. She, however, ignored her words and continued to read. She complains of many such pin-pricks.

Communicative counselling has been given to make her believe that in the Indian family structure coexistence of persons of different generations with incoherent beliefs is unavoidable and had to be accepted as fact of life. The counselling has made the desired impact. Her tension has disappeared and she has become normal.

Awakening of her love for her small child, and of her obligation to protect him from getting emotional shocks as a consequence of her own emotional and psychic imbalances and upheavals, has been of great help. She has become conscious of the importance of her role as a mother in bringing up of the child, and of the influence her moods and behaviour might have on the child's mental health. It was put into her mind that it was necessary that she should get her mind diverted to other matters so that she could be able to avoid the effect of the hatred and discord radiating from her mother-in-law.

At the same time the husband was counselled to request his mother to behave sympathetically while dealing with Sunita and also, if necessary, to give her the warning that for the avoidance of tension in the family, it may be better for her to go back to live with her other son. He has responded well to the suggestion and promised to do the needful.

Sunita has become very happy, her tension has melted away. The purpose of emergency visit was achieved.

She has taken the book *Psychodynamics of Emotions*, and says she will translate it into Tamil.

Fourth Session

Sometime after the last session Sunita had informed on phone: "I am very happy, very-very happy". She was trying to take interest in other matters and attempting to develop hobbies.

During the session, she complained only of one pin-prick. Her mother-in-law had put flowers in front of the pictures of all the deities, except that of Sai Baba in whom Sunita has faith.

C. Everyone has the right to believe in any deity and not to have faith in any other. For some gods godmen, one may have special devotion and may not believe in the divinity of some others. It is not necessary for your mother-in-law to place flowers at Sai Baba's feet if she did not believe in him. It is open to you to place flowers of worship at his feet if you want. You should not feel offended, particularly when Sai Baba never asked or desired anybody to place flowers at his feet when he was alive.

Sunita has been conditioned to cope with unpleasant situations by controlling her thought through the teachings and blessing of Sai Baba.

S. I know he needs nothing and wants nothing, he only gives.

C. Whenever you apprehend unpleasantness you should visualise Sai Baba and that he is asking you to become calm; remember his hand, it asks you to keep calm and leave all your problems to him. This will help you remain calm and happy. Put all your worries at his feet, it would be much better to surrender all your problems to him and treat them as flowers of devotional offering, place such flowers at his feet every morning and every evening.

Fifth Session

S. Sai Baba has helped me to ward off much of my tension and made me feel happy. But I am again feeling disturbed. My elder son has come from the hostel for Diwali. I wish to cook for him, but my mother-in-law is not permitting me, and insists that she will herself do the cooking for him, and I should keep away.

C. Sunita, please be more charitable and let your mother-in-law do as she wills, that will give her pleasure without making you lose anything. You should also feel happy and let everyone know you are happy, because otherwise the whole atmosphere in the house will become tense, and your son will feel unhappy. Participate in whatever happens in the house; eat and enjoy the food your mother-in-law cooks. It is good to get a meal without making any effort. Remember also that true pleasure lies in giving happiness to others. Happiness always reflects back to the person who gives it.

S. One thing more serious which gives me tension is that I have to live constantly in fear of being criticised. I cannot even drink a cup of tea or eat anything in front of others, I have to take it to my room to avoid criticism.

C. You must learn to have courage to do what you believe is right. You must never live in fear. Fear is always of something happening in the future, instead of fearing a future ghost, wait till it comes and then face it. There is ninety-nine per cent chance that what you fear will never happen. You said you believe in Durga, so whenever need be, remember Goddess Durga and derive courage from Her. She is the embodiment of courage, confidence, faith, and power. That is why She is called 'the incarnation of power' 'Shakti'. Durga (Shakti) and Her image are meant to induce in you the spirit of confidence, courage, faith and power. Durga is non-violent in the sense that She does not kill any person but destroys only the spirit of revenge, cowardice and violence from the individual's mind. Be a Durga in the true sense: a woman full of love, compassion, power, vigour and strength. Face the Demon when it comes and destroy it as Durga did. But the truth is that Demons only create fear, they never appear.

Sixth Session

S. Although my agony has been very much reduced by counselling, a hidden deep-roted sorrow still continues to trouble me. There is something I want to disclose, but my husband has always prevented me from coming out with it on the pretext that it would make his family's private matters become public, and this he would not tolerate. Today I got the chance to come alone as he is out on professional work.

Mine was not a love-marriage. It was also not just an arranged marriage but a marriage under pressure and distress. (She wanted to elaborate, but for fear of her husband restrained herself and did not proceed further in detail). After marriage I was treated just like a machine for production of children, and till my first son was born, I was treated with contempt both by my husband and his mother. There was no love, only hatred and isolation. I was treated as an unwanted intruder in the family.

My husband before my marriage had an affair with another girl and wanted to marry her, but she was much too smart with high educational qualifications to accept him; another reason for rejection by the girl was the demand of dowry by his mother.

On his failure to get that girl he was married to me against his will. He did not approve the match but got married. Life afterward remained full of miseries. It was only after more than a year that he said that he had finally accepted the loss of his first love and was getting reconciled to the new situation.

His mother never liked me and always reminded my husband that I was not married to him by his choice, and was not the girl of his liking and his dreams. This has been a source of continued ill-will against me. My mother-in-law uses this as a tool to make my husband dislike me.

In due course I got pregnant; my husband on the advice of his mother got the foetus aborted. When I became pregnant again my husband did not insist on abortion and the elder son was born. My husband showed no interest in the child, never touched or loved him. It was only when he became eight or nine months old and began to speak that he accepted the child.

I again got in the family way, but my mother-in-law got it aborted. This happened once again. So I had two further abortions against my will. My husband insisted that his mother could not be wrong in asking for abortion. By that time my own mother had died and I was too weak to resist, all by myself.

My mother-in-law had made her other daughters-in-law too suffer the same fate.

C. Have your wounds not healed yet?

S. No. Even though I had not suffered any physical or sexual disability or dysfunctioning, I suffered psychological shock which has continued; even now when I think of abortions, I feel the trauma.

C. You should forget the events now because they have now lost their significance. Moreover, the process is irreversible, you can't get back the aborted foetuses. Why worry about them particularly when you have now got another child ?

S. But the other son was born nine years after the first. He came because of the failure of the contraceptive measures. This time I refused abortion and my husband supported me.

C. So now the chapter of pregnancies and abortions is over. It is time to feel happy about the children you have.

S. Yes, I am quite happy with my children. My husband also is happy with the birth of the second child. My mother-in-law is not.

C. She seems to think that you three (you and your two children) are strangers who have intruded into her exclusive domain, the domain of her son's love.

S. She shows clear discrimination in her daily behaviour towards us; for instance, she will give whole milk to my husband but will mix water in the milk given to the children, similarly she will give only the curd water to us, and the thick curd only to her son...

C. Don't worry about all these small things, milk is important but children get their nutrition from many other things, it is the entire food that counts, neither you nor the children are suffering from any nutritional deficiency, so forget it.

You know she is eighty-five and cannot be changed.

S. Yes, I know that, and I am trying to remain conscious of that, but...

C. No 'ifs' and 'buts', just accept things as they are.

S. Do you think my elder son is not growing up properly because of what I did during the time he was in my womb. I was not getting enough food, so I used to stealthily keep a few chapatis away from the sight of my mother-in-law and eat them whenever I got the opportunity. [Sunita feels guilty, it is apparent from her face.]

C. No, no. It was necessary for you to get full nutrition and you managed to get it. There was no element of malice in your behaviour, you did what any wise mother-to-be would do in the circumstances in which you were. It could have absolutely no psychological impact on your child who was born fully normal and is still not suffering from any psychic ailment. There is no reason for you to have the feeling of guilt or shame. You are unnecessarily suffering from a feeling of guilt when you should feel proud for acting with wisdom. You have suffered for so many years without any reason, now get free of this feeling of guilt.

S. Yes, I should.

C. Feel happy, you have done no wrong for which you should feel guilty or ashamed.

Sunita laughs, happiness comes on her face. She feels as if a great burden has been lifted off her head, and she can now live with a clean heart.

S. My husband had permitted me to talk to you only about the son and not myself but I could not resist. By opening before you I have got immense relief. I feel as if something which was lying buried and weighing heavily on my heart has gone. For years I have unnecessarily suffered from fear and a feeling of guilt and shame, and self-condemnation. Today I feel relieved. I must say again that now I am very happy. I am enjoying real freedom.

C. *Shanti-sukham* (Peace and happiness) ?

S. Yes, *Shanti-sukham*.

Sunita is no more the same Sunita who had come on the day of the first session, broken, depressed, nervous, without confidence and faith in herself. Today she looks like a woman of substance, full of courage, confidence and faith in herself; she has regained her lost self.

PSYCHIC COMA

— Frozen consciousness
— Awakening the slumbering mind

3
Psychic Coma

It is possible for the mind to go into a psychic coma and create an emotional blockade. One of the concepts of the dynamics of human reactions and behaviour is that an individual's earlier experience tends to take emotional precedence over subsequent impressions. Much depends on the depth, impregnability, and intensity of the impression the earlier experience makes on the emotional field of the individual's conscious and, more particularly, sub-conscious mind, and similarly on the quality of subsequent experience. When the earlier impressions refuse to be altered by subsequent experiences, mind loses its dynamism and the consciousness becomes static. This leads to the blockade and freezing of the stream of thoughts, feelings and emotions, the result is psychic coma. In normal flow of human life, successive impressions form a movie–like pictorial series, and when this movement stops, an emotional freeze occurs and a coma-like psychic situation develops.

Psychic coma is not the same as the hypnotic state of dormancy. Unlike what happens in hypnosis, the unified personality of the individual does not become the blend of multiple personalities. It is also not a situation in which some particular type of personality is voluntarily induced in the individual and made to obey the suggestions given to it. In 'Psychic Coma', nothing of the sort happens. Psychic coma is caused when through a process of involuntary emotional impact on human consciousness certain aspects of personality become dormant, non-active, and non-responsive. Psychic coma involves prolonged forgetfulness of certain aspects of one's life, and creates unawareness of some part of memory. Hypnosis can, of course, be used to activate and awaken the hibernating thoughts, feelings and emotions.

The mental blockade in a psychic coma stops the flow of positivity, and the mind begins brooding, pondering and musing on the specific situation at which the consciousness has come to stay. It seems as if the flow of thoughts has stopped and the stream of life has become a stagnant pool. In this pool arise, emerge and soar only the tides of depressing thoughts, stagnating feelings, glum emotion, and Depressing waves of fear, sorrow and frustration. At times this blockade also creates obsessional-compulsive discorders (OCD), and similar behavioural problems.

Once a person goes into psychic coma, the thinking process halts and the mind gets chocked, memories existing in the conscious and the sub-conscious mind lose their dynamism and go into stupor; they cease to move forward and produce only still photographs of feelings, emotions, and thoughts lying embedded in the consciousness of the individual. When mind becomes inert, negativity takes over; and, when negativity becomes the master and begins to rule the consciousness, it leads to depression and allied symptoms.

If the coma comes as a consequence of an emotional shock, the blockade makes the mind stuck-up in that situation. For instance, if the trauma and shock are the result of rape or something like it, which make the woman feel defiled and polluted, her mind gets blocked at that situation and she develops the OCD of long and repeated washing and cleaning of the body, and allied symptoms. She may go on cleaning her whole body or parts of it which she feels have been defiled, including her mouth and teeth, repeatedly for hours together; or may go on washing her clothes. Such and other symptoms may occur even when the mind gets blocked-up as a consequence of a frustrated love affair, particularly when love in its full bloom is destroyed by the lover, for no fault of one's own. The blockade may come even at a time when she had begun to regard herself as the lover's wife. In that case she might continue to behave as a married woman, observing the rituals prescribed for wives.

Sometimes blockade may occur without there being an apparent cause or a known traumatic event. It may even be some hidden fear in one's sub-consciousness of which the person may not be aware. The psychic coma so produced, may also create stagnation in the mind. It might bring confusion in thought. It may even make the person become too superstitious, and suffer from the irrational fear of the unknown. Sometimes he/she might go on performing rituals in order to atone one's assumed and imaginary sins and moral lapses.

There are innumerable factors, having manifold characteristics and multifarious attributes that create psychic coma. They might appear independently or in combinations. Psychic coma and blockade may sometimes come through a slow, long-drawn process. Happenings and incidents that bring about the ultimate state of psychic coma and blockade might start in childhood, and continue till late in life. A person may before actually slipping into psychic coma, continue to live without realising the effect of the blockade which might be slowing down the thinking process. The individual might have suffered various kinds of traumatic experiences some of which he/she might have felt and some which may have passed unnoticed, but not without making their impact on the individual's emotional life.

Lack of friends can become a contributory factor and loss of a spouse can by itself create a freeze. It all depends on the individual's make-up, and the emotional situations one lives through in life. Psychic coma, does not necessarily lead to withdrawal or alienation. The inter-personal relationships continue, but they become distressing for those who have to deal with the person whose consciousness has got stuck-up at a particular point. A situation of conflicts arises because a static consciousness cannot function harmoniously with dynamic consciousness of normal persons. Behaviour of a person with frozen consciousness becomes unpalatable to persons who have open, active consciousness; and when the behavioural patterns of the two become incompatible, a stressful situation arises. Their inter-personal relationship comes under strain, and their inter-se behaviour makes them draw away from each other. In turn, that leads to loss of communication, and the emotional coma becomes more intractable and feelings of anxiety and insecurity become more difficult to tackle.

Psychic coma cripples a person's life and makes him/her become oblivious of past experiences of happiness, and get absolutely absorbed in the miseries responsible for the psychic stalemate. He/she begins to live in the changed mood-pattern. It makes the individual assume a static existence in which the mind gets stuck-up to a particular situation, and becomes unable to see beyond a set of fixed thoughts. It seems as if the consciousness has gone in hibernation, and has become dormant. Such a dormant consciousness becomes prone to despondency, and causes loss of confidence and self-esteem. The slumbering benumbed consciousness makes a person lose his/her real personality, and instead acquire a truncated and distracted personal image of oneself.

All types of psyhic coma, including OCDs, affect the dynamism of the brain and cause a type of mental hibernation. Its extent, intensity, and duration may vary, but the general impact remains the same-loss of mental dynamism. That means partial disuse of the brain and failure to use its full psychic capabilities. The trauma leads to coma, which causes disuse of the brain and then the circle begins again and results in gradual increase of mental hibernation. The process continues with the consequence that the coma goes on becoming worse and more distressing. Effort has got to be made to curtail mental hibernation by making the brain engaged in as many and as varied activities as might be possible.

What is needed in such a situation is to give a cleansing treatment to the mental screen on which non-changing emotional impressions have been recorded. Age regression becomes necessary so that the person might return to the former stages of psychic life when such impressions were photographed on the mental screen. The memories lodged in the sub-consciousness have to be brought to the level of consciousness and then given a reconditioning treatment, so that the still photographs may gain new life and acquire continuity, fluidity and dynamism. Once the blockade is removed and the mind is reactivated, consciousness automatically comes out of the coma, gets awakened, and the whole life regains its lost continuity.

RUMA AND JYOTI

What ? will I go to hell where there will be no God?

I don't know, but wait till death comes; don't worry about it so long you are alive. Think only of life, never of death or what will happen thereafter. When that happens, we will see about it, your fear will not help you. So be concerned only with living happily in this world and do not get concerned about your time in heaven or hell?

Diagnostic Scan

Ruma was a teacher, she voluntarily retired ten years back. Took tuitions. Now doing nothing. Age sixty-two years.

Uneasiness and worry.

Short breath.

No inclination to do anything, depression.

Ruma looks haggard, weak, sick, aged beyond her age.

She is full of fear.

Feels insecure.

She used to sing Ghazals.

[When asked to sing, she said she did not remember anything.]

She is not ready and willing (probably she is unable) to disclose anything from which inferences about her fears may be drawn. When I had written just half a page about her case she became very restless, and jumped up.

R. What have you written? What are you writing?

C. Just don't get scared, I am writing only what you have said. Read it.

R. I haven't got my reading glasses.

C. Then listen to what I have written. (She heard and seemed to be satisfied. She settled down but could not get out of the zone of suspicion. She called for her sister Jyoti sitting in the next room. Jyoti came in and was asked to read it out to satisfy her. She read it out. Ruma was still feeling restless, breathless, and full of fear. After a while she became a little calm).

C. Well, you try to remember your past, were you ever in love with a man who ditched you ? Did you have any troublesome affair ? Did you ever find yourself cheated, or let down?

Did you ever have any trouble during your service as teacher?

(She did not respond. Even on being coaxed by her sister to cooperate and give replies, she remained unmoved).

C. Anyway, if you will not tell anything, I will hypnotise you, and make you tell everything that is troubling you.

She became more restless and began entreating:

R. No, no please don't hypnotise me.

Still she did not come out with anything except that there was no man in her life because of whom she might have had problems.

Her sister Jyoti said: She refuses to disclose anything even to me or my husband. There was some trouble with her share in a property belonging to their parents. Their elder sister had grabbed Ruma's share and that caused her some anxiety but not a shock. That sister died about two years ago and Ruma has got back her share, which she has sold.

Ruma has invested all her savings and has comfortable income, out of which she pays to Jyoti Rs. 1000 approximately every month as her contribution to household expenses.

According to Jyoti, Ruma sometimes sings among friends, but takes no interest in anything, she is not willing to undertake any responsibility.

After very mild hypnosis (of which she did not become conscious), counselling has been given and she has responded and has shown her willingness:

(1) to undertake giving tuition to teach conversational Bangla (Bengali);

(2) to listen to the tapes and sing to herself Ghazal's and Bhajans of her liking;

(3) to try not to think about the past or worry about the future and to live only in the present;

(4) not to let seeds of misery (unpleasant or depressing thoughts and moods) enter or grow in her mind;

(5) to encourage only hopeful and pleasant thoughts to enter and grow in her mind, and to make all efforts to remain happy;

(6) to make effort to see that her sister does not feel miserable because of her, and try to make her happy;

(7) to take interest in household chores.

Finally, after the long counselling session was over she said she was now feeling much better and was having a feeling of well-being.

Ruma was advised to start giving tuition in conversational Bangla. One young man who was taking a job in Bangladesh was sent to her and she agreed to teach him Bangla. Regular teaching exercise brought a big change in her. She had found a purpose. Every morning she would get ready and give tuition with keen interest. It benefited both the teacher and the student. Her condition improved, her confidence was restored, and so was her self-esteem. The experiment was continued and gradual change came over her.

Second Session

Her appearance has changed; fear and tension have subsided. There is no more breathlessness (short breathing), or nervousness.

Ruma is today not the same shattered woman as she was on the last occasion. There is no fear or tension or nervousness on her face. She appears to be more composed.

She was asked to sing a song. On the last occasion she had refused, saying she did not remember any, and with her breathlessness (shortness of breath) was unable to sing. Today, she sang very well, there was no problem, her breathing was normal and she could sing without difficulty. This has given her confidence.

Ruma claims she has many obsessive compulsions. She is now sixty-two and they have become part of her life, such as checking things again and again and taking long time in bathing, etc.

C. Let them be as they are, don't worry about them, they have become part of your personality, accept them willingly and learn to live with them.

R. So, I will never be cured ?

C. They are not diseases but part of your habits, so there is no question of their being cured.

R. But nasty thoughts always come and disturb me.

C. There are three types of thoughts: beneficial, of no consequence and injurious. First two are not nasty, only the third one is. When they come just begin to sing, your nasty thoughts will go and you will become happy.

R. Will nasty thoughts continue to come?

C. There are no nasty thoughts in your mind. The only thought you have been talking of is about your feeling that you are troubling your sister, but that is wrong, she feels comfortable and happy with you.

R. I am always full of fears.

C. Your fear of future is baseless. You are having fear of death, of loss of your sister's love, and loss of people's respect for you.

Why do you fear death?

R. I don't know. What I will tell God when I go to heaven?

C. Don't worry about it. God may not ask you any questions.

R. What? will I go to hell, where there will be no God?

C. I don't know, but wait till death comes; don't worry about it so long you are alive. Think only of life, never of death or what will happen thereafter. When that happens we will see about it, your fear will not help you. So be concerned only with living happily in this world and do not get concerned about your time in heaven or hell?

You are a talented person, one who can teach and sing. Sing whenever you think you are getting unwelcome thoughts or thoughts that you call nasty. Let all your thoughts get lost in the sound of your music.

Ruma was made to listen to the tape on hypno-sleep and positive thinking (Stress-Management tape). She became quite relaxed. However, when she got up, she said:

R. I did not see any fairies, I did not see the fairies dancing or singing; even though I had opened my eyes and became quite alert, I did not see the fairies. (The tape makes reference to fairies coming and dancing).

C. Fairies can't be seen with these eyes, they entered your mind and were dancing and singing there, so how could you see them. They will henceforth control your thoughts and give you happiness.

From now on you will never have negative and nasty thoughts. Whenever you get them, think of those fairies and sing with them.

Try to calm your agitated mind, imagine your mind becoming calm like still water in a bucket. Become calm and still.

Ruma was made to speak and repeat positive thoughts and beliefs. She smiled and smiled broadly. (Her sister said she did not remember when she had last seen Ruma smile, and smile so broadly.)

Third Session

Overall, Ruma is in better shape. She also gave a song recital.

She describes her fears:

1. *Insanity* : When she was twelve years old she had seen one man called Kaka who was thought to be insane and that had developed in her the fear of insanity. Later he died in a mental hospital. She still fears she may become insane like him.

It was a case of pre-natal insanity. She is given counselling to make her believe that she is normal and suffers from no abnormality, and there is no reason for her to fear insanity. Her attitude has changed and her fear of insanity has almost gone...

2. *Insecurity* :

(*a*) She never married, had no intimate friends or even an adopted child. Never enjoyed security or the protection of the husband or anyone else. Lived all alone. Now as she remains ill she has developed the feeling of insecurity, she has heart problem, wears a pacemaker, and suffers from other ailments too.

(*b*) Ageing process has meant loss of physical strength and reduced her capacity to work. All this has made her full of fear of the future.

(*c*) Illness and general debility has caused loss of confidence and feeling of insecurity.

(*d*) Loss of mental alertness and memory has made her feel inferiority.

(*e*) Fear of becoming listless and inactive. This is due to her existing physical and mental health which is at a low ebb.

General counselling has been given to restore her sense of security.

3. She thinks Joyti feels disgusted and annoyed with her.

This is correct to some extent. Jyoti and her husband have become disgusted with her behaviour, particularly of not letting Jyoti have freedom to go anywhere or enjoy her quiet or to have private moments with her husband. Ruma like a mad person runs after her whenever she is going out. Ruma is conscious of it and feels guilty and ashamed.

C. Don't try to remain too such attached to or dependent on Jyoti. You have already been living alone, continue to do so in Jyoti's house too. She has allowed you to become some sort of a paying guest but has not bargained to let you interfere with her life. You must leave her alone. She has undertaken to help you only in case of need. You must realise that Jyoti has the right to live her own life, in the way she likes, and has also the right to enjoy privacy.

R. I know and I will try not to give her any further trouble.

C. Why not go to some temple in the evening and join in singing, etc.

R. I do not sing *bhakti* songs or *bhajans*.

C. That does not matter, you sing very well and will find no difficulty in singing in chorus with others. From today you must go.

R. I shall.

Fourth Session

Ruma is generally looking well. However, she is having breathlessness. After fifteen minutes of counselling her breathing has become normal.

She is given a song—Bujhe deep ko sone do... (Let the extinguished tamp sleep...) for singing. After some hesitation on the ground that she did not know how to give a tune or music to a song, she succeeded in singing it well. She has been given suggestions to make her develop more and more confidence in her ability to sing, and to devote more time to it so that she might be able to do something creative and better than just singing *ghazals* and *bhajans* in their conventional tunes.

She has been made to see that she has talent for reciting poems and singing songs, and deserved to be classed as a good teacher because she was a respected teacher in a very prestigious school in Dehradun. It was with great difficulty that the idea could go through to make her believe that she is more talented than her sister and need not pester her by asking her to make decisions on her behalf for little things like selecting clothes for her or doing little odd jobs. Gradually she came to accept that she was capable of making and taking decisions.

C. It is nothing but slavery to let your sister make decisions for and on behalf of you. Both of you have lived different types of life and your thinking patterns are not the same. Her decisions will not always be what you will like them to be. That will cause stress and tension, though it will remain invisible to you, but will adversely affect your consciousness. So, decide everything yourself, that will give you contentment and happiness. From today you should be independent.

Ruma remains silent, but by gestures showed that the idea is acceptable to her.

She also agreed to cook lunch everyday, and that too of her own choice.

Intervening Session—Jyoti

Things, however, did not improve for Jyoti, and she came alone leaving Ruma at home. She is very tense, more than she was on previous occasions when she came with Ruma. She is upset and disturbed because of Ruma's behaviour. It has become intolerable for her to put up with that behaviour of Ruma where she clings to her constantly and asks for help and assistance. All that Ruma utters is irrelevant and unimportant, complains Jyoti. She also clings to Jyoti whenever Joyti has to go out for marketing or other odd jobs. Jyoti finds her life has become unbearable.

On the one hand Jyoti wants to feel great by thinking she has given support to a relative whom no one else is ready to accept, and in the other, she has in her subconscious mind a feeling of samllness that she has— become a joint operator of all the accounts, etc. of Ruma, which means she will become the owner of all her assets to the exclusion of all other sisters and brothers when Ruma dies. There is also a will written by Ruma which is with Jyoti's elder daughter.

Jyoti herself needed counselling to get from the suffering caused by the disgusting behaviour of her sister who is mentally and emotionally not normal. She feels offended and frustrated.

C. You should feel proud of what you are doing, you are doing something to help a sister whom no other relative is prepared to help.

J. That is so, but I feel disgusted, it makes me sick. (Tears appear in her eyes, she wipes them).

C. Develop in yourself the feeling of self-importance of being a benefactor in so much as you are helping a sick person, whose sufferings are far greater than yours. You are acting like a great nurse, a Mother Teresa; feel the satisfaction of doing good to others, of making someone happier, making someone relieved of mental agony.

J. Let her pray to God, why does she not go and pray to God for help, I have been asking her to do so.

C. She sees God in you, she believes you are the living God; instead of running to the stone God, she prefers a living God, that is why she clings to you and prays for relief from her agonies. Try to see with her eyes, the eyes seeking your love and compassion. Just give a little bit of your compassion, your love. That will give happiness to you also.

(Jyoti's face becomes calm, tension disappears, she feels happy)

J. May I come with Ruma.

C. Yes, please do.

Fifth Session

Further counselling has been given to make Ruma acquire greater self-confidence and self-esteem, and to end her dependence on Jyoti.

She is still very nervous and feels she may not be able to live without clinging to Jyoti.

Various strategies have been used to inculcate in her greater self-confidence.

She is particularly counselled to be independent, accept things as they are, give up worrying about her helplessness, and feel buoyant and cheerful.

Sixth Session

Ruma appeared to be better, she came all by herself, without Jyoti. Intensive counselling was continued to revive self-confidence in her.

R. I have given tune to that song, now I can sing it.

She sang the song beautifully with good melody. She complained it was a song of grief, and she wanted a song to generate cheerfulness. She was given sparkling song. She gave tune to the new song also and sang it with gusto and enthusiasm. The two songs seemed to have brought new life to Ruma, she had shaken off her mental listlessness and intellectual coma.

She had brought two copies of *Togore's Gitanjali* one in Bangla and another in Sanskrit (translation). She also sang a song from *Gitanjali*. She felt delighted and moved, she felt as if she had found something which touched her heart, and which she had missed all along.

R. I am feeling upset because Jyoti has to go to Calcutta to stay with her son for sometime.

C. This has come to you as a blessing in disguise from God. Accept it with gratitude, treat it as an opportunity to revive your past freedom, to become independent, and to get back your lost confidence and self-esteem. [She has begun to see a ray of hope, and to feel she might regain confidence in herself.]

The input of the idea that she was one of the most talented women in the locality made her gather some of her lost sense of self-esteem. She began to open up. She described how she had specialised in Hindi literature, had studied the history of Hindi literature, and was the teacher of Hindi language in a very prestigious school, and also taught mathematics. She sang a song to give evidence of her love of music. She also recalled her talent in dramatics. When discussion was focussed on the works of Tagore, in the field of literature, music, painting, and dramatics, Ruma began to feel elated; she began to see the hidden light of life within herself. Self-introspection brought a revival of her lost self-esteem..

Seventh Session

Ruma is all smiles, full of confidence, her voice is natural, full-throated and resonant, she talks as if misfortune had never plagued her.

Ruma said that during the last four or five days she had undergone a complete transformation, her old self had revived, her entire life had regained its vitality, her memory had come back, and she was feeling absolutely at ease. She is surprised at the sudden change that has come in her life and wonders how she had lost everything and got everything back.

She says she no more feels dependent on Jyoti and does no longer cling to her apron. Last two evenings till about 11.00 p.m. she had to spend alone as her sister and brother-in-law had gone to attend a wedding function, and she felt quite at home reading a book of stories.

She said she could now recall all the songs that she knew earlier, and was now able to recite poems and sing songs. While coming here she remembered a *ghazal* of Bahadur Shah Zafar, the last one he wrote. She sang the *ghazal* with fervour, her voice was resonant, had volume and melody.

She has begun to talk to people; her silence, her isolation, her withdrawal has gone; during the last few days she has been having friendly chat and conversation with people. She feels this is a great and miraculous change. She says she is now perfectly well. She is completely transformed.

She remembered the first day of counselling and said: On the first day I had refused to speak when you asked me to talk; I had felt hopelessly nervous, and even lost my balance on being provoked to speak. Today I can talk, and talk. I can describe everything. I used to keep silent and cling to my sister for protection, but now things have changed. Since the last counselling, I am having normal conversation with everyone. I feel I am now as normal as ever I was. I can remember and see my whole life as a movie in flesh and blood.

She remembers her early life and makes a disclosure which might have had something to do with the serious type of depression and introversion into which she had fallen. Her father never showed any concern for her. He used to go to club after returning from work, and then came, had a drink, dinner and slept; she always felt neglected and insecure. It was this sense of insecurity which had overtaken her and made her existence blank and desolate. For all practical purposes she had sunk into an intellectual coma. Now she has got over her feeling of insecurity and regained self-esteem and self-confidence. She has come out of her consciousness coma.

The strongest piece of counselling, out of the whole series, which seems to have changed her, was the rekindling into her mind the suppressed desire and dormant love for literature, music, art, and dramatics. Her father, she confessed, was against Tagore and would not allow his books, art, or dramatics of any kind enter the house.

Making her give tune and music to the two songs made her go into the process of creating something new. It activated her mind which was in search of doing something that would bring acclamation and recognition. Her participation in discussions about fine arts, painting, literature and dramatics energised her mind and made her rise above the level she had sunk to, and helped her in ascending to the level she was unconsciously aspiring for. Her psychological and intellectual coma had disappeared and she became once again vibrant and lively.

On going back I slept, it was a most relaxing sleep. When I woke up I found something magical had happened. I felt I have unconsciously gained something invaluable. Immediately came to my mind the legend of Sudama and Krishna. It seemed you gave me nothing but I had received everything, happiness and peace of mind.

Diagnostic Scan

Pratibha is an ordinary looking woman of forty-three, mother of three. She looks morose, lacks self-confidence, and has low self-esteem. She is M.A. She is religious, or rather is a woman who tries to find escape through religion, trying to get some help from some god. She was made to sing something so that her thoughts and feelings could be understood better. With great hesitation she sang a Hindi song: [Live in the way, God makes you live.]

Pratibha is suffering from depression, dejection and is disinterested in life. She has normal sex-life. She complains that her husband drinks alcohol in the evening and goes on postponing dinner. Many a time he takes dinner late in the night after she retires. He remains glued to T.V. and goes to bed at about 1 a.m. Pratibha is very unhappy, remains morose and depressed, her daughters try to console her.

General counselling was given to boost-up self-confidence and self-esteem.

C. Pratibha, remember that misery and happiness are both born in the mind and also cultivated by human mind, they can be given the desired direction by deliberate positive thinking. You seem to have chosen to remain miserable, try to change your thinking, decide to be happy. Instead of looking at the dark side of your domestic life, try to be happy.

Try to love yourself. Decide to remain happy. Decide to once again go in for honeymoon and romance; I don't mean unrestricted sex, but unrestricted love. Try to do everything that brings you joy, that makes your husband happy, makes your children dance and sing. Why do you live so shabbily ? Please have better make-up on your face, dress better, live more like a woman in love than a woman who has been rejected by her husband, a wife for whom the husband has no time to spare. Make your husband see that your company is more pleasant than that of the characters on the small screen.

P. I don't know if it is possible, but I shall try.

C. I don't want you to sing any more your silly songs of desperation and surrender, sing songs of joy, merriment and love. Just paint, sing and dance, dance like a fairy. Why not become a fairy?

P. All your suggestions look utopian, I do not know if I can give practical shape to your world of dreams and imageries.

C. Let us wait and see. But go with the determination that you desire to be happy ever hereafter, and would never let any thought enter your mind that may create a state of despondency, hopelessness or helplessness.

P. Okay.

Second Session—Three days later (*on phone*)

P. On going back I slept, it was a most relaxing sleep. When I woke up I found something magical had happened. I felt I have unconsciously gained something invaluable. Immediately came to my mind the legend of Sudama and Krishna. It seemed you gave me nothing, but I had received everything, happiness and peace of mind.

C. It is very good that you have received a little bit of happiness.

P. It all seems a bit magical to me, I don't know how long will this bliss last. This morning, my husband also expressed surprise. He wondered how this sudden change had come in the house. I had not informed him about my visit to you.

(Her daughter Sonia takes the phone).

S. Mother is very happy, there is remarkable change in her.

C. I am glad all of you are happy. Let her keep it up, make her listen to and sing with you the songs that bring thrill and joy in life.

Next Session

Pratibha is now a changed woman, her despondency, depression, and hopelessness have gone. She is full of life and is in high spirits. She has gained confidence and self-esteem. She is laughing and joking.

P. I still lack confidence.

C. Don't look at confidence in its abstract form. Do you lack confidence in cooking food, or doing household chores?

P. No, I don't. I know I can cook what I like, and I have no difficulty. Similarly I feel no problem in doing other household chores.

C. Then it is clear you don't lack confidence. What special dish are you making for dinner tonight?

P. I have not thought of it; well I shall make, *'karhi'* he also likes it. But the problem is he will eat too much and it is not good for him, he has diabetes and high blood pressure.

C. Have you ever measured them? Anyway, don't worry about it and go ahead. You have decided to be happy, so think only of the good dinner all of you are going to have tonight. No more any depressing thoughts.

P. Okay. I will think only of giving a treat to the family this evening, and enjoy the dinner.

C. That is right, what about painting, music and dancing?

P. I have not yet gathered material for painting, but hope to do it very soon.

C. You can start with just a blank paper, pencil and eraser. Make a few bad sketches on the paper and laugh. What about dancing and singing? How far have you gone?

P. I direct my daughters and correct them when they practise dancing.

C. That shows you know dancing.

P. Yes, in my early years, I was the best dancer amongst my friends, I could dance very well. But after marriage everything is finished.

C. Dancing, one can never forget. From now on you will give directions to your daughters by demonstrating and not just telling them how to do it. Can you do it?

P. Yes, I can. I know the art much better than them, I can teach them by demonstrating. But...

C. What is this 'but' ? Have you seen the film. *Hum Aapke Hain Kaun*, and *Khubsoorat* ? You can be Madhuri Dikshit.

P. Yes, and Rekha.

C. Right, you will dance and sing only to get *nirmal anand*. (Pure happiness).

P. Will you like to hear me sing?

C. Certainly, come on.

Pratibha sings the song:... *Deevanoo se Poonchho...* [It is a love song].

C. Pratibha, I never knew you sing so well. It is wonderful. What a change from *Jis Vidhi Rakhe Ram* to *Deevanon se Poochho*. It is superb you have a marvellous voice. Do the people in your family know a Lata Mangeshkar lives in the house?

P. No, I have never sung in the house, my husband is not interested. Years and years have slipped by and no music came out from my lips. It was only to obey your command that I started singing again, and here I am singing before you.

C. I am happy that you have revived your talent. Believe me, you have sung the song with perfection, I wish you could sing the whole day, and I could listen the whole day. I do not want to pamper you, I mean it. You try this magic today on your husband and children, sing before everyone. I know they will be surprised, but I am sure they will feel very happy, and that will give happiness to you too.

P. I know my daughters will be very happy, and the younger one will begin to dance.

C. You can be sure about your husband too. He will just love and kiss you for this song. In any case, you will be singing mainly for your own happiness. Enjoy your singing, feel happy while singing, treat it as your meditation. Dance and sing, laugh and laugh, be happy and fill yourself with joy of living and life of love. With you the whole family will get immersed in love and happiness. Try it Pratibha, try it. You are a woman of multi-faceted talents, let the whole world know of your talents.

(Pratibha is too shy to speak, but her silence and smile shows her inner happiness).

P. But my husband does not think I am worth anything.

C. He needs to know you better. You are a wonderful person, you are charming and pleasant to talk to. I enjoy talking to you, I wish I could talk to you for hours and hours. Your conversation is jovial, you make me laugh and feel happy, there is wit and humour in what you talk. You are full of intelligence and emotions, it is this that makes you a pleasant person.

P. You are the only person who thinks I am a talented person and pleasant to talk to. At home I am just a simple housewife with no accomplishment.

C. No Pratibha, you are what your name indicates: 'Pratibha' a woman of radiance, wisdom and charm.

Showering of such appreciation induced in her the desired feelings, and she attempted and succeeded in living up to the standards set out in the conversation. It has made a positive dent on her sleeping psyche and she has effectively woken up to face the new challenges. She does not want to fail in my estimation, and has started playing the role of a new woman, a woman she unconsciously dreamt to be. She got the appreciation for which she was starving and which had brought depression in her life. Everyone craves for recognition. Pratibha was craving to get recognition and appreciation of her suppressed talents. The therapy has awakened her sleeping mind and brought out in the open her suppressed talents that were lying bured in her mind and which were keen to blossom and bloom. The release of her suppressed unconscious ambitions has given her the wings to fly high, fly like a free bird who is being gazed at by someone in an appreciative mood.

Next Session

P. For the last three days I am again in a miserable state.

C. Why, what has happened?

P. My son is coming, and also my younger sister is coming.

C. So you should be happy that they are coming. You are upset probably because you are making too much preparation to let everything appear excellent. Don't be a perfectionist, don't worry, just let things happen and you will be happy.

P. That is not the problem, my sister runs a beauty-parlour, remains well-groomed with a beautician's professional make-up, and that is the problem. She has always been a problem for me.

C. Is she very smart and more beautiful, attractive and charming than you?

P. Yes, she is in her early thirties, and my husband always had an amorous corner for her in his heart. Even in my presence he says "I love you".

C. Don't worry about that, it is nothing. In Indian society a man is normally permitted to have a little fun with his wife's younger sister. How old is your husband now?

P. He is about fifty, but that makes no difference to him. My sister is married but her husband never comes with her.

C. Don't take things very seriously, enjoy all this as fun for a few days she is staying with you.

P. She will stay for quite some time, she will spend the vacation here, and make my life hell.

C. Pratibha, you have no option, so make the best of it, enjoy her company and take things sportingly, it will lessen your agony. I don't know but their relationship may be just of brother-in-law and sister-in-law or of good friends. Well, she is married and can understand the feelings of a wife if her husband tries to go beyond the limits of permissible behaviour in his relationship with another woman, and you can hope she will keep your husband under restraint.

P. But my husband drinks and knows no limits of permissible social behaviour with a young woman even in the presence of his own wife.

C. It might also be due to his treating her as a guest of honour, because she is his wife's younger sister. Moreover, now the things have changed, the whole environment in your house has changed, and he may not like to spoil it by his imprudent behaviour. You should think positive and behave as if there is nothing special happening in the house. Treat her just as you did when you lived together as sisters before marriage. Do not treat her as a guest who requires five-star treatment or needs to be entertained by anyone. If you will treat her just as your younger sister with sisterly affection and not as a guest, the whole atmosphere in the house will change and your husband will also behave with her more like a relation than a stranger who can take liberty with a young friend.

P. I shall try this 'mantra' also.

Next Session (*on phone*)

C. How are you, Pratibha? Has your charming young sister arrived?

P. Yes, she has come. I have applied your medicine and I find it is working wonderfully. All of us are happy and relaxed, we are all enjoying and having a good time.

C. What about *Jija Ji* ?

P. Oh, he too is acting fine, there is no problem.

C. Okay. Remember no special treatment, a sister is only a sister.

P. Yes.

Next Session

P. Things have been generally good, there has been nothing very disturbing; however, there is something which always annoys and worries me.

C. Tell me what?

P. Only last evening we had dinner, immediately thereafter he (my husband) went to bed and slept. I wished something else, and in spite of my caressing he did not open his eyes. I wanted to talk, to have a little chit-chat and..., but he continued sleeping till morning. I had a sleepless night and in the morning I felt very uneasy, tired, fatigued, and disturbed. The result was that I became agitated, and my maid and the children had to suffer. Later I felt very bad for taking out my rage on my servant and the children.

C. I have told you how to cope with your angry mood, did you apply the calming down method?

P. No.

C. So, try it next time. [She is given general counselling for coping with her problems]

P. I don't get sound sleep.

C. That is all due to your mind remaining churned up with unnecessary worries. Now you have learnt more coping strategies and will find no difficulty in calming down. Just try relaxation when you don't get sleep. And, remember that more will you worry about insomnia, less sleep will you get. So forget insomnia. Even if you do not sleep one night it does not matter, even keeping awake for two or three nights does not affect the functioning of the mind and body. Leave it to your sub-conscious mind, it will take care of your insomnia. Further, it is difficult to know how much have you slept in the night, the period during which you sleep is not recorded by your conscious mind and hence when you wake up you think you have not slept at all, that makes you sad and frustrated. Don't you think your feeling of sleeplessness may be due to your mind not correctly recording your sleep?

P. Yes, I think it is so. I must have slept for sometime. I felt still worse because my husband just got up normally, fully relaxed, took tea and breakfast and went to work as if nothing had happened.

C. So that is your real problem. You were annoyed because your husband had denied you the pleasure you wanted to have in the night. Pratibha, be happy don't be upset because your husband is not unhappy, you should rather feel happy because he is happy. Even the loss of one night's pleasure does not matter very much.

P. Since I came to you I did have a number of pleasant nights, but that occurs only when he desires and not when I want.

C. Anyway, even when he wants, you do get the enjoyment alright, so do not worry as to who takes the initiative, otherwise it will spoil your happiness.

(Pratibha feels happy and smiles)

P. Come on, Pratibha, give me some good music.

[Pratibha sings two songs].

C. Oh, it is wonderful, you are a very good singer, your voice has resonance and is steady, it seems as if the songs come from deep down your heart. Please keep up, develop this talent more and more. Let singing be your meditation. Whenever you find yourself slipping into or moving towards an unpleasant mood, just sing, and if possible also dance with your music.

P. I do not sing before anyone, no one, not even my husband, has ever heard my musical voice. It is only before you that I feel courage and sing; sometimes I sing when I am alone and sure no one is listening.

C. Don't be shy of singing before others, it is a great gift you have, utilise if for your own happiness, and also for the happiness of others.

P. I shall now get ready with more songs and sing before you. I had recollected and practised only these two songs, and that too only for you. Nobody ever talks about my merits or talents, and no one has ever made me feel that I too have something worthy of praise or appreciation.

C. Don't worry about receiving praises. You have to sing for your own joy; singing, I can see, gives you immense pleasure and untold happiness, enjoy it as much as you can without being concerned about receiving praises from others.

(Pratibha laughs with joy)

P. I never laugh, I don't know why I do it here.

C. It is because here you feel fully relaxed. Always remain relaxed and laugh.

DEATH AND GRIEF

— **Birth and death—the two terminals**
— **Drama of life**
— **Trauma of death**
— **Mourning—a negative process**

4
Death and Grief

"The goal of all life is death"
(*Sigmund Freud*)

Death is the normal consequence of birth, it is the natural end of a journey, an inevitable termination of every person's journey through life. Death must come, life's journey must end. We have to accept death as the *finale* of life's music. We cannot escape facing the reality of death, it is as real as life itself. Then what is the grievance?

Death is a wonderful phenomenon, it permits everyone to go on the journey without ever realising that there is a point of termination in his own life also. It never disturbs the peace and happiness of persons while they are still continuing their journey. It does not require anyone to think of it, and thus spoil the holiday by becoming conscious of the fact that the holiday has to end one day. One can, therefore, throughout the life enjoy the pleasure of living. It is a festival, and its beauty must not be marred by the thought of death, the end of the festival. Till the end comes, life must be treated as a continuing and non-ending festival, even death should be enjoyed as a part of the festival. Death is entitled to a treatment similar to that of life itself, because death by itself is nothing, it has no independent existence. Till the end it is life. Death is only another name of life.

Life itelf is a drama in which the individuals go on acting their parts without being aware of the story of the play, or how will it end. The story goes on unfolding itself with changing circumstances. It is full of suspense and action. The screen goes on rising and coming down. It is in a way made-up of a series of dramas some of which are comedies, some tragedies and some others are melodramatic. Life's drama is a beautiful amalgam of tragedies and comedies, psychological situations and just vacancies. It is this intermixing of the variant situations that makes life full of colors although the colors are always not pleasant. But it is really this panorama of variant colors that makes life liveable.

There can be no play or drama more realistic than the actual drama of life in which there are all types of characters playing their roles. In fact, each individual plays all the roles, and lives through the various dramatic situations. There is no director to direct the play, and the story always remains a mystery. The actor does not know the next scene. He has to act and react according to his own intellect, emotions, feelings, and experiences. It is this which gives life a constant sense of suspense and creates the desire to move on into the next scene, sometimes with hope and sometimes with despair. Each actor has to play the role till the last scene in his journey to the finish, and if not, the actor gets drowned in the sea of distress. But till the river of life reaches its end the person has got to go on, swimming, floating or just drifting.

Somethings are inevitable and irreversible, still people refuse to accept them as such. Death is one of them. Everyone knows that death is inevitable, final and irreversible. The stage of life existing prior to the coming of death, a situation in which a person was alive cannot be reverted to. Things cannot be made to happen or to happen in a different manner producing different results. Death cannot be reconverted into life, it is an irreversible event, an unchallengeable truth.

Death has to be accepted as a fact of life. It is no use living in a world of make-belief. Death is a process which oblitberates everything, only memories of the past can remain; there can be no present and no future with respect to a person who is no more, who will never be any more. One can continue to live with a person who is no more, only in the realm of memories, memories of emotional ties, memories that we want should never die. They are only delusions, non-existent and live only in the subconscious mind, and appear from time to time in our conscious mind.

Practical wisdom requires the realisation and acceptance of the factual reality of death—the final washing away of everything, the ultimate obliteration of the living being. There can be no return and no come-back of the past. However, this does not mean despair, despondency, or melancholia. Life is a continuing process, people come, play their role, and go away. Others come and become part of the existence and so on. The play must go on whether one is there or not. Everyone has to realise this truth and continue to participate in the grand show accepting the fact that when the role of an actor ends, he must leave the stage. In order to overcome the trauma of death, death must be seen as a part and phase of this ongoing drama of life.

Death, however, induces various kinds of traumatic reactions, they differ from person to person; normally loss of life produces such feelings as:

(1) anger,
(2) guilt,
(3) bitterness,
(4) regret,
(5) longing and searching, (to convince one self that the person still exists and bereavement is not called for)
(6) the need to establish blame,
(7) anxiety,
(8) fear,
(9) (*i*) helplessness
(*ii*) loneliness
(*iii*) self-reproach
(*iv*) loss of identity, and
(*v*) isolation.

All these reactions do not develop in all person. Much depends on the emotional state of the individual and the circumstances in which death occurs. However, the basic anxiety of the person in each case is to find solace and escape from the event of death which is the most dreaded thing in the mind of men who do not understand the true meaning, character and implication of death and consider it something unnatural coming down as a bolt from the blue.

Sometimes, the individual who suffers the shock of someone's death, begins to consider himself/herself intrinsically responsible for the loss of life, and develops all or some of the above mentioned reactions and feelings. And, in order to reduce their severity tries the transference thereof to other persons. Unconsciously the person tries to establish his/her innocence and projects himself/herself as a victim of the tragedy. Yet, the same unconscious mind doubts its authenticity and makes the person suffer the unabating pain of deprivation. In addition, the feeling of guilt and shame also develops in the subconscious mind and enhances the trauma.

The various traumatic reactions produced by death get blended with the memories of experiences which the individual had with the deceased. These memories get mingled-up and become a subconscious reality. They continue to remind the person that his/her beloved is no more, and has become just a dream, never to come back, never again to be alive. It is this feeling of permanent deprivation that makes one unhappy. One tries to live in the world of dreams to avoid the feeling of deprivation, or having the vision of reality. It brings frustration and pain.

It is not possible to cleanse the subconscious mind totally of the memories of the event and they continue to appear and disappear. They find their way in dreams where they adopt symbolic forms and give vent to feelings hidden in the subconscious mind and struggling to find escape. Dreams, whether they come during sleep or wakefulness, are generally the expressions and manifestations of concealed desires. For instance, a dream involving kissing and embracing without either resistance or withdrawal, may just be a sub-conscious visual expression of a concealed desire, and unconscious wish that the deceased be still alive. But if in the dream one sees resistance or withdrawal by the partner, or something like that, it might be a reminder of an unsuccessful or unhappy amorous event; but that too makes alive the memory of the deceased person and the desire that he/she be still alive. A dream is generally a manifestation of memorised pictures of past happenings lying deep in the subconscious mind. Continuing of memories connected with the deceased only prolong the trauma. Earlier they disappear, better it is.

Grieving on the death of an individual only helps in preserving the memories and is counter-productive. Still people grieve and mourn. This is because death causes deprivation and a vacuum in the life of the survivors. Death no longer looks like something of a fictitious nature, something which we talk about and forget, something that is a matter of semantic conversation. The survivor suddenly sees that death means total loss, total deprivation, the final end of a life, something that will never let the person come back to the original form. Thus death becomes a final departure. This sense of total deprivation gives a severe shock and causes intense agony and grief. It is this irreversible deprivation that disturbs the human psyche.

Death brings different degrees of deprivation to different persons, depending on the type of relationship he had with the deceased person. Loss of a spouse or a child causes maximum sense of deprivation. Death of a relative, a friend, or acquaintance, and sometimes even of an unknown person, brings sadness and misery in the life of individuals. Death has always been regarded as the most painful event in human life, and thus a matter for grieving.

Relatives, friends and acquaintances try to help the deprived victims in having disengagement from the deceased. Death calls for total estrangement, the emotional cord has to be finally cut to get final disengagement. Here, the sympathisers and mourners play a role, they take away the body and make the grieving persons cremate or bury the body and this makes them accept the truth that it is lost forever. They also lend their moral support to help them cope with the trauma of emotional deprivation, and thus help in accepting final departure of the deceased. Sharing of grief by sincere and well-meaning persons helps in reducing the grief. By giving them the opportunity to cry and weep they help in lessening the burden of grief. But this has to be for a very limited duration and should not be allowed to prolong. Agony shared is agony reduced, but agony prolonged is agony enhanced.

With the passage of time, however, the event of death slips into the domain of memories, and the individual succeeds in incorporating them into one's life experiences. These memories do not easily die, but although they surface occasionally, they do not cause trauma, and one manages to survive, cope and carry on. With the passage of time they adopt a neutral character and lose their emotional overtones, and new thoughts, feelings and events become predominant constituents of the individual's personality. That is how one enters the present, leaving behind the traumatic past.

By feeling grief or developing the feeling of grief, the person unconsciously tries to punish himself. Grieving causes sadness and produces misery. By imposing misery and suffering on oneself, the person tries to get some sort of relief, and to atone for what has happened. A wife or husband subconsciously feels the guilt of failure to save the life of the spouse, and begins to entertain the belief of being a failure, a person unable to save the life of the person he/she loved. Gradually, in some cases (rare) this turns into a phobia and the person begins to regard himself/herself guilty of causing the death of the spouse. It is this feeling of guilt which makes him/her impose on one-self the punishment of self-suffering. He/she begins to suffer agony and other debilitating emotions resulting in complete physical and psychological ill-health. Women are more prone to this feeling than men.

What a person, however, needs is to understand that he/she is not guilty and there is no cause for him/her to feel shame or remorse or sadness for the event of death. One should not forget that no individual can or does have control over death of any person, not even ones own. The body goes through a life-long process, and then stops functioning. No person is or can be responsible for the coming of the end of time, the end of life. One has only to accept the reality that anyone who is born must die.

Religious people have sought to teach the same thing by taking resort to the theories of destiny, fate and God. They say life and death are in the hands of God or destiny, meaning thereby that no one is or can be responsible for anybody's death, and that death comes of its own. Hence, the expression of grief as a method of atoning for the death of any person is meaningless. What is needed is the acceptance of the truth that death is inevitable, it is only an unavoidable consequence of birth and part of life.

Mouring is counter productive, instead of reducing it enhances and prolongs the misery.

People bereave and mourn mainly to calm down their own nerves. They grieve for the loss of their own happiness which they may have been having from the company of the dead. They grieve not for the dead, but only for themselves. They mourn the loss of their own happiness, which they fear will no more be available after the death of that person.

They forget that very often death brings to the deceased person relief from the multiple pains and agonies of life. Life is a continuous process of misery and joy; with death not only the joy of living but also the misery of life ends. Why feel sorry? Why shed tears? Why not rejoice in the completion of a journey by a beloved one? Why feel sad? Why not glorify the event which marks the end of the journey, which the deceased persons had to complete. The deceased may have even preferred that no one should mourn on his death, or shed tears, and may have wished everyone to share his joy of completing the life's journey.

When a person suffers bereavement, he/she becomes too self-centered and looks only to his/her own deprivation, misery and loss of happiness. He/she totally fails to look at the event from the point of view of the person who has died, and for whose loss she bereaves. Maybe the deceased was suffering from an agonising pain and death might have come as a relief to him.

Listen to his inaudible words:

"And now time has come when we must report : I to my death, you to go on living."

SMRITI

Smriti's attachment to her dead son has ended. She has won liberation. The umbilical cord has been finally cut, she is no more crazy about her dead child, her feeling of guilt and shame has also died out.

Diagnosatic Scan

Smriti—young married woman of twenty-three. She has done her B.A. (Hons.) and lives in Mumbai with her husband Vinayak and his parents. Married three years back, she gave birth to a child last year. but he died after a few months. Her parents live in Delhi.

The shocking memories of her child's death always haunt her. Smriti looks tense, nervous, afraid, and miserable. Her mind gets blank and thoughtlessness engulfs her, it seems as if her life was all a vacuum. She does not get proper sleep during night. She has developed symptoms of withdrawal, goes into depression, is disinterested in life or living. Always thinks of the dead child.

Other problems in her life have contributed a great deal to her misery and forced her to attempt suicide.

Behaviour of her husband, Vinayak, and his mother was so abnormal that it made Smriti profoundly depressed. Her husband often came wholly frustrated from office and remained in high tension. Before the son was born she used to help him in completing and finishing his unfinished office work and that used to calm him down. But since the birth and death of the child she was not able to do so with the result that Vinayak gets angry and begins to beat himself with his hands and sometimes with his leather belt saying: as he cannot beat Smriti, he will beat himself because his misery was all due to Smriti; this used to frighten her and make her shiver.

She did not then understand that Vinayak's behaviour was the result of his own tensions for which she was not responsible, and she had no reason to feel guilty for the same and develop the feelings of guilt and shame.

It is a case of transference of guilt, and transference of punishment. He is unable to beat Smriti because she is innocent, so he punishes himself in order to escape his own frustration and feeling of guilt. But that makes the whole environment tense and develops in Smriti the feeling of shame and guilt. Thus, indirectly the husband achieves his objective of transferring the guilt to Smriti and making her suffer for it.

Another way in which Vinayak used to punish Smriti was to decree that for one, two or three days he will not speak to her. The duration would depend on the severity of fault, which, he thinks, Smriti was guilty of. It may be as insignificant a thing as the table not being cleared of papers, etc., in the manner he wished. Smriti used to get stunned and feel great pain (emotional) because of such acts of Vinayak. His mother also sometimes imposed the same type of punishment on Smriti by withdrawing herself and not speaking to her. It is very likely that when Vinayak was a child or young boy her mother used to punish him like this. Now he practies this on Smriti.

Smriti's miserable life became intolerable to her when the child was operated upon. Depression overtook her and she attemped suicide by consuming Baygon. She admitted having made the attempt because she felt discarded, depressed and helpless, and had lost the desire to live any more. It appears that she attempted suicide for various reasons: the feeling of guilt for giving birth to a defective baby, inability to bear the sight of operated portions on the body of the child, unsympathetic and hostile behaviour of her husband and his parents, and general tension in the house where accusations were always being hurled at her.

After her attempt to commit suicide her mother-in-law questioned her husband: Will he at this age get her sent to jail for killing Smriti? She feared she may be charged for attempting to kill the daughter-in-law. This made her husband fly into rage and he became so tense that he forced Smriti to leave the house.

The child was born with perforated stomach, and had no chance of survival. She became very upset when operation was performed in Mumbai without any hope of recovery. Everyone became sore and began to blame Smriti. She was condemned and turned out of the house. She went to Ghaziabad to stay with a relative where the child died. Her husband was not there, and the shock Smriti got was beyond her to bear.

Smriti is open to listen to reason. She has a keen desire to overcome the shock.

Counselling

[General counselling was given to her to make her get out of the trauma]

C. Smriti, just think what was the child except a biological product. In your ovary some egg got inseminated with your husband's sperm and the fertilised egg developed into an embryo and became the final product, the child. The end product had a manufacturing defect—perforated stomach—and was not capable of surviving, so it died after four months.

You have unnecessarily developed a feeling of guilt. You were not responsible for the baby been born with perforated stomach, nor were you responsible for the death of the child. Death is not in human hands. It is fated, and in the present case the child was born with a manufacturing defect and was bound to die sooner or later, the sooner, the better.

Life is a process of constant adjustment to the changing situations as they crop up. Life is dynamic, it remains in the process of a continuous change. So you must move forward with courage and hope, and face the loss of the child as a matter which was beyond your control. You were destined to have that child only for four months. Why mourn?

You are still very young and the first child was born in a normal delivery process. So there is every reason to believe and hope that you will very soon give birth to another child. The new one may be a better one, fully developed, without a biological manufacturing defect. You have the option to forget the past and have a new healthy child or to continue to live with the memory of your dead defective child.

S. I would like to have a new one who is normal. But the memory of the old one still persists to make me sad.

C. Do you not realise that the child would never have lived a happy life with a serious physical deformity ? It was good that you have been spared a long life of agony and suffering. Now you can look forward to having a new child. You must nurture in your mind the desire to conceive and give birth to a new child for which the necessary pre-condition is the wiping off the memory of the dead child and your liberation from your depressive attachment to the dead child. It is necessary for you to understand that the sick child is dead and gone and will never come back. The whole drama of birth and death of the child is over, it has gone into oblivion. You must accept the reality.

S. My attachment with that child was deep because in him I saw the image and incarnation of my own father who had died when I was only four. After my father's death my mother had remarried. The step-father has given me full love and affection and I never felt the loss of my father. Still I could not forget my father, I revered him and saw his reincarnation in my son.

C. Do you believe in the theory of death and reincarnation?

S. I do believe in reincarnation.

C. Anyway, is it not unethical to think of your revered father in the shape of a sick or dead child?

S. Yes, now at least, as the child is not alive it is not right to think of reincarnation and see my father having a second death after twenty years.

C. Do you know the legend about Gautam Buddha's encounter with the woman whose son had died and she wanted him to give back life to her son?

S. No, I do not.

C. Buddha asked the wailing woman to bring a little water from some house where death had never taken its toll, and by sprinkling of that water on the child's body, life will come back. The woman went from house to house and came back empty-handed. There was no house (family) where death had not taken toll of some life.

Buddha told her that death was inevitable and was the natural consequence of birth. His teachings consoled that woman.

[At this stage in a hypnotic manner I told her: "I can bring back your son to life. Would you like to have him back, that rickety sick child with perforated stomach?"

S. Pat came the reply, "No, no, after having heard you I do not want him back".

(Maybe this was just impulsive, but it was certainly not superficial; rather it came from the depth of her heart. She meant what she said)

C. So, forget the dead child, and hope that very soon you will have a healthy child.

S. I am feeling much better now. I am relieved.

Smriti's attachment to her dead son is gone. She has won liberation. The umbilical cord has been finally cut. She is no more crazy about her dead child, her feeling of guilt and shame is gone.

Another Session

Smriti says she is in a very good condition now. She has also been listening to the tape on positive thinking and stress management and feels she is having great peace of mind. She is having good sleep. Her fear of the people's company has also decreased, she had gone out and met two friends. But her fear of the future continues, she has no shelter and no security, she has no place to go to. She says, "my husband has closed my entry into his house, what am I to do, where am I to go?"

General and specific counselling has been given to allay her fears and restore her confidence.

Final Session

The whole scenario has changed, her husband has come. He too has been given counselling, he no longer thinks Smriti to be guilty or an inanimate object which can be rejected and discarded at his will. He has talked to her, and has taken her to live with him for a few days with a relative of his.

He has also assured her that in future he would behave better and would no more resort to imposing on Smriti the punishment of self-withdrawal and going into silence. She is determined to play a positive role. She is full of courage and confidence. The 'silence' punishment, she agrees, did not prohibit her from loving, caressing, kissing, embracing or hugging. She will resort to all of this in order to end the curse of silence, and finally remove it from the family's punishment code.

Smriti is very happy. Last evening she cooked food at the house of her in-laws where she was staying with her husband. She also met and conversed with people, she has overcome the fear of meeting and facing people. Her confidence has been fully restored and her fear which had led to her withdrawal has disappeared.

Smriti is now a changed person, a new woman; so is her husband, a man with a better understanding of the psyche of a woman and his role as a lover and a husband.

Smriti finally goes back to Mumbai with her husband with rekindled feelings of love, courage, faith and confidence.

SHABNAM

I really suffer more because of the friends and relatives who come to mourn, they always remind me of my sorrow and grief. They are really not grieved, but pose to be deeply shocked by my husband's death.

Diagnostic Scan and Counselling

Trauma and shock caused by death of her husband make Shabnam (in her fifties) weep, tears often flow from her eyes, she remains disheartened and depressed. Her sleep is no longer sound. She weeps like a child who has lost a dear toy.

C. You look quite brave, your face shows confidence, and you appear to have high degree of self-esteem. Why do you mourn for your husband who was ill and suffering and whom death brought relief from agony?

S. I think I should not. I really suffer more because of the friends and relatives who come to mourn, they always remind me of my sorrow and grief. They are really not grieved, but pose to be deeply shocked by my husband's death. Once while going to the doctor I met quite a few persons on the way, each asked me about my condition. By replying to their endless repetitive queries, I developed high B.P. by the time I reached the doctor.

C. It was because they made you develop more grief. Each time a question was asked about your emotional health your grief was revived, and your tension mounted up.

S. Yes.

C. But you can't help it, this has become a part of our culture. You should learn to ignore it. If you will remain generally composed, it will be easier for you to overcome these shocks. It is better to smile and change the topic without giving them reply to their awkward queries.

Her daughter intervenes: Mummy even otherwise continues thinking about *Abbu* and remains depressed.

S. I cannot help it, tears come automatically.

C. Subconsciously you do invite tears. You have to divert your mind to other things, that will help you in forgetting your loss, which is, as you know, irreparable.

What you need is not weeping at the loss which was inevitable, and necessary to bring to your husband relief from suffering, but to look forward to a peaceful future, a future with broader horizons. You need more happiness to overcome the shock. Do you know: happiness given is happiness received; sorrow given is sorrow received. Try to feel you are not alone; why only feel, you are in fact not alone. You do not belong to a husband-wife nuclear family, but to a larger family—a family consisting of you and your children. Think of that big family of yours, whose happiness depends now entirely on you. If you will be miserable, they will be miserable, if you will be happy they will be happy too.

Think also of your husband whom you loved so much. Will it be his wish to see you miserable and weeping, or to see you happy and smiling? You know very well what will be his will.

S. He will certainly not wish me to be miserable and weeping, he always wished me to be happy and smiling. He always made effort to make me happy.

C. Then try to behave as he had desired. If you will do this your trauma will slowly wither away, and in doing this you will only be fulfilling the wish of your husband. Mourning develops a negative emotion and makes you sad. Try instead to fulfil your husband's desire of making you, your daughter and every other member of the family, happy and contented.

Please develop more concern, compassion and love for your daughter. Just look at her, how sad she feels in your sadness. Don't transfer your own sadness to her. Try to make her happy by yourself becoming happy.

S. I shall try to remain calm and relaxed.

C. Try also for the diversion of your mind to positive and pleasant activities, it is a good method of reducing agony. Mind becomes locked up to a particular thought and continues to remain locked up unless diverted to some other brainwork. You can also not think in vacuum, so think about something other than the demise of your husband, about someone other than your husband. Think of problems which other members of your family are facing and try to resolve them with the aid of your wisdom and wide experience. Have you not been acting as the pivotal point in the family circle? Does not everyone look to you for guidance?

S. Yes, they do. I play an important role in the family.

C. Then continue to play that role, now it is more important. That will surely reduce your feeling of loneliness. Loneliness is felt more acutely when the mind has no occupation, so try to live a wholesome life forgetting the deprivation. The loss cannot be resurrected, only the vacuum can be filled by some sort of purposeful mental occupation. Keep yourself as much occupied in day-to-day activities as you can without feeling tense.

S. I also think so, I shall try to forget the tragedy by diverting my thoughts to something purposeful. After all, it was the will of Allah. I had no say in the matter and have to accept His will gracefully.

C. You know there are three kinds of thinking: One is purposeful, the other purposeless, and the third is that which causes harm to oneself and/ or to others. Thinking about bereavement and grief falls in the second and the third categories, it causes unhappiness to everyone, in any case it serves no purpose. So avoid such thoughts and divert your thoughts to happier things. That will bring you peace and relaxation.

S. I am already feeling relieved and hope to overcome the grief in due course of time. My daughter loves me very much and always worries about me, it is she who made me come to you. All my children and grandchildren are very much concerned about me. I feel pained to see them unhappy.

C. Everything depends on how you look at life. Everyone in the family has suffered a severe blow by the sad demise of the head of the family, all of you have to stand together and face the loss. Now you have become the head of the family and a great responsibility has come on your shoulders to keep the family happy. I have no doubt that the way you look at life, you shall be able to win peace of mind for yourself and bring joy and happiness to everyone else.

S. I wish I may succeed, I am sure by the grace of God I shall succeed.

C. Certainly you will. And then your very smart daughter is there to help you.

S. But she has to live with her husband and her in-laws.

D. That does not matter, I shall always be with you whenever you will need me.

C. She is already by your side, you can always depend on her.

S. Yes, that is so, she is always there to give me solace.

C. You do not anymore need solace, you will from now be extending solace to her and everyone else.

S. Yes, I shall.

ANATOMY OF HAPPINESS

— **Maximisation of pleasure**
— **Minimisation of pain**
— **God, Fate, Destiny**
— **Equanimity with no pleasure and no pain**
— **Conscious control of mind**

5
Anatomy of Happinesss

"That man lives happy and in command of himself, who from day to day can say, I have lived. Whether clouds obscure, or the sun illumines the following day, that which is past is beyond recall". (Horace: Carmina, iii, 29,41).

Happiness and unhappiness are only the condensed and capsular versions of the two basic states of human consciousness. The state in which the mind is agitated, frustrated, upset, perturbed, ruffled, tumultuous; or feels uneasiness is the state of consciousness called unhappiness. The state in which there is no agitation, commotion or strife in the mind, and it is calm, peaceful and serene is the state of consciousness called happiness. However, dynamic activism and activated dynamism of mind are not to be confused with the state of mental agitation, they are quite different and produce entirely different outputs. Similarly emotional tranquility doesnot mean or include psychic slumber or emotional stagnancy, hibernation or passivity.

In the state of happiness, the mind experiences love, ecstacy, delight and joy; and in the state of unhappiness it experiences agony pain, misery and depression. Human mind constantly goes on living in the two states of consciousness, experiencing emotions according to the happenings in one's life. Sometimes, both happiness and unhappiness exist simultaneously, sometimes they appear singly. It may look odd, but in life, happiness and misery always live as twins, they always exist together. As a matter of fact, nothing ever exists all alone, everything exists along with its opposite, then alone can it be experienced. One is never totally happy or totally miserable; one is always relatively happy or relatively miserable. If the level and field of happiness is higher and wider than that of misery, one experiences happiness; if the reverse is the situation, he experiences misery and feels unhappy.

Normally every person desires to remain happy. Happiness is a subjective feeling which is experienced by an individual in his/her consciousness. How this feeling originates has been a matter of debate. The two basic approaches are: maximisation of pleasure and minimisation of pain. There is a third approach, basically Indian, it requires maintenance of equanimity by avoidance of both the states, rather remaining unaffected by either of them: pleasure or pain.

The first is the hedonist approach, which emphasises that happiness is the outcome of the satisfaction derived from material success, comfort, luxuries, and increasing consumption of goods and services. The principle is: satisfaction of desire brings pleasure, and pleasure gives the feeling of happiness. The reverse of the theory is that failure in the achievement of desires brings pain and unhappiness. This approach leads to continued effort to the increasing of desires, and also to the ever-increasing pain and unhappiness. There is always a competition going on between achievement and failure, leading respectively to feelings of pleasure and pain. When the quantum of pleasure outweighs the stress created during the pursuit of pleasure, the resultant is the feeling of happiness; and when the reverse happens, it causes misery. In all attempts to get higher degree of pleasure some element of risk of failure is involved, but very often higher is the risk, greater is the joy of success.

The second approach advocates the serene acceptance of the inevitable, and the notion of right living in harmony with natural forces in the social environment. It emphasises the harmonisation of one's behaviour with the innumerable forces created by thoughts, emotions, and behaviour of all who make the social environment. This approach accepts that adverse situations are generally the cause of pain and are inevitable, it is accordingly best to live in harmony with them so that the conflict is avoided and pain is not suffered. Absence of pain helps a person remain calm and enjoy peace of mind, which is deemed to be the basic foundation and necessary component of happiness.

The principle of maintaining happiness through minimisation of pain differs from the theory of acquiring happiness by maximisation of pleasure, essentially because of their differing concepts of happiness. While one regards natural and undisturbed flow of life in the state of tranquillity as happiness, the other considers the activation of the sensations and the body and its being in a state of dynamism as happiness. The pursuit of pleasure theory of happiness depends on increasing consumption of material goods and services that satisfy the physical body sensations. The other theory depends on reverse action. They differ also because the pleasure theory is essentially homeostatic, while the pain-avoidance theory is not essentially so. The pursuit of pleasure doctrine depends invariably on the intrinsic and fundamental cycle of arousal and release. It is undeniable that the experience of pleasure is limited to the individual's inherited and conditioned capacities of the organism; pleasures arising from such achievements can produce positive subjective states, but they do not lead to a change of organism or enhance the capacity to feel the pleasure or happiness.

The avoidance of pain by curbing one's drives, and coping with external changes, may superficially look homeostatic, but it has some elements which do lead the organism to change. It makes the organism become less sensitive to psychic pressures and better suited to cope with the psychic impact of external pressures and environmental changes.

Very often one resorts to find relief by cultivating faith in God, fate, and destiny. This is also a method to minimise pain and suffering and thereby gain the feeling of happiness.

All the three terms God, fate, and destiny are incapable of any precise definition, they mean different things to different people. The concepts of God, fate and destiny, however, play an important role in the life of individuals. They help in relieving a person of his feeling of guilt, rather preventing the feeling of guilt affect the individual. They help in shifting the responsibility of a particular event or situation, and as a consequence help the person in accepting things as they are. They help in relieving tension that might get generated due to adverse happenings, events, and situations.

If a person believes in the supreme power of God, and also believes that nothing happens except in accordance with His will, then he/she can easily succeed in getting disassociated from his own actions and inactions, and feel relieved. He might in this way avoid self-condemnation and self-reproach; which cause distressing tension which produces pain and agony.

Similarly, belief in fate and destiny can give comfort to a person in situations that produce tension and cause unhappiness. One can accept such situations as inevitable, and thus prevent him from holding himself responsible for the same, and also from thinking that he could have defused the situation, or made things happen in a different or more favourable way. Once he accepts what had happened had to happen, because that was fated or destined, he gets disconnected with the event and succeeds in keeping free of the feeling of guilt which is generally responsible for a person's unhappiness. The belief in God, fate and destiny thus helps in coping with an adverse situation. However, that requires a complete effacement of one's own individuality and personality. It may be better to accept this and see the same idea in a more scientific way. There are innumerable factors that influence every individual's thoughts, feelings and behaviour. They make their impact continuously on existing situations and make them fluid. It is impossible to foresee or give shape to things and happenings as they are the product of innumerable factors on which the individual has no control. In the making of any particular situation, an individual's role is insignificant, hence no person can hold himself responsible or accountable for the same. It can therefore, be termed as fated or destined. Hence, for minimisation of pain, one should remain convinced that he is not guilty of creating a bad situation

However, acceptance of fate or destiny, by whatever name called, cannot take the individual beyond the point of avoiding the sense of guilt for an adverse situation. It cannot by itself either end the situation that creates misery or agony or make a situation where you might get and enjoy positive happiness. Suffering whether it is caused by the voluntary act of an individual or the will of God or fate or destiny, has the same damaging effect on the individual's psyche, ultimately it is the effect and not the source that is relevant. Misery, sorrow and depression do not automatically change into joy and happiness by the acceptance of the plea that it was fated or destined. Positive steps have to be taken to end the trauma even though it may be caused by ill-luck.

The third alternative is more positive, it tries to bring a change in the organism by keeping the mind free from the onslaught of both pleasure and pain. By regular practice of strategies that curb one's desire and craving for materialistic objects, such as food, sex, rest, intoxication and the like, a change occurs in the organism; and that helps in the promotion of positive emotions and elimination of negative emotions. Positive emotions bring happiness and negative emotions cause unhappiness. Happiness is really the state of mind in which it gets filled up with positivity and becomes immune to negativity.

However, these three modes, ways, strategies for gaining happiness are neither conflicting, nor excluding, and not even non-cooperative with each other. And at the same time none of the three strategies is self-sufficient, all-embracing or exhaustive. Each contributes to the realisation of the ultimate goal of getting happiness. Both, arousal of pleasure and reduction of pain produce rewarding states, indispensable for maintaining the psychic process on a stable plane, from where one might take the life to experience higher degrees of happiness. Any activity which is enjoyable generates positive emotions and promotes happiness. An enjoyable activity is one in which one gets so involved that nothing detracts him/her from pursuing it, and the doing of which itself becomes its own reward. Most of the creative activities like painting, music, dancing, etc., fall in this category and bring not only relief from tension, stress, depression and boredom, but give positive happiness. Similar are the activities which involve physical and mental dynamism, like games, sports, and different kinds of adventures. Every human activity that counteracts negative emotions like hate, anger, fear, sorrow, and anxiety, reduces pain and misery and helps in generating positive emotions.

The person whose thinking becomes blurred with negativity begins to develop such emotions and feelings that block his way to positivity and produce unhappiness. The reduction of negativity reduces pain, and growth of positivity enhances pleasure. Both added together tend to minimise pain and maximise pleasure.

Happiness being a subjective feeling is capable of having qualitative variations. The ladder of happiness starts from the bottom of unhappiness scale, which is the stage of agony. The top rung of the ladder in the zone of unhappiness, represents feeling of unpleasantness, discomfort and uneasiness, in between are the rungs representing annoyance, distress, irritation, anger, anxiety, grief, misery, pain, sadness, sorrow, suffering, torment, wretchedness, depression and similar feelings. Similarly, in the zone of positive happiness the steps in the ladder vary from simple pleasure to blissful happiness and rapturous delight. In between are steps representing happiness of different shades, varying according to qualitative content of pleasantness they produce. They include such feelings as cheerfulness, contentment, delight, elation, gladness, joy, jubilation, thrill, bliss, and the feelings of equanimity, tranquillity, peace, and the like, which make the person reach the ultimate stage where mind becomes absolutely calm.

Blissful happiness finds a welcome entry when the mind is free from turbulence and is calm. When there is storm in the mind, it gets agitated and loses its calm, then psychological functioning gets disturbed and psychosomatic stresses appear. When the mind is calm the entire body functions peacefully, and experiences become delightful.

It is possible to train the mind to enjoy normally the happiness which is qualitatively of a higher order. It is also possible to learn to stay permanently in the happiness zone, and never to sink into the zone of unhappiness or at least, never to descend below a particular level. Everyone has a particular belt in the two zones into which he usually stays, and only occasionally moves up and down. If a person stays in an emotionally stable situation this movement is reduced to minimum. Through a process of learning and training one can neutralise all upheavals which tend to push a person down into the zone of unhappiness. An understanding of the causes of these disturbing feelings can prevent their cropping-up in the mind. In intimate relationships and behavioural matters love and understanding play an important role in controlling negative feelings, love being a powerful positive emotion succeeds in counteracting negative emotions, and takes the mind back into the happiness zone.

Emotions, thoughts and feelings constitute the structural frame of happiness. They play decisive role in determining the anatomy of happiness. Mental stress is generally responsible for creating unhappiness. People normally spend more of their time mentally stressed than mentally relaxed. General mental attitude plays a vital role in keeping the mind stressed or relaxed. Meditation and like exercises usually help in promoting and maintaining mental calm and keeping the mind relaxed.

Happiness and unhappiness have direct bearing on human behaviour. Conversely, behaviour affects his mood and produces happiness as well as unhappiness. Hence, control of behaviour and giving it proper direction becomes important. One must learn and develop a hebavioural pattern to match the desired mood, the mood that enjoys and radiates gaiety and cheerfulness.

Experience of happiness can be made more rewarding by improving one's skill of performing an activity, and heightening the capacity of feeling happiness. For instance, every person can get some pleasure from music, but if he learns music he gets higher degree of pleasure out of it, and can even appreciate and enjoy classical music. If he himself learns to sing or play a musical instrument he would get far greater pleasure and might ultimately get meditational happiness. Learning helps in the enhancement, and maximisation of pleasure in every field of activity, may it be music, dance, drama, painting, or any other field of creative activity which involves experiencing of emotions, feelings and cognitive thinking. It applies equally to all other activities; games, sports, cooking, interior decoration, body care, etc., all give enhanced happiness on acquisition of proficiency in them. Every advancement in this direction through learning and acquisition of wider knowledge helps in experiencing deeper happiness.

Human mind has very wide horizons, it travels up and down the scale of time. Through the memory lane it can travel to any time zone in one's life, and through day-dreaming it can go to any period in future. While travelling through the channels of time one can re-enact happy and sad moments experienced in the past, and also dream of experiencing happiness and unhappiness in the future. It gives choice to live in a way one likes. By reviving pleasant memories, one can develop positive emotions, and also experience happiness which may be called 'recalled' happiness. And, by thinking of darkness suffered in the past, the individual can recreate the moments of unhappiness and experience what may be called the 'haunted unhappiness'. In the same way one can experience happiness and unhappiness by dramatising the future and experiencing it as if it were the present. By converting the future time-zone into the liveable present, the individual attempts to create an imaginary world believing it to be a real one, and perceives different kinds of emotions and feelings. He passes through pleasant and unpleasant phases of his own creation which are bereft of all reality and are more the product of subconscious illusions and inspirations than of conscious thinking. What he experiences is only 'fancied happiness' and 'Feared unhappiness'. It serves no real purpose to live in the world of fancies and images of events dead or unborn. One should enjoy the reality rather than run after iliusion.

ASHA AND RAKESH

I don't advocate 'forgetfulness' but its contrary: 'awareness'. Be aware of everything and accept their reality, and instead of fighting with reality, live with it as a partner. Don't deny but accept what is, as it is. I am not asking you to efface your individuality but to look at things with greater practicability; change them if you can, accept them if you cannot. The sole objective is to avoid conflict and thereby prevent avoidable stress.

GO SLOW, treat the world as a place for enjoyment, and life an entertaining comedy. Live life in an easy, relaxed way, that is the natural way to live.

Diagnostic Scan

Asha is a lady with posed happiness on her face. Maybe nearing sixty, a bit plump well-built, well-groomed.

Rakesh, Asha's husband is in his sixties, looking sick, frail and dejected.

Asha came with the idea of getting counselling for her husband. Rakesh was silent, only Asha was speaking.

Asha said I should better ask him his problems. She looked tense, though she continued saying there was no problem with her. She plays bridge twice a week and that relieves her of all her stress. A few minutes later, however, she was wiping her tears; she had broken down.

Her life, ever since marriage, had been an ordeal and a tragedy. There was something wrong with her husband, but her mother-in-law and husband's elder sister continued to curse her for not bearing a child. This was a continuous source of unhappiness and tension for her. She could never remain in peace, and had a sad and sorrowful youth.

Finally, they adopted a girl child Madhu, many years later, who is about twenty now.

Her failure to have a child of her own has been a continued source of misery. She feels it was because of her husband that she had to remain without her own issue.

Rakesh retired as Customs Commissioner. Asha tries to impress that he was a very honest officer and because of it he had to suffer during his tenure in office, and finally a year before his retirement he was suspended, superseded and charged with corruption. This had shattered his life, he is now sixty-five. Both suffered social humiliation, though ultimately he was found to be not guilty.

He suffered various types of illnesses, including a special type of Parkinson's disease, which maims a person, but there is no shaking of hands, etc. The medicines had some side effects and one night he suffered an attack which caused death of certain cells in his brain which control motor action of muscles. He is not paralysed, but all his muscles are in a state of latent paralysis or coma.

If somebody makes him do it, he moves his limbs, etc., otherwise he remains quite stiff, sits straight without moving his limbs or head. He has stiff neck, probably has spondylitis. When asked to look around and up, he complained he got reeling sensation. He hardly winks, his whole face and eyes look stressed. He says he has a feeling of stiffness all over. Yoga exercises make his body come into action, but muscles always remain under stress.

He takes walk—two kilometre in two hours, with someone to walk along.

He cannot easily get up from the chair. He feels uncomfortable in the straight-back chair.

He walks in slow motion.

Asha says that he always tries to get help and support, and that he purposely does this, otherwise he is physically not unfit to get up or get going.

He will not help himself even to get a glass of water, or put his plate in the kitchen.

He desires that someone should look to all his needs. Today he even made his daughter give him a shave. He will always try to find someone to shave his face and do even little things for him.

He is always trying to escape from activity. He will occasionally not even flush the latrine. Asha feels agitated and irritated as she dislikes dirty and stinking bathroom. She has to go and pull the flush chain. She likes cleanliness.

He is also in the habit of disturbing everything. While moving about in the room, he will remove and change positions of things in his way and make everything in a disorderly condition. Asha has to find the things and replace them.

He will walk on the carpet with dirty shoes. Even today while coming here he picked up her handkerchief from the clothes she had taken out for wearing. She searched but could not find it. It was only when she sat in the car, she discovered he was holding it in his hand.

He talks with great difficulty, only answers questions and that too with difficulty and in the minimum of words. He initiates no conversation, neither does he participate.

He is suffering from tension of the body, as also mental tension. For sometime he is not getting good sleep, otherwise he takes calmpose and medicines for B.P., etc.

He says he is fond of reading, but does not read because of his eyes.

Sometime back there was some illness, they say it was the side effect of some medicine, which had made him lose most of his higher mental faculties, but now he is okay. Maybe, the effect is still continuing which has made him dumb (almost) non-responsive, and seriously diminished his capacity to take initiatives.

Maybe he had a big shock for being charged of corruption, superseded and compulsorily retired before age of superannuation. Maybe, he was honest and is still suffering from shame. Whatever be the cause, he has developed negativism and has lost hope of recovery, accepted miserableness as his lot, which has rendered his body stiff, mind dull, and the whole body inert.

The only reason he gives for his tension is that he feels concerned and miserable because of his inability to help his wife and for putting a lot of extra burden on her for managing his finances, etc.

Counselling

He has been given counselling to make him change his attitude and learn thinking more positively, and for living a normal life. He has also been counselled to give up the fear of ill-health, and to think of health and not illness. He should accept his physical and mental states as they are, they should he accepted as representing his normal health and he should learn to live happily with the same, practise strategies for relaxation of muscles and mind, and let positive thoughts enter his consciousness. Meditation will help in getting relaxation.

Asha

Asha says she gets fits and convulsions when she becomes very agitated. She develops anger at the abnormal and disgusting behaviour of her husband, it is a constant source of tension for her. She thinks both his action and inaction are deliberate and meant to make her feel small and disturbed and to put her to shame. This leads her to suffer fits and convulsions. She frequently weeps, feels frustration and helplessness.

Asha does not want to live with her husband and desires to get separation, but finds it not possible. The reason is her feeling of duty towards him.

She finds it impossible to deal with and tolerate his miserable and irritating behaviour.

She practies meditation but not correctly with the result that instead of relaxation she gets more stress.

C. Don't you think individuals have very little control over situations that control human life?

A. No.

C. I think things happen mainly under force of circumstances and the individual has a very limited role to play.

A. It is Tao's philosophy, I don't believe in Taoism.

C. Even *Gita* says that things happen, and man acts only as a tool and a medium. Does it not appear to you that you never had played and still play no role in determining and modulating your husband's existing pitiable condition and his obnoxious behaviour?

A. Yes I have played no role in making him what he has become.

C. Do you think you can do much in changing the behaviour of your husband?

A. No, I know things are beyond my control.

C. Then will it not be better to accept it as inevitable?

A. I know I am helpless. Even though I will like to get separation, circumstances will not let me have my will fulfilled.

C. I don't think a woman of substance and confidence like you should accept this in the spirit of despondency. If you want separation, you can get it; but deep in your heart you do not want it. Be brave and do whatever you want. If you do not want him as he is, then reject him, but that is not likely to bring you greater happiness. Your attachment to your husband is not superficial, it is genuine. Remember, it is not receiving but giving that brings blissful happiness. The little happiness you are getting in your life is because of this. It is an oasis of happiness in the desert of unhappiness, and that is what really matters.

A. Yes, I think you are right.

She is also suffering with what I call Post-Retirement Trauma (P.R.T.). As the wife of a Customs Commissioner she enjoyed many privileges including the luxury of servants and high social status, where people will even artificially try to keep her in good humour. With the (disgraced) retirement every privilege has disappeared. She, rather they, have been reduced to the status of common middle-class persons with a tainted image. They have no servants. She does not keep a servant because of the condition of her husband, she feels it is risky to leave the house to a servant with an invalid husband. She has to do all the domestic chores in addition to managing such affairs which normally the husband would have done. She is over-worked, is always short of time and consequently under tension. The tension ultimately leads her to develop frustration, and resort to crying and weeping. That makes her indulge in cursing her fate, and getting fits and convulsions.

C. Please try to keep relaxed, that will help you to cope with depressing circumstances and adverse situations.

A. I shall try to face the situations and circumstances with the maximum courage at my command. I promise never to shed tears again.

C. Accept with grace and equanimity what is not changeable. You should also try to lower down a bit your standards of cleanliness, orderliness, etc. that will give you peace of mind and relaxation.

A. They have become my obsessions but I shall try my best.

Second Session

A. For four or five days after the last counselling my husband was very much better, he began to go round and do some work as well, there was general improvement, but things changed again to what they were earlier.

C. What about your ownself?

A. There is a long history, I had a number of surgical operations. Surgery had begun with my gynaecological problems, there were glands in my breasts too, which needed surgery. My right leg is almost paralysed, but I have not accepted defeat and am continuing to live with all the ailments, treating myself as normal.

C. You are a woman of great courage and confidence. As you have accepted to live with your own physical problems, why not extend it further and accept your husband also in the same spirit?

A. I am accepting my husband in the condition he is. The acceptance, no more, is under any sort of compulsion like helplessness, compassion or sympathy.

I am a changed person since my last counselling. I feel relaxed, I stay relaxed.

The reason for my not getting separation was due to my sense of duty towards him. That has now become the reason for my taking so much care of him, and feeling so much concerned about his welfare.

C. That is right, but don't treat your relationship as propelled by the sense of duty, treat it just as part of your normal behaviour. It is really your love and not duty which makes you accept him with all his shortcomings. Don't mar your nobleness by the input of duty. Duty implies some sort of compulsion, but your attitude is prompted by your free will and not any compulsion.

A. I understand the distinction.

C. All you require to do is to let things go as they do. Just remain a participant in the drama of life without getting involved in it, I mean emotionally involved.

A. I get the point, I have to play my role in the drama of life as an actor does. I shall no more worry about my husband having any faults. I am used to accept every odd. From the very time I got married I had faced a very agonishing behaviour of my mother-in-law and elder sister-in-law. The sister-in-law had a feeling that by keeping the four brothers docile she could always have an upper hand in the family. All the four brothers including my husband have been docile, inert, and have formed the habit of withdrawal from work and responsibility. They all suffer from escapism.

I still remember the occasion when he exhibited his attitude of withdrawal, escapism, and refusal to take responsibility. He wanted to perform *Shradha* of his father and asked me to make preparations. I arranged everything and cooked food and called the priest, but he disappeared and never turned up, with the result *Shradha* was not performed, and in the night the food was sent to a temple.

C. It seems probably it is the same attitude that has now taken a magnified shape. He wants every responsibility to be taken by you and he should remain just an onlooker. In the process he creates more problems for you. So take the whole thing lightly and feel relaxed.

A. She smiles.

C. Well, can you think of any background for this type of behaviour which is certainly not normal for a person who has held such a responsible post in the government.

A. The early childhood of my husband is probably responsible for his attitude of withdrawal and escapism. He spent all his time with a Muslim woman *ayah* (governess) and had no attachment with the family or involvement in the affairs of the family. He was never entrusted with any responsibility. It was only when I came into his life, things changed and the influence of the governess ended.

C. But it continued to control his sub-conscious mind and behaviour.

A. He also had involvement with a girl before marriage.

C. Did you also have boyfriends or affairs?

A. No. I had some friends but no emotional involvement with any boy.

C. I think in view of what you have said it would be better to do a little bit of age regression of your husband. Will you stay or go out?

A. I am prepared to listen to any disclosures he may make during the age-regression exercise, that will not affect my feelings or behaviour towards him.

Age-regression is done. During age-regression he seemed to be overturning his thoughts, feelings and events in his mind, but when it came to expressing them, he spoke out only of one insignificant event, viz., that when he was ten, his father had said he had flat foot. He did not speak anything about his personal life or the events during his earlier life. (Further attempt was not made.)

He named two persons who were responsible for his suspension and removal from service, but said he did not know the reason. He insists that charges of corruption against him were baseless, and he was found not guilty, but it was this event which had shattered him and pushed him into the situation and condition in which he presently is.

Counselling Rakeṣh

C. You know you were innocent and falsely implicated in the case, so forget the event and free your mind of its traumatic effect. That will help you overcome the trauma. You have revealed it during the process of age-regression, now reproduce the whole thing into writing. That will strengthen your belief that you were victimised for no fault of yours and you were a victim of conspiracy and malice. You should reinforce your feeling of innocence by making inputs to strengthen that belief. Your sub-conscious mind must get the signal of your innocence.

You should try to come out of the trauma, and begin swimming again in the stream of life; begin a new normal life. You should no longer drift in the stream of life.

R. I shall try my best to become more and more self-reliant on both physical and emotional planes.

C. Please write a biographical sketch of your experiences, both good and bad. Get involved in hobbies and activities like painting, etc. You have a lot to tell the world, please write something like your memoir.

Asha

C. You need to adopt a different life-style. You are running faster than time, as if you were in a race. Give up planning for the morrow. Live just today, just minute by minute.

GO SLOW, treat the world as a place for enjoyment, and life an entertaining comedy. Live life in an easy relaxed way, that is the natural way to live.

A. I have already started treating life as a drama.

Third Session

Daughter

Asha while describing unsavoury behaviour of her husband, spoke of his behaviour towards Madhu (daughter).

A. He asks Madhu to massage his body or to do something like rubbing it lightly. He makes Madhu even to shave his face.

C. I do not approve of such behaviour. All this shows he is trying to communicate with Madhu via 'body-touch language'. Where a young girl of about twenty is involved it may be indicative of its having sexual overtones. In any case, precautionary measures are necessary to be taken for the well-being of Madhu's emotional health.

A. How can I do it?

C. Ask Madhu to stop being involved in body-touch communications. Many times many things happen without being intended. Precaution is always better and desirable. It is essential that Madhu should be prevented from having any body contact with her adoptive father, so that body communication may not take place.

Some incidents in the life of your husband, which you mentioned earlier are sufficient for a guess that he maybe psychologically starving for sex in its broadest sense. Body touch of a young girl is a way of sexual fulfilment. In this case it may not be so but in the interest of the girl it may be necessary to take precaution.

Moreover, it will also retard his recovery because he will feign illness to gain access to the girl. He will try more and more to invoke compassion, sympathy and pity in order to get greater attention of the young girl. Body-touch language communication will be sought by him in increasing degrees, and that will lead him unconsciously to feign illness of a nature that may require support—physical and even psychological. He will develop symptoms that will make him more and more dependent on others.

Madhu need not be and should not be totally briefed, she should only be told that for the sake of the father's health it is necessary that all supportive aid be withdrawn and he be made to become more and more self-reliant.

A. I was myself not happy with his behaviour. Now I shall take immediate steps to prevent such behaviour.

C. All you need, Asha, is to remain relaxed without worrying about what is going on. Cultivate an attitude of non-involvement which poets and philosophers describe by referring to Lotus flower. You already have it, you only need to strengthen it.

A. The counselling is helping me to remain happier.

Fourth Session

A. During the time since the last session Rakesh has felt general improvement in his well-being and more relaxation in his muscles and joints. I took this early appointment because I thought momentum should not be allowed to be lost.

Rakesh has been made to listen to hypno-sleep tape. When he reached the stage of hypno-sleep, inputs were made reminding him of the emphasis laid by Sigmund Freud on sexual aetiology—the role of sex on the behavioural pattern of an individual.

He was made to go back to the age of five to ten the period he had spent with the Ayah out of house. Progressively he was made to make a self-analysis concerning the events, thoughts and feelings relating to sex, particularly suppression of sexual instinct and desire. He did not desire to speak so he was asked to relate to himself in his mind in non-vocal words, his thoughts and feelings connected with any significant event involving his sex-life. This process took him on to his present day life in which he is doing overt acts of body-touch communication with his daughter.

Asha was also made to undergo age-regression. She said she was suffering from frustration, and it was continuing since her youth. She describes the events:

(*a*) I was a very bright student, and reasonably hoped to get through in I.A.S. At the time of marriage it was agreed that I will be allowed to appear in the I.A.S. examination, but after marriage my father-in-law, and more particularly my mother-in-law refused to permit me and I got a shock, my dream and ambition of becoming an IAS officer was frustrated.

(*b*) My husband had mumps, and also suffered shrinking of testicles, which affected my sex-life. Even though my father-in-law was a doctor, nothing was done. This became for me a matter of continuing disgust and disappointment. I could not conceive and bear a child. It has remained a life-long source of anxiety for me. As a last resort I adopted a daughter and became completely involved in her.

(*c*) I am a strict disciplinarian, my husband is of the opposite nature, and I had frequently to suffer distress while dealing with the child. This has also been a cause of disgust and suppressed anger throughout my life.

(*d*) My husband always suffered from inferiority complex because I was culturally on a higher plane; I also played better tennis, better bridge, and was a better conversationalist. His inferiority complex with its overtones had an indirect depressing effect on me.

(*e*) Husband's illness and his progressive withdrawal from his daily routine jobs resulted in putting real psychological stress and burden on me. It developed in me the feelings of desperation and frustration.

(*f*) Retirement with stressful accusations of corruption had also a very depressing influence on the psyche of both.

(g) All his contemporaries who were similarly placed (we live in the colony of officers) are having a happier life, they have servants and other comforts of life which I do not have. I have to work like a horse all day, remain over-worked and consequently over-stressed.

Her circumstances have landed her into a comparatively deplorable situation. This has developed in her not only inferiority complex but also repulsion and hatred against her husband whom she regards responsible for the situation in which she is.

Counselling

C. How many of these women hold Ph.D?

A. None.

C. How many have studied or gone abroad for the purpose of higher studies?

A. None, I believe.

C. How many have the will or capability to read a whole lot of history, literature, etc. like you?

A. None, I think.

C. How many play good tennis?

A. None better than me, none comes even near me.

C. How many play good bridge better than you, or even upto your standard?

A. Again the answer is none.

C. So you see you have got many sterling qualities which you can be proud of. It is a person's personality and not material possessions that are relevant. You have no cause to feel inferior for that reason. You can also afford a servant, it is only for good reasons you do not employ one. It is the intrinsic worth of a person that really matters.

A. I know that, but all of them look so happy.

C. When you had come initially I had thought you to be a very happy person. It was only when your eyes began to speak through the flowing tears, I could see your real face. The mask had been lifted and your concealed self had appeared. Everyone wears a mask, and nobody is what she/he looks. Happiness lies within and not on the surface.

A. Of course it is so, and since the counselling has commenced I have been feeling happier, my tensions have become almost non-existent.

However, I find difficulty in accepting completely the things as they are. Compromising with existing situations and circumstances is not in my nature. I cannot believe in Taoist philosophy.

C. Taoism is a form of religion or a religious philosophy, what I am saying is only a practical way of avoiding tension. By asking you to compromise with situations which are not changeable at individual's will, I am only asking you to treat the inevitable as inevitable and to live through life having minimum conflict with the existing situations, which are neither of your creation nor can be altered at your will.

What is necessary is to forget the past and to live in the present, the present as it is.

A. It is a good philosophy, a practical philosophy.

C. I think it is not a philosophy, but an action-plan.

A. Very well, I shall follow this action-plan from now.

C. Have you read *Gitanjali*.

A. Yes, its translation in English.

C. But that does not let you hear the hidden music in the songs of Tagore. Read the original. Then you will hear the divine music of Tagore. Every verse in it is a song where the whole nature comes to life, you feel the music of birds, dance of flowers, beauty of the rising sun and the colourful moon dancing through the sky. Enjoy life like Tagore, let it be a beautiful dream, where everything seems pleasant, gives happiness, and brings peace of mind.

A. I have already begun participating in the music of pretty birds and the dance of beautiful flowers.

[Asha feels happy and relaxed.]

C. What about your fits and convulsions?

A. (Asha smiles) They have gone with the wind.

KARUNA

I was twenty at the time of marriage, wholly ignorant of what marriage meant. I was not mentally prepared for the marriage and had no idea of what was going to happen. I was suffering from fear—fear of the new life.

Scanning

Karuna does not look very cheerful; from her face it seems she is under some kind of hidden stress.

She is living in a city in the hilly area. Her life is confined to the Army campus, meeting armed forces wives, attending dinners and parties with some dance, etc.

Her two sons have grown up.

Karuna has crossed forty. She feels dejected. She complains she has lost interest in everything. She does not find glamour in dressing-up like other women. She acts automatically without any zest.

In the normal course she accepts withdrawal and does not insist on getting done things of her choice. She does not interfere with the choice of TV programmes, but lets her husband and sons tune in any programme of their choice. That is why she does not see any serial, she has really lost interest in TV programmes.

This is one of the instances to illustrate her mental condition—withdrawal and lack of enthusiasm and possibly loss of interest in things in which other persons are generally interested, or in which she too was interested till sometime ago. She thinks this state of detachment and non-involvement had started since the time of her marriage.

K. I was twenty at the time of marriage, wholly ignorant of what marriage meant. I was not mentally prepared for the marriage and had no idea of what was going to happen. I was suffering from fear—fear of the new life. I feared that I would no longer be able to do things that interest me, my old interests will die because I was changing from childhood to womanhood with the ringing of the wedding bells. I would not, I thought, be able to continue learning music or keeping up my other interests; and in fact my fears came out to be true. Everything changed, a new life began. I had now become a married woman with responsibilities of running the house and looking to the comforts of others. Everything was so new and came with such suddenness that I felt lost and developed some sort of latent fear. It is this fear, I do not know, which seems to have made me draw away, from activities that require initiative.

Now the things appear to be more serious as they are leading to further withdrawal, and making me feel depression now and then.

Counselling

C. Your fear was really a fear of a new life. You were feeling you were entering an unknown world, a world of the grown-ups, the world of adults. That makes a person lose self-confidence and more seriously self-esteem. All these years you have suffered from low self-esteem. Low self-esteem also causes depression. Generally phobic anxiety coexists with depression. A person suffering from this disorder tries to escape from the situations she has to face, that is what had made you draw way from life.

K. Yes, I did want to escape and always tried to evade and avoid. That continued long enough and has become part of my life.

C. But now you have seen that your fears had no basis and nothing you feared ever happened in your life. Instead of your experiencing the situations you feared, you received love and affection from everyone.

K. Yes, that is so, still I always felt diffident, fearful, nervous, and scared to do anything which meant assertion of my will. Probably I always remained conscious of not committing any mistake.

C. It was all a result of your deep-rooted fear of the unknown. Now your experience has shown that there was really no cause for your fear and everyone was cooperative and desirous of making you feel happy.

K. Yes, and I always have had my way, my say.

C. Now, let us leave the past and come to the present. Do you today have any fears?, if so of what?

K. No, I cannot think of anything specific.

C. Think of the sub-conscious fears which you had before you got married, and tell me which one still worries you.

K. I do not think I have now any fears, whatever lurking hazy fears I had, I think, with the counselling have gone way and I am feeling relieved. Everyone, my husband, sons, relatives and friends are all cooperative and friendly. They are always ready to help me. I do not have any feeling of isolation. I feel no threat.

C. You see, your fear was only a fear of alienation and isolation, and of condemnation by those who mattered to you and whose love and concern you cared to get. Now you find that your apprehensions have no basis, so you are feeling relief and freedom from anxiety and fear.

K. Of course I am feeling happy and relaxed. I feel as if I never had any fears.

C. Certainly you had none, they were only of the nature of dreams, now you have woken up and the dream has disappeared.

K. Yes, that is so but I am still not having positive happiness which I am longing for. Ambitions I had before my marriage still remain unfulfilled.

C. What were your ambitions?

K. I wanted to gain proficiency in music, to do painting and all other things which a young girl normally wishes to do in order to get recognition and admiration.

C. Karuna, you are still trying to become the same young girl of twenty which you were before marriage, that can never be. You have to treat that period as dead and gone. You have to live in the present, you must develop new interests suitable to your age and circumstances. All you need is to accept your middle-age, and to treat yourself as a matured middle-aged woman.

Your life has now undergone a semi-circle. Your children have grown-up, your husband has become more involved in other matters, you too have changed and entered the state of new maturity. You must try new experiments with life. Try to have new goals, new interests suitable to your matured life.

By changing over to the new phase of life, you have not lost anything, you have only shed your old feathers and acquired new ones, to make you fly better.

K. I will try to do something to create fresh interest in life, such as making paintings, writing something about the life of native women of the mountains, and doing some other intellectual activities.

C. Don't confine your interest to things in the outside world, but enjoy the daily life, enjoy your food, enjoy your own existence.

K. But I now eat only for the sake of eating without caring least for taste.

C. This is not right. Revive your interest in cooking food, dressing yourself attractively, and appearing in presentable style in parties, why even at home. Your husband will love it, and his love will bring you greater happiness.

K. I will try not to withdraw myself from life, but enter into it once again with renewed enthusiasm.

C. You must understand that life is meant to be lived and enjoyed and not to be discarded and thrown away as being of no value. You have still to see that the children reach adulthood with honours. It will give you immense pleasure.

K. I know my mission is not yet over, I still have a duty towards my children and my husband; my happiness ultimately depend on their happiness.

C. No, the situation is otherwise, their happiness depends on your happiness. If you are dejected and unhappy, everyone will become unhappy. Your withdrawal from life will mean deprivation of love to everyone, and life without love will not be worth living. Do not act as being propelled by duty but by love.

Make yourself involved in every facet of life, become once again the light of the family, the lamp from which everyone may get light of happiness. Love yourself, fall in love with yourself: that will give you interest in life and living.

K. Lamp seems to have already come into my hand. I am feeling relaxed, my disinterest in life seems to be disappearing. I do not think I shall have any more withdrawal syndromes and depressive moods.

C. No, never.

USHA

Motherhood is good, conceiving a child is good, but it becomes a curse when the mother fails or refuses to deliver the child. You are still preserving the embryo in the womb of your consciousness. You have got to cut the umbilical cord of emotional attachment and deliver the child (embryo) out of your mind. Just complete the process of producing the child. It is necessary to cut the umbilical cord, not only the biological but also the psychological and emotional umbilical cord. It will be good for both of you.

Diagnostic Scan

Usha complained that her elder son was having too much anger and behaved in a manner that irritates her. She wanted him to be treated.

It, however, appeared that Usha was herself living in a state of serious tension. She originally denied but later admitted she was often boiling with rage and anger. Sometimes she and her husband also quarrel, but says this is just normal husband/wife domestic fight.

Usha suffers from high blood pressure and takes regular medicines.

Usha had a religious Guru before her marriage, and even now she goes to him. Her husband also accompanies her. She says she gets peace in meeting him, but is unable to explain what is the nature of that tension which takes her to the Guru for solace. She appears to be living in an unsettled emotional state.

She says she has a general feeling of insecurity, but is not in a position to speak out the circumstances that lead her to feel insecure. She has no apparent reason to feel insecure. She is a working woman and has good independent income.

Making her travel back in life reveals that in her childhood (age: 10-12 years) she used to dream she was about to fall in the deep water below, or something like it. She also felt as if someone will beat her. Feeling of insecurity and fear has continued till today.

Today her dreams have become a reality, she suffers violence at the hands of her son, is not protected by her husband and feels fallen and insecure.

Counselling

General counselling has been given to make her come out of her problems. It has been conveyed to her that she was now a grown-up strong woman who can protect not only that little Usha but also the grown-up Usha as she now is.

She has been put under a very mild hypnosis and made to develop higher self-esteem, self-confidence, and self-reliance. She has been counselled to become more loving towards all, particularly the son against whom she has complaint. Instead of always trying to point out that he was not working sufficiently at his studies, she should show more affectionate understanding of the situation, and give him a little longer rope to act according to his will. What is needed is cultivation of positive emotions, particularly the emotion of love.

It was impressed on her that her tension radiates all round and influences even her son. If she becomes calm by overcoming her own tension, her son will also become calm and may not remain as much exercised as he at present does.

Second Session

Usha reported she felt better.

She has now revealed the real cause (as she says) of her voes. After her marriage her husband's elder brother was married to Kanta who was about two years elder to her. According to Usha, Kanta is a real devil and she began playing her devilish game soon after her marriage. She made everyone dislike Usha, she did all types of ragging to make Usha's life miserable. In the joint family Usha's position became very deplorable. She was going out for a job, and had a minor son. Kanta managed to turn out the maid; and caring of the child also became a problem; the mother-in-law was already an inconvenient factor; further, every moment Kanta did something to make the mother-in-law lose her temper and abuse Usha. This made her life suffocating and very miserable.

Her husband was also always a cause of her agony. He used to return late (sometimes very late) in night. He was spending the evenings playing cards, as he informed Usha. Life was unhappy for Usha, her child too suffered due to neglect.

Although Usha had left the family house ten years ago, she still feels she is haunted by Kanta. She gets nightmares of her tortures. Kanta is constantly haunting her mind and vexing her. Whenever she meets Kanta, she gets a new wound.

C. Please do not worry any more about Kanta. Do not recall memories of misery and agony you suffered because of Kanta. More you will try to force her out, more aggressively will she come back in your subconscious mind. Just take it easy, let her stay where she is, and she will slowly walk out of your mind, leaving you free. Only way to get rid of an evil or devil is to open the gates of your mind to let it walk out. Feel relaxed to let her have easy passage out.

U. I shall try to forget the past and cease to think of that evil woman. However, I am facing torture everyday. Every now and then my husband goes into rage, so does the elder son.

C. They probably feel neglected, it would be better if you start showing some more concern for him and your son.

U. My son has nothing to do with me except demand of food and clothes, and to show temper if I say anything which he does not like.

C. That is one part. Now tell me why do you feel insecurity?

U. It is because I do not have a house of my own. The house I live in is of my husband. I am saving money to buy a house.

C. There is no sense in it, and with your present income you will take years and years to build a new house. Instead of saving for the house, you should think of some income-yielding investment. Your fear of losing the house is baseless.

U. Yes, it is.

C. Then give up the feeling of insecurity. It is your house, you have a right to live in it, and you can be confident that no one will ever turn you out of the house.

Third Session

U. I am again in great distress. I am worried about my son, he does not devote sufficient time to his studies, and goes out with his friends, even when I ask him to stay at home and study. What is more serious and annoying is that he abuses me in unbecoming language, and even becomes violent and beats me. I am spending so much money on him, giving him all comforts, good food, clothes, etc., and in return I get only-abuses and blows.

Usha has come with her problem child, about seventeen years old, he is studying in class XII.

U. I cannot tolerate my mother repeatedly asking me, rather pestering me, for studying at home. I go to school and for tuition for two hours, and also study at home whenever I like. I do not need to be goaded, that makes me lose my temper.

C. Usha, you should not buy misery in exchange of your concern for the betterment of your son. It is not worth it, do not let your peace be disturbed by asking him to study at home. Why invite abuses and violence against yourself if you can avoid? Let him study as he likes, he is now quite grown up, leave it to him. So long you will go on asking him to study, he will go on resisting, as he does not want to obey your commands. If you stop, it will develop a sense of responsibility in him which is more important than studying without a will.

U. How can I see him sitting idle and not studying, his future is at stake?

C. I know you are too much concerned about your son's future, you wish him to reach great heights, but nothing of that type is in your hand. He will himself try to reach the height he can, let him try. Become more rational, reduce your concern him, let him blossom on his own, give him freedom, let him fly like a free bird.

That will give freedom to you as well. Enjoy your freedom, freedom without strings. It will bring you peace and happiness, and most certainly save you from suffering the pain of being abused and physically assaulted by your own son.

[Further counselling given on the same line.]

Fourth Session

Usha still lives in severe tension. She has headache. Acupressure on temples has relieved her of pain.

U. I am distressed, I have high blood-pressure. I am taking medicines, but still diastolic B.P is on higher side. Throughout the day, even in office, I am thinking of my son, and worrying about his bad behaviour and gloomy future. I know it does me no good and causes only stress, but I can't help.

C. Why are you so much concerned about your son, specially when your emotional relationship with him is only of a negative and distressing character. Just think, you conceived him and carried him for nine months in you womb, thereafter your body expelled it out, and all biological relationship was severed by the cutting of the umbilical cord. You only played the role of a biological machine in producing the child. Better get away from the involvement which gives you pain and distress. Do your duty in helping him to grow up, but do it without emotional involvement. It may be little difficult, but that is the only wise thing to do. If you do not want to live under constant stress and distress, you have no option but to get yourself liberated from your emotional involvement with your son.

Did you have a tension-laden mind during pregnancy?

U. Yes, I did not have a happy life as I have already told you, and I always lived in tension during pregnancy.

C. That might have injected tension in the embryo. I don't know, he may have born with in-built tension. Anyway, that is not very relevant at this stage. Today you have to discover how to keep your calm in the environment of tension.

You must learn to cope with stress. The tape on stress management will help you.

Decide to remain happy, free of tension, otherwise you will have nothing but high B.P., headache, and misery.

U. I always try, but fail to stop tension and anger gripping me.

C. You require more practice of coping strategies you have learnt. Let things happen as they do.

U. I shall try to keep calm and learn to put in practice the philosophy of 'Let Go'.

C. That will help you in getting peace of mind.

U. It is a curse to be a mother.

C. It is not a curse to be a mother, motherhood is normally a pleasant experience; at least it should not be a curse.

Motherhood is good, conceiving a child is good, but it becomes a curse when the mother fails or refuses to deliver the child. You are still preserving the embryo in the womb of your consciousness. You have got to cut the umbilical cord of emotional attachment and deliver the child (embryo) out of your mind. Just complete the process of producing the child. It is necessary to cut the umbilical cord, not only the biological but also the psychological, the emotional umbilical cord. It will be good for both of you.

U. I do not understand this.

C. It means detachment. Live with your child, but live like a mother who has given birth to a child and leaves him independent to grow up. Just keep a watch from a distance, I mean emotional distance, emotional detachment. Simply because you have given birth to the son you do not cease to be what you were, an independent and a free individual. Your attachment with the son is killing your individuality, your personality, your very existence as a person, as a woman. Live without being too much concerned about him. Get detached, live your own life in the way which gives you maximum happiness.

U. Maybe I shall be able to do it.

C. I am sure you will. Decide not to let your peace be disturbed by your son. Once you inculcate the feeling of detachment nothing will give you tension. Please do not let the behaviour of your son disturb your peace of mind.

General counselling has been given to make her leave things to God, as she believes in God.

U. I feel I should leave things to God and feel relieved of all worries about the future of myself and my son.

C. Yes, and you will get the peace of mind you so keenly desire.

After some time Usha phoned that the counselling about remaining detached had done her a lot of good; and that now she was feeling completely relaxed as her son had passed the exam and joined a professional course in another city.

RANJANA

It may be good to remain concerned about oneself and to think about one's own tensions; but it is better to love someone else and forget one's own sorrows.

Ranjana's husband works as a manager in a company, he complains about depression and failure in achievement in his job, remains sad and feels disinterested in life. He worries about difficulties he might face in regard to higher education of children though they are only thirteen and six. He also becomes tense because his wife, very often, feels disgusted with him and wants to go to her parent's house. He is rather confused and is not sure about what makes him sad and depressed.

Ranjana looks morose, and does not seem to be in very good health. She is lean and thin, but knows her mind well and is clear in her thoughts. She is talented and has done M.Com., she can sing classical music. She lives at home and spends her time in doing domestic chores and looking after children.

When her husband was sent to another room and she was alone, she disclosed:

R. My husband always feels he has failed in life. All his colleagues have got promoted to the rank of executives, he has not gone up, so feels frustrated. Our living in the Company's colony has also added to this problem. His colleagues who have got promotion, live in better houses while we occupy the house meant for junior officers.

C. Do you also feel inferiority because of this?

R. No, left to myself I would not feel anything, but when I see him depressed and frustrated, I also get a depressing feeling.

C. Because you are his *ardhangini* (being half)

R. Yes, 'better half'.

C. No, 'worse half', because instead of transferring your own feelings of contentment to him, you take on to yourself his feelings of frustration. Don't do this. This makes you both sad and depressed, but if you brush aside his feeling of inferiority and transfer to him your own feeling of contentment, both of you will become happier.

How many women in the colony who occupy better houses or are wives of higher officers, are as highly educated as you are, or can sing like you? How many of them know classical music?

R. I don't think many, some can, but just sing a few songs. I don't know of anyone who sings classical music.

C. So, you see you are the most talented woman in the colony. Real status of a person or his/her worth is not to be measured by the office he holds, the salary he gets, or the house occupies but by his/her personal qualities. Don't you agree?

R. Yes, I do.

C. How much difference would it have made if your husband had got the promotion?

R. Not much, and now he is being transferred on promotion.

C. Will you mind singing a tune? I wish to know if you really have something you should be proud of Ranjana sings.

C. Oh, it is wonderful, how much time do you devote to music everyday?

R. Nothing. I had learnt classical music, and I wish to learn more, but I am presently occupied in the bringing-up of my children only.

C. Can't you spare an hour a day for practising music? Singing, particularly classical music, is the best form of meditation, it means complete involvement, it gives maximum relaxation and happiness. And, the happiness you get continues even after you stop singing Please sing everyday; it will not only fill you with happiness, but the whole atmosphere in the house, the whole environment will begin to vibrate with happiness; even your husband will feel the change, your happiness will make him happy as well. How much time can you spare for music?

R. One hour, from five to six in the evening.

C. Mr. Goswami, why do you not encourage your wife to sing?

G. She is too shy, she doesn't sing.

C. Did you hear her melodious voice while you were in the other room?

G. No, I was busy watching T.V.

C. She is not at all shy, music came naturally from her on my request. She will love to sing if you will only show a little interest in listening. From now on she is going to practise singing one hour everyday from five to six.

G. In the morning?

C. No, in the evening, she will not disturb you in the morning, and she will finish before you come back from work.

G. I shall be very happy if she will revive her interest in music. I know she is an accomplished singer, she had learnt music for quite sometime when she was young.

C. It may be good to remain concerned about oneself, and to think about one's own tension but it is better to love someone else and forget one's own sorrows. Your wife is the best person available for being loved. You had loved her intensely once, please revive that love, she will love to be loved by you. That will make her happy, and that happiness will reflect back to you. In addition it will make you forget your office blues and give you happiness. Why do you want to cultivate misery by bringing home the problems of your office? You are suffering from nothing except jealousy. You feel dejected and depressed because most of your colleagues got promotion before you and are occupying positions higher than you in the same establishment. May be your estimate about yourself is erroneous, they might be superior to you in doing the job, or there may be something wrong in the system. Anyway there is no reason for you to feel inferior or ashamed.

G. I realise, I might have been over-estimating my capabilities and performance. I have got what I deserved. Anyway, now I am getting the promotion.

C. So, the problem is now over.

G. I realise I should not carry home the worries of the office and make my wife unhappy.

C. Just one thing more. Try to make your wife positively happy by showering more of your love on her. By giving her more love, you will yourself feel happier. Fall in love with her once again, celebrate her birthday with gusto, give her a Valentine card.

G. I realise the significance of what you are trying to convey. Instead of worrying about my own miseries, I should think more about her happiness, which really means our happiness, everyone's happiness.

C. Yes.

DEEPALI

Children have to be controlled. I dislike any disturbance in the house. I cannot tolerate if somebody disturbs anything, I get upset and find myself left with no option but to punish the guilty.

Diagnostic Scan

F. (Deepali's father) Deepali as fallen in bad company, and has developed bad habits. Last evening she wanted to go to Meerut to play handball as a member of the team. I did not think it was right for her to go, and for that she wept and cried the whole night.

(All except Deepali go to the waiting room)

D. My parents do not allow me freedom to move about with friends, and my elder brother always acts like a policeman and always quarrels with me taking objection to whatever I do.

The real cause for their trying to find fault with me is that all of them dislike my friendship with a boy who is twenty-one. They dislike him mainly because he has a different religion and is supposed by them to be a vagabond. He lives with his maternal uncle who has a factory. He says he is doing some correspondence course and also learning computer work.

C. Is he a regular student anywhere?

D. No.

C. That means he is doing nothing in particular, and gets pocket money from his uncle. There are chances of his getting spoiled. He may be just trying to play with your growing youth. Do you have any body-contact with him? Kissing, hugging?

D. No, we only talk. I like him, I like talking to him. I do not meet him in isolation, but always in the company of friends.

C. Do you never talk to him when you are not in the company of your friends?

D. Except when I talk to him on phone. Everyone in the family objects to my telephone talks. I like him so I talk to him.

C. There is nothing wrong in talking to him, but you have to be cautious. You know at this age a girl is very vulnerable, she is in the process of blooming and is sexually and emotionally attractive, and is also prone to get attracted to young men. Young men, particularly in the age group of twenty to twenty-five, try to take advantage of the situation, they become romantically friendly with girls in their teens. You are only fifteen and are good-looking so it is very likely that your friend might be thinking of taking advantage of your inexperience. Let him remain your friend but do not let him become your boyfriend and date you. By the way, I feel you know music and sing?

D. Yes, I sing very well, I have also learnt Bharatanatyam and I dance.

C. So I have guessed right. Your interest in music and dance makes you more attractive and more desirable. You need to be more cautious, particularly when your boyfriend does nothing, is neither in a school nor is working and might be having money to spare and spend on girls for pleasure.

D. I know that. I do not mix with him, or go out with him.

C. Do you know that a girl's emotions can be aroused also by pleasant conversation, and complimentary words? Friendly talk is always the beginning of a love affair.

What is your ambition?

D. I want to be a musician like Lata Mangeshkar and a dancer like Hema Malini.

C. Then you will have to devote all your thought and energy to the learning of classical music and classical dance. Both Lata and Hema have practised for at least ten hours a day, and they still go on practising. How much time do you spend on these?

D. Nothing, I have no teacher.

Deepali's parents enter.

C. Well, you must put Deepali in some school to learn dance and music along with her studies in the school. She needs diversion and diversion towards a cause which may be dear to her.

F. I shall see to it that she gets proper coaching.

C. It seems Deepali is in search of attention and affection, she needs someone who is prepared to listen to her as a friend. Is she receiving sufficient love and attention in the family? How is the general atmosphere in the house? Is it peaceful or tense?

M. Deepali and her brother always fight.

D. What can I do, he objects to everything I do and fights with me, I also retaliate.

C. Why don't you as a mother control your son? You should yourself tell Deepali whatever you think is wrong and what is right. You cannot delegate your authority to your son who is just two years elder to her. Do you also generally become angry like your son, or you keep your calm?

M. I also get angry, all of us fight.

C. And also beat each other?

M. Yes.

C. With hands or sticks?

M. Hands.

C. So the father alone stays calm.

M. No, no, he is no exception.

C. Do you two also get involved amongst yourselves and fight.

M. Yes, only husband-wife fight.

F. Children have to be controlled. I dislike any disturbance in the house. I cannot tolerate if somebody disturbs anything, I get upset and find myself left with no option but to punish the guilty.

C. You are suffering from what is called OCD—obsessive compulsive disorder.

F. Probably. I am very emotional and I lose my emotional balance very easily and very quickly.

C. So, your house is Kurukshetra (where the battle of Mahabharat was fought), open for all.

[Counselling is given to make them think more rationally, behave more peacefully, and develop greater tolerance for each other.]

They all smile.

C. Do you want happiness or misery?

F. Of course, happiness.

C. Alright then you do:

1. Take a tape-recorder and as soon as arguments begin to develop heat, press the button. If the main actors in the fight cannot do it, let some non-participant press the button. Thereafter play the tape and listen, you will find there was no real reason to have a violent fight, everything was due to misunderstanding. Everyone thinks he is right and the other is wrong and tries to force his views on the other, and on failure to subdue the other, resorts to verbal and physical violence in utter frustration, just avoid this process. Let everyone have his views, everyone has the freedom of thought, no one has the right to force his thoughts on others. One has to learn respecting the opinions of others, no one is always right or always wrong.

2. After each confrontation, take a pen and paper and write down the whole incident; this will make you see things in a new light.

3. Impose a twenty-four hours moratorium on all fights. The time begins to run from now. All of you have now entered into a twenty-four hour truce and nobody will violate it.

This moratorium and truce is renewable after every twenty-four hours. Continue it as long as possible. Try to do it for a week till we have the next session.

Do you agree.

F,M,D. Yes we do.

C. Try to communicate with each other in an atmosphere of love and understanding.

Next Session

Deepali has been put under a music teacher, she has started learning music. She wanted to know the type of music she should learn. She has been guided with a view to make her treat music as meditation, and to think of attaining high-class proficiency.

C. How much time are you devoting in practising music at home?

D. Not much.

C Let me hear what have you learnt.

D. Deepali recites the notes.

C. There is still some trembling, your voice is not yet stable, you need greater concentration, devotion, and practice.

D. I realise the voice does have trembling, I shall now devote more time.

C. Practise with devotion, and full concentration, so that you might sing like Lata. Treat music as your meditation. Well, how is your love-bird?

D. Fine. We are having talks and even exchange glances as we are neighbours and can see each other from our balconies.

C. Like Romeo and Juliet, Juliet used to look from the balcony and Romeo looked at her from the street. But probably she was not so young. You have not yet become eighteen, you are only fifteen, you are still a bud in the stage of blossoming. You will find romance much more enchanting after you have fully blossomed. Wait for three years and then enjoy the fun. I think it would be better for you to wait a little and let youself become a girl with greater charm, then you will get and enjoy higher degree of happiness. Make yourself worthy and deserving of a higher intensity of love from someone who is also worthy of making love with a girl who is someone special and not just a girl, develop your faculties and talents a little more before you let the honey-bees come.

Your brother has promised not to act as your policing guardian for one month, during this period he will try to be more friendly and will not fight with you. You also reciprocate. Just go and talk to him, ask him to give you the card I gave him which contains the inscription: "For every minute of anger you lose sixty seconds of Joy" You have got to talk to him.

[Deepali goes hesitatingly, but then smiles and talks to him and reads the inscription.]

Deepali's father and mother have stated that although they have not been able to use the tape-recorder or write down the happenings, there has come a general improvement in the domestic climate, things have changed, and the atmosphere is now quite peaceful. Violence has almost retreated into the backyard.

No, no, just the reverse. He has the freedom to live in Rome as he may desire, but we have to live and behave in Rome (Home) as the ROMAN desires.

Diagnostic Scan and Counselling

Lolitha is smart and healthy, outspoken and pleasant. She has done B.A. and is studying for B.Ed. to become a teacher.

Her husband runs a factory, goes to work at 9 a.m. on week days. On Sundays he goes to club at 11 a.m. and returns at 10 in the night. He returns home only after drinking four pegs or more, smokes heavily, eats and sleeps.

C. You look quite calm and contented, except for a little bit of tension everything seems to be Okay.

L. It is so because I have adopted a passive attitude of tolerance and do no more enter into arguments with him. I also make the children, particularly the son who is very outspoken, to remain submissive and not to argue. In this way I manage to maintain peace in my home.

C. You are a diplomat. You know how to manage the family. Why don't you manage your husband too? If you change his behaviour, you can get peace in the house.

L. That is beyond me. He is incorrigible. I have tried, but he is not prepared either to reduce his drink or smoking. That spoils the atmosphere in the house, but he does not care.

C. He must be driving after drinking, and that may be dangerous.

L. Yes, but he doesn't care. He says he knows his job, and nothing will happen.

C. Anyway, what has brought you here?

L. The problem of my children, specially of my son. They do not devote sufficient time to their studies. The teacher complains to me during parent-teacher meetings, and I have no answer. The problem is mostly with the son. He is very good in Hindi and Arithmetic. He writes good Hindi and can solve sums mentally with efficiency. The problem is with English. He has aversion to English and says it is a bad foreign language, and does not want to learn it. The problem arises because his father thinks English is the status symbol in social life, and the son must learn to speak fluently because his friends' children do. He blames me for not talking in English and for conversing in Hindi with my children.

C. So the problem is not with the child but with the father. Your son has proficiency in Hindi and arithmetic, that is enough. He is only seven yet, and will gradually get interested in English too as he grows. Anyway, you get some books of fairy tales and nursery rhymes, and read them out to him. That will create in him a liking for English.

L. He does like listening to poems when my daughter reads them. But he is very naughty and over-active.

C. There is nothing wrong in being naughty or over-active. You too are very active, and maybe your husband was naughty when he was a child.

L. Maybe. I certainly am and love to be quite active, I do not like lethargy. Maybe, I don't know, I too might have been naughty as a child.

There is, however, one thing bad and objectionable about his behaviour. Once there was an unruly boy with him in the class and from him he had learnt abusive words. However, I have succeeded in making him give up the use of abusive language. But he continues to smack his classmates, and his elder sister.

C. That is, of course, anti-social behaviour and has to be controlled. May I know if you or your husband also indulge in such a behaviour?

L. I do not, except rarely, but my husband of course does not spare the child. He is always full of liquor inside, and whenever the boy resists, argument develops and he hits the boy before I manage to intervene. The son also objects to his being kissed by him as he does not like the smell of alcohol or smoke. This also make him feel offended and he resists.

C. The problem is really with your husband.

L. I know, but I can do nothing about it.

C. Let us concentrate presently on the child's behaviour. You can adopt the common method of controlling a wrong behaviour by reward for behaving in a particular manner. Offer him a chocolate or something if he does not hit anyone on a particular day. By and by you can increase the period of controlled abstinence.

L. I think this will work, he likes chocolates.

C. How is your life otherwise, financially and domestically?

L. It is not in a good shape. My husband will spend as much as he would like on his drinks, smoking, and club activities, but give only a bare minimum for household expenses. I have to maintain complete account and he will check and see that nothing has been purchased except what he desired. I cannot purchase even such small things as body lotion or face cream for myself or the children. Even small eatables I cannot purchase which the children like and crave for. He will buy them only ice cream of Mother Dairy and nothing else.

With him we do not get even the marketing pleasure. He would take us to a shop, and we have to select whatever is available there, and then return home.

C. It would be much better if you involve him more in your life, why not go out on a picnic some day?

L. Then the cost of petrol comes in the way. He will say it will mean wastage of petrol, the result is that we cannot go anywhere and have always to stay in the house. Can you imagine that during the entire long summer vacation we have to stay inside the house. I have become used to it, but the children get bored as during the vacation they have not even the school to go to.

C. Why don't you do something to earn a little money by doing some work in the house itself?

L. I do not want to work at home, I also need outing, I wish to mix with people, to enjoy human company. That is why I am doing B.Ed. so that I might join some school as a teacher. My daughter also says so.

C. It means you are having financial crunch and the children feel its pinch. At the same time you are feeling the need for freedom to breathe fresh air and social interaction with people of your age. Don't you ever enjoy a holiday?

L. Once a week we have it.

C. How?

L. On Sundays he religiously goes to club at about eleven in the morning and returns not before ten in the night. During this period he does not even phone, so we have free time all to ourselves.

C. So on Sundays you have a field-day, do what you like, eat what you like.

L. Yes, and we enjoy to the full. We even go out, have picnic and do the real little marketing with the little money I somehow manage to save. We visit shops, reject things, do bargaining and then purchase. That gives us the pleasure of marketing.

C. It is wonderful, you dupe him and save, and get real fun from it.

L. Not always, one month I saved a thousand rupees by cutting expenses; however, on checking the accounts he found it, and my next month's allowance was reduced. It looks all so funny. One day jokingly my daughter said I should inflate prices in the account book.

C. It is really funny, a man can spend unlimited amount on himself and become so calculating when it comes to the expenses of the family.

L. We have a real field-day on Sundays. We live leisurely. All things become free from control, they can be where they are. Only late in the evening the house is tidied up, things are placed in order, so that when he arrives, he may feel nothing has happened in the house during his absence. He wants us to remain under strict discipline.

C. As disciplined as he is?

L. No, no, just the reverse. He has the freedom to live in Rome as he may desire but we have to live and behave in Rome (Home) as the ROMAN desires.

He considers he is virtue personified, and all others are faltering mortals living around him. Is it not wonderful?

C. It is. Does he also become violent?

L. With great effort and sacrifice I have succeeded in keeping him within bound of non-violence. It is only by avoiding all argument, and by not making any suggestions of any kind I am maintaining peaceful environment in the house.

C. And also remaining so jovial, happy, and peaceful. You deserve congratulation. I think other women should copy you and follow the way you are handling your husband.

Next Session

C. Yes, Lolitha what's the matter?

L. Everything is good, but I do not know why I have to prepare myself for the whole week and gather sufficient courage just to ask my husband for money, even small amounts, for running the house.

C. It is because you feel guilt and shame in asking for money. You feel subconsciously that you are begging, you feel shame and probably also guilt.

L. I do not ask for unnecessary expenditure, even then his response is scornful, he will condemn me for asking money. This hurts me as it is quite contrary to my nature, my culture.

C. You have had this treatment for the last ten years, this should be sufficient to make you understand his nature. You know you are doing nothing wrong in asking for money, it is your right to get it, you are not a beggar begging for alms, you should realise that you are the mistress of the house and have the right to demand money for household expenses, why only for household expenses, you are entitled to get money for your personal expenses too.

L. I know I do nothing wrongful or shameful in asking for money, but feel hurt when he asks hundred questions before giving even paltry sums.

C. He has no business to treat you as a manager or servant. You should realise that you are his wife and the children belong to both of you, and you are entitled to be treated as an equal partner. Running of the house and maintenance of the children is as important as earning money.

L. I see I have been totally misunderstanding the nature of our relationship.

C. He should really feel ashamed for his behaviour, you should not. You should face the situation bravely without the feeling of shame and guilt. That will remove your fear and give you courage to demand whatever you need. Always remember that you are his wife and not a beggar asking for alms, and he is your husband and the children's father under a duty to pay for your living a comfortable life.

L. From now, I am going to change my attitude. I realise that my fear was due to my feeling that I was going to commit a shameful act. I will no more beg but demand as of right. No more fear, no more shame, no more guilt.

C. That is like a brave woman, who understands not only her own rights and rights of the children but also the duties of the husband. Be brave and accept your husband's comments and resentments as arising out of his erroneous understanding of his duties as a husband and a father. Of course, you neither can, nor should, try to teach him his duties, let him realise them himself.

L. Yes, I have only to mould my own attitude and life-style, and my own thoughts. From henceforth I shall behave like a wife and a mother and feel proud in behaving like that.

C. Yes, no more have the feeling of being a beggar, no more the feeling of shame and guilt. That is the key to all your problems. You are not yet enjoying the husband-wife relationship on the basis of equality but more on the basis of superiority and inferiority; the relationship is more like that of a supporter and dependent, not of a husband and wife having mutuality of rights, obligations and responsibilities.

L. That seems to be so.

C. Then change your outlook, it will ultimately make your relationship more rational and sweeter.

L. I shall try. I hope I shall succeed in making our relationship happier.

C. For marital happiness you need trust and confidence, and not fear. Trust and confidence can exist only between equals, so treat yourself his equal because you are his equal.

Remember the words of Bickerstaffe :

Let men say what'er they will
Woman, woman, rules them still.

L. (Lolitha laughs) I feel grand, elated, a real princess.

C. So you are. However, I would like to add a word of caution. Your husband is addicted to drinking and smoking, and that has made his ego a little bit unruly and inflated; his unhealthy ego needs to be properly handled. That does not mean you should fear him, you need only to tackle him a little diplomatically. The way you have developed yourself, you shall find no difficulty in doing so. You are required to bring a change not in his concepts, but in your own attitude, your own concept of yourself, your own status in the family. I am not asking you to be arrogant, but only to see things in their true perspective.

L. I quite understand what you mean. I realise I am not a beggar but a wife in its true sense, and I am sure I shall be able to play my role well.

C. I too am sure about your wisdom and talent to play the role as a superstar.

Next Session

L. Some days back I had a very bad time.

C. What happened?

L. My husband did not turn up in the night. I waited and waited for him, but with no result. I could not sleep the whole night, really I was so worried that it was impossible to sleep. He turned-up only at five in the morning, and the only explanation was that after an official meeting he started drinking and playing Rummy with friends. In the morning I had splitting headache, like of which I had never experienced. The doctor came and said it was tension and stress that had caused the headache and vomiting.

C. It was your accumulated tension, worry, and fear that had caused the trouble. Better you learn some relaxation exercises to relieve your stress. Too much of concern made you worry and caused tension. Try to take things lightly.

L. However, that had a good effect on my husband. Since then, whenever he has to return very late, he informs me on phone.

C. It gives you relief and prevents tension overtaking your nerves.

L. It is extremely good, it is really the victory of your love. What about your financial aspect?

L. Oh, a big breakthrough. I have taken agency for selling a health drink. There are concentrates of three drinks, one for reducing weight, the other for increasing weight, and the third for maintaining weight.

C. How much have you earned?

L. Two thousand in fifteen days.

C. Marvellous.

L. However, I am still looking forward to a teaching job, after finishing B.Ed. I shall take-up computer course. I want a job which can take me out of this house. I want to go out and meet people, have interaction with adults.

C. That will give you the relaxation you so badly need. You are suffering from a sort of stagnation, your feelings have choked-up and they want ventilation.

L. Inside the house, I feel boredom. I feel frustration on seeing myself doing nothing when I have capacity and capability to work and earn.

C. Of course, that is your problem, and I am happy you have gained awareness of the problem. Once you know the problem, its resolution becomes just a matter of time.

Most creditable of your achievements, however, is your winning back the love and concern of your husband.

L. That is of course my greatest win. I feel really happy, the tension lying buried deep in my mind seems to have gone. Now I feel quite relaxed, no longer do I feel I am living in a house where my husband was only a stranger.

C. The fear of your husband's displeasure and the feeling of alienation have both disappeared, and that has brought you peace of mind.

L. Yes, that is so. Now I feel I am the woman I dreamt to be: fearless, confident and loving.

SHRADDHA

Let every day be a day of rejoicing, every night a honeymoon.

Diagnostic Scan

Shraddha is a smart, pleasant looking girl of 24. She is educated. Normal health.

Shraddha gets distressed at the behaviour of Varun, a technical (Engineering) employee in the same organisation. He tries to find defects and mistakes in her work without justifiable reason. Her performance at work is generally, rather always, according to her, good. Still Varun tries to interfere to find some fault, Shraddha is working as secretary to the Managing Director and Varun does not come in the picture, he has, strictly speaking, no role to play in her functioning. Varun's behaviour makes Shraddha tense and distressed.

Counselling

C. Shaddha, you need to be a little thick-skinned. You have to accept even the things which are not pleasant. You have to learn, to be tolerant about the views of others even if, according to you, they are wrong. There is no harm in listening to criticism of your work, even from a person not directly connected with the job. You are still at the start of your career, you have been working only for the last three or four months and have still a long way to go. So learn to be tolerant.

S. I shall try to be more tolerant. I am not quite happy with secretary's job, although with my qualifications it is the most suitable job for me. Sometimes I think of starting my own computer related independent free-lance job. I do not see much future in this job. Moreover, I do not like to be in the company of irritating people.

C. It is of no use worrying about what happens in the office. You should live in the present and forget it as soon as it slips into the past, and do not worry about the future, which is unknown, otherwise you will generate in yourself fear of the future with no benefit to yourself.

S. But I do not like being put to fault for doing nothing wrong.

C. Maybe it is so, but don't carry it home, your husband does not need it. You have to treat the office blues as part of official work and not a gift for taking home. Whatever situation arises in the office should be dealt with then and there, and then forgotten. There are people who try to gain importance by finding fault with others. Those who have nothing of their own to claim as an achievement, try to belittle what others do, so as to feel themselves superior. You should not take too such things seriously. You just change yourself a little and give him the importance craves for from a smart young lady like you. It is only a veiled manifestation of his sex instinct. It does not mean anything, it has no teeth to bite. You try to change your attitude and act like a friend to Varun and to all those who criticise or try to pull you down. That will bring a remarkable change in their behaviour.

Shraddha, as regards your discontent with the present job, it is only your uncomfortable present that makes you look at your future with fear, and makes you miserable. Your fear of the unknown future is baseless as it may turn out to be entirely different from what you imagine. It is better to take a brighter view of the future.

S. I realise how foolish I have been. I have been worrying for nothing. From now I shall think and behave differently. I shall try to see things in their true perspective and thus avoid everything that is negative and pessimistic.

C. What about positive aspects of your life, negativity can be counteracted more easily by doing positive activities that give you pleasure.

S. I am interested in Western music and dance. I have also done some paintings and that used to give me total satisfaction.

C. Then start painting again, and treat it as your meditation, get fully absorbed in whatever you do, that is what I mean by meditation. Let your whole life become a meditation full of pleasant moments, fun and frolic. Does your husband also dance?

S. Yes, both of us can dance.

C. So from now on dance in the evening, every evening, play the cassettes and dance.

The idea is to make you so filled up with happiness that you may forget everything unpleasant including the pin-pricks in the office. The happiness should be so intense that there remains no place for misery in your life. When there is full sunshine, a little darkness in the corner automatically vanishes, darkness cannot enter a room flooded with light.

Second Session

S. I am very happy, my life has become a life of perpetual honeymoon.

C. This is very good.

S. I am also doing some meditation. I just try to concentrate on the spot in the middle of my eyes, but I have all along to fight with the incoming thoughts. By this meditation I do not get any peace or pleasure.

C. At your age and the way you are made, you have to have a different type of meditation, the meditation, you are practising is not suitable for you. Best meditation for you is dance and music. It should not be a ritual but a source of true pleasure. You should get absorbed in it and enjoy. That will generate divine love and ecstasy in you, and bring real joy and happiness.

[Shraddha felt very happy during the whole session and wanted to repay it in some way].

C. If I succeed in bringing even a ray of happiness in someone's life I feel amply rewarded. Happiness is not a saleable or purchaseable commodity. Go and be happy.

Let every day be a day of rejoicing, every night a honeymoon.

[Shraddha smiles].

S. It has already become so. For me now, everyday is a day of rejoicing, every night a honeymoon.

Intermission Epilogue

It seems anomalous to write the concluding page when the book still continues running, when tears still remain flooding youthful eyes and the sparkle of smile still continues to elude innocent faces. But it is only an intermission epilogue.

Maybe, the book has at times given you the disquieting sense that you were yourself the character involved in the cases in the book, and may be struggling to find the way out for yourself and everybody else to make life really worth living.

These cases indirectly try to offer solutions to various problems you might yourself be facing. You must have noticed that in every case the counsellor tries to make friends with the person needing support, and works to establish a relationship of faith and confidence. You can become your own counsellor by becoming your own confidante.

Let your subconsciousness open-up, and make your conscious mind become a witness to all your hidden anger, fury, grudge, suspicions, fears, and everything that troubles your mind and disturbs your peace. That will make your whole consciousness become your friend and philosopher, and come forward to guide you. It will make you more relaxed, peaceful and blissful.

'Relationship stress' is generally caused by a person's inability to cope with an uncomfortable situation into which one is involuntarily driven by the wrong behaviour of someone else. Many such situations have been considered in this book. Pinpoint the cases in which situations like yours have been faced by characters therein and follow the behavioural pattern gradually adopted by the suffering individual in those cases. Just become an optimist and a positive thinker.

Madonna's song, I feel, has already started ringing in your ears:

Papa don't preach,
I'm in trouble deep.

If not, please begin singing it. Everyone has the right to be happy in one's own way. You should be 'you' and only 'you'. Listen to your consciousness, and behave as it commands. It is better that you always keep a mirror in front of you so that your personality and behaviour may never deceive you. If you ever think it would be better to have a mask, then instead of wearing the mask, let your whole personality get a transformation, and let you become the new character of your dream, in the drama of life. You can then play the role of your choice and participate in that grand drama in the way you like.

A final word and no more:

Please choose to become a character who believes in making every day a day of celebration and every night a night of rejoicing. And, go on playing this beautiful role to make your life a things of beauty, a joy for ever.

INDEX